Nonlinear Dynamical Systems with Applications

Nonlinear Dynamical Systems with Applications

Editors

Shengda Zeng
Stanisław Migórski
Yongjian Liu

MDPI • Basel • Beijing • Wuhan • Barcelona • Belgrade • Manchester • Tokyo • Cluj • Tianjin

Editors
Shengda Zeng
Guangxi Colleges and Universities Key Laboratory of Complex System Optimization and Big Data Processing
Yulin
China

Stanisław Migórski
Faculty of Mathematics and Computer Science
Jagiellonian University
Krakow
Poland

Yongjian Liu
Faculty of Mathematics and Computer Science
Yulin Normal University
Yulin
China

Editorial Office
MDPI
St. Alban-Anlage 66
4052 Basel, Switzerland

This is a reprint of articles from the Special Issue published online in the open access journal *Axioms* (ISSN 2075-1680) (available at: www.mdpi.com/journal/axioms/special_issues/nonlinear_dynamical_systems).

For citation purposes, cite each article independently as indicated on the article page online and as indicated below:

LastName, A.A.; LastName, B.B.; LastName, C.C. Article Title. *Journal Name* **Year**, *Volume Number*, Page Range.

ISBN 978-3-0365-7997-9 (Hbk)
ISBN 978-3-0365-7996-2 (PDF)

Contents

axioms

MDPI

Editorial

Editorial: Overview and Some New Directions

Shengda Zeng [1,2,*], Stanislaw Migórski [2] and Yongjian Liu [1]

[1] Guangxi Colleges and Universities Key Laboratory of Complex System Optimization and Big Data Processing, Yulin Normal University, Yulin 537000, China; liuyongjianmaths@126.com
[2] Faculty of Mathematics and Computer Science, Jagiellonian University, 30348 Krakow, Poland; stanislaw.migorski@uj.edu.pl
* Correspondence: zengshengda@163.com

1. Overview of the Published Papers

The Special Issue contains eleven accepted and published submissions to a Special Issue of the MDPI journal Axioms on the subject of "Nonlinear Dynamical Systems with Applications". In this volume, the invited authors have submitted their latest results on nonlinear dynamical systems and related various applications. All papers have been accepted after a rigorous reviewing process.

In their study [1], Sarem H. Hadi, Maslina Darus and Alina Alb Lupaş considered a class of Janowski-type (p,q)-convex harmonic functions involving a generalized q-Mittag–Leffler function. This research aims to present a linear operator $\mathcal{L}_{p,q}^{\rho,\sigma,\mu} f$ by utilizing the q-Mittag–Leffler function and to introduce the subclass of harmonic p,q-convex functions $\mathcal{HT}_{p,q}(\vartheta,\mathcal{W},\mathcal{V})$ related to the Janowski function. For the harmonic p-valent functions f class, they investigated the harmonic geometric properties, such as coefficient estimates, convex linear combination, extreme points, and Hadamard product. Finally, the closure property was derived via using the subclass $\mathcal{HT}_{p,q}(\vartheta,\mathcal{W},\mathcal{V})$, and the theory of fractional q-calculus operators in geometric function theory was developed.

In another study [2], Barić, Josipa provided a research article on the Levinson's functional in time-scale settings. In their paper, a Levinson functional on time scales was introduced using the integral inequality of Levinson's type in the terms of Δ-integral for convex (concave) functions on time-scale sets, and the relevant properties of Levinson functionals were obtained, such as superadditivity and monotonicity. Then, the authors defined some new types of functionals using weighted generalized and power means on time scales, and proved their properties. These can be employed in future works to obtain refinements and converses of known integral inequalities on time scales.

The research of Gunasekaran Nallaselli, Arul Joseph Gnanaprakasam, Gunaseelan Mani, Ozgur Ege, Dania Santina and Nabil Mlaiki in reference [3] involves a study on fixed-point techniques under the α-$\digamma$-convex contraction with an application. In this paper, they consider several classes of mappings related to the class of α-Σ-contraction mappings by introducing a convexity condition and establish some fixed-point theorems for such mappings in complete metric spaces. The result extends and generalizes the well-known results on α-admissible and convex contraction mappings, and many others in the existing literature. An illustrative example is also provided to exhibit the utility of their main results. Finally, they derive the existence and uniqueness of a solution to an integral equation to support their main result and provide a numerical example to validate the application of their obtained results. In this paper, the authors extend and generalize their main theorem into an α-Σ-convex contraction of seven possible values (with rational type) in complete metric spaces inspired and motivated by previous research. Examples and applications to integral equations are provided to illustrate the usability of their obtained results.

The authors of reference [4], Xiaolan Yuan and Yusheng Zhou, produce a design of state-dependent switching rules for second-order switched linear systems revisited. For switched systems, differential equations are used to describe the dynamic behavior of the

Citation: Zeng, S.; Migórski, S.; Liu, Y. Editorial: Overview and Some New Directions. *Axioms* **2023**, *12*, 553. https://doi.org/10.3390/axioms12060553

Received: 1 June 2023
Accepted: 2 June 2023
Published: 4 June 2023

continuous characteristic, which are marked as subsystems. A piecewise constant function is adopted to describe the discrete characteristic, which is referred to as a switching rule. An important part of hybrid systems, switched systems have been exhibited in many practical fields. This paper focuses on the asymptotic stability of second-order switched linear systems with positive real part conjugate complex roots for each subsystem. Compared with available studies, a more appropriate state-dependent switching rule is designed to stabilize a switched system with the phase trajectories of two subsystems rotating outward in the same direction or the opposite direction. Finally, several numerical examples are used to illustrate the effectiveness and superiority of the proposed method.

In the research presented in reference [5], Xinyue Zhu, Wei Li and Xueping Luo considered stability for a class of differential set-valued inverse variational inequalities in finite dimensional spaces. In this paper, the authors introduce and study a new class of differential set-valued inverse variational inequalities in finite dimensional spaces. By applying a result to differential inclusions involving an upper semi-continuous set-valued mapping with closed convex values, the authors first prove the existence of Carathéodory weak solutions for differential set-valued inverse variational inequalities. Then, using the existence result, the authors establish the stability for the differential set-valued inverse variational inequality problem when the constraint set and the mapping are perturbed by two different parameters. The closedness and continuity of Carathéodory weak solutions with respect to the two different parameters are obtained.

Some novel conditions for the stability results for a class of fractional-order quasi-linear impulsive integro-differential systems with multiple delays are discussed by Mathiyalagan Kalidass, Shengda Zeng and Mehmet Yavuz [6]. First, the existence and uniqueness of mild solutions for the considered system are discussed using contraction mapping theorem. Then, novel conditions for the Mittag–Leffler stability (MLS) of the considered system are established by using well-known mathematical techniques, and further, the two corollaries are deduced, which provides some new results. Finally, an example is provided to illustrate the applications of the results. The Mittag–Leffler stability of a fractional-order system (FOS) has not been fully investigated, which motivated the authors of the present study. Thus, in this study, the existence and uniqueness of solutions and MLS analysis of the impulsive quasi-linear FOS with multiple time delays are established using the well-known fixed point theorems and Mittag–Leffler approach. Furthermore, the main contribution of this paper lies in deriving new stability conditions for the fractional-order quasi-linear system with nonlocal conditions, multiple time delays and impulses. Novel conditions for the Mittag–Leffler stability of FOSs are established. The existence and uniqueness of mild solutions for the FOS are discussed with help of the contraction mapping principle. Finally, an example is provided to show the applicability of the results.

For the study presented in reference [7], Yunru Bai, Leszek Gasinski, and Nikolaos S. Papageorgiou consider nonlinear eigenvalue problems for the Dirichlet $(p,2)$-Laplacian. The authors consider a nonlinear eigenvalue problem driven by the Dirichlet $(p,2)$-Laplacian. The parametric reaction is a Carathéodory function, which exhibits $(p-1)$-sublinear growth as $x \to \infty$ and as $x \to 0^+$. Using variational tools and truncation and comparison techniques, the authors prove a bifurcation-type theorem describing the spectrum as $\lambda > 0$ varies. The authors also prove the existence of a smallest positive eigenfunction for every eigenvalue. Finally, the authors indicate how the result can be extended to (p,q)-equations $(q \neq 2)$.

Considering the importance of the nutrient-phytoplankton, in reference [8], Ruizhi Yang, Liye Wang and Dan Jin consider Hopf bifurcation analysis of a diffusive nutrient-phytoplankton model with time delay. One of the most complex and difficult problems in water pollution treatment is the prevention and control of algal bloom. Due to the complexity of the pollution source and the difficulty factor of material removal, a lot of energy is required, but it is not very effective. Therefore, scientists are searching for better methods to prevent and cure algal bloom, especially using mathematical models, in order to find reasonable prevention and cure measures. In this paper, the authors studied a nutrient-phytoplankton model with time delay and diffusion term. The authors studied the Turing instability, local stability, and the existence of Hopf bifurcation. Some formulas are obtained to determine the direction of the bifurcation and the stability of periodic solutions by the central manifold theory and normal form method. Finally, the conclusion is verified through numerical simulation.

New results on the Darboux transformation and N-soliton solutions of Gerdjik ov-Ivanov equation on a time–space scale equation are presented by Huanhe Dong, Xiaoqian Huang, Yong Zhang, Mingshuo Liu and Yong Fang in [9]. The Gerdjikov–Ivanov (GI) equation is one type of derivative nonlinear Schrödinger equation that is widely used in quantum field theory, nonlinear optics, weakly nonlinear dispersion water waves and other fields. In this paper, the coupled GI equation on a time–space scale is deduced from Lax pairs and the zero curvature equation on a time–space scale, which can be reduced to the classical and the semi-discrete GI equation by considering different time–space scales. Furthermore, the Darboux transformation (DT) of the GI equation on a time-space scale is constructed via gauge transformation. Finally, N-soliton solutions of the GI equation are provided through applying its DT, which is expressed by the Cayley exponential function. One-solition solutions are obtained at three different time–space scales ($\mathbb{X} = \mathbb{R}$, $\mathbb{X} = \mathbb{C}$, $\mathbb{X} = \mathbb{K}_p$).

The research of Dumitru Motreanu is presented in [10]. The result concerns two Dirichlet boundary value problems whose differential operators in the principal part exhibit a lack of ellipticity and contain a convection term (depending on the solution and its gradient). They are driven by a degenerated (p, q)-Laplacian with weights and a competing (p, q)-Laplacian with weights, respectively. The notion of competing (p, q)-Laplacians with weights is considered for the first time. The author presents existence and approximation results that hold under the same set of hypotheses for the convection term for both problems. The proofs are based on weighted Sobolev spaces, Nemytskij operators, a fixed-point argument and finite dimensional approximation. A detailed example illustrates the effective applicability of the results.

New results are obtained concerning the global directed dynamic behaviors of a Lotka–Volterra competition-diffusion-advection system by Lili Chen, Shilei Lin and Yanfeng Zhao in [11]. Motivated by the aforementioned studies, the authors investigate the problem of the global directed dynamic behaviors of a Lotka–Volterra advection system between two organisms in heterogeneous environments, where the two organisms are competing for different fundamental resources, their advection and diffusion strategies follow the dispersal towards a positive distribution, and the functions of inter-specific competition ability are variable. This paper investigates the problem of the global directed dynamic behaviors of a Lotka–Volterra competition-diffusion-advection system between two organisms in heterogeneous environments. The two organisms not only compete for different basic resources, but also the advection and diffusion strategies follow the dispersal towards a positive distribution. By virtue of the principal eigenvalue theory, the linear stability of the co-existing steady state is established. Furthermore, the classification of dynamical behaviors is shown by utilizing the monotone dynamical system theory. This work can be seen as a further development of a competition–diffusion system.

2. Conclusions

The eleven papers published in the Special Issue on "Nonlinear Dynamical Systems with Applications" concern a broad range of subjects regarding Janowski-Type (p, q)-convex harmonic functions, Levinson's functional, fixed-point techniques, dynamical systems, differential set-valued inverse variational inequalities, fractional-order quasilinear impulsive integro-differential systems, nonlinear eigenvalue problems, the nutrient–phytoplankton problem, Gerdjikov–Ivanov equation and dynamic behaviors. Researchers interested in nonlinear dynamical systems with applications and related topics will find interesting insights and inspiring results in this volume.

Conflicts of Interest: The authors declare no conflict of interest.

References

1. Hadi, S.H.; Darus, M.; Alb Lupaş, A. A Class of Janowski-Type (p,q)-Convex Harmonic Functions Involving a Generalized q-Mittag-Leffler Function. *Axioms* **2023**, *12*, 190. [CrossRef]
2. Barić, J. Levinson's Functional in Time Scale Settings. *Axioms* **2023**, *12*, 141. [CrossRef]
3. Nallaselli, G.; Gnanaprakasam, A.J.; Mani, G.; Ege, O.; Santina, D.; Mlaiki, N. A Study on Fixed-Point Techniques under the α-Σ-Convex Contraction with an Application. *Axioms* **2023**, *12*, 139. [CrossRef]
4. Yuan, X.; Zhou, Y. The Design of State-Dependent Switching Rules for Second-Order Switched Linear Systems Revisited. *Axioms* **2022**, *11*, 566. [CrossRef]
5. Zhu, X.; Li, W.; Luo, X. Stability for a Class of Differential Set-Valued Inverse Variational Inequalities in Finite Dimensional Spaces. *Axioms* **2022**, *11*, 475. [CrossRef]
6. Kalidass, M.; Zeng, S.; Yavuz, M. Stability of Fractional-Order Quasi-Linear Impulsive Integro-Differential Systems with Multiple Delays. *Axioms* **2022**, *11*, 308. [CrossRef]
7. Bai, Y.; Gasinski, L.; Papageorgiou, N.S. Nonlinear Eigenvalue Problems for the Dirichlet $(p,2)$-Laplacian. *Axioms* **2022**, *11*, 58. [CrossRef]
8. Yang, R.; Wang, L.; Jin, D. Hopf Bifurcation Analysis of a Diffusive Nutrient—Phytoplankton Model with Time Delay. *Axioms* **2022**, *11*, 56. [CrossRef]
9. Dong, H.; Huang, X.; Zhang, Y.; Liu, M.; Fang, Y. The Darboux Transformation and N-Soliton Solutions of Gerdjikov-Ivanov Equation on a Time-Space Scale. *Axioms* **2021**, *10*, 294. [CrossRef]
10. Motreanu, D. Degenerated and Competing Dirichlet Problems with Weights and Convection. *Axioms* **2021**, *10*, 271. [CrossRef]
11. Chen, L.; Lin, S.; Zhao, Y. Global Directed Dynamic Behaviors of a Lotka-Volterra Competition-Diffusion-Advection System. *Axioms* **2021**, *10*, 195. [CrossRef]

axioms

MDPI

Article

A Class of Janowski-Type (p, q)-Convex Harmonic Functions Involving a Generalized q-Mittag–Leffler Function

Sarem H. Hadi [1,2,*,†], **Maslina Darus** [2,†] and **Alina Alb Lupaş** [3,†]

1 Department of Mathematics, College of Education for Pure Sciences, University of Basrah, Basrah 61001, Iraq
2 Department of Mathematical Sciences, Faculty of Science and Technology, Universiti Kebangsaan Malaysia, Bangi 43600, Selangor, Malaysia
3 Department of Mathematics and Computer Science, University of Oradea, 1 Universitatii Street, 410087 Oradea, Romania
* Correspondence: sarim.hadi@uobasrah.edu.iq or p110974@siswa.ukm.edu.my
† These authors contributed equally to this work.

Abstract: This research aims to present a linear operator $\mathcal{L}_{p,q}^{\rho,\sigma,\mu} f$ utilizing the q-Mittag–Leffler function. Then, we introduce the subclass of harmonic (p, q)-convex functions $\mathcal{HT}_{p,q}(\vartheta, \mathcal{W}, \mathcal{V})$ related to the Janowski function. For the harmonic p-valent functions f class, we investigate the harmonic geometric properties, such as coefficient estimates, convex linear combination, extreme points, and Hadamard product. Finally, the closure property is derived using the subclass $\mathcal{HT}_{p,q}(\vartheta, \mathcal{W}, \mathcal{V})$ under the q-Bernardi integral operator.

Keywords: harmonic p-valent functions; the q-Mittag–Leffler function; (p, q)-convex functions; extreme points; Hadamard product; closed convex hulls; q-Bernardi integral operator

MSC: 05A30; 30C45; 11B65; 47B38

Citation: Hadi, S.H.; Darus, M.; Alb Lupaş, A. A Class of Janowski-Type (p, q)-Convex Harmonic Functions Involving a Generalized q-Mittag–Leffler Function. *Axioms* **2023**, *12*, 190. https://doi.org/10.3390/axioms12020190

Academic Editors: Shengda Zeng, Stanisław Migórski, Yongjian Liu and Palle E.T. Jorgensen

Received: 28 November 2022
Revised: 21 January 2023
Accepted: 10 February 2023
Published: 11 February 2023

1. Main Concepts of Quantum Calculus

Quantum calculus, often known as q-calculus (or q-analysis), is a method for studying calculus that is similar to traditional calculus but focused on finding q-analogous conclusions without the need for limits. The q-differential equations are generally defined on the scale T_q, where T and q are the time and scale index, respectively. Euler and Jacobi devised the fundamental formulae of q-calculus in the eighteenth century. Jackson ([1,2]) introduced and developed the concepts of q-derivative and q-integral. Moreover, the geometries of q-analysis were found in many studies presented on quantum groups. It has also been identified that there is a relationship between q-integral and q-derivative. With the expansion of the q-calculus study, many relevant facts have also been explored, including the q-Gamma and q-Beta functions, the q-Laplace transform, and the q-Mittag–Leffler function. The theory of q-calculus operators has been recently applied in the areas of ordinary fractional calculus, optimal control problems, finding solutions to the q-difference and q-integral equations, and q-transform analysis (see [3,4]). Furthermore, certain classes of functions that are analytic in $\mathbb{U}$ using fractional q-calculus operators were investigated by numerous research (for example, see [5–12]).

This paper aims to further develop the theory of fractional q-calculus operators in geometric function theory. Initially, this study provides some essential definitions and concepts of q-calculus and symmetric q-calculus, which have been employed in this research.

This work begins with the basic concepts and, consequently, an in-depth analysis of our proposed applications of the q-calculus. Throughout this paper, assume that $0 < q < 1$. The following definitions provide an introduction to the q-calculus operators for a complex-valued function f:

Let $\mathcal{S}(p)$ be the class of analytic and multivalent functions f in the open unit disc $\mathbb{U} = \{z \in \mathbb{C} : |z| < 1\}$ with the normalized form:

$$f(z) = z^p + \sum_{j=p+1}^{\infty} a_j z^j, \quad (p \in \mathbb{N}). \tag{1}$$

Definition 1. *For $0 < q < 1$, the q-number $[\kappa]_q$ is expressed by*

$$[\kappa]_q := \begin{cases} \dfrac{1-q^\kappa}{1-q} & (\kappa \in \mathbb{C}) \\ \sum\limits_{\kappa=0}^{n-1} q^j & (\kappa = n \in \mathbb{N}). \end{cases}$$

Definition 2 ([1])**.** *The q-derivative operator $\mathfrak{D}_q$ is given by*

$$\mathfrak{D}_q f(z) = \frac{f(qz) - f(z)}{(q-1)z} \ (z \neq 0).$$

The q-derivative of the function f in (1) *is given by*

$$\mathfrak{D}_q f(z) = [p]_q z^{p-1} + \sum_{j=p+1}^{\infty} [j]_q a_j z^{j-1}.$$

The q-factorial indicated by $[j]_q!$ is defined by

$$[j]_q! = \begin{cases} [j]_q [j-1]_q \ldots [2]_q [1]_q, & j = 1, 2, 3, \ldots, \\ 1 & j = 0, \end{cases}$$

so that

$$\begin{aligned} f'(z) &:= \lim_{q \to 1^-} \mathfrak{D}_q \left\{ [p]_q z^{p-1} + \sum_{j=p+1}^{\infty} [j]_q a_j z^{j-1} \right\} \\ &= p z^{p-1} + \sum_{j=p+1}^{\infty} j a_j z^{j-1}. \end{aligned}$$

The q-Gamma function is defined by

$$\Gamma_q(\varrho) = (1-q)^{1-\varrho} \prod_{k=0}^{\infty} \frac{1-q^{k+1}}{1-q^{k+\varrho}} = (1-q)^{1-\varrho} \frac{(q;q)_\infty}{(q^\varrho;q)_\infty},$$

where $(\varrho; k)_q$ the q-Pochhammer is given as

$$(\varrho; k)_q = (\varrho)_q (\varrho+1)_q (\varrho+2)_q \cdots (\varrho+k-1)_q = \frac{(\varrho;q)_n}{(1-q)^n}, \quad (\varrho \in \mathbb{R}, k \in \mathbb{N}).$$

Obviously,

$$\Gamma_q(\varrho+1) = [\varrho]_q \Gamma_q(\varrho) \text{ and } \Gamma_q(1) = 1.$$

In the following section, we have introduced some concepts of harmonic p-valent functions and the Mittag–Leffler function. Then, we have derived a number interesting results regarding p-valent functions related to the operator $\mathcal{L}_{p,q}^{\rho,\sigma,\mu} f(z)$. Furthermore, this paper demonstrates some of the geometric results of the operator $\mathcal{L}_{p,q}^{\rho,\sigma,\mu} f(z)$.

2. Harmonic Functions, Definitions and Motivation

In the complex domain $\mathcal{D} \subset \mathbb{U}$, if the values u and v are real harmonic, then the continuous function $f = u + iv$ is called the harmonic function in $\mathcal{D}$. In any simply connected domain $\mathcal{D}$, the function f can be stated by

$$f = \mathcal{F} + \overline{\mathcal{G}}, \tag{2}$$

where both $\mathcal{F}$ and $\mathcal{G}$ are analytic functions in $\mathcal{D}$. The function $\mathcal{F}$ is called analytic of f, and $\mathcal{G}$ the conjugate-analytic (or co-analytic) of f. Clunie and Sheil-Small [13] discovered that $|\mathcal{F}'(z)| > |\mathcal{G}'(z)|$ is a necessary and sufficient condition for the harmonic functions (2) to be locally multivalent and sense-preserving in $\mathcal{D}$ (also, see [14]).

Let $\mathcal{H}(p,j)$ be the family of harmonic multivalent functions $f = \mathcal{F} + \overline{\mathcal{G}}$ that are orientation keeping the open unit disc $\mathbb{U} = \{z : |z| < 1\}$. The analytic functions $\mathcal{F}$ and $\mathcal{G}$ are defined by

$$\mathcal{F} = z^p + \sum_{j=p+1}^{\infty} a_j z^j \quad \text{and} \quad \mathcal{G} = \sum_{j=p}^{\infty} d_j z^j$$

and

$$f = \mathcal{F} + \overline{\mathcal{G}} = z^p + \sum_{j=p+1}^{\infty} a_j z^j + \sum_{j=p}^{\infty} \overline{d_j z^j}, \tag{3}$$

where $p \geq 1$ and $|d_p| < 1$.

The family $\mathcal{H}(1,j) = \mathcal{H}(j)$ of harmonic univalent functions is presented by Jahangiri et al. [15] (also see [16–21]).

Furthermore, we consider the subclass $\widetilde{\mathcal{H}}(p,j)$ of the family $\mathcal{H}(p,j)$ that consists of functions $f = \mathcal{F} + \overline{\mathcal{G}}$, where the functions $\mathcal{F}$ and $\mathcal{G}$ are defined as below:

$$\mathcal{F}(z) = z^p - \sum_{j=p+1}^{\infty} |a_j| z^j \quad \text{and} \quad \mathcal{G}(z) = -\sum_{j=p}^{\infty} |d_j| z^j, \quad (|d_p| < 1). \tag{4}$$

Recently, many studies have emphasized the concept of p-valent harmonic functions and their applications (for example, see [22–26]).

If the analytic functions $f, h \in \mathcal{H}(p,j)$, then the function f is subordinate to the function h, denoted by $(f \prec h)$, if there exists a Schwarz function Φ with

$$\Phi(0) = 0, \ |\Phi(z)| < 1, \quad (z \in \mathbb{U}),$$

such that

$$f(z) = h(\Phi(z)).$$

In addition, we get the following equivalence if the function h is univalent in $\mathbb{U}$:

$$f(z) \prec h(z) \Leftrightarrow f(0) = h(0) \text{ and } f(\mathbb{U}) \subset h(\mathbb{U}).$$

We now mention the well-known Mittag–Leffler function $E_\sigma(z)$ provided by Mittag–Leffler [27], which is defined by

$$E_\sigma(z) = \sum_{j=0}^{\infty} \frac{z^j}{\Gamma(\sigma j + 1)}, \quad (\sigma, z \in \mathbb{C}, \mathcal{R}(\sigma) > 0),$$

where $\mathcal{R}, \Gamma$ are the real part and the gamma function, respectively.

Within chaotic, stochastic, and dynamic systems, partial differential equations, and statistical distributions, many considerations can be seen in applying this function. Wiman [28] defined the Mittag–Leffler function with two parameters

$$E_{\sigma,\mu}(z) = \sum_{j=0}^{\infty} \frac{z^j}{\Gamma(\sigma j + \mu)}, \quad (\sigma, \mu, z \in \mathbb{C}, \mathcal{R}(\sigma) > 0, \mathcal{R}(\mu) > 0).$$

Shukla and Prajapati [29] provided the Mittag–Leffler function with three parameters $E^{\rho,k}_{\sigma,\mu}(z)$ as follows:

$$E^{\rho,k}_{\sigma,\mu}(z) = \sum_{j=0}^{\infty} \frac{(\rho)_{kj}}{\Gamma(\mu + \sigma j)} \frac{z^j}{j!}, \quad (\sigma, \mu, \rho, z \in \mathbb{C}, \mathcal{R}(\sigma) > 0, \mathcal{R}(\mu) > 0, \mathcal{R}(\rho) > 0),$$

where $k \in (0,1) \bigcup \mathbb{N}$ and $(\rho)_{kj} = \frac{\Gamma(\rho+kj)}{\Gamma(\rho)}$ is the generalized Pochhammer symbol.

The Mittag–Leffler function plays a vital role in solving fractional order differential and integral equations. It has recently become a subject of rich interest in the field of fractional calculus and its applications. Numerous research has been conducted on the theory of the Mittag–Leffler function. For more review, Bansal and Prajapat [30] (also Srivastava and Bansal [31]) investigated geometric properties of the Mittag–Leffler function $E_{\sigma,\mu}(z)$. In addition, many other researchers studied properties of the Mittag–Leffler function, including starlikeness, convexity, and differential subordination (see [32–35]). In the fact, the generalized Mittag–Leffler function $E_{\sigma,\mu}(z)$ is still vastly used in geometric function theory and a variety of applications (see [36]).

Hadi et al. [37] defined a generalized q-Mittag–Leffler function with three parameters as below:

$$\mathcal{E}^{\rho}_{\sigma,\mu}(q;z) = z + \sum_{j=2}^{\infty} \frac{(\rho)_{kj}}{\Gamma_q(\mu + \sigma j)} \frac{z^j}{j!}, \quad (\sigma, \mu, \rho \in \mathbb{C}, \mathcal{R}(\sigma) > 0, \mathcal{R}(\mu) > 0, \mathcal{R}(\rho) > 0). \tag{5}$$

We note that if $q \to 1^-$, we have the Mittag–Leffler function defined by Shukla and Prajapati [29].

Motivated by the importance of studying the applications of quantum calculus and the Mittag–Leffler function in the physical and mathematical sciences, we first present a new linear operator $\mathcal{L}^{\rho,\sigma,\mu}_{p,q} f$, which is defined by the q-Mittag–Leffler function with harmonic p-valent functions. Then, we use this operator to introduce a subclass of Janowski (p,q)-convex harmonic functions. For the harmonic p-valent functions f, we investigate some harmonic geometric properties, including coefficient estimates, convex hulls, convex linear combination, extreme point, and Hadamard product. Furthermore, we derive the closure property under the q-Bernardi integral operator.

Now, we introduce the function $\mathcal{M}^{\rho}_{\sigma,\mu}(p,q;z) \in \mathcal{S}(p)$ related to the q-Mittag–Leffler function in (5) as follows:

$$\begin{aligned} \mathcal{M}^{\rho}_{\sigma,\mu}(p,q;z) &= \frac{\Gamma_q(\sigma+\mu) z^{p-1}}{(\rho)_k} \left(\mathcal{E}^{\rho}_{\sigma,\mu}(q;z) - \frac{1}{\Gamma_q(\mu)} \right) \\ &= z^p + \sum_{j=p+1}^{\infty} \frac{\Gamma_q(\sigma+\mu)\Gamma(\rho+jk)}{\Gamma_q(\sigma j+\mu)\Gamma(\rho+k) j!} z^j, \quad (p \geq 1; z \in \mathbb{U}), \end{aligned} \tag{6}$$

where $\sigma, \mu, \rho \in \mathbb{C}, \mathcal{R}(\sigma) > 0, \mathcal{R}(\mu) > 0, \mathcal{R}(\rho) > 0$, and $(\rho)_{kj} = \frac{\Gamma(\rho+kj)}{\Gamma(\rho)}$.

From the function $\mathcal{M}^{\rho}_{\sigma,\mu}(p,q;z)$, we define a linear operator $\mathcal{L}^{\rho,\sigma,\mu}_{p,q} : \mathcal{S}(p) \to \mathcal{S}(p)$ as follows:

$$\begin{aligned} \mathcal{L}^{\rho,\sigma,\mu}_{p,q} f(z) &= \mathcal{M}^{\rho}_{\sigma,\mu}(p,q;z) * f(z) \\ &= z^p + \sum_{j=p+1}^{\infty} \frac{\Gamma_q(\sigma+\mu)\Gamma(\rho+jk)}{\Gamma_q(\sigma j+\mu)\Gamma(\rho+k)j!} a_j z^j. \end{aligned} \tag{7}$$

When $q \to 1^-, k = 1, \sigma = 0$, and $\rho = 1$, then $\mathcal{L}^{\rho,\sigma,\mu}_{p,q} f(z) = f(z)$.

Remark 1. *If $\mathcal{R}(\sigma) > \max\{0, \mathcal{R}(k) - 1\}$ and $\mathcal{R}(k) > 0$, the following operators are obtained*

1. *If $q \to 1^-$, we find the operator $\mathcal{L}^{\rho,\sigma,\mu}_{p} f(z)$ investigated by Xu and Liu [38].*
2. *When $q \to 1^-$ and $p = 1$, we find the operator $\mathcal{L}^{\rho,\mu}_{\sigma} f(z)$ investigated by Attiya [39].*

For $f \in \mathcal{H}(p,j)$ in the form (3), we define the operator $\mathcal{L}^{\rho,\sigma,\mu}_{p,q} f$ as follows:

$$\mathcal{L}^{\rho,\sigma,\mu}_{p,q} f(z) = \mathcal{L}^{\rho,\sigma,\mu}_{p,q} \mathcal{F}(z) + \overline{\mathcal{L}^{\rho,\sigma,\mu}_{p,q} \mathcal{G}(z)}, \tag{8}$$

where

$$\mathcal{L}^{\rho,\sigma,\mu}_{p,q} \mathcal{F}(z) = z^p + \sum_{j=p+1}^{\infty} \psi_q a_j z^j,$$

$$\mathcal{L}^{\rho,\sigma,\mu}_{p,q} \mathcal{G}(z) = \sum_{j=p}^{\infty} \psi_q d_j z^j$$

and $\psi_q = \frac{\Gamma_q(\sigma+\mu)\Gamma(\rho+jk)}{\Gamma_q(\sigma j+\mu)\Gamma(\rho+k)j!}$.

We define the class $\mathcal{HT}_{p,q}(\vartheta, \mathcal{W}, \mathcal{V})$ using the operator $\mathcal{L}^{\rho,\sigma,\mu}_{p,q} f$ in (8) as follows:

Definition 3. *A multivalent functions $f = \mathcal{F} + \overline{\mathcal{G}} \in \mathcal{H}(p,j)$ is said to be in the class $\mathcal{HT}_{p,q}$ $(\vartheta, \mathcal{W}, \mathcal{V})$ if*

$$\frac{\mathfrak{D}_q(z\mathfrak{D}_q \mathcal{L}^{\rho,\sigma,\mu}_{p,q} f(z))}{\mathfrak{D}_q(\mathcal{L}^{\rho,\sigma,\mu}_{p,q} f(z))} \prec ([p]_q - \vartheta)\frac{1+\mathcal{W}z}{1+\mathcal{V}z} + \vartheta, \tag{9}$$

or equivalently

$$\frac{\mathfrak{D}_q(z\mathfrak{D}_q \mathcal{L}^{\rho,\sigma,\mu}_{p,q} f(z))}{\mathfrak{D}_q(\mathcal{L}^{\rho,\sigma,\mu}_{p,q} f(z))} \prec \frac{[p]_q + \{(\mathcal{W}-\mathcal{V})([p]_q - \vartheta) + \mathcal{V}[p]_q\}z}{1+\mathcal{V}z}.$$

Utilizing of the subordination principle, $f \in \mathcal{HT}_{p,q}(\vartheta, \mathcal{W}, \mathcal{V})$ if and only if there is a Schwarz function φ such that

$$\frac{\mathfrak{D}_q(z\mathfrak{D}_q \mathcal{L}^{\rho,\sigma,\mu}_{p,q} f(z))}{\mathfrak{D}_q(\mathcal{L}^{\rho,\sigma,\mu}_{p,q} f(z))} = \frac{[p]_q + \{(\mathcal{W}-\mathcal{V})([p]_q - \vartheta) + \mathcal{V}[p]_q\}\varphi(z)}{1+\mathcal{V}\varphi(z)},$$

that is

$$\left| \frac{\frac{\mathfrak{D}_q(z\mathfrak{D}_q \mathcal{L}^{\rho,\sigma,\mu}_{p,q} f(z))}{\mathfrak{D}_q(\mathcal{L}^{\rho,\sigma,\mu}_{p,q} f(z))} - [p]_q}{\mathcal{V}\frac{\mathfrak{D}_q(z\mathfrak{D}_q \mathcal{L}^{\rho,\sigma,\mu}_{p,q} f(z))}{\mathfrak{D}_q(\mathcal{L}^{\rho,\sigma,\mu}_{p,q} f(z))} - \{(\mathcal{W}-\mathcal{V})([p]_q - \vartheta) + \mathcal{V}[p]_q\}} \right| < 1, \tag{10}$$

where $0 \le \vartheta < [p]_q, -1 \le \mathcal{V} < \mathcal{W} \le 1$, and $\mathcal{L}^{\rho,\sigma,\mu}_{p,q} f(z)$ is defined in (8).

We also define

$$\widetilde{\mathcal{H}}\mathcal{T}_{p,q}(\vartheta, \mathcal{W}, \mathcal{V}) = \mathcal{HT}_{p,q}(\vartheta, \mathcal{W}, \mathcal{V}) \bigcap \widetilde{\mathcal{H}}(p,j).$$

Example 1. *If* $k = 1, \sigma = 0$, *and* $\rho = 1$, *the class* $\mathcal{HT}_{p,q}(\vartheta, \mathcal{W}, \mathcal{V})$ *would reduce to the following subclass* $\mathcal{HK}_{p,q}(\vartheta, \mathcal{W}, \mathcal{V})$

$$\frac{\mathfrak{D}_q(z\mathfrak{D}_q f(z))}{\mathfrak{D}_q(f(z))} \prec ([p]_q - \vartheta)\frac{1+\mathcal{W}z}{1+\mathcal{V}z} + \vartheta. \tag{11}$$

3. A Set of Main Results

To demonstrate the geometric properties for the class $\mathcal{HT}_{p,q}(\vartheta, \mathcal{W}, \mathcal{V})$, the necessary and sufficient condition must first be proved.

Unless otherwise stated, in this paper, we suppose that $0 \leq \vartheta < [p]_q, -1 \leq \mathcal{V} < \mathcal{W} \leq 1$ and $0 < q < 1$.

Theorem 1. *Let* $f = \mathcal{F} + \overline{\mathcal{G}} \in \mathcal{H}(p, j)$ *in the form* (3), *then* $f \in \mathcal{HT}_{p,q}(\vartheta, \mathcal{W}, \mathcal{V})$ *if the following inequality holds:*

$$\begin{aligned} &\sum_{j=p+1}^{\infty} \{(1+\mathcal{V})[j]_q([j]_q - [p]_q) - (\mathcal{W} - \mathcal{V})([p]_q - \vartheta))\}\psi_q|a_j| \\ &\quad + \sum_{j=p}^{\infty}\{(1+\mathcal{V})[j]_q([j]_q - [p]_q) - (\mathcal{W} - \mathcal{V})([p]_q - \vartheta))\}\psi_q|d_j| \\ &\quad \leq (\mathcal{V} - \mathcal{W})([p]_q - \vartheta)[p]_q, \end{aligned} \tag{12}$$

where $\psi_q = \frac{\Gamma_q(\sigma+\mu)\Gamma(\rho+jk)}{\Gamma_q(\sigma j+\mu)\Gamma(\rho+k)j!}$.

Proof. Suppose that the inequality (12) is correct, it follows from (10) that

$$\begin{aligned} &|\mathfrak{D}_q(z\mathfrak{D}_q\mathcal{L}_{p,q}^{\rho,\sigma,\mu} f(z)) - [p]_q\mathfrak{D}_q\mathcal{L}_{p,q}^{\rho,\sigma,\mu} f(z)| \\ &\qquad - \left|\mathcal{V}\mathfrak{D}_q(z\mathfrak{D}_q\mathcal{L}_{p,q}^{\rho,\sigma,\mu} f(z)) - [(\mathcal{W}-\mathcal{V})([p]_q - \vartheta) + \mathcal{V}[p]_q]\mathfrak{D}_q\mathcal{L}_{p,q}^{\rho,\sigma,\mu} f(z)\right| \\ &= |\sum_{j=p+1}^{\infty} [j]_q([j]_q - [p]_q)\psi_q a_j z^{j-1} + \sum_{j=p}^{\infty}[j]_q([j]_q - [p]_q)\psi_q\overline{d_j z^{j-1}}| \\ &\qquad - | - (\mathcal{W}-\mathcal{V})([p]_q - \vartheta)[p]_q z^{p-1} \\ &\qquad + \sum_{j=p+1}^{\infty} [-\mathcal{V}[j]_q([j]_q - [p]_q) + (\mathcal{W}-\mathcal{V})([p]_q - \vartheta)]\psi_q a_j z^{j-1} \\ &\qquad + \sum_{j=p}^{\infty}[-\mathcal{V}[j]_q([j]_q - [p]_q) + (\mathcal{W}-\mathcal{V})([p]_q - \vartheta)]\psi_q\overline{d_j z^{j-1}}| \\ &\leq -(\mathcal{V}-\mathcal{W})([p]_q - \vartheta)[p]_q|z|^{p-1} \\ &\qquad + \sum_{j=p+1}^{\infty} [(1+\mathcal{V})[j]_q([j]_q - [p]_q) - (\mathcal{W}-\mathcal{V})([p]_q - \vartheta)]\psi_q|a_j||z|^{j-1} \\ &\qquad + \sum_{j=p}^{\infty}[(1+\mathcal{V})[j]_q([j]_q - [p]_q) - (\mathcal{W}-\mathcal{V})([p]_q - \vartheta)]\psi_q|d_j||z|^{j-1} \\ &< -(\mathcal{V}-\mathcal{W})([p]_q - \vartheta)[p]_q \\ &\qquad + \sum_{j=p+1}^{\infty} [(1+\mathcal{V})[j]_q([j]_q - [p]_q) - (\mathcal{W}-\mathcal{V})([p]_q - \vartheta)]\psi_q|a_j| \\ &\qquad + \sum_{j=p}^{\infty}[(1+\mathcal{V})[j]_q([j]_q - [p]_q) - (\mathcal{W}-\mathcal{V})([p]_q - \vartheta)]\psi_q|d_j|, \end{aligned}$$

thus, we observe

$$-(\mathcal{V}-\mathcal{W})([p]_q-\vartheta)[p]_q + \sum_{j=p+1}^{\infty}[(1+\mathcal{V})[j]_q([j]_q-[p]_q)-(\mathcal{W}-\mathcal{V})([p]_q-\vartheta)]\psi_q a_j + \sum_{j=p}^{\infty}[(1+\mathcal{V})[j]_q([j]_q-[p]_q)-(\mathcal{W}-\mathcal{V})([p]_q-\vartheta)]\psi_q d_j \leq 0.$$

Consequently, utilizing the maximum modulus theorem, we obtain

$$\left|\frac{\frac{\mathfrak{D}_q(z\mathfrak{D}_q\mathcal{L}_{p,q}^{\rho,\sigma,\mu}f(z))}{\mathfrak{D}_q(\mathcal{L}_{p,q}^{\rho,\sigma,\mu}f(z))}-[p]_q}{\mathcal{V}\frac{\mathfrak{D}_q(z\mathfrak{D}_q\mathcal{L}_{p,q}^{\rho,\sigma,\mu}f(z))}{\mathfrak{D}_q(\mathcal{L}_{p,q}^{\rho,\sigma,\mu}f(z))}-\{(\mathcal{W}-\mathcal{V})([p]_q-\vartheta)+\mathcal{V}[p]_q\}}\right|<1.$$

Therefore, $f \in \mathcal{HT}_{p,q}(\vartheta,\mathcal{W},\mathcal{V})$.

For the following harmonic function, the coefficient bound (12) is sharp

$$\begin{aligned} f(z) = & z^p + \sum_{j=p+1}^{\infty}\frac{(\mathcal{V}-\mathcal{W})([p]_q-\vartheta)[p]_q}{[(1+\mathcal{V})[j]_q([j]_q-[p]_q)-(\mathcal{W}-\mathcal{V})([p]_q-\vartheta)]\psi_q}\nu_{1,j}z^j \\ & + \sum_{j=p}^{\infty}\frac{(\mathcal{V}-\mathcal{W})([p]_q-\vartheta)[p]_q}{[(1+\mathcal{V})[j]_q([j]_q-[p]_q)-(\mathcal{W}-\mathcal{V})([p]_q-\vartheta)]\psi_q}\bar{\nu}_{2,j}\bar{z}^j, \end{aligned} \tag{13}$$

with $\sum_{j=p+1}^{\infty}|\nu_{1,j}|+\sum_{j=p}^{\infty}|\nu_{2,j}|=1$. □

When $k=1, \sigma=0$, and $\rho=1$, Theorem 1 becomes

Corollary 1. *Let $f=\mathcal{F}+\overline{\mathcal{G}}\in\mathcal{H}(p,j)$ in the form* (3)*, then $f\in\mathcal{HK}_{p,q}(\vartheta,\mathcal{W},\mathcal{V})$ if the following inequality holds:*

$$\begin{aligned} & \sum_{j=p+1}^{\infty}\{(1+\mathcal{V})[j]_q([j]_q-[p]_q)-(\mathcal{W}-\mathcal{V})([p]_q-\vartheta))\}|a_j| \\ & \quad + \sum_{j=p}^{\infty}\{(1+\mathcal{V})[j]_q([j]_q-[p]_q)-(\mathcal{W}-\mathcal{V})([p]_q-\vartheta))\}|d_j| \\ & \quad \leq (\mathcal{V}-\mathcal{W})([p]_q-\vartheta)[p]_q. \end{aligned} \tag{14}$$

Next, we prove that the inquality (12) is necessary and sufficient condition for the class $\widetilde{\mathcal{HT}}_{p,q}(\vartheta,\mathcal{W},\mathcal{V})$.

Theorem 2. *Let $f=\mathcal{F}+\overline{\mathcal{G}}\in\widetilde{\mathcal{H}}(p,j)$ in the form* (4)*. Then the harmonic function $f\in\widetilde{\mathcal{HT}}_{p,q}(\vartheta,\mathcal{W},\mathcal{V})$ if and only if the inequality condition* (12) *holds.*

Proof. Since $\widetilde{\mathcal{HT}}_{p,q}(\vartheta,\mathcal{W},\mathcal{V})\subset\mathcal{HT}_{p,q}(\vartheta,\mathcal{W},\mathcal{V})$, then the sufficient condition holds by the previous Theorem 1. Now, we have to prove just the necessity condition.
Let $f\in\widetilde{\mathcal{HT}}_{p,q}(\vartheta,\mathcal{W},\mathcal{V})$, from (10) yields

$$\left|\frac{\frac{\mathfrak{D}_q(z\mathfrak{D}_q\mathcal{L}_{p,q}^{\rho,\sigma,\mu}f(z))}{\mathfrak{D}_q(\mathcal{L}_{p,q}^{\rho,\sigma,\mu}f(z))}-[p]_q}{\mathcal{V}\frac{\mathfrak{D}_q(z\mathfrak{D}_q\mathcal{L}_{p,q}^{\rho,\sigma,\mu}f(z))}{\mathfrak{D}_q(\mathcal{L}_{p,q}^{\rho,\sigma,\mu}f(z))}-\{(\mathcal{W}-\mathcal{V})([p]_q-\vartheta)+\mathcal{V}[p]_q\}}\right|=$$

$$\left|\frac{-\sum_{j=p+1}^{\infty}[j]_q([j]_q-[p]_q)\psi_q|a_j|z^{j-1}-\sum_{j=p}^{\infty}[j]_q([j]_q-[p]_q)\psi_q|d_j|\bar{z}^{j-1}}{(\mathcal{V}-\mathcal{W})([p]_q-\vartheta)[p]_q z^{p-1}-\sum_{j=p+1}^{\infty}\mathcal{A}_q|a_j|z^{j-1}-\sum_{j=p}^{\infty}\mathcal{A}_q|d_j|\bar{z}^{j-1}}\right|<1,$$

where $\mathcal{A}_q = [\mathcal{V}[j]_q([j]_q - [p]_q) - (\mathcal{W} - \mathcal{V})([p]_q - \vartheta)]\psi_q$.

For $z = r < 1$, we deduce that

$$\frac{\sum_{j=p+1}^{\infty}[j]_q([j]_q - [p]_q)\psi_q|a_j|r^{j-1} + \sum_{j=p}^{\infty}[j]_q([j]_q - [p]_q)\psi_q|d_j|r^{j-1}}{(\mathcal{V} - \mathcal{W})([p]_q - \vartheta)[p]_q r^{p-1} - \sum_{j=p+1}^{\infty}\mathcal{A}_q|a_j|r^{j-1} - \sum_{j=p}^{\infty}\mathcal{A}_q|d_j|r^{j-1}} < 1. \tag{15}$$

When $r \to 1$, if condition (12) is not satisfied, inequality (15) is also not satisfied. In the range $(0,1)$, we may, thus, identify at least one $z_0 = r_0$ for which the quotient (15) is greater than 1. This conflicts with the prerequisite for $f \in \widetilde{\mathcal{HT}}_{p,q}(\vartheta, \mathcal{W}, \mathcal{V})$, hence the proof is complete. □

In the next result, we establish the extreme points of closed convex hulls of the subclass $\widetilde{\mathcal{HT}}_{p,q}(\vartheta, \mathcal{W}, \mathcal{V})$.

Theorem 3. *The function $f \in \widetilde{\mathcal{HT}}_{p,q}(\vartheta, \mathcal{W}, \mathcal{V})$ if and only if*

$$f(z) = \sum_{j=p}^{\infty}(\vartheta_j \mathcal{F}_j + \aleph_j \mathcal{G}_j), \tag{16}$$

where $\mathcal{F}_p = z^p$,

$$\mathcal{F}_j = z^p - \frac{(\mathcal{V} - \mathcal{W})([p]_q - \vartheta)[p]_q}{[(1+\mathcal{V})[j]_q([j]_q - [p]_q) - (\mathcal{W} - \mathcal{V})([p]_q - \vartheta)]\psi_q} z^j; \ (j = p+1, p+2, \ldots)$$

and

$$\mathcal{G}_j = z^p - \frac{(\mathcal{V} - \mathcal{W})([p]_q - \vartheta)[p]_q}{[(1+\mathcal{V})[j]_q([j]_q - [p]_q) - (\mathcal{W} - \mathcal{V})([p]_q - \vartheta)]\psi_q} \overline{z}^j; \ (j = p, p+1, \ldots),$$

with $\sum_{j=p}^{\infty}(\vartheta_j + \aleph_j) = 1, \vartheta_j \geq 0$, and $\aleph_j \geq 0$.

Particularly, the extreme points of the subclass $\widetilde{\mathcal{HT}}_{p,q}(\vartheta, \mathcal{W}, \mathcal{V})$ are $\{\mathcal{F}_j\}$ and $\{\mathcal{G}_j\}$.

Proof. Let f be defined as below

$$\begin{aligned} f(z) = \sum_{j=p}^{\infty}(\vartheta_j \mathcal{F}_j + \aleph_j \mathcal{G}_j) &= \sum_{j=p}^{\infty}(\vartheta_j + \aleph_j) z^p \\ &- \sum_{j=p}^{\infty} \frac{(\mathcal{V} - \mathcal{W})([p]_q - \vartheta)[p]_q}{[(1+\mathcal{V})[j]_q([j]_q - [p]_q) - (\mathcal{W} - \mathcal{V})([p]_q - \vartheta)]\psi_q} \vartheta_j z^j \\ &- \sum_{j=p}^{\infty} \frac{(\mathcal{V} - \mathcal{W})([p]_q - \vartheta)[p]_q}{[(1+\mathcal{V})[j]_q([j]_q - [p]_q) - (\mathcal{W} - \mathcal{V})([p]_q - \vartheta)]\psi_q} \aleph_j \overline{z}^j. \end{aligned} \tag{17}$$

We deduce from (17) and (4) that

$$|a_j| = \frac{(\mathcal{V} - \mathcal{W})([p]_q - \vartheta)[p]_q}{[(1+\mathcal{V})[j]_q([j]_q - [p]_q) - (\mathcal{W} - \mathcal{V})([p]_q - \vartheta)]\psi_q} \vartheta_j$$

and

$$|d_j| = \frac{(\mathcal{V} - \mathcal{W})([p]_q - \vartheta)[p]_q}{[(1+\mathcal{V})[j]_q([j]_q - [p]_q) - (\mathcal{W} - \mathcal{V})([p]_q - \vartheta)]\psi_q} \aleph_j.$$

Now

$$\sum_{j=p+1}^{\infty} \frac{[(1+\mathcal{V})[j]_q([j]_q-[p]_q)-(\mathcal{W}-\mathcal{V})([p]_q-\vartheta)]\psi_q}{(\mathcal{V}-\mathcal{W})([p]_q-\vartheta)[p]_q}|a_j| + \sum_{j=p}^{\infty} \frac{[(1+\mathcal{V})[j]_q([j]_q-[p]_q)-(\mathcal{W}-\mathcal{V})([p]_q-\vartheta)]\psi_q}{(\mathcal{V}-\mathcal{W})([p]_q-\vartheta)[p]_q}|d_j| = \sum_{j=p}^{\infty}(\vartheta_j+\aleph_j)-\vartheta_p = 1-\vartheta_p \leq 1.$$

Thus, Theorem 2 leads to the result $f \in \widetilde{\mathcal{HT}}_{p,q}(\vartheta, \mathcal{W}, \mathcal{V})$.

Conversely: Let $f \in \widetilde{\mathcal{HT}}_{p,q}(\vartheta, \mathcal{W}, \mathcal{V})$, then

$$|a_j| \leq \frac{(\mathcal{V}-\mathcal{W})([p]_q-\vartheta)[p]_q}{[(1+\mathcal{V})[j]_q([j]_q-[p]_q)-(\mathcal{W}-\mathcal{V})([p]_q-\vartheta)]\psi_q}$$

and

$$|d_j| \leq \frac{(\mathcal{V}-\mathcal{W})([p]_q-\vartheta)[p]_q}{[(1+\mathcal{V})[j]_q([j]_q-[p]_q)-(\mathcal{W}-\mathcal{V})([p]_q-\vartheta)]\psi_q}.$$

Letting

$$\vartheta_j = \frac{[(1+\mathcal{V})[j]_q([j]_q-[p]_q)-(\mathcal{W}-\mathcal{V})([p]_q-\vartheta)]\psi_q}{(\mathcal{V}-\mathcal{W})([p]_q-\vartheta)[p]_q}|a_j|; \quad (j = p+1, p+2, \ldots)$$

and

$$\aleph_j = \frac{[(1+\mathcal{V})[j]_q([j]_q-[p]_q)-(\mathcal{W}-\mathcal{V})([p]_q-\vartheta)]\psi_q}{(\mathcal{V}-\mathcal{W})([p]_q-\vartheta)[p]_q}|d_j|; \quad (j = p, p+1, \ldots),$$

with $\sum_{j=p}^{\infty}(\vartheta_j+\aleph_j) = 1$.
We get the result $f(z) = \sum_{j=p}^{\infty}(\vartheta_j\mathcal{F}_j + \aleph_j\mathcal{G}_j)$, after substituting the values of $|a_j|$ and $|d_j|$ from the above relations in (4). □

Theorem 4. *The subclass $\widetilde{\mathcal{HT}}_{p,q}(\vartheta, \mathcal{W}, \mathcal{V})$ is a convex set of the functions $f = \mathcal{F} + \overline{\mathcal{G}} \in \widetilde{\mathcal{H}}(p, j)$.*

Proof. Let $f_i \in \widetilde{\mathcal{HT}}_{p,q}(\vartheta, \mathcal{W}, \mathcal{V})$ given by

$$f_i(z) = z^p - \sum_{j=p+1}^{\infty} |a_{i,j}|z^j - \sum_{j=p}^{\infty} \overline{|d_{i,j}|z^j}, \quad (i = 1, 2). \tag{18}$$

Then, for $0 \leq \daleth \leq 1$

$$\mathcal{J}(z) = \daleth f_{1,j}(z) + (1-\daleth) f_{2,j}(z) = z^p - \sum_{j=p+1}^{\infty} (\daleth|a_{1,j}| + (1-\daleth)|a_{2,j}|)z^j - \sum_{j=p}^{\infty}(\daleth|d_{1,j}| + (1-\daleth)|d_{2,j}|)\overline{z}^j,$$

also belongs to the subclass $\widetilde{\mathcal{HT}}_{p,q}(\vartheta, \mathcal{W}, \mathcal{V})$.

By the result of Theorem 2, we get

$$\begin{aligned}
&\beth\Big[\sum_{j=p+1}^{\infty}\{(1+\mathcal{V})[j]_q([j]_q-[p]_q)-(\mathcal{W}-\mathcal{V})([p]_q-\vartheta))\psi_q\}|a_{1,j}| \\
&\qquad+\sum_{j=p}^{\infty}\{(1+\mathcal{V})[j]_q([j]_q-[p]_q)-(\mathcal{W}-\mathcal{V})([p]_q-\vartheta))\psi_q\}|d_{1,j}|\Big] \\
&+(1-\beth)\Big[\sum_{j=p+1}^{\infty}\{(1+\mathcal{V})[j]_q([j]_q-[p]_q)-(\mathcal{W}-\mathcal{V})([p]_q-\vartheta))\psi_q\}|a_{2,j}| \\
&\qquad+\sum_{j=p}^{\infty}\{(1+\mathcal{V})[j]_q([j]_q-[p]_q)-(\mathcal{W}-\mathcal{V})([p]_q-\vartheta))\psi_q\}|d_{2,j}|\Big] \\
&\qquad\leq \beth((\mathcal{V}-\mathcal{W})([p]_q-\vartheta)[p]_q)+(1-\beth)((\mathcal{V}-\mathcal{W})([p]_q-\vartheta)[p]_q) \\
&\qquad=(\mathcal{V}-\mathcal{W})([p]_q-\vartheta)[p]_q.
\end{aligned}$$

Here the subclass $\widetilde{\mathcal{HT}}_{p,q}(\vartheta, \mathcal{W}, \mathcal{V})$ is convex set, because $\mathcal{J} \in \widetilde{\mathcal{HT}}_{p,q}(\vartheta, \mathcal{W}, \mathcal{V})$. □

Theorem 5. *We have*

$$\mathcal{E}\widetilde{\mathcal{HT}}_{p,q}(\vartheta, \mathcal{W}, \mathcal{V}) = \{\mathcal{F}_j : j = \{p, p+1, \ldots\}\} \bigcup \{\mathcal{G}_j : j = \{p+1, p+2, \ldots\}\},$$

where

$$\begin{aligned}
\mathcal{F}_p &= z^p, \\
\mathcal{F}_j &= z^p - \frac{(\mathcal{V}-\mathcal{W})([p]_q-\vartheta)[p]_q}{[(1+\mathcal{V})[j]_q([j]_q-[p]_q)-(\mathcal{W}-\mathcal{V})([p]_q-\vartheta)]\psi_q} z^j, \\
\mathcal{G}_j &= -\frac{(\mathcal{V}-\mathcal{W})([p]_q-\vartheta)[p]_q}{[(1+\mathcal{V})[j]_q([j]_q-[p]_q)-(\mathcal{W}-\mathcal{V})([p]_q-\vartheta)]\psi_q} \overline{z}^j.
\end{aligned} \tag{19}$$

Proof. Suppose that $0 < \beth < 1$ and

$$\mathcal{G}_j = \beth f_1 + (1-\beth) f_2,$$

where $f_1, f_2 \in \widetilde{\mathcal{HT}}_{p,q}(\vartheta, \mathcal{W}, \mathcal{V})$ are defined in (18).

From (12), we obtain

$$|d_{j,1}| = |d_{j,2}| = \frac{(\mathcal{V}-\mathcal{W})([p]_q-\vartheta)[p]_q}{[(1+\mathcal{V})[j]_q([j]_q-[p]_q)-(\mathcal{W}-\mathcal{V})([p]_q-\vartheta)]\psi_q}$$

and as result, $a_{1,n} = a_{2,n} = 0$ for $n \in \{p+1, p+2, \ldots\}$ and $d_{1,n} = d_{2,n} = 0$ for $n \in \{p+1, p+2, \ldots\} \setminus \{j\}$.

Thus, it follows that $\mathcal{G}_j = f_1 = f_2$, hence $\mathcal{G}_j \in \widetilde{\mathcal{HT}}_{p,q}(\mu, \mathcal{W}, \mathcal{V})$.

Similarly, we can satisfy that the functions $\mathcal{F}_j$ in (19) are also extreme points of $\widetilde{\mathcal{HT}}_{p,q}(\vartheta, \mathcal{W}, \mathcal{V})$.

Now, let the function f in (18) belongs to the extreme points of the class $\widetilde{\mathcal{HT}}_{p,q}(\vartheta, \mathcal{W}, \mathcal{V})$ and f is not of the form (19).

Then there exists $n \in \{p+1, p+2, \ldots\}$, such that

$$0 < |a_n| < \frac{(\mathcal{V}-\mathcal{W})([p]_q-\vartheta)[p]_q}{[(1+\mathcal{V})[n]_q([n]_q-[p]_q)-(\mathcal{W}-\mathcal{V})([p]_q-\vartheta)]\psi_q}, \tag{20}$$

or

$$0 < |d_n| < \frac{(\mathcal{V}-\mathcal{W})([p]_q-\vartheta)[p]_q}{[(1+\mathcal{V})[n]_q([n]_q-[p]_q)-(\mathcal{W}-\mathcal{V})([p]_q-\vartheta)]\psi_q}. \tag{21}$$

If (20) is satisfied, we have

$$\beth = \frac{[(1+\mathcal{V})[n]_q([n]_q-[p]_q)-(\mathcal{W}-\mathcal{V})([p]_q-\vartheta)]\psi_q|a_n|}{(\mathcal{V}-\mathcal{W})([p]_q-\vartheta)[p]_q}, \ \phi = \frac{1}{1-\beth}(f-\beth\mathcal{F}_n),$$

we get $0<\beth<1$, $\mathcal{F}_n \neq \phi$, and $f=\beth\mathcal{F}_n+(1-\beth)\phi$. Hence $f \notin \mathcal{E}\widetilde{\mathcal{H}\mathcal{T}}_{p,q}(\vartheta,\mathcal{W},\mathcal{V})$.

Similarly, if (21) is satisfied, we also have

$$\beth = \frac{[(1+\mathcal{V})[n]_q([n]_q-[p]_q)-(\mathcal{W}-\mathcal{V})([p]_q-\vartheta)]\psi_q|a_n|}{(\mathcal{V}-\mathcal{W})([p]_q-\vartheta)[p]_q}, \ \nu = \frac{1}{1-\beth}(f-\beth\mathcal{G}_n),$$

thus $0<\beth<1$, $\mathcal{G}_n \neq \nu$, and $f=\beth\mathcal{G}_n+(1-\beth)\nu$. Hence $f \notin \mathcal{E}\widetilde{\mathcal{H}\mathcal{T}}_{p,q}(\vartheta,\mathcal{W},\mathcal{V})$. □

4. Hadamard Product Property

The Hadamard product and the closed under a convex linear combination of the subclass $\widetilde{\mathcal{H}\mathcal{T}}_{p,q}(\vartheta,\mathcal{W},\mathcal{V})$ are provided in the following results.

The Hadamard product of harmonic functions with negative coefficient is given by

$$(f*h)(z) = z^p - \sum_{j=p+1}^{\infty}|a_{1,j}a_{2,j}|z^j - \sum_{j=p}^{\infty}|d_{1,j}d_{2,j}|\overline{z}^j, \tag{22}$$

where

$$f(z) = z^p - \sum_{j=p+1}^{\infty}|a_{1,j}|z^j - \sum_{j=p}^{\infty}|d_{1,j}|\overline{z}^j \tag{23}$$

and

$$h(z) = z^p - \sum_{j=p+1}^{\infty}|a_{2,j}|z^j - \sum_{j=p}^{\infty}|d_{2,j}|\overline{z}^j. \tag{24}$$

Theorem 6. *If $f,h \in \widetilde{\mathcal{H}\mathcal{T}}_{p,q}(\vartheta,\mathcal{W},\mathcal{V})$, then $f*h \in \widetilde{\mathcal{H}\mathcal{T}}_{p,q}(\vartheta,\mathcal{W},\mathcal{V})$.*

Proof. Let $f,h \in \widetilde{\mathcal{H}\mathcal{T}}_{p,q}(\vartheta,\mathcal{W},\mathcal{V})$. Since $h \in \widetilde{\mathcal{H}\mathcal{T}}_{p,q}(\vartheta,\mathcal{W},\mathcal{V})$, we find that $|a_{2,p}|<1$ and $|d_{2,p}|<1$. Then from the Hadamard product $f*h$, we obtain

$$\begin{aligned}
&\sum_{j=p+1}^{\infty}\{(1+\mathcal{V})[j]_q([j]_q-[p]_q)-(\mathcal{W}-\mathcal{V})([p]_q-\vartheta))\}\psi_q|a_{1,j}||a_{2,j}| \\
&\quad+\sum_{j=p}^{\infty}\{(1+\mathcal{V})[j]_q([j]_q-[p]_q)-(\mathcal{W}-\mathcal{V})([p]_q-\vartheta))\}\psi_q|d_{1,j}||d_{2,j}| \\
&\leq \sum_{j=p+1}^{\infty}\{(1+\mathcal{V})[j]_q([j]_q-[p]_q)-(\mathcal{W}-\mathcal{V})([p]_q-\vartheta))\}\psi_q|a_{1,j}| \\
&\quad+\sum_{j=p}^{\infty}\{(1+\mathcal{V})[j]_q([j]_q-[p]_q)-(\mathcal{W}-\mathcal{V})([p]_q-\vartheta))\}\psi_q|d_{1,j}| \\
&\leq (\mathcal{V}-\mathcal{W})([p]_q-\vartheta)[p]_q.
\end{aligned}$$

Hence $f*h \in \widetilde{\mathcal{H}\mathcal{T}}_{p,q}(\vartheta,\mathcal{W},\mathcal{V})$. □

Theorem 7. *Let $f_s(z) = z^p - \sum_{j=p+1}^{\infty}|a_{j,s}|z^j - \sum_{j=p+1}^{\infty}|d_{j,s}|\overline{z}^j$ $(s=1,2,\dots)$ be in the subclass $\widetilde{\mathcal{H}\mathcal{T}}_{p,q}(\vartheta,\mathcal{W},\mathcal{V})$. Then the function*

$$\mathcal{J}(z) = \sum_{s=1}^{m}\eta_s f_s(z), \quad (\eta_s \geq 0, \sum_{s=1}^{\infty}\eta_s = 1),$$

also belongs to the subclass $\widetilde{\mathcal{HT}}_{p,q}(\vartheta,\mathcal{W},\mathcal{V})$. This means $\widetilde{\mathcal{HT}}_{p,q}(\vartheta,\mathcal{W},\mathcal{V})$ is closed under convex linear combination.

Proof. Since $f_s \in \widetilde{\mathcal{HT}}_{p,q}(\vartheta,\mathcal{W},\mathcal{V})$, then

$$\begin{aligned}\sum_{j=p+1}^{\infty}&\{(1+\mathcal{V})[j]_q([j]_q-[p]_q)-(\mathcal{W}-\mathcal{V})([p]_q-\vartheta))\}\psi_q|a_{j,s}|\\&+\sum_{j=p}^{\infty}\{(1+\mathcal{V})[j]_q([j]_q-[p]_q)-(\mathcal{W}-\mathcal{V})([p]_q-\vartheta))\}\psi_q|d_{j,s}|\\&\leq(\mathcal{V}-\mathcal{W})([p]_q-\vartheta)[p]_q.\end{aligned}$$

Now,

$$\mathcal{J}(z)=z^p-\sum_{j=p+1}^{\infty}(\sum_{s=1}^{\infty}\eta_s|a_{j,s}|)z^j-\sum_{j=p}^{\infty}(\sum_{s=1}^{\infty}\eta_s|d_{j,s}|)\overline{z}^j. \tag{25}$$

From (25) and (17), we conclude that

$$\begin{aligned}&\sum_{j=p+1}^{\infty}\frac{\{(1+\mathcal{V})[j]_q([j]_q-[p]_q)-(\mathcal{W}-\mathcal{V})([p]_q-\vartheta))\}\psi_q}{(\mathcal{V}-\mathcal{W})([p]_q-\vartheta)[p]_q}(\sum_{s=1}^{\infty}\eta_s|a_{j,s}|)\\&+\sum_{j=p}^{\infty}\frac{\{(1+\mathcal{V})[j]_q([j]_q-[p]_q)-(\mathcal{W}-\mathcal{V})([p]_q-\vartheta))\}\psi_q}{(\mathcal{V}-\mathcal{W})([p]_q-\vartheta)[p]_q}(\sum_{s=1}^{\infty}\eta_s|d_{j,s}|)\\&=\sum_{s=1}^{\infty}\eta_s\{\sum_{j=p+1}^{\infty}\frac{\{(1+\mathcal{V})[j]_q([j]_q-[p]_q)-(\mathcal{W}-\mathcal{V})([p]_q-\vartheta))\}\psi_q}{(\mathcal{V}-\mathcal{W})([p]_q-\vartheta)[p]_q}(|a_{j,s}|)\\&+\sum_{j=p}^{\infty}\frac{\{(1+\mathcal{V})[j]_q([j]_q-[p]_q)-(\mathcal{W}-\mathcal{V})([p]_q-\vartheta))\}\psi_q}{(\mathcal{V}-\mathcal{W})([p]_q-\vartheta)[p]_q}(|d_{j,s}|)\}\\&\leq\sum_{s=1}^{\infty}\eta_s=1.\end{aligned}$$

Hence, $\mathcal{J}\in\widetilde{\mathcal{HT}}_{p,q}(\vartheta,\mathcal{W},\mathcal{V})$. □

5. Closure Property

Next, we prove the closure property of the subclass $\widetilde{\mathcal{HT}}_{p,q}(\vartheta,\mathcal{W},\mathcal{V})$ under the q-Bernardi integral operator for p-valent functions (see [40]), which is given by

$$\mathcal{B}^p_{\omega,q}f(z)=\frac{[p+\omega]_q}{z^\omega}\int_0^z t^{\omega-1}f(t)d_qt\ \ (\omega>-p,z\in\mathbb{U}). \tag{26}$$

Definition 4. *For $f\in\widetilde{\mathcal{H}}(p,j)$, we define the q-Bernardi integral operator for p-valent functions $\mathcal{I}^p_{\omega,q}f:\widetilde{\mathcal{H}}(p,j)\to\widetilde{\mathcal{H}}(p,j)$ as follows:*

$$\begin{aligned}\mathcal{I}^p_{\omega,q}f(z)=&\frac{[p+\omega]_q}{z^\omega}\int_0^z t^{\omega-1}[t^p-\sum_{j=p+1}^{\infty}a_jt^j-\sum_{j=p}^{\infty}\overline{d_jt^j}]d_qt\\=&z^p-\sum_{j=p+1}^{\infty}\frac{[p+\omega]_q}{[j+\omega]_q}|a_j|z^j-\sum_{j=p}^{\infty}\frac{[p+\omega]_q}{[j+\omega]_q}|d_j|\overline{z}^j,\ (\omega>-p,z\in\mathbb{U}).\end{aligned} \tag{27}$$

Then

$$\mathcal{I}^p_{\omega,q}f(z)=\mathcal{I}^p_{\omega,q}\mathcal{F}(z)+\overline{\mathcal{I}^p_{\omega,q}\mathcal{G}(z)}. \tag{28}$$

Theorem 8. *If $f\in\widetilde{\mathcal{HT}}_{p,q}(\vartheta,\mathcal{W},\mathcal{V})$, then $\mathcal{I}^p_{\omega,q}f\in\widetilde{\mathcal{HT}}_{p,q}(\vartheta,\mathcal{W},\mathcal{V})$.*

Proof. Since $f \in \widetilde{\mathcal{HT}}_{p,q}(\vartheta, \mathcal{W}, \mathcal{V})$, by Theorem 2, we conclude that

$$\begin{aligned} \sum_{j=p+1}^{\infty} & \{(1+\mathcal{V})[j]_q([j]_q - [p]_q) - (\mathcal{W}-\mathcal{V})([p]_q - \vartheta))\}\psi_q |a_j| \\ & + \sum_{j=p}^{\infty}\{(1+\mathcal{V})[j]_q([j]_q - [p]_q) - (\mathcal{W}-\mathcal{V})([p]_q - \vartheta))\}\psi_q |d_j| \\ & \leq (\mathcal{V}-\mathcal{W})([p]_q - \vartheta)[p]_q. \end{aligned} \tag{29}$$

We have to prove

$$\begin{aligned} \sum_{j=p+1}^{\infty} & \{(1+\mathcal{V})[j]_q([j]_q - [p]_q) - (\mathcal{W}-\mathcal{V})([p]_q - \vartheta))\}\psi_q \frac{[p+\omega]_q}{[j+\omega]_q} |a_j| \\ & + \sum_{j=p}^{\infty}\{(1+\mathcal{V})[j]_q([j]_q - [p]_q) - (\mathcal{W}-\mathcal{V})([p]_q - \vartheta))\}\psi_q \frac{[p+\omega]_q}{[j+\omega]_q} |d_j| \\ & \leq (\mathcal{V}-\mathcal{W})([p]_q - \vartheta)[p]_q, \end{aligned} \tag{30}$$

and we observe that the inequality (30) is correct, if

$$\frac{[p+\omega]_q}{[j+\omega]_q} \leq 1.$$

Since $p \leq j$, then the inequality (30) is satisfied, and this yields to the result. □

6. Concluding Remarks

Recently, the q-calculus and its applications have received great attention in several fields of mathematical and physical sciences (especially quantum physics), as well as an affirmation of the importance of the Mittag–Leffler function in the structure of fractional calculus. In this paper, we have introduced the subclass of q-convex harmonic p-valent functions connected with the q-Mittag–Leffler function. For this harmonic subclass, we have obtained the necessary and sufficient condition, convex hulls, convex linear combination, extreme point, and Hadamard product. Finally, this research has investigated the closure property for this class employing the q-Bernardi integral operator for harmonic p-valent functions.

The outcomes of this study may be beneficial to investigate several different classes of univalent (or p-valent) functions connected to various fields, notably those that use the generalized q-Mittag–Leffler function. Therefore, the findings of this paper can facilitate new research works in Geometric Function Theory and related subjects, such as differential subordination notions, the upper bounds of Fekete–Szegö inequality, and Hankel determinant. For more details on the suggested works, see [33,41,42].

It should be noted that the Fox–Wright hypergeometric function ${}_q\Psi_s$ is much more general than many of the expansions of the Mittag–Leffler function. The survey of the more complicated and general case of the Srivastava–Wright operator (see [43,44]), defined by the Fox–Wright function ${}_q\Psi_s$, is a recent interesting subject in Geometric Function Theory. Many properties of the Srivastava–Wright operator can be found in several recent works (see [30,39,45,46]).

Author Contributions: Conceptualization, S.H.H. and M.D.; methodology, M.D.; software, A.A.L.; validation, M.D. and A.A.L.; formal analysis, M.D. and A.A.L.; investigation, S.H.H.; resources, S.H.H. and M.D.; data curation, M.D.; writing—original draft preparation, S.H.H.; writing—review and editing, M.D. and A.A.L.; visualization, A.A.L.; supervision, M.D.; project administration, M.D.; funding acquisition, A.A.L. and S.H.H. All authors have read and agreed to the published version of the manuscript.

Funding: This research received no external funding.

Institutional Review Board Statement: Not applicable.

Informed Consent Statement: Not applicable.

Data Availability Statement: Not applicable.

Conflicts of Interest: The authors declare no conflict of interest.

References

1. Jackson, F.H. On q-difference equations. *Am. J. Math.* **1910**, *32*, 305–314. [CrossRef]
2. Jackson, F.H. On q-definite integrals. *Q. J. Pure Appl. Math.* **1910**, *41*, 193–203.
3. Abdeljawad, T.; Benli, B.; Baleanu, D. A generalized q-Mittag-Leffler function by q-captuo fractional linear equations. *Abstr. Appl. Anal.* **2012**, *2012*, 546062. [CrossRef]
4. Abdeljawad, T.; Baleanu, D. Caputo q-fractional initial value problems and a q-analogue Mittag-Leffler function. *Commun. Nonlinear Sci. Numer. Simul.* **2011**, *16*, 4682–4688. [CrossRef]
5. El-Deeb, S.M.; Bulboacă, T. Differential sandwich-type results for symmetric functions connected with a Q-analog integral operator. *Mathematics* **2019**, *7*, 1185. [CrossRef]
6. Frasin, B.A.; Murugusundaramoorthy, G.A. Subordination results for a class of analytic functions defined by q-differential operator. *Ann. Univ. Paedagog. Crac. Stud. Math.* **2020**, *19*, 53–64. [CrossRef]
7. Hadi, S.H.; Darus, M. Differential subordination and superordination of a q-derivative operator connected with the q-exponential function. *Int. J. Nonlinear Anal. Appl.* **2022**, *13*, 5865416.
8. Hadi, S.H.; Darus, M. (p,q)-Chebyshev polynomials for the families of biunivalent function associating a new integral operator with (p,q)-Hurwitz zeta function. *Turk. J. Math.* **2022**, *46*, 25. [CrossRef]
9. Khan, B.; Srivastava, H.M.; Tahir, M.; Darus, M.; Ahmad, Q.Z.; Khan, N. Applications of a certain q-integral operator to the subclasses of analytic and bi-univalent functions. *AIMS Math.* **2021**, *6*, 1024–1039. [CrossRef]
10. Shah, S.A.; Noor, K.I. Study on the q-analogue of a certain family of linear operators. *Turkish J. Math.* **2019**, *43*, 2707–2714. [CrossRef]
11. Shamsan, H.; Latha, S. On generalized bounded mocanu variation related to q-derivative and conic regions. *Ann. Pure Appl. Math.* **2018**, *17*, 67–83. [CrossRef]
12. Srivastava, H.M.; Hadi, S.H.; Darus, M. Some subclasses of p-valent γ-uniformly type q-starlike and q-convex functions defined by using a certain generalized q-Bernardi integral operator. *Rev. Real Acad. Cienc. Exactas Fis. Nat. Ser. A Mat.* **2023**, *117*, 50. [CrossRef]
13. Clunie, J.; Sheil-Small, T. Harmonic univalent functions. *Ann. Acad. Sci. Fenn.* **1984**, *9*, 3–25. [CrossRef]
14. Lewy, H. On the non-vanishing of the Jacobian in certain one-to-one mappings. *Bull. Amer. Math. Soc.* **1936**, *42*, 689–692. [CrossRef]
15. Jahangiri, J.M.; Kim, Y.C.; Srivastava, H.M. Construction of a certain class of harmonic close-to-convex functions associated with the Alexander integral transform. *Integral Transform. Spec. Funct.* **2003**, *14*, 237–242. [CrossRef]
16. Aldweby, H.; Darus, M. A Subclass of harmonic univalent functions associated with q-analogue of Dziok-Srivatava operator. *ISRN Math. Anal.* **2013**, *2013*, 382312.
17. Darus, M.; Al-Shaqsi, K. On certain subclass of harmonic univalent functions. *J. Anal. Appl.* **2008**, *6*, 17–28.
18. Al-Shaqsi, K.; Darus, M. On subclass of harmonic starlike functions with respect to k-symmetric points. *Int. Math. Forum* **2007**, *2*, 2799–2805. [CrossRef]
19. Elhaddad, S.; Aldweby, H.; Darus, M. Some properties on a class of harmonic univalent functions defined by q -analogue of Ruscheweyh operator. *J. Math. Anal.* **2018**, *9*, 28–35.
20. Oshah, A.; Darus, M. A subclass of harmonic univalent functions associated with generalized fractional differential operator. *Bull. Calcutta Math. Soc.* **2015**, *107*, 205–218.
21. Khan, M.F. Certain new class of harmonic functions involving quantum calculus. *J. Funct. Spaces* **2022**, *2022*, 6996639. [CrossRef]
22. Ahuja, O.P.; Jahangiri, J.M. Multivalent harmonic starlike functions. *Ann. Univ. Mariae Curie-Sklodowska* **2001**, *55*, 1–13.
23. Ahuja, O.P.; Jahangiri, J.M. Multivalent harmonic starlike functions with missing coefficients. *Math. Sci. Res. J.* **2003**, *7*, 347–352.
24. Aouf, M.K.; Moustafa, A.O.; Adwan, E.A. Subclass of multivalent harmonic functions defined by Wright generalized hypergeometric functions. *J. Complex Anal.* **2013**, *2013*, 397428. [CrossRef]
25. Yaşar, E.; Yalçın, S. Partial sums of starlike harmonic multivalent functions. *Afr. Math.* **2015**, *26*, 53–63. [CrossRef]
26. Çakmak, S.; Yalçın, S.; Altınkaya, S. A new class of Salagean-type multivalent harmonic functions defined by subordination. *Iran. J. Sci. Technol. Trans. Sci.* **2020**, *44*, 1899–1904. [CrossRef]
27. Mittag-Leffler, G.M. Sur la nouvelle function $E\alpha(x)$. *CR Acad. Sci. Paris* **1903**, *137*, 554–558.
28. Wiman, A. Uber den fundamental satz in der theory der funktionen. *Acta Math.* **1905**, *29*, 191–201. [CrossRef]
29. Shukla, A.K.; Prajapati, J.C. On a generalization of Mittag-Leffler function and its properties. *J. Math. Anal. Appl.* **2007**, *336*, 797–811. [CrossRef]
30. Bansal, D.; Prajapat, J.K. Certain geometric properties of the Mittag-Leffler functions. *Complex Var. Ellip. Equ.* **2016**, *61*, 338–350. [CrossRef]

31. Srivastava, H.M.; Bansal, D. Close-to-convexity of a certain family of q-Mittag-Leffer functions. *J. Nonlinear Var. Anal.* **2017**, *1*, 61–69.
32. Agarwal, P.; Chand, M.; Certain, J.S. Integrals involving generalized Mittag-Leffler functions. *Proc. Natl. Acad. Sci. India Sect. A* **2015**, *85*, 359–371. [CrossRef]
33. Aouf, M.K. Fekete-Szegö properties for classes of complex order and defined by new generalization of q-Mittag Leffler function. *Afr. Mat.* **2022**, *33*, 15. [CrossRef]
34. Bas, E.; Acay, B. The direct spectral problem via local derivative including truncated Mittag-Leffler function. *Appl. Math. Comput.* **2020**, *367*, 124787. [CrossRef]
35. Cang, Y.-L.; Liu, J.-L. A family of multivalent analytic functions associated with Srivastava-Tomovski generalization of the Mittag-Leffler function. *Filomat* **2018**, *32*, 4619–4625. [CrossRef]
36. Paneva-Konovska, J. Series in Mittag-Leffler functions: Inequalities and convergent theorems. *Fract. Calc. Appl. Anal.* **2010**, *13*, 403–414.
37. Hadi, S.H.; Darus, M.; Park, C.; Lee, J.R. Some geometric properties of multivalent functions associated with a new generalized q-Mittag-Leffler function. *AIMS Math.* **2022**, *7*, 11772–11783. [CrossRef]
38. Xu, Y.-H.; Liu, J.-L. Convolution and Partial Sums of Certain Multivalent Analytic Functions Involving Srivastava–Tomovski Generalization of the Mittag–Leffler Function. *Symmetry* **2018**, *10*, 597. [CrossRef]
39. Attiya, A.A. Some applications of Mittag-Leffler function in the unit disk. *Filomat* **2016**, *30*, 2075–2081. [CrossRef]
40. Shi, L.; Khan, Q.; Srivastava, G.; Liu, J.-L.; Arif, M. A study of multivalent q-starlike functions connected with circular domain. *Mathematics* **2019**, *7*, 670. [CrossRef]
41. Aouf, M.K.; Seoudy, T.M. Certain subclasses of multivalently non-Bazilevic functions involving a generalized Mittag–Leffler function. *ROMAI J.* **2019**, *15*, 13–24.
42. Yassen, M.F. Subordination results for certain class of analytic functions associated with Mittag-Leffler function. *J. Comp. Anal. Appl.* **2019**, *26*, 738–746.
43. Srivastava, H.M.; Tomovski, Z. Fractional calculus with an integral operator containing a generalized Mittag-Leffler function in the kernal. *Appl. Math. Comput.* **2009**, *211*, 198–210. [CrossRef]
44. Kiryakova, V. Criteria for univalence of the Dziok-Srivastava and the Srivastava-Wright operators in the class A. *Appl. Math. Comput.* **2011**, *218*, 883–892. [CrossRef]
45. Srivastava, H.M. On an extension of the Mittag-Leffler function. *Yokohama Math. J.* **1968**, *16*, 77–88.
46. Srivastava, H.M. Some Fox-Wright generalized hypergeometric functions and associated families of convolution operators. *Appl. Anal. Discrete Math.* **2007**, *1*, 56–71.

axioms

Article

Levinson's Functional in Time Scale Settings

Josipa Barić

Faculty of Electrical Engineering Mechanical Engineering and Naval Architecture, University of Split, 21000 Split, Croatia; jbaric@fesb.hr

Abstract: We introduce the Levinson functional on time scales using integral inequality of Levinson's type in the terms of Δ-integral for convex (concave) functions on time scale sets and investigate its properties such as superadditivity and monotonicity. The obtained properties are used to derive the bounds of the given Levinson's functional and those results provide a refinement and the converse of the known Levinson's inequality on time scales. Further, we define new types of functionals using weighted generalized and power means on time scales, and prove their properties which can be employed in future works to obtain refinements and converses of known integral inequalities on time scales.

Keywords: Levinson's inequality; Jensen's functional; time scale calculus

MSC: 26D15; 26A51; 28A25

Citation: Barić, J. Levinson's Functional in Time Scale Settings. *Axioms* **2023**, *12*, 141. https://doi.org/10.3390/axioms12020141

Academic Editor: Hari Mohan Srivastava

Received: 30 December 2022
Revised: 19 January 2023
Accepted: 28 January 2023
Published: 30 January 2023

1. Introduction

In [1], authors Baloch, Pečarić and Praljak introduced a knew class of functions, $\mathcal{K}_1^c(I)$ proving that $\mathcal{K}_1^c(I)$ is the largest class of functions for which Levinson's inequality hold under Mecer's assumptions. J. Barić, J. Pečarić and D. Radišić obtained in [2] Levinson's type inequalities in time scale settings by using the class $\mathcal{K}_1^c(I)$ and some known results regarding integral inequalites for convex (concave) functions on time scale sets. Constructing the Levinson functional on a time scale, as a difference between the right-hand side and left-hand side of the Levinson inequality on time scale, we get the opportunity to investigate known time scale integral inequalities in other directions using the properties and boundaries of new functionals.

The known Levinson's inequality ([3]) was proved in 1964 in the following theorem.

Theorem 1. *For $c \in \mathbf{R}$, $c > 0$, let $f : (0, 2c) \to \mathbb{R}$ satisfy $f''' \geq 0$ and let p_i, x_i, y_i, $i = 1, 2, \ldots, n$, be such that $p_i > 0$, $\sum_{i=1}^n p_i = 1$, $0 \leq x_i \leq c$, and*

$$x_1 + y_1 = x_2 + y_2 = \cdots = x_n + y_n = 2c. \tag{1}$$

Then,

$$\sum_{i=1}^n p_i f(x_i) - f(\overline{x}) \leq \sum_{i=1}^n p_i f(y_i) - f(\overline{y}), \tag{2}$$

where $\overline{x} = \sum_{i=1}^n p_i x_i$ and $\overline{y} = \sum_{i=1}^n p_i y_i$ are the weighted arithmetic means.

In ([4]), Popoviciu generalized Levinson's inequality proving (2) is true if f is 3-convex function.

By rescaling axes, P. S. Bullen proved in [5], in 1973, that if $f : [a, b] \to \mathbb{R}$ is 3-convex and p_i, x_i, y_i, $i = 1, 2, \ldots, n$, are such that $p_i > 0$, $\sum_{i=1}^n p_i = 1$, $a \leq x_i, y_i \leq b$, $x_i + y_i = c$ and

$$\max\{x_1, \ldots, x_n\} \leq \min\{y_1, \ldots, y_n\}, \tag{3}$$

then (2) holds.

In 2010, Mercer ([6]) improved the Levinson inequality proving that if $f : [a, b] \to \mathbb{R}$ satisfies $f''' \geq 0$ and $p_i, x_i, y_i, i = 1, 2, \ldots, n$, are such that $p_i > 0$, $\sum_{i=1}^{n} p_i = 1$, $a \leq x_i, y_i \leq b$ and $\max\{x_1, \ldots, x_n\} \leq \min\{y_1, \ldots, y_n\}$, inequality (2) holds if (1) is weakened by

$$\sum_{i=1}^{n} p_i (x_i - \overline{x})^2 = \sum_{i=1}^{n} p_i (y_i - \overline{y})^2. \tag{4}$$

In this paper, we base our main results on Levinson's type inequality on time scale ([2]) proved for the functions belonging in a new class of functions, $\mathcal{K}_1^c(I)$, defined as follows.

Definition 1. *Let $f \colon I \to \mathbb{R}$ and $c \in I^0$, where I^0 is the interior of the interval I. We say that $f \in \mathcal{K}_1^c(I)$, (resp.$f \in \mathcal{K}_2^c(I)$), if there exists a constant λ such that the function $F(x) = f(x) - \frac{\lambda}{2}x^2$ is concave (respectively, convex) on $(-\infty, c] \cap I$ and convex (respectively, concave) on $I \cap [c, \infty)$.*

The authors proved that $\mathcal{K}_1^c(I)$ is the largest class of functions for which Levinson's inequality holds under Mercer's assumptions. For function f, which belongs to class $\mathcal{K}_1^c(I)$, we say that it is 3-convex at point c. Therefore, the class $\mathcal{K}_1^c(I)$ generalizes 3-convex functions in the following sense: a function is 3-convex on I if and only if it is 3-convex at every $c \in I^0$.

Before citing the main results that are our motivation for the new results, let us briefly introduce some basic properties of the theory of time scale calculus in the next chapter.

2. Preliminaries

The theory of time scales is attributed to Stefan Hilger and was started in his PhD thesis [7]. It represents a unification of the theory of difference equations and the theory of differential equations, unifying integral and differential calculus with the calculus of finite differences. It has applications in any field that requires simultaneous modelling of discrete and continuous cases. Many interesting results, properties and applications regarding time scale calculus can be found in [8–11] and the books [12–14].

Now, we briefly introduce the basics on time scale calculus that we need in the rest of the article, using the same notations as in [13].

A *time scale* $\mathbb{T}$ is defined as any closed subset of the set of real numbers $\mathbb{R}$. Notice that the two most representative examples of time scales are $\mathbb{R}$ and $\mathbb{Z}$. In order to unify the approaches and theories for the sets that may or may not be connected, we introduce the concept of jump operators so, for $t \in \mathbb{T}$, we define the *forward jump operator* $\sigma : \mathbb{T} \to \mathbb{T}$ by

$$\sigma(t) = \inf\{s \in \mathbb{T} : s > t\}$$

and the *backward jump operator* by

$$\rho(t) = \sup\{s \in \mathbb{T} : s < t\}.$$

The convention here is $\inf \emptyset = \sup \mathbb{T}$ (i.e., $\sigma(t) = t$ if $\mathbb{T}$ has a maximum t) and $\sup \emptyset = \inf \mathbb{T}$ (i.e., $\rho(t) = t$ if $\mathbb{T}$ has a minimum t). If $\sigma(t) > t$, then we say that t is *right-scattered*, and if $\rho(t) < t$, then we say that t is *left-scattered*. Points that are right-scattered and left-scattered at the same time are called *isolated*. Additionally, if $\sigma(t) = t$, then t is said to be *right-dense*, and if $\rho(t) = t$, then t is said to be *left-dense*. Points that are simultaneously right-dense and left-dense are called *dense*. The mapping $\mu : \mathbb{T} \to [0, \infty)$ defined by

$$\mu(t) = \sigma(t) - t$$

is called the *graininess function*. If $\mathbb{T}$ has a left-scattered maximum M, then we define $\mathbb{T}^\kappa = \mathbb{T} \setminus \{M\}$; otherwise $\mathbb{T}^\kappa = \mathbb{T}$. If $f : \mathbb{T} \to \mathbb{R}$ is a function, then we define the function $f^\sigma : \mathbb{T} \to \mathbb{R}$ by

$$f^\sigma(t) = f(\sigma(t)) \quad \text{for all} \quad t \in \mathbb{T}.$$

Definition 2. *Let $f : \mathbb{T} \to \mathbb{R}$ and $t \in \mathbb{T}^{\kappa}$. We define the* delta derivative *of f at t as a number $f^{\Delta}(t)$ (provided it exists) with the property that given any $\varepsilon > 0$, there is a neighborhood U of t such that*

$$\left|f(\sigma(t)) - f(s) - f^{\Delta}(t)(\sigma(t) - s)\right| \le \varepsilon|\sigma(t) - s| \quad \text{for all} \quad s \in U.$$

f is delta differentiable on $\mathbb{T}^{\kappa}$ provided $f^{\Delta}(t)$ exists for all $t \in \mathbb{T}^{\kappa}$.

Definition 3. *A function $f : \mathbb{T} \to \mathbb{R}$ is called* rd-continuous *if it is continuous at all right-dense points in $\mathbb{T}$ and its left-sided limits are finite at all left-dense points in $\mathbb{T}$. We denote by C_{rd} the set of all rd-continuous functions. We say that f is rd-continuously delta differentiable (and write $f \in C^1_{rd}$) if $f^{\Delta}(t)$ exists for all $t \in \mathbb{T}^{\kappa}$ and $f^{\Delta} \in C_{rd}$.*

Definition 4. *A function $F : \mathbb{T} \to \mathbb{R}$ is called a* delta antiderivative *of $f : \mathbb{T} \to \mathbb{R}$ if $F^{\Delta}(t) = f(t)$ for all $t \in \mathbb{T}^{\kappa}$. Then, if $a \in \mathbb{T}$, the* delta integral *is defined by*

$$\int_a^t f(s)\Delta s = F(t) - F(a), \quad a, t \in \mathbb{T}.$$

Notice that *every rd-continuous function has a delta antiderivative.*

In what follows, we use the same notations and approaches as in [15] [Chapter 5] and recall briefly the introduction of Lebesgue Δ-integrals. For $[a, b] \subset \mathbb{T}$, we say it is a time scale interval if

$$[a, b] = \{t \in \mathbb{T} : a \le t \le b\}, \quad a, b \in \mathbb{T},\ a \le b.$$

Let μ_{Δ} be the Lebesgue Δ-measure on $[a, b]$ and $f : [a, b] \to \mathbb{R}$ be a μ_{Δ}-measurable function. Then, the Lebesgue Δ-integral of f on $[a, b]$ can be written as $\int_{[a,b]} f d\mu_{\Delta}$, $\int_{[a,b]} f(t)\, d\mu_{\Delta}(t)$ or $\int_{[a,b]} f(t)\Delta(t)$. All theorems of the general Lebesgue integration theory, including the Lebesgue dominated convergence theorem, hold also for Lebesgue Δ-integrals on time scale $\mathbb{T}$ and the relation between the Lebesgue Δ-integral and the Riemann Δ-integral is given in the following way: if f is Riemann Δ-integrable from a to b, then f is Lebesgue Δ-integrable on $[a, b]$ and

$$R\int_a^b f(t)\, \Delta t = L \int_{[a,b]} f(t)\, \Delta t,$$

where R and L denote the Riemann and Lebesgue integrals, respectively, $[a, b]$ is a closed bounded interval in $\mathbb{T}$ and f is a bounded real valued function on $[a, b]$.

In this article, the integrals in our results are related to Lebesgue Δ-integrals and Lebesgue Δ-measure od $[a, b]$, but according to the properties of time scale theory, all results given here are true and can be rewritten for Cauchy delta integral, Cauchy nabla integral, α-diamond integral and multiple versions of Riemann and Lebesgue integrals.

Here are some properties of the Lebesgue delta integral.

Theorem 2. *If $a, b, c \in \mathbb{T}$, $\alpha \in \mathbb{R}$ and $f, g \in C_{rd}$, then*

(i) $\int_a^b (f(t) + g(t))\, d\mu_{\Delta}(t) = \int_a^b f(t) d\mu_{\Delta}(t) + \int_a^b g(t)\, d\mu_{\Delta}(t);$

(ii) $\int_a^b \alpha f(t)\, d\mu_{\Delta}(t) = \alpha \int_a^b f(t)\, d\mu_{\Delta}(t);$

(iii) $\int_a^b f(t)\, d\mu_{\Delta}(t) = -\int_b^a f(t)\, d\mu_{\Delta}(t);$

(iv) $\int\limits_a^b f(t)\,d\mu_\Delta(t) = \int\limits_a^c f(t)\,d\mu_\Delta(t) + \int\limits_c^b f(t)\,d\mu_\Delta(t)$;

(v) $\int\limits_a^a f(t)\,d\mu_\Delta(t) = 0$;

(vi) *if* $f(t) \geq 0$ *for all* t, *then* $\int\limits_a^b f(t)\,d\mu_\Delta(t) \geq 0$.

The Jensen inequality on time scales via the Δ-integral is proved in [8] by Agarwal, Bohner and Peterson.

Applying weighted Jensen's inequality on time scales ([16]), the authors in [2] established weighted Levinson's type inequality in the settings of time scale calculus and proved the following theorem.

Theorem 3. *Let* $a_i, b_i \in \mathbb{T}$, $a_i < b_i$, $i = 1,2$ *and suppose* $I \subset \mathbb{R}$ *is an interval. Assume* $w_i \in C_{\text{rd}}([a_i, b_i], \mathbb{R})$, $i = 1,2$, *are non-negative functions such that* $\int_{a_i}^{b_i} w_i(t)\,d\mu_\Delta(t) > 0$ *and* $[a_i, b_i]$, $i = 1,2$, *are time scale intervals. Let* $f_i \in C_{\text{rd}}([a_i, b_i], I)$, $i = 1,2$, *and suppose there exists* $c \in I^0$ *such that*

$$\sup_{x\in[a_1,b_1]} f_1(x) \leq c \leq \inf_{x\in[a_2,b_2]} f_2(x). \tag{5}$$

If

$$\overline{\mathcal{D}}_{[a_1,b_1]}(w_1, f_1) = \overline{\mathcal{D}}_{[a_2,b_2]}(w_2, f_2) \tag{6}$$

then the inequality

$$\begin{aligned} &\Phi\left(\frac{\int_{a_2}^{b_2} w_2(t) f_2(t)\,d\mu_\Delta(t)}{\int_{a_2}^{b_2} w_2(t)\,d\mu_\Delta(t)}\right) - \frac{\int\limits_{a_2}^{b_2} w_2(t)\Phi(f_2(t))\,d\mu_\Delta(t)}{\int_{a_2}^{b_2} w_2(t)\,d\mu_\Delta(t)} \\ &\leq \Phi\left(\frac{\int_{a_1}^{b_1} w_1(t) f_1(t)\,d\mu_\Delta(t)}{\int_{a_1}^{b_1} w_1(t)\,d\mu_\Delta(t)}\right) - \frac{\int\limits_{a_1}^{b_1} w_1(t)\Phi(f_1(t))\,d\mu_\Delta(t)}{\int_{a_1}^{b_1} w_1(t)\,d\mu_\Delta(t)} \end{aligned} \tag{7}$$

holds for every function $\Phi \in \mathcal{K}_1^c(I)$, *where the term* $\overline{\mathcal{D}}_{[a,b]}(w, f)$ *denotes following expression*

$$\overline{\mathcal{D}}_{[a,b]}(w, f) = \frac{\int\limits_a^b w(t)(f(t))^2\,d\mu_\Delta(t)}{\int_a^b w(t)\,d\mu_\Delta(t)} - \left(\frac{\int\limits_a^b w(t) f(t)\,d\mu_\Delta(t)}{\int_a^b w(t)\,d\mu_\Delta(t)}\right)^2.$$

If the function Φ *is contained in* $\mathcal{K}_2^c(I)$, *then the sign of inequality* (7) *is reversed.*

This theorem will be our starting point in defining Levinson's functional.

3. Definition of Levinson's Functional on Time Scales and Its Properties

Recently, many authors investigated the concept of the Jensen functional as a difference between the right-hand side and the left-hand side of the Jensen inequality regarding different kinds of environments (discrete cases, integral cases, linear sets of real-valued functions, time scale sets, etc.) The benefit of investigating those new functionals lies in their properties, which yield to new generalizations of known inequalities.

In [17], authors defined Jensen's functional on time scales by

$$\mathcal{J}_{\mathbb{T}}(\Phi, f, p; \mu_\Delta) = \int_a^b p(\Phi \circ f)\, d\mu_\Delta - \int_a^b p\, d\mu_\Delta \Phi \left(\frac{\int_a^b pf\, d\mu_\Delta}{\int_a^b p\, d\mu_\Delta} \right), \tag{8}$$

where $\Phi \in C(I, \mathbb{R})$, $f : [a, b] \to \mathbb{R}$ is Δ-integrable and $p : [a, b] \to \mathbb{R}$ is non-negative and Δ-integrable such that $\int_a^b p\, d\mu_\Delta > 0$.

In this section, we define Levinson's functional on time scales and prove some of its properties.

Definition 5. *Let $a_i, b_i \in \mathbb{T}$, $a_i < b_i$, $i = 1, 2$ and suppose $I \subset \mathbb{R}$ is an interval. Assume $w_i \in C_{rd}([a_i, b_i], \mathbb{R})$, $i = 1, 2$, are non-negative functions such that $\int_{a_i}^{b_i} w_i(t)\, d\mu_\Delta(t) > 0$. Let $f_i \in C_{rd}([a_i, b_i], I)$, $i = 1, 2$, and suppose there exists $c \in I^0$ such that* (5) *is fulfilled. Then, we define Levinson's functional on time scales by*

$$\mathcal{L}_{\mathbb{T}}(\Phi, f_1, f_2, w_1, w_2; \mu_\Delta) = \mathcal{J}_{\mathbb{T}}(\Phi, f_2, w_2; \mu_\Delta) - \mathcal{J}_{\mathbb{T}}(\Phi, f_1, w_1; \mu_\Delta), \tag{9}$$

where $\mathcal{J}_{\mathbb{T}}(\Phi, f_i, w_i; \mu_\Delta)$, $i = 1, 2$, denotes Jensen's functionals on time scales defined by (8) *and continuous function $\Phi \in \mathcal{K}_1^c(I)$ (or $\Phi \in \mathcal{K}_2^c(I)$).*

Remark 1. *From the main statement of Theorem 3 it is obvious that*

$$\mathcal{L}_{\mathbb{T}}(\Phi, f_1, f_2, w_1, w_2; \mu_\Delta) \geq 0, \tag{10}$$

for every continuous function $\Phi \in \mathcal{K}_1^c(I)$. If continuous function $\Phi \in \mathcal{K}_2^c(I)$, then the sing in (10) *is reversed.*

Remark 2. *Since the Levinson functional is related to a class $\mathcal{K}_1^c(I)$ or $\mathcal{K}_2^c(I)$, we will use Definition 1 to express it by the terms of convex or concave function as it will be substantial in proving our new results. In order to obtain that, we start with Jensen's functional on time scales $\mathcal{J}_{\mathbb{T}}(\Phi, f_i, w_i; \mu_\Delta)$, $i = 1, 2$. According to Definition 1, for $\Phi \in \mathcal{K}_1^c(I)$, there exists a constant λ such that $F(x) = \Phi(x) - \frac{\lambda}{2}x^2$ is concave on $(-\infty, c] \cap I$ and convex on $I \cap [c, \infty)$ so, for $i = 1, 2$, we can write*

$$\begin{aligned}
\mathcal{J}_{\mathbb{T}}(\Phi, f_i, w_i; \mu_\Delta) &= \int_{a_i}^{b_i} w_i \left(F \circ f_i + \frac{\lambda}{2} f_i^2 \right) d\mu_\Delta \\
&- \int_{a_i}^{b_i} w_i\, d\mu_\Delta \cdot \left[F \left(\frac{\int_{a_i}^{b_i} w_i f_i\, d\mu_\Delta}{\int_{a_i}^{b_i} w_i\, d\mu_\Delta} \right) + \frac{\lambda}{2} \left(\frac{\int_{a_i}^{b_i} w_i f_i\, d\mu_\Delta}{\int_{a_i}^{b_i} w_i\, d\mu_\Delta} \right) \right] \\
&= \mathcal{J}_{\mathbb{T}}(F, f_i, w_i; \mu_\Delta) + \frac{\lambda}{2} \left[\int_{a_i}^{b_i} w_i f_i^2\, d\mu_\Delta - \frac{\left(\int_{a_i}^{b_i} w_i \cdot f_i\, d\mu_\Delta \right)^2}{\int_{a_i}^{b_i} w_i\, d\mu_\Delta} \right].
\end{aligned}$$

For simplicity, let us denote

$$\sigma_i(f_i, w_i) = \int\limits_{a_i}^{b_i} w_i f_i^2 \, d\mu_\Delta - \frac{\left(\int\limits_{a_i}^{b_i} w_i \cdot f_i \, d\mu_\Delta \right)^2}{\int\limits_{a_i}^{b_i} w_i \, d\mu_\Delta}.$$

Now, Jensen's functional on time scales can be rewritten in the following form

$$\mathcal{J}_{\mathbb{T}}(\Phi, f_i, w_i; \mu_\Delta) = \mathcal{J}_{\mathbb{T}}(F, f_i, w_i; \mu_\Delta) + \frac{\lambda}{2} \cdot \sigma_i(f_i, w_i) \tag{11}$$

and Levinson's functional on time scales, defined by (9)*, can be expressed via convex (concave) functions as*

$$\begin{aligned} \mathcal{L}_{\mathbb{T}}(\Phi, f_1, f_2, w_1, w_2; \mu_\Delta) \quad &= \quad \mathcal{J}_{\mathbb{T}}(F, f_2, w_2; \mu_\Delta) - \mathcal{J}_{\mathbb{T}}(F, f_1, w_1; \mu_\Delta) \\ &\quad + \frac{\lambda}{2} \cdot [\sigma_2(f_2, w_2) - \sigma_1(f_1, w_1)]. \end{aligned} \tag{12}$$

In the following theorem, we derive the superadditivity property of the Levinson functional on time scales.

Theorem 4. *Let $a_i, b_i \in \mathbb{T}$, $a_i < b_i$, $i = 1, 2$ and suppose $I \subset \mathbb{R}$ is an interval. Assume $w_i, \phi_i \in C_{rd}([a_i, b_i], \mathbb{R})$, $i = 1, 2$, are non-negative functions such that $\int_{a_i}^{b_i} w_i \, d\mu_\Delta > 0$, $\int_{a_i}^{b_i} \phi_i \, d\mu_\Delta > 0$, $\int_{a_i}^{b_i} (w_i + \phi_i) \, d\mu_\Delta > 0$. Let $f_i \in C_{rd}([a_i, b_i], I)$, $i = 1, 2$, and suppose there exists $c \in I^0$ such that* (5) *is fulfilled. If*

$$\sigma_1(f_1, w_1) + \sigma_1(f_1, \phi_1) - \sigma_1(f_1, w_1 + \phi_1) = \sigma_2(f_2, w_2) + \sigma_2(f_2, \phi_2) - \sigma_2(f_2, w_2 + \phi_2) \tag{13}$$

then, for every continuous function $\Phi \in \mathcal{K}_1^c(I)$, we have

$$\mathcal{L}_{\mathbb{T}}(\Phi, f_1, f_2, w_1 + \phi_1, w_2 + \phi_2; \mu_\Delta) \geq \mathcal{L}_{\mathbb{T}}(\Phi, f_1, f_2, w_1, w_2; \mu_\Delta) + \mathcal{L}_{\mathbb{T}}(\Phi, f_1, f_2, \phi_1, \phi_2; \mu_\Delta). \tag{14}$$

If continuous function $\Phi \in \mathcal{K}_2^c(I)$, then the sing in (14) *is reversed.*

Proof. Suppose $\Phi \in \mathcal{K}_1^c(I)$ is continuous. According to Definition 1, there exists a constant λ such that $F(x) = \Phi(x) - \frac{\lambda}{2}x^2$ is convex on $I \cap [c, \infty)$. Using (11) and superadditivity of the Jensen functional on time scales, we obtain

$$\mathcal{J}_{\mathbb{T}}(\Phi, f_2, w_2 + \phi_2; \mu_\Delta) = \mathcal{J}_{\mathbb{T}}(F, f_2, w_2 + \phi_2; \mu_\Delta) + \frac{\lambda}{2}\sigma_2(f_2, w_2 + \phi_2)$$

$$\geq \mathcal{J}_{\mathbb{T}}(F, f_2, w_2; \mu_\Delta) + \mathcal{J}_{\mathbb{T}}(F, f_2, \phi_2; \mu_\Delta) + \frac{\lambda}{2}\sigma_2(f_2, w_2 + \phi_2) \tag{15}$$

$$\begin{aligned} &= \mathcal{J}_{\mathbb{T}}(\Phi, f_2, w_2; \mu_\Delta) - \frac{\lambda}{2}\sigma_2(f_2, w_2) + \mathcal{J}_{\mathbb{T}}(\Phi, f_2, \phi_2; \mu_\Delta) \\ &\quad - \frac{\lambda}{2}\sigma_2(f_2, \phi_2) + \frac{\lambda}{2}\sigma_2(f_2, w_2 + \phi_2) \end{aligned} \tag{16}$$

Furthermore, according to Definition 1, for continuous function $\Phi \in \mathcal{K}_1^c(I)$ and taken constant λ, $F(x) = \Phi(x) - \frac{\lambda}{2}x^2$ is concave on $(-\infty, c] \cap I$, therefore, we can write

$$\begin{aligned} &\mathcal{J}_{\mathbb{T}}(\Phi, f_1, w_1 + \phi_1; \mu_\Delta) \leq \mathcal{J}_{\mathbb{T}}(\Phi, f_1, w_1; \mu_\Delta) + \mathcal{J}_{\mathbb{T}}(\Phi, f_1, \phi_1; \mu_\Delta) \\ &\quad - \frac{\lambda}{2}\sigma_1(f_1, w_1) - \frac{\lambda}{2}\sigma_1(f_1, \phi_1) + \frac{\lambda}{2}\sigma_1(f_1, w_1 + \phi_1). \end{aligned} \tag{17}$$

Now, since

$$\mathcal{L}_{\mathbb{T}}(\Phi, f_1, f_2, w_1 + \phi_1, w_2 + \phi_2; \mu_\Delta) = \mathcal{J}_{\mathbb{T}}(\Phi, f_2, w_2 + \phi_2; \mu_\Delta) - \mathcal{J}_{\mathbb{T}}(\Phi, f_1, w_1 + \phi_1; \mu_\Delta)$$

the required property (14) of superadditivity of Levinson's functional on time scales follows by adding up (15) and (17) and taking into account the assumption (13). If continuous function $\Phi \in \mathcal{K}_2^c(I)$, then the sing in (14) will be reversed since F is convex on $(-\infty, c] \cap I$ and concave on $I \cap [c, \infty)$ and the inequality signs in (15) and (17) are reversed. □

In the next corollary, we will use the property of superadditivity to prove the monotonicity of Levinson's functional on time scales.

Corollary 1. *Let w_i, ϕ_i, f_i satisfy the hypotheses of Theorem 4 for $i = 1, 2$. Suppose there exists $c \in I^0$ such that* (5) *is fulfilled. If*

$$\sigma_1(f_1, w_1 - \phi_1) = \sigma_2(f_2, w_2 - \phi_2) \tag{18}$$

$$\sigma_1(f_1, \phi_1) - \sigma_1(f_1, w_1) = \sigma_2(f_2, \phi_2) - \sigma_2(f_2, w_2) \tag{19}$$

then Levinson's functional on time scale is increasing, that is, $w_i \geq \phi_i$ for $i = 1, 2$, implies

$$\mathcal{L}_{\mathbb{T}}(\Phi, f_1, f_2, w_1, w_2; \mu_\Delta) \geq \mathcal{L}_{\mathbb{T}}(\Phi, f_1, f_2, \phi_1, \phi_2; \mu_\Delta) \tag{20}$$

for continuous function $\Phi \in \mathcal{K}_1^c(I)$. If continuous function $\Phi \in \mathcal{K}_2^c(I)$, then (20) *holds in reverse order.*

Proof. Taking into account condition (19), we can apply superadditivity of the Levinson functional in the following way.

$$\begin{aligned} &\mathcal{L}_{\mathbb{T}}(\Phi, f_1, f_2, w_1 - \phi_1 + \phi_1, w_2 - \phi_2 + \phi_2; \mu_\Delta) \\ &\geq \mathcal{L}_{\mathbb{T}}(\Phi, f_1, f_2, w_1 - \phi_1, w_2 - \phi_2; \mu_\Delta) + \mathcal{L}_{\mathbb{T}}(\Phi, f_1, f_2, \phi_1, \phi_2; \mu_\Delta), \end{aligned}$$

i.e.

$$\begin{aligned} &\mathcal{L}_{\mathbb{T}}(\Phi, f_1, f_2, w_1, w_2; \mu_\Delta) \\ \geq\ &\mathcal{L}_{\mathbb{T}}(\Phi, f_1, f_2, w_1 - \phi_1, w_2 - \phi_2; \mu_\Delta) + \mathcal{L}_{\mathbb{T}}(\Phi, f_1, f_2, \phi_1, \phi_2; \mu_\Delta). \end{aligned}$$

From (18) we have

$$\mathcal{L}_{\mathbb{T}}(\Phi, f_1, f_2, w_1 - \phi_1, w_2 - \phi_2; \mu_\Delta) \geq 0$$

so inequality (20) is true. If continuous function $\Phi \in \mathcal{K}_2^c(I)$, the sign in (20) is reversed according to Remark 1. □

In the next result, we obtain bounds for the Levinson functional on time scales assuming the positivity of the required functionals.

Theorem 5. *Suppose $a_i, b_i \in \mathbb{T}$, $a_i < b_i$, $i = 1, 2$, and $I \subset \mathbb{R}$ is an interval. Let $w_i \in C_{\mathrm{rd}}([a_i, b_i], \mathbb{R})$, $i = 1, 2$ be non-negative functions such that $\int_{a_i}^{b_i} w_i \, d\mu_\Delta > 0$ and suppose w_i are bounded. Let $m_i = \inf_{x \in [a_i, b_i]} w_i(x)$, $M_i = \sup_{x \in [a_i, b_i]} w_i(x)$, $i = 1, 2$. Let $f_i \in C_{\mathrm{rd}}([a_i, b_i], I)$ and suppose there exists $c \in I^0$ such that* (5) *holds. If*

$$\sigma_1(f_1, w_1) = \sigma_2(f_2, w_2), \tag{21}$$

$$\sigma_1(f_1, w_1 - min\{m_1, m_2\}) = \sigma_2(f_2, w_2 - min\{m_1, m_2\}) \tag{22}$$

and

$$\sigma_1(f_1, 1) = \sigma_2(f_2, 1), \tag{23}$$

then

$$\mathcal{L}_{\mathbb{T}}(\Phi, f_1, f_2, w_1, w_2; \mu_\Delta) \geq min\{m_1, m_2\}\mathcal{L}_{\mathbb{T}}(\Phi, f_1, f_2, 1, 1; \mu_\Delta) \tag{24}$$

holds for continuous function $\Phi \in \mathcal{K}_1^c(I)$ and $\mathcal{L}_{\mathbb{T}}(\Phi, f_1, f_2, 1, 1; \mu_\Delta)$ denotes the non-weighted Levinson's functional on time scales. If conditions (21), (23) are fulfilled and condition (22) is replaced by

$$\sigma_1(f_1, max\{m_1, m_2\} - w_1) = \sigma_2(f_2, max\{m_1, m_2\} - w_2) \tag{25}$$

then

$$\mathcal{L}_{\mathbb{T}}(\Phi, f_1, f_2, w_1, w_2; \mu_\Delta) \leq max\{m_1, m_2\}\mathcal{L}_{\mathbb{T}}(\Phi, f_1, f_2, 1, 1; \mu_\Delta). \tag{26}$$

If continuous function Φ belongs to $\mathcal{K}_2^c(I)$ then (24) and (26) are reversed.

Proof. In order to prove (24), we use the monotonicity property (20), taking $\phi_i(x) = \min\{m_1, m_2\}$, $x \in [a_i, b_i]$, $i = 1, 2$. Since $w_i(x) \geq \min\{m_1, m_2\}$, $i = 1, 2$, applying (20), we obtain

$$\begin{aligned} \mathcal{L}_{\mathbb{T}}(\Phi, f_1, f_2, w_1, w_2; \mu_\Delta) &\geq \mathcal{L}_{\mathbb{T}}(\Phi, f_1, f_2, \min\{m_1, m_2\}, \min\{m_1, m_2\}; \mu_\Delta) \\ &= \min\{m_1, m_2\}\mathcal{L}_{\mathbb{T}}(\Phi, f_1, f_2, 1, 1; \mu_\Delta) \end{aligned}$$

thus, inequality (24) holds. Inequality (26) follows from the same reasoning. □

Remark 3. *Rewritting inequalities (24) and (7) in expanded forms, it can easily be seen that inequality (24) represents a refinement of the Levinson inequality (7) in Theorem 3 and inequality (26) yields a converse of (7).*

Example 1. *Taking in (9) that $\mathbb{T} = \mathbb{Z}$, $[a_1, b_1] = \{1, 2, \ldots, n\}$, $[a_2, b_2] = \{1, 2, \ldots, m\}$, $n, m \in \mathbb{N}$ and $f_1(i) = x_i$, $w_1(i) = w_{1i}$, $f_2(j) = y_j$, $w_2(j) = w_{2j}$, $i \in \{1, 2, \ldots, n\}$, $j \in \{1, 2, \ldots, m\}$, we obtain the following discrete form of Levinson's functional (9)*

$$\begin{aligned} &\mathcal{L}(\Phi, x, y, w_1, w_2) = \mathcal{J}(\Phi, y, w_2) - \mathcal{J}(\Phi, x, w_1) \\ &= \sum_{j=1}^{m} w_{2j}\Phi(y_j) - \sum_{i=1}^{n} w_{1i}\Phi(x_i) + \sum_{i=1}^{n} w_{1i}\Phi\left(\frac{\sum_{i=1}^{n} w_{1i}x_i}{\sum_{i=1}^{n} w_{1i}}\right) - \sum_{j=1}^{m} w_{2j}\Phi\left(\frac{\sum_{j=1}^{m} w_{2j}y_j}{\sum_{j=1}^{m} w_{2j}}\right) \end{aligned}$$

where I is an interval, $c \in I^0$, $\Phi \in \mathcal{K}_1^c(I)$, $x = (x_1, \ldots, x_n) \in I \cap (-\infty, c]$, $y = (y_1, \ldots, y_m) \in I \cap [c, +\infty)$, $w_1 = (w_{11}, \ldots, w_{1n}) \in \mathbb{R}_+^n$, $w_2 = (w_{21}, \ldots, w_{2m}) \in \mathbb{R}_+^m$. Under these notations, if

$$\sum_{i=1}^{n} w_{1i}x_i^2 - \frac{\left(\sum_{i=1}^{n} w_{1i}x_i\right)^2}{\sum_{i=1}^{n} w_{1i}} \leq \sum_{j=1}^{m} w_{2j}y_j^2 - \frac{\left(\sum_{j=1}^{m} w_{2j}y_j\right)^2}{\sum_{j=1}^{m} w_{2j}}, \tag{27}$$

$$\sum_{i=1}^{n}(w_{1i} - \gamma)x_i^2 - \frac{\left(\sum_{i=1}^{n}(w_{1i} - \gamma)x_i\right)^2}{\sum_{i=1}^{n}(w_{1i} - \gamma)} \leq \sum_{j=1}^{m}(w_{2j} - \gamma)y_j^2 - \frac{\left(\sum_{j=1}^{m}(w_{2j} - \gamma)y_j\right)^2}{\sum_{j=1}^{m}(w_{2j} - \gamma)} \tag{28}$$

and

$$\sum_{i=1}^{n} x_i^2 - \frac{\left(\sum_{i=1}^{n} x_i\right)^2}{n} \leq \sum_{j=1}^{m} y_j^2 - \frac{\left(\sum_{j=1}^{m} y_j\right)^2}{m}, \tag{29}$$

then

$$\mathcal{L}(\Phi, x, y, w_1, w_2) \geq \gamma \mathcal{L}(\Phi, x, y, 1, 1)$$

where $\gamma = min\{w_{1i}, w_{2j} : 1 = 1, \ldots, n; j = 1, \ldots, m\}$. *If conditions* (27) *and* (29) *are true and* (28) *is replaced by*

$$\sum_{i=1}^{n}(\Gamma - w_{1i})x_i^2 - \frac{\left(\sum_{i=1}^{n}(\Gamma - w_{1i})x_i\right)^2}{\sum_{i=1}^{n}(\Gamma - w_{1i})} \leq \sum_{j=1}^{m}(\Gamma - w_{2j})y_j^2 - \frac{\left(\sum_{j=1}^{m}(\Gamma - w_{2j})y_j\right)^2}{\sum_{j=1}^{m}(\Gamma - w_{2j})} \tag{30}$$

where $\Gamma = max\{w_{1i}, w_{2j} : 1 = 1, \ldots, n; j = 1, \ldots, m\}$, *then*

$$\mathcal{L}(\Phi, x, y, w_1, w_2) \leq \Gamma \mathcal{L}(\Phi, x, y, 1, 1)$$

In the case when $n = m$, $w_{1i} = w_{2i}$, $i = 1, \ldots, n$ *and the condition* (1) *is fulfilled, i.e., the distribution of points* x_i, y_i *around the* c *is symmetric, then* (27)–(30) *hold with equality signs.*

Example 2. *Suppose* $\mathbb{T} = \mathbb{R}$ *and* $a_i, b_i \in \mathbb{R}$, $i = 1, 2$. *Then, the Levinson functional* (9) *becomes*

$$\int_{a_2}^{b_2} w_2(t)[\Phi(f_2(t))]\, d\mu(t) - \int_{a_2}^{b_2} w_2(t)\, d\mu(t) \cdot \Phi\left(\frac{\int_{a_2}^{b_2} w_2(t) f_2(t)\, d\mu(t)}{\int_{a_2}^{b_2} w_2(t)\, d\mu(t)}\right)$$
$$- \int_{a_1}^{b_1} w_1(t)[\Phi(f_1(t))]\, d\mu(t) + \int_{a_1}^{b_1} w_1(t)\, d\mu(t) \cdot \Phi\left(\frac{\int_{a_1}^{b_1} w_1(t) f_1(t)\, d\mu(t)}{\int_{a_1}^{b_1} w_1(t)\, d\mu(t)}\right),$$

where $w_i : [a_i, b_i] \to \mathbb{R}$ *are non-negative integrable functions such that* $\int_{a_i}^{b_i} w_i(t)\, d\mu(t) > 0$, $f_i : [a_i, b_i] \to \mathbb{R}$ *are integrable and* $\Phi \in \mathcal{K}_1^c(I)$.

4. Applications to Weighted Generalized Means

Weighted generalized mean is defined in [17] as follows.

Definition 6. *Let* $\chi \in C(I, \mathbb{R})$ *be strictly monotone,* $I \subset \mathbb{R}$ *is an interval. Assume* $f : [a, b] \to I$ *is* Δ*-integrable and* $w : [a, b] \to \mathbb{R}$ *is non-negative and* Δ*-integrable such that* $\int_a^b w\, d\mu_\Delta > 0$. *Weighted generalized mean on time scales is defined as*

$$\mathcal{M}_\chi(f, w; \mu_\Delta) = \chi^{-1}\left(\frac{\int_a^b w(\chi \circ f)\, d\mu_\Delta}{\int_a^b w\, d\mu_\Delta}\right)$$

provided that all integrals are well defined.

Applying the definition of Levinson's functional on time scales, in the following theorem, we establish new Levinson's type functional in the terms of generalized means and prove its properties. The obtained properties can be used to improve some known inequalities on time scales.

Theorem 6. *Assume $\chi, \psi \in C(I, \mathbb{R})$ are strictly monotone, $I \subset \mathbb{R}$ is an interval. Let w_i, ϕ_i, f_i satisfy the hypotheses of Theorem 4 for $i = 1, 2$ such that the functional*

$$\int_{a_2}^{b_2} w_2 \, d\mu_\Delta \cdot \left[\chi(\mathcal{M}_\chi(f_2, w_2; \mu_\Delta)) - \chi(\mathcal{M}_\psi(f_2, w_2; \mu_\Delta))\right]$$
$$- \int_{a_1}^{b_1} w_1 \, d\mu_\Delta \cdot \left[\chi(\mathcal{M}_\chi(f_1, w_1; \mu_\Delta)) - \chi(\mathcal{M}_\psi(f_1, w_1; \mu_\Delta))\right]$$
$$+ \frac{\lambda}{2} \cdot [\sigma_2(\psi \circ f_2, w_2) - \sigma_1(\psi \circ f_1, w_1)] \tag{31}$$

is well defined. Denoting (31) *by $\mathcal{G}(f_1, f_2, w_1, w_2; \mu_\Delta)$, we obtain that if $\chi \circ \psi^{-1}$ is convex and following conditions are fulfilled:*

$$\sigma_1(\psi \circ f_1, w_1) = \sigma_2(\psi \circ f_2, w_2), \tag{32}$$

$$\sigma_1(\psi \circ f_1, \phi_1) - \sigma_1(\psi \circ f_1, w_1 + \phi_1) = \sigma_2(\psi \circ f_2, \phi_2) - \sigma_2(\psi \circ f_2, w_2 + \phi_2), \tag{33}$$

then (31) *is superadditive, i.e.,*

$$\mathcal{G}(f_1, f_2, w_1 + \phi_1, w_2 + \phi_2; \mu_\Delta) \geq \mathcal{G}(f_1, f_2, w_1, w_2; \mu_\Delta) + \mathcal{G}(f_1, f_2, \phi_1, \phi_2; \mu_\Delta). \tag{34}$$

Moreover, if $\chi \circ \psi^{-1}$ is concave, then (31) *is subadditive, that is, inequality* (34) *holds in reverse order.*

Proof. We start by replacing, in definition (12) of Levinson's functional on time scales, function F by $\chi \circ \psi^{-1}$ and function f_i by $\psi \circ f_i$, $i = 1, 2$. It follows that

$$\mathcal{L}_{\mathbb{T}}(\Phi, \psi \circ f_1, \psi \circ f_2, w_1, w_2; \mu_\Delta) = \mathcal{J}_{\mathbb{T}}\left(\chi \circ \psi^{-1}, \psi \circ f_2, w_2; \mu_\Delta\right)$$
$$- \mathcal{J}_{\mathbb{T}}\left(\chi \circ \psi^{-1}, \psi \circ f_1, w_1; \mu_\Delta\right) + \frac{\lambda}{2} \cdot [\sigma_2(\psi \circ f_2, w_2) - \sigma_1(\psi \circ f_1, w_1)]$$
$$= \int_{a_2}^{b_2} w_2 \cdot \left[\left(\chi \circ \psi^{-1}\right) \cdot (\psi \circ f_2)\right] d\mu_\Delta - \int_{a_2}^{b_2} w_2 \, d\mu_\Delta \cdot \left(\chi \circ \psi^{-1}\right) \circ \left(\frac{\int_{a_2}^{b_2} w_2 \cdot (\psi \circ f_2) \, d\mu_\Delta}{\int_{a_2}^{b_2} w_2 \, d\mu_\Delta} \right)$$
$$- \int_{a_1}^{b_1} w_1 \left[\left(\chi \circ \psi^{-1}\right) \cdot (\psi \circ f_1)\right] d\mu_\Delta - \int_{a_1}^{b_1} w_1 \, d\mu_\Delta \cdot \left(\chi \circ \psi^{-1}\right) \circ \left(\frac{\int_{a_1}^{b_1} w_1 \cdot (\psi \circ f_1) \, d\mu_\Delta}{\int_{a_1}^{b_1} w_1 \, d\mu_\Delta} \right)$$
$$+ \frac{\lambda}{2} \cdot [\sigma_2(\psi \circ f_2, w_2) - \sigma_1(\psi \circ f_1, w_1)]$$

(according to Definition 6 and condition (32), we continue as follows)

$$= \int_{a_2}^{b_2} w_2 \cdot (\chi \circ f_2)\, d\mu_\Delta - \int_{a_2}^{b_2} w_2\, d\mu_\Delta \cdot \chi(\mathcal{M}_\psi(f_2, w_2; \mu_\Delta))$$
$$- \int_{a_1}^{b_1} w_1 \cdot (\chi \circ f_1)\, d\mu_\Delta + \int_{a_1}^{b_1} w_1\, d\mu_\Delta \cdot \chi(\mathcal{M}_\psi(f_1, w_1; \mu_\Delta))$$
$$= \int_{a_2}^{b_2} w_2\, d\mu_\Delta \cdot \chi(\mathcal{M}_\chi(f_2, w_2; \mu_\Delta)) - \int_{a_2}^{b_2} w_2\, d\mu_\Delta \cdot \chi(\mathcal{M}_\psi(f_2, w_2; \mu_\Delta))$$
$$- \int_{a_1}^{b_1} w_1\, d\mu_\Delta \cdot \chi(\mathcal{M}_\chi(f_1, w_1; \mu_\Delta)) + \int_{a_1}^{b_1} w_1\, d\mu_\Delta \cdot \chi(\mathcal{M}_\psi(f_1, w_1; \mu_\Delta))$$
$$= \int_{a_2}^{b_2} w_2\, d\mu_\Delta \cdot \left[\chi(\mathcal{M}_\chi(f_2, w_2; \mu_\Delta)) - \chi(\mathcal{M}_\psi(f_2, w_2; \mu_\Delta))\right]$$
$$- \int_{a_1}^{b_1} w_1\, d\mu_\Delta \cdot \left[\chi(\mathcal{M}_\chi(f_1, w_1; \mu_\Delta)) - \chi(\mathcal{M}_\psi(f_1, w_1; \mu_\Delta))\right]$$

Now, the superadditivity property (34) follows immediately from Theorem 4 and conditions (32) and (33). □

Corollary 2. *Assume $\chi, \psi \in C(I, \mathbb{R})$ are strictly monotone, $I \subset \mathbb{R}$ is an interval. Let w_i, ϕ_i, f_i satisfy the hypotheses of Theorem 4 for $i = 1, 2$ such that the functional $\mathcal{G}(f_1, f_2, w_1, w_2; \mu_\Delta)$ defined by* (31) *is well defined. If*

$$\sigma_1(\psi \circ f_1, w_1 - \phi_1) = \sigma_2(\psi \circ f_2, w_2 - \phi_2) \tag{35}$$

and

$$\sigma_1(\psi \circ f_1, \phi_1) - \sigma_1(\psi \circ f_1, w_1) = \sigma_2(\psi \circ f_2, \phi_2) - \sigma_2(\psi \circ f_2, w_2) \tag{36}$$

then, the Levinson's type functional (31) *is increasing, that is, $w_i \geq \phi_i$ for $i = 1, 2$, implies*

$$\mathcal{G}(f_1, f_2, w_1, w_2; \mu_\Delta) \geq \mathcal{G}(f_1, f_2, \phi_1, \phi_2; \mu_\Delta). \tag{37}$$

Moreover, if $\chi \circ \psi^{-1}$ is concave, then (31) *is decreasing, that is, inequality* (37) *holds in reverse order.*

Proof. Monotonicity property (37) follows from the proof of Theorem 6, monotonicity properties of the Levinson functional on time scales obtained in Corollary 1 and conditions (35) and (36). □

In the next definition, we introduce weighted generalized power mean ([17]).

Definition 7. *Suppose $r \in \mathbb{R}$, $I \subset \mathbb{R}$ is an interval. Assume $f : [a, b] \to I$ is positive and Δ-integrable and $w : [a, b] \to \mathbb{R}$ is non-negative and Δ-integrable such that $\int_a^b w\, d\mu_\Delta > 0$. Weighted generalized power mean on time scales is defined as*

$$\mathcal{M}^{[p]}(f, w; \mu_\Delta) = \begin{cases} \left(\frac{\int_a^b w f^p \, d\mu_\Delta}{\int_a^b w \, d\mu_\Delta} \right), & p \neq 0, \\ \exp\left(\frac{\int_a^b w \ln(f) \, d\mu_\Delta}{\int_a^b w \, d\mu_\Delta} \right), & p = 0. \end{cases}$$

provided that all integrals are well defined.

The following theorem establishes another Levinson's type functional in terms of generalized power mean and proves its properties using the functional obtained in Theorem 6.

Theorem 7. *Let $p, q \in \mathbb{R}$ and $p \neq 0$. Assume w_i, ϕ_i, f_i satisfy the hypotheses of Theorem 4 for $i = 1, 2$ such that the functional*

$$\begin{aligned} & \int_{a_2}^{b_2} w_2 \, d\mu_\Delta \cdot \left\{ \left[\mathcal{M}^{[q]}(f_2, w_2; \mu_\Delta) \right]^q - \left[\mathcal{M}^{[p]}(f_2, w_2; \mu_\Delta) \right]^q \right\} \\ & - \int_{a_1}^{b_1} w_1 \, d\mu_\Delta \cdot \left\{ \left[\mathcal{M}^{[q]}(f_1, w_1; \mu_\Delta) \right]^q - \left[\mathcal{M}^{[p]}(f_1, w_1; \mu_\Delta) \right]^q \right\} \\ & + \frac{\lambda}{2} \cdot \left[\sigma_2({f_2}^p, w_2) - \sigma_1({f_1}^p, w_1) \right] \end{aligned} \tag{38}$$

is well defined. Denoting (38) *by $\mathcal{P}(f_1, f_2, w_1, w_2; \mu_\Delta)$, we obtain that if $max\{0, p\} < q < min\{0, p\}$ and the following conditions are fulfilled:*

$$\sigma_1({f_1}^p, w_1) = \sigma_2({f_2}^p, w_2), \tag{39}$$

$$\sigma_1({f_1}^p, \phi_1) - \sigma_1({f_1}^p, w_1 + \phi_1) = \sigma_2({f_2}^p, \phi_2) - \sigma_2({f_2}^p, w_2 + \phi_2), \tag{40}$$

then (38) *is superadditive, i.e.,*

$$\mathcal{P}(f_1, f_2, w_1 + \phi_1, w_2 + \phi_2; \mu_\Delta) \geq \mathcal{P}(f_1, f_2, w_1, w_2; \mu_\Delta) + \mathcal{P}(f_1, f_2, \phi_1, \phi_2; \mu_\Delta). \tag{41}$$

If $0 < q < p$ or $p < q < 0$, then (38) *is subadditive, that is, inequality* (41) *holds in reverse order.*

Proof. Substituting in (31) that $\chi(x) = x^q$ and $\psi(x) = x^p$, $x > 0$, if $p \neq 0$, we obtain (38). Since now $(\chi \circ \psi^{-1})(x) = x^{\frac{q}{p}}$ and $(\chi \circ \psi^{-1})'' = \frac{g(q-p)}{p^2} x^{\frac{q}{p}-2}$, we conclude that, if $\max\{0, p\} < q < \min\{0, p\}$, then $\chi \circ \psi^{-1}$ is convex and if $0 < q < p$ or $p < q < 0$, then $\chi \circ \psi^{-1}$ is concave so property (41) follow from Theorem 6. If $p = 0$, then taking $\chi(x) = x^q$ and $\psi(x) = \ln(x)$, $x > 0$ in Theorem 6, we obtain $(\chi \circ \psi^{-1})(x) = x^{qx}$ so $\chi \circ \psi^{-1}$ is convex for $q \neq 0$ and results follow from Theorem 6. □

Corollary 3. *Assume $p, q \in \mathbb{R}$ and $p \neq 0$. Let w_i, ϕ_i, f_i satisfy the hypotheses of Theorem 4 for $i = 1, 2$ such that the functional $\mathcal{P}(f_1, f_2, w_1, w_2; \mu_\Delta)$ defined by* (38) *is well defined. If*

$$\sigma_1({f_1}^p, w_1 - \phi_1) = \sigma_2({f_2}^p, w_2 - \phi_2) \tag{42}$$

and

$$\sigma_1({f_1}^p, \phi_1) - \sigma_1({f_1}^p, w_1) = \sigma_2({f_2}^p, \phi_2) - \sigma_2({f_2}^p, w_2) \tag{43}$$

then the functional (38) *is increasing, that is, $w_i \geq \phi_i$ for $i = 1, 2$, implies*

$$\mathcal{P}(f_1, f_2, w_1, w_2; \mu_\Delta) \geq \mathcal{P}(f_1, f_2, \phi_1, \phi_2; \mu_\Delta). \tag{44}$$

If $0 < q < p$ *or* $p < q < 0$*, then* (38) *is decreasing, that is, inequality* (44) *holds in reverse order.*

Proof. Monotonicity property (44) follows from the proof of Theorem 7, monotonicity properties of the Levinson functional on time scales obtained in Corollary 1 and conditions (42) and (43). □

5. Conclusions

In this paper, we established the Levinson functional on time scales utilizing integral inequality of Levinson's type in the terms of Δ- integral for convex (concave) functions on time scale sets and proved the properties of superadditivity and monotonicity. Using obtained properties, we derived the bounds of the Levinson's functional on time scales. Applying the same methods in the rest of the article, we constructed new Levinson's types of functionals using weighted generalized and power means on time scales and proved their properties regarding superadditivity and monotonicity. In future investigations, using the same reasoning as in Theorem 5, the bounds for the functionals in Theorem 6 and Theorem 7 can be obtained. Furthermore, a new type of functionals can be constructed using the methods of Theorem 6 and Theorem 7 and some specific forms of functions χ and ψ, and then properties of superadditivity and monotonicity can be easily proved as well as the bounds of obtained new functionals. Derived properties can then be used to improve some known inequalities on time scales.

Funding: This research received no external funding.

Data Availability Statement: Not applicable.

Conflicts of Interest: The author declares no conflict of interest.

References

1. Baloch, I.A.; Pečarić, J.; Praljak, M. Generalization of Levinson's inequality. *J. Math. Inequal.* **2015**, *9*, 571–586. [CrossRef]
2. Barić, J.; Pečarić, J.; Radišić, D. Integral inequalities of Levinson's type in time scale settings. *Math. Inequalities Appl.* **2019**, *22*, 1477–1491. [CrossRef]
3. Levinson, N. Generalization of an inequality of Ky Fan. *J. Math. Anal. Appl.* **1964**, *8*, 133–134. [CrossRef]
4. Popoviciu, T. Sur une inealite de N. Levinson. *Mathematica* **1964**, *6*, 301–306.
5. Bullen, P.S. An inequality of N. Levinson. *Publ. Elektrotehn. Fak. Ser. Mat. Fiz.* **1973**, *No. 412/460*, 421–460.
6. Mercer, A. Short proof of Jensen's and Levinson's inequalities. *Math. Gaz.* **2010**, *94*, 492–495. [CrossRef]
7. Hilger, S. Ein Maßkettenkalkül mit Anwendung auf Zentrumsmannigfaltigkeiten. Ph.D. Thesis, Universität Würzburg, Würzburg, Germany, 1988.
8. Agarwal, R.P.; Bohner, M.; Peterson, A. Inequalities on time scale: A survey. *Math. Inequalities Appl.* **2001**, *4*, 535–557. [CrossRef]
9. Barić, J.; Bohner, M.; Jakšić, R.; Pečarić, J. Converses of Jessen's inequality on time scales. *Math. Notes* **2015**, *98*, 11–24. [CrossRef]
10. Hilger, S. Analysis on measure chains -a unified approach to continuous and discrete calculus. *Results Math.* **1990**, *18*, 18–56. [CrossRef]
11. Hilger, S. Differential and difference calculus unified. *Nonlinear Anal.* **1997**, *30*, 143–166. [CrossRef]
12. Barić, J.; Bibi, R.; Bohner, M.; Nosheen, A.; Pečarić, J. *Jensen Inequalities on Time Scales, Theory and Applications*; Monograph in inequalities; Element: Zagreb, Croatia, 2015.
13. Bohner, M.; Peterson, A. *Dynamic Equations on Time Scales*; Birkhäuser: Boston, MA, USA; Basel, Switzerland; Berlin, Germany, 2001.
14. Kaymakcalan, B.; Lakshmikantham, V.; Sivasundaram, S. *Dynamic Systems on Measure Chains*; Kluwer Academic Publishers: Dordrecht, The Netherlands, 1996.
15. Bohner, M.; Peterson, A. *Advances in Dynamic Equations on Time Scales: An Introduction with Applications*; Birkhäuser: Boston, MA, USA, 2003.
16. Wong, F.H.; Yeh, C.C.; Lian, W.C. An extension of Jensen's inequality on time scales. *Adv. Dyn. Syst. Appl.* **2006**, *1*, 113–120.
17. Anwar, M.; Bibi, R.; Bohner, M.; Pečarić, J. Jensen's functionals on time scales. *J. Funct. Spaces Appl.* **2012**, *2012*, 384045. [CrossRef]

axioms

MDPI

Article

A Study on Fixed-Point Techniques under the α-$\mathcal{F}$-Convex Contraction with an Application

Gunasekaran Nallaselli [1], Arul Joseph Gnanaprakasam [1], Gunaseelan Mani [2], Ozgur Ege [3], Dania Santina [4] and Nabil Mlaiki [4,*]

1 Department of Mathematics, College of Engineering and Technology, Faculty of Engineering and Technology, SRM Institute of Science and Technology, SRM Nagar, Kattankulathur 603203, Tamil Nadu, India
2 Department of Mathematics, Saveetha School of Engineering, Saveetha Institute of Medical and Technical Sciences, Chennai 602105, Tamil Nadu, India
3 Department of Mathematics, Ege University, Bornova, 35100 Izmir, Turkey
4 Department of Mathematics and Sciences, Prince Sultan University, Riyadh 11586, Saudi Arabia
* Correspondence: nmlaiki2012@gmail.com or nmlaiki@psu.edu.sa

Abstract: In this paper, we consider several classes of mappings related to the class of α-$\mathcal{F}$-contraction mappings by introducing a convexity condition and establish some fixed-point theorems for such mappings in complete metric spaces. The present result extends and generalizes the well-known results of α-admissible and convex contraction mapping and many others in the existing literature. An illustrative example is also provided to exhibit the utility of our main results. Finally, we derive the existence and uniqueness of a solution to an integral equation to support our main result and give a numerical example to validate the application of our obtained results.

Keywords: α-admissible; $\mathcal{F}$-contraction; fixed point; α^*-admissible; α-$\mathcal{F}$-convex contraction; integral equation

MSC: 47H10; 54H25

Citation: Nallaselli, G.; Gnanaprakasam, A.J.; Mani, G.; Ege, O.; Santina, D.; Mlaiki, N. A Study on Fixed-Point Techniques under the α-$\mathcal{F}$-Convex Contraction with an Application. *Axioms* **2023**, *12*, 139. https://doi.org/10.3390/axioms12020139

Academic Editors: Shengda Zeng, Stanisław Migórski, Yongjian Liu and Hsien-Chung Wu

Received: 27 December 2022
Revised: 23 January 2023
Accepted: 28 January 2023
Published: 29 January 2023

1. Introduction and Preliminaries

In recent years, a great number of papers have presented generalizations of the well-known Banach–Picard contraction principle. Čirić [1] investigated the generalized contraction and extension of Banach's contraction to combine x, y, Tx, and Ty of all six possible values for all $x, y \in X$ and T a self-mapping on a metric space. In 1982, Istrăţescu [2] proposed a generalization of seven contraction principle values by introducing a "convexity" condition for the mapping iterates. He deduced that these conditions might be adapted for other classes of mappings to obtain some extensions of known fixed-point results. Alghamdi et al. [3] proved a generalization of the Banach contraction principle to the class of convex contractions in non-normal cone metric spaces. In 2015, Miculescu et al. [4] obtained a generalization of Istrăţescu's fixed-point theorem concerning convex contractions. In 2017, Miculescu et al. [5] obtained a generalization of Matkowski's fixed-point theorem and Istrăţescu's fixed-point theorem of convex contraction of a comparison function ϕ such that $d(f^{[m]}(x), f^{[m]}(y)) \leq \phi(\max d(x,y), d(f(x), f(y)), \ldots, d(f^{[m-1]}(x), f^{[m-1]}(y)))$ for all $x, y \in X$. Latif et al. [6] introduced the new concepts of partial generalized convex contractions and partial generalized convex contractions of order two. Moreover, they established some approximate fixed-point results in a metric space endowed with an arbitrary binary relation and some approximate fixed-point results in a metric space endowed with a graph. In 2022, Latif et al. [7] established fixed points in the setting of metric spaces for generalized multivalued contractive mappings with respect to the w_b-distance . In 2013, Miandaragh et al. [8] expanded the concept of convex contractions to generalized convex contractions and generalized convex contractions of order two. In the same year, they proved some approximate fixed-point results in the setting of generalized α-convex contractive mapping in [9]. Wardowski [10] introduced the F-contraction and proved a new fixed-point theorem concerning the F-contraction. Samet et al. [11] introduced a new concept of α–ψ-contractive-type mappings and established fixed-point theorems for such mappings in complete metric spaces. Asem and Singh proved some fixed-point theorems on a Meir–Keeler proximal contraction for non-self-mappings in [12]. Following that [13,14], Karapinar established some fixed-point theorems in different metric spaces for the concept of α-admissible mapping. Recently, Khan et al. [15] discussed the concepts of (α, p)-convex contraction and asymptotically T^2-regular sequence and demonstrated that an (α, p)-convex contraction reduced to a two-sided convex contraction. Yildirim [16] introduced a definition of the F-Hardy–Rogers contraction of Nadler type and also proved some fixed-point theorems for such mappings using Mann's iteration process in complete convex b-metric spaces. Singh et al. [17] discussed an α-$\digamma$-convex contraction of six possible values (without rational type) in complete metric spaces. Eke et al. [18] introduced the convexity condition to some classes of contraction mappings, such as the Chatterjea contractive mapping and the Hardy and Rogers contractive mapping, and proved the fixed points of these maps in complete metric spaces. Following that, some works on the generalization of such classes of mappings in the setting of various spaces [19–34] appeared.

Singh et al. [17] discussed an α-$\digamma$-convex contraction of six possible values (without rational type) and proved the fixed points of these maps in complete metric spaces. In this paper, we extend and generalize their main theorem into an α-$\digamma$-convex contraction of seven possible values (with rational type) in the setting of complete metric spaces inspired and motivated by Singh et al. [17]. Examples and applications to integral equations are provided to illustrate the usability of our obtained results.

Throughout this paper, we use the following notations: $\mathbb{R}$ represents $(-\infty, +\infty)$, $\mathbb{R}_+$ is $(0, +\infty)$, and $\mathbb{R}_+^0$ represents $[0, +\infty)$.

Definition 1 ([11])**.** *Let $\Gamma : \Lambda \to \Lambda$ be a self-mapping on a nonvoid set Λ and $\alpha : \Lambda \times \Lambda \to [0, \infty)$ be a mapping. Then, Γ is said to be α-admissible if for all $\eta, \mathfrak{m} \in \Lambda, \alpha(\eta, \mathfrak{m}) \geq 1 \Rightarrow \alpha(\Gamma\eta, \Gamma\mathfrak{m}) \geq 1$.*

Example 1. *Let $\Lambda = (-\infty, \infty)$ and define $\Gamma : \Lambda \to \Lambda$ by*

$$\Gamma\eta = \begin{cases} ln|\eta|, & \text{if } \eta \neq 0; \\ 3, & \text{else.} \end{cases}$$

Define $\alpha : \Lambda \times \Lambda \to [0, \infty)$ by

$$\alpha(\eta, \mathfrak{m}) = \begin{cases} 3, & \text{if } \eta \geq \mathfrak{m}; \\ 0, & \text{else.} \end{cases}$$

Then, Γ is α-admissible as $\alpha(\eta, \mathfrak{m}) \geq 1 \Rightarrow \alpha(\Gamma\eta, \Gamma\mathfrak{m}) \geq 1$ for $\eta \geq \mathfrak{m}$ and $\alpha(\eta, \mathfrak{m}) = \alpha(\mathfrak{m}, \eta)$, for all $\eta = \mathfrak{m}$.

Definition 2 ([13])**.** *Let $\Gamma : \Lambda \to \Lambda$ be a self-mapping and $\alpha : \Lambda \times \Lambda \to (-\infty, +\infty)$ be a mapping. Then, we say that Γ is triangular α-admissible if*

(Γ_1) *$\alpha(\eta, \mathfrak{m}) \geq 1 \Rightarrow \alpha(\Gamma\eta, \Gamma\mathfrak{m}) \geq 1$, for all $\eta, \mathfrak{m} \in \Lambda$;*
(Γ_2) *$\alpha(\eta, \mathfrak{o}) \geq 1$ and $\alpha(\mathfrak{o}, \mathfrak{m}) \geq 1$ imply $\alpha(\eta, \mathfrak{m}) \geq 1$, for all $\eta, \mathfrak{m}, \mathfrak{o} \in \Lambda$.*

Example 2. *Let $\Lambda = [0, +\infty), \Gamma\eta = \eta^2 + e^\eta$ and*

$$\alpha(\eta, \mathfrak{m}) = \begin{cases} 1, & \text{if } \eta, \mathfrak{m} \in [0, 1]; \\ 0, & \text{else.} \end{cases}$$

Hence, Γ is a triangular α-admissible mapping.

Definition 3 ([14]). *Let $\Lambda \neq \emptyset$ and let Γ be an α-admissible mapping on Λ. Then, Λ has the property (H) if for each $\eta, \mathfrak{m} \in Fix(\Gamma)$, there exists $\mathfrak{o} \in \Lambda$ such that $\alpha(\eta, \mathfrak{o}) \geq 1$ and $\alpha(\mathfrak{o}, \mathfrak{m}) \geq 1$.*

Definition 4 ([17]). *An α-admissible mapping Γ is said to be α^*-admissible, if for each η, $\mathfrak{m} \in Fix(\Gamma) \neq \emptyset$, we get $\alpha(\eta, \mathfrak{m}) \geq 1$. If $Fix(\Gamma) = \emptyset$, then Γ is called vacuously α^*-admissible.*

Example 3. *Let $\Lambda = [0, \infty)$ and $\Gamma : \Lambda \to \Lambda$ by $\Gamma\eta = 3 + \eta$, for all $\eta \in \Lambda$. Define a mapping $\alpha : \Lambda \times \Lambda \to [0, \infty)$ by*

$$\alpha(\eta, \mathfrak{m}) = \begin{cases} \mathbf{e}^{(\eta - \mathfrak{m})}, & \text{if } \eta \geq \mathfrak{m}; \\ 0, & \text{else}. \end{cases}$$

Then, Γ is α-admissible. Since Γ has no fixed point, we have $Fix(\Gamma) = \emptyset$, and Γ is vacuously α^*-admissible.

Example 4. *Let $\Lambda = [0, \infty)$ and $\Gamma : \Lambda \to \Lambda$ by $\Gamma\eta = \frac{\eta^3}{9}$, for all $\eta \in \Lambda$. Define $\alpha : \Lambda \times \Lambda \to [0, \infty)$ by*

$$\alpha(\eta, \mathfrak{m}) = \begin{cases} 1, & \text{if } \eta, \mathfrak{m} \in [0, 3]; \\ 0, & \text{else}. \end{cases}$$

Clearly, Γ is α-admissible and $Fix(\Gamma) = \{0, 3\}$. Then, Γ is α^*-admissible.

Example 5. *Let $\Lambda = [0, \infty)$ and define $\Gamma : \Lambda \to \Lambda$ by $\Gamma\eta = \sqrt{\frac{\eta(\eta^2+6)}{5}}$, for all $\eta \in \Lambda$. Define $\alpha : \Lambda \times \Lambda \to [0, \infty)$ by*

$$\alpha(\eta, \mathfrak{m}) = \begin{cases} 1, & \text{if } \eta, \mathfrak{m} \in [0, 2]; \\ 0, & \text{else}. \end{cases}$$

Clearly, Γ is α-admissible and $Fix(\Gamma) = \{0, 2, 3\}$. Note that Γ is not α^*-admissible, since $\alpha(\eta, 3) = 0$ for $\eta \in \{0, 2\}$.

Definition 5 ([10]). *For a nonvoid set Λ, a function $\mathcal{Q} : \Lambda \times \Lambda \to \mathbb{R}_+^0$ is said to be metric if it satisfies the following conditions:*

1. $\mathcal{Q}(\eta, \mathfrak{m}) \geq 0$ *and* $\mathcal{Q}(\eta, \mathfrak{m}) = 0$ *if and only if* $\eta = \mathfrak{m}$.
2. $\mathcal{Q}(\eta, \mathfrak{m}) = \mathcal{Q}(\mathfrak{m}, \eta)$, *for all* $\eta, \mathfrak{m} \in \Lambda$.
3. $\mathcal{Q}(\eta, \mathfrak{m}) \leq \mathcal{Q}(\eta, \mathfrak{o}) + \mathcal{Q}(\mathfrak{o}, \mathfrak{m})$, *for all* $\eta, \mathfrak{m}, \mathfrak{o} \in \Lambda$.

In addition, the pair $(\Lambda, \mathcal{Q})$ is called a metric space.

Definition 6 ([10]). *Let $\digamma \in \Im$ be the set of all mappings $\digamma : \mathbb{R}_+ \to \mathbb{R}$ satisfying the stipulations:*

(F_1) *$\digamma$ is strictly nondecreasing, i.e., for all $\delta, \epsilon \in \mathbb{R}_+$ such that $\delta < \epsilon \implies \digamma(\delta) < \digamma(\epsilon)$;*
(F_2) *For each sequence $\{\delta_\beta\}_{\beta \in \mathbb{N}}$, $\lim_{\beta \to \infty} \delta_\beta = 0 \Leftrightarrow \lim_{\beta \to \infty} \digamma(\delta_\beta) = -\infty$;*
(F_3) *There exists $\mathbf{k} \in (0, 1)$ such that $\lim_{\delta \to 0^+} \delta^{\mathbf{k}} \digamma(\delta) = 0$.*

Definition 7 ([10]). *A mapping $\Gamma : \Lambda \to \Lambda$ is said to be an $\digamma$-contraction on a metric space $(\Lambda, \mathcal{Q})$ if there exists $\digamma \in \Im$ and $\mu > 0$ such that for all $\eta, \mathfrak{m} \in \Lambda$,*

$$\mathcal{Q}(\Gamma\eta, \Gamma\mathfrak{m}) > 0 \implies \mu + \digamma(\mathcal{Q}(\Gamma\eta, \Gamma\mathfrak{m})) \leq \digamma(\mathcal{Q}(\eta, \mathfrak{m})). \tag{1}$$

Example 6 ([10]). *The following functions $\digamma : \mathbb{R}_+ \to \mathbb{R}$ are in $\Im$:*

(i) $\digamma(\delta) = ln\delta$;
(ii) $\digamma(\delta) = ln\delta + \delta$;

(*iii*) $\digamma(\delta) = \frac{-1}{\sqrt{\delta}}$;
(*iv*) $\digamma(\delta) = ln(\delta^2 + \delta)$.

The following theorem was proved by Wardowski [10].

Theorem 1 ([10]). *Let $(\Lambda, \mathcal{Q})$ be a complete metric space and $\Gamma : \Lambda \to \Lambda$ be an $\digamma$-contraction. Then, we get*

(*i*) $\mathfrak{o} \in \Lambda$ *is the unique fixed point of* Γ;
(*ii*) *For all* $\eta \in \Lambda$, *the sequence* $\{\Gamma^{\beta}\eta\}$ *is convergent to* $\mathfrak{o} \in \Lambda$.

Definition 8 ([1]). *Let Γ be a self-mapping on a metric space $(\Lambda, \mathcal{Q})$. Then, we say that Γ is orbitally continuous on Λ if $\lim_{\mathfrak{k}\to\infty} \Gamma^{\beta_{\mathfrak{k}}}\eta = \mathfrak{o}$ implies that $\lim_{\mathfrak{k}\to\infty} \Gamma^{\beta_{\mathfrak{k}}}\eta = \Gamma\mathfrak{o}$.*

Let $\Gamma : \Lambda \to \Lambda$ be a self-mapping on a nonvoid set Λ. Define $Fix(\Gamma) = \{\eta : \Gamma\eta = \eta,\ for\ all\ \eta \in \Lambda\}$.

We establish some fixed-point theorems on an α-$\digamma$-convex contraction of possible seven values included rational type with an application to integral equations, inspired by Singh et al. [17].

2. Main Results

First, we introduce the concept of "α-$\digamma$-convex contraction" with examples.

Definition 9. *A self-mapping Γ on Λ is said to be an α-$\digamma$-convex contraction, if there exist two functions $\alpha : \Lambda \times \Lambda \to [0, \infty)$ and $\digamma \in \Im$ such that for all $\eta, \mathfrak{m} \in \Lambda$,*

$$\mathcal{Q}^{\flat}(\Gamma^2\eta, \Gamma^2\mathfrak{m}) > 0 \implies \mu + \digamma(\alpha(\eta, \mathfrak{m})\mathcal{Q}^{\flat}(\Gamma^2\eta, \Gamma^2\mathfrak{m})) \leq \digamma(\mathfrak{p}^{\flat}(\eta, \mathfrak{m})), \tag{2}$$

where $\flat \in [1, \infty)$, $\mu > 0$ and

$$\mathfrak{p}^{\flat}(\eta, \mathfrak{m}) = \max\{\mathcal{Q}^{\flat}(\eta, \mathfrak{m}), \mathcal{Q}^{\flat}(\eta, \Gamma\eta), \mathcal{Q}^{\flat}(\Gamma\eta, \Gamma^2\eta), \mathcal{Q}^{\flat}(\mathfrak{m}, \Gamma\mathfrak{m}), \mathcal{Q}^{\flat}(\Gamma\mathfrak{m}, \Gamma^2\mathfrak{m}), \frac{\mathcal{Q}^{\flat}(\eta, \Gamma\mathfrak{m}) + \mathcal{Q}^{\flat}(\mathfrak{m}, \Gamma\eta)}{2}, \frac{\mathcal{Q}^{\flat}(\Gamma\eta, \Gamma^2\mathfrak{m}) + \mathcal{Q}^{\flat}(\Gamma\mathfrak{m}, \Gamma^2\eta)}{2}\}. \tag{3}$$

Example 7. *Let $\digamma(\mathfrak{r}) = \ln(\mathfrak{r}), \mathfrak{r} > 0$. Obviously, $\digamma \in \Im$. Let Γ be a self-mapping on a metric space $(\Lambda, \mathcal{Q})$. We postulate that the convex contraction of type 2 ([2]) putting $\alpha(\eta, \mathfrak{m}) = 1$, for all $\eta, \mathfrak{m} \in \Lambda$, $\mathbf{e}^{-\mu} = \mathbf{k} = \sum_{\mathfrak{k}=1}^{7} \alpha_{\mathfrak{k}} < 1$ and $\alpha_{\mathfrak{k}} \geq 0$ for all $\mathfrak{k} = 1, 2, ..., 7$.*

$$\begin{aligned}\mathcal{Q}(\Gamma^2\eta, \Gamma^2\mathfrak{m}) \leq\ & \alpha_1\mathcal{Q}(\eta, \mathfrak{m}) + \alpha_2\mathcal{Q}(\eta, \Gamma\eta) + \alpha_3\mathcal{Q}(\Gamma\eta, \Gamma^2\eta) \\ & + \alpha_4\mathcal{Q}(\mathfrak{m}, \Gamma\mathfrak{m}) + \alpha_5\mathcal{Q}(\Gamma\mathfrak{m}, \Gamma^2\mathfrak{m}) + \alpha_6\left(\frac{\mathcal{Q}(\eta, \Gamma\mathfrak{m}) + \mathcal{Q}(\mathfrak{m}, \Gamma\eta)}{2}\right) \\ & + \alpha_7\left(\frac{\mathcal{Q}(\Gamma\eta, \Gamma^2\mathfrak{m}) + \mathcal{Q}(\Gamma\mathfrak{m}, \Gamma^2\eta)}{2}\right),\end{aligned}$$

where $\eta, \mathfrak{m} \in \Lambda$ with $\eta \neq \mathfrak{m}$. Then, we obtain

$$\begin{aligned}\alpha(\eta, \mathfrak{m})\mathcal{Q}(\Gamma^2\eta, \Gamma^2\mathfrak{m}) &= \mathcal{Q}(\Gamma^2\eta, \Gamma^2\mathfrak{m}) \\ &\leq \sum_{\mathfrak{k}=1}^{7} \alpha_{\mathfrak{k}} \max\Big\{\mathcal{Q}(\eta, \mathfrak{m}), \mathcal{Q}(\eta, \Gamma\eta), \mathcal{Q}(\Gamma\eta, \Gamma^2\eta), \mathcal{Q}(\mathfrak{m}, \Gamma\mathfrak{m}), \mathcal{Q}(\Gamma\mathfrak{m}, \Gamma^2\mathfrak{m}), \\ &\quad \frac{\mathcal{Q}(\eta, \Gamma\mathfrak{m}) + \mathcal{Q}(\mathfrak{m}, \Gamma\eta)}{2}, \frac{\mathcal{Q}(\Gamma\eta, \Gamma^2\mathfrak{m}) + \mathcal{Q}(\Gamma\mathfrak{m}, \Gamma^2\eta)}{2}\Big\},\end{aligned}$$

which implies that

$$\alpha(\eta,\mathfrak{m})\mathcal{Q}(\Gamma^2\eta,\Gamma^2\mathfrak{m}) \leq \mathbf{k}\mathfrak{p}^1(\eta,\mathfrak{m}) = \mathbf{e}^{-\mu}\mathfrak{p}^1(\eta,\mathfrak{m}).$$

Applying the natural logarithm on both sides, we get

$$\mu + F(\alpha(\eta,\mathfrak{m})\mathcal{Q}(\Gamma^2\eta,\Gamma^2\mathfrak{m})) \leq F(\mathfrak{p}^1(\eta,\mathfrak{m})).$$

Therefore,

$$\mathcal{Q}(\Gamma^2\eta,\Gamma^2\mathfrak{m}) > 0 \implies \mu + F(\alpha(\eta,\mathfrak{m})\mathcal{Q}(\Gamma^2\eta,\Gamma^2\mathfrak{m})) \leq F(\mathfrak{p}^1(\eta,\mathfrak{m})),$$

for all $\eta,\mathfrak{m} \in \Lambda$. *We conclude that* Γ *is an* α-F*-convex contraction with* $\flat = 1$.

Example 8. *Let* $\Lambda = [0,1]$ *with* $\mathcal{Q}(\eta,\mathfrak{m}) = |\eta - \mathfrak{m}|$. *Define a mapping* $\Gamma : \Lambda \to \Lambda$ *by* $\Gamma\eta = \frac{\eta^2}{2} + \frac{5}{16}$, *for all* $\eta \in \Lambda$ *with* $\alpha(\eta,\mathfrak{m}) = 1$, *for all* $\eta,\mathfrak{m} \in \Lambda$. *Then,* Γ *is* α*-admissible. Now, we get* Γ *is nonexpansive, since we obtain*

$$|\Gamma\eta - \Gamma\mathfrak{m}| = \frac{1}{2}|\eta^2 - \mathfrak{m}^2| \leq |\eta - \mathfrak{m}|, \; for\ all\ \eta,\mathfrak{m} \in \Lambda.$$

Setting $F \in \Im$ *such that* $F(\mathfrak{x}) = \ln\mathfrak{x}, \mathfrak{x} > 0$. *Then, for all* $\eta,\mathfrak{m} \in \Lambda$ *with* $\eta \neq \mathfrak{m}$, *we obtain*

$$\begin{aligned}
\alpha(\eta,\mathfrak{m})|\Gamma^2\eta,\Gamma^2\mathfrak{m}| &= |\Gamma^2\eta,\Gamma^2\mathfrak{m}| \\
&= \frac{1}{512}(|(64\eta^4 + 80\eta^2 - 64\mathfrak{m}^4 - 80\mathfrak{m}^2)|) \\
&\leq \frac{1}{512}(64|\eta^4 - \mathfrak{m}^4| + 80|\eta^2 - \mathfrak{m}^2|) \\
&\leq \frac{1}{2}|\Gamma\eta - \Gamma\mathfrak{m}| + \frac{5}{16}|\eta - \mathfrak{m}| \\
&\leq \frac{13}{16}\max\{|\Gamma\eta - \Gamma\mathfrak{m}|, |\eta - \mathfrak{m}|\} \\
&\leq e^{-\mu}\mathfrak{p}^1(\eta,\mathfrak{m}),
\end{aligned}$$

where $-\mu = \ln(\frac{13}{16})$. *Applying the logarithm on both sides, we have*

$$\mu + F(\alpha(\eta,\mathfrak{m})\mathcal{Q}(\Gamma^2\eta,\Gamma^2\mathfrak{m})) \leq F(\mathfrak{p}^1(\eta,\mathfrak{m})).$$

We conclude that Γ *is an* α-F*-convex contraction with* $\flat = 1$.

Example 9. *Define* $\Gamma : [0,1] \to [0,1]$ *by* $\Gamma\eta = \frac{1-\eta^2}{2}$, *for all* $\eta \in [0,1]$ *and* $\alpha(\eta,\mathfrak{m}) = 1$, *for all* $\eta,\mathfrak{m} \in [0,1]$, *with usual metric* $\mathcal{Q}(\eta,\mathfrak{m}) = |\eta - \mathfrak{m}|$. *Then,* Γ *is* α*-admissible. Setting* $F \in \Im$ *such that* $F(\mathfrak{x}) = ln\mathfrak{x}, \mathfrak{x} > 0$. *Then, for all* $\eta,\mathfrak{m} \in [0,1]$ *with* $\eta \neq \mathfrak{m}$, *we obtain*

$$|\Gamma\eta,\Gamma\mathfrak{m}| = \frac{1}{2}|\eta^2 - \mathfrak{m}^2| \leq |\eta - \mathfrak{m}|$$

and

$$\begin{aligned}
\alpha(\eta,\mathfrak{m})|\Gamma^2\eta,\Gamma^2\mathfrak{m}| &= |\Gamma^2\eta,\Gamma^2\mathfrak{m}| \\
&= \frac{1}{8}(|2\eta^2-\eta^4-2\mathfrak{m}^2+\mathfrak{m}^4|) \\
&= \frac{1}{8}(2|\eta^2-\mathfrak{m}^2|+|\eta^4-\mathfrak{m}^4|) \\
&\le \frac{1}{2}|\eta-\mathfrak{m}|+\frac{1}{4}|\eta^2-\mathfrak{m}^2| \\
&= \frac{1}{2}|\eta-\mathfrak{m}|+\frac{1}{2}|\Gamma\eta-\Gamma\mathfrak{m}| \\
&\le 1.\max\{|\eta-\mathfrak{m}|,|\Gamma\eta-\Gamma\mathfrak{m}|\} \\
&\le e^{-\mu}\mathfrak{p}^1(\eta,\mathfrak{m}).
\end{aligned}$$

where $-\mu=\ln(1)$*. Applying the logarithm on both sides, we get*

$$\mu+\digamma(\alpha(\eta,\mathfrak{m})\mathcal{Q}(\Gamma^2\eta,\Gamma^2\mathfrak{m}))\le\digamma(\mathfrak{p}^1(\eta,\mathfrak{m})).$$

However, by $\mu=-\ln(1)$*, there does not exist any* $\mu>0$ *such that*

$$\mu+\digamma(\alpha(\eta,\mathfrak{m})\mathcal{Q}(\Gamma^2\eta,\Gamma^2\mathfrak{m}))\le\digamma(\mathfrak{p}^1(\eta,\mathfrak{m})).$$

Therefore, Γ *is not an* α*-*$\digamma$*-convex contraction with* $\flat=1$*. Now, we see*

$$|\Gamma\eta-\Gamma\mathfrak{m}|^2=\frac{1}{4}|\eta^2-\mathfrak{m}^2|^2\le|\eta-\mathfrak{m}|^2$$

and

$$\begin{aligned}
\alpha(\eta,\mathfrak{m})(|\Gamma^2\eta,\Gamma^2\mathfrak{m}|^2) &= \frac{1}{64}|2\eta^2-\eta^4-2\mathfrak{m}^2+\mathfrak{m}^4|^2 \\
&\le \frac{1}{64}(4|\eta^2-\mathfrak{m}^2|^2+|\eta^4-\mathfrak{m}^4|^2) \\
&= \frac{1}{16}|\eta^2-\mathfrak{m}^2|^2+\frac{1}{64}|\eta^4-\mathfrak{m}^4|^2 \\
&\le \frac{1}{4}|\eta-\mathfrak{m}|^2+\frac{1}{16}|\eta^2-\mathfrak{m}^2|^2 \\
&\le \frac{5}{16}\max\{|\eta-\mathfrak{m}|^2,|\Gamma\eta-\Gamma\mathfrak{m}|^2\} \\
&\le \frac{5}{16}\mathfrak{p}^2(\eta,\mathfrak{m}) \\
&= e^{-\mu}\mathfrak{p}^2(\eta,\mathfrak{m}).
\end{aligned}$$

Applying the logarithm on both sides, we get

$$\mu+\digamma(\alpha(\eta,\mathfrak{m})\mathcal{Q}(\Gamma^2\eta,\Gamma^2\mathfrak{m}))\le\digamma(\mathfrak{p}^2(\eta,\mathfrak{m})),$$

where $-\mu=\ln\frac{5}{16}$*. Therefore,* Γ *is an* α*-*$\digamma$*-convex contraction with* $\flat=2$*.*

Now, first, we prove the Lemma through an α-$\digamma$-convex contraction.

Lemma 1. *Let* $(\Lambda,\mathcal{Q})$ *be a complete metric space,* $\Gamma:\Lambda\to\Lambda$ *a given map, and let* $\alpha:\Lambda\times\Lambda\to[0,\infty)$ *be a mapping. Suppose that the following affirmations hold:*

(*i*) *There exists* $\flat\in[1,\infty)$ *and* $\mu>0$ *such that for all* $\eta,\mathfrak{m}\in\Lambda$*,*

$$\mathcal{Q}^\flat(\Gamma^2\eta,\Gamma^2\mathfrak{m})>0\implies\mu+\digamma(\alpha(\eta,\mathfrak{m})\mathcal{Q}^\flat(\Gamma^2\eta,\Gamma^2\mathfrak{m}))\le\digamma(\mathfrak{p}^\flat(\eta,\mathfrak{m})),$$

where

$$\mathfrak{p}^{\flat}(\eta,\mathfrak{m}) = \max\{\mathcal{Q}^{\flat}(\eta,\mathfrak{m}), \mathcal{Q}^{\flat}(\eta,\Gamma\eta), \mathcal{Q}^{\flat}(\Gamma\eta,\Gamma^2\eta), \mathcal{Q}^{\flat}(\mathfrak{m},\Gamma\mathfrak{m}), \mathcal{Q}^{\flat}(\Gamma\mathfrak{m},\Gamma^2\mathfrak{m}), \frac{\mathcal{Q}^{\flat}(\eta,\Gamma\mathfrak{m}) + \mathcal{Q}^{\flat}(\mathfrak{m},\Gamma\eta)}{2}, \frac{\mathcal{Q}^{\flat}(\Gamma\eta,\Gamma^2\mathfrak{m}) + \mathcal{Q}^{\flat}(\Gamma\mathfrak{m},\Gamma^2\eta)}{2}\}.$$

(*ii*) Γ *is* α*-admissible;*
(*iii*) *There exists* $\eta_0 \in \Lambda$ *such that* $\alpha(\eta_0,\Gamma\eta_0) \geq 1$.

Define a sequence $\{\eta_\beta\}$ *in* Λ *by* $\eta_{\beta+1} = \Gamma\eta_\beta = \Gamma^{\beta+1}\eta_0$, *for all* $\beta \geq 0$, *then* $\{\mathcal{Q}^{\flat}(\eta_\beta,\eta_{\beta+1})\}$ *is a strictly decreasing sequence in* Λ.

Proof. Let $\eta_0 \in \Lambda$ be such that $\alpha(\eta_0,\Gamma\eta_0) \geq 1$ and define a sequence $\{\eta_\beta\}$ by $\eta_{\beta+1} = \Gamma\eta_\beta$, for all $\beta \in \mathbb{N} \cup \{0\}$. By (ii), we have

$$\alpha(\eta_0,\eta_1) = \alpha(\eta_0,\Gamma\eta_0) \geq 1 \Rightarrow \alpha(\eta_2,\eta_3) = \alpha(\Gamma\eta_1,\Gamma^2\eta_0) \geq 1.$$

Inductively, we obtain $\alpha(\eta_\beta,\eta_{\beta+1}) \geq 1$, for all $\beta \geq 0$. Postulating that $\eta_\beta \neq \eta_{\beta+1}$ for all $\beta \geq 0$, then $\mathcal{Q}^{\flat}(\eta_\beta,\eta_{\beta+1}) > 0$, for all $\beta \geq 0$. Let $\mathfrak{v} = \max\{\mathcal{Q}^{\flat}(\eta_0,\eta_1), \mathcal{Q}^{\flat}(\eta_1,\eta_2)\}$. From (3), taking $\eta = \eta_0$ and $\mathfrak{m} = \eta_1$, we obtain

$$\begin{aligned}
\mathfrak{p}^{\flat}(\eta_0,\eta_1) &= \max\{\mathcal{Q}^{\flat}(\eta_0,\eta_1), \mathcal{Q}^{\flat}(\eta_0,\Gamma\eta_0), \mathcal{Q}^{\flat}(\Gamma\eta_0,\Gamma^2\eta_0), \mathcal{Q}^{\flat}(\eta_1,\Gamma\eta_1), \mathcal{Q}^{\flat}(\Gamma\eta_1,\Gamma^2\eta_1), \\
&\quad \frac{\mathcal{Q}^{\flat}(\eta_0,\Gamma\eta_1) + \mathcal{Q}^{\flat}(\eta_1,\Gamma\eta_0)}{2}, \frac{\mathcal{Q}^{\flat}(\Gamma\eta_0,\Gamma^2\eta_1) + \mathcal{Q}(\Gamma\eta_1,\Gamma^2\eta_0)}{2}\} \\
&= \max\{\mathcal{Q}^{\flat}(\eta_0,\eta_1), \mathcal{Q}^{\flat}(\eta_0,\eta_1), \mathcal{Q}^{\flat}(\eta_1,\eta_2), \mathcal{Q}^{\flat}(\eta_1,\eta_2), \mathcal{Q}^{\flat}(\eta_2,\eta_3), \\
&\quad \frac{\mathcal{Q}^{\flat}(\eta_0,\eta_2) + \mathcal{Q}^{\flat}(\eta_1,\eta_1)}{2}, \frac{\mathcal{Q}^{\flat}(\eta_1,\eta_3) + \mathcal{Q}(\eta_2,\eta_2)}{2}\} \\
&= \max\{\mathcal{Q}^{\flat}(\eta_0,\eta_1), \mathcal{Q}^{\flat}(\eta_1,\eta_2), \mathcal{Q}^{\flat}(\eta_2,\eta_3), \frac{\mathcal{Q}^{\flat}(\eta_0,\eta_2)}{2}, \frac{\mathcal{Q}^{\flat}(\eta_1,\eta_3)}{2}\} \\
&= \max\{\mathcal{Q}^{\flat}(\eta_0,\eta_1), \mathcal{Q}^{\flat}(\eta_1,\eta_2), \mathcal{Q}^{\flat}(\eta_2,\eta_3)\}.
\end{aligned} \tag{4}$$

By (F_1) and $\alpha(\eta_0,\eta_1) \geq 1$, by (2) and (4), we obtain

$$\begin{aligned}
F(\mathcal{Q}^{\flat}(\eta_2,\eta_3)) &= F(\mathcal{Q}^{\flat}(\Gamma^2\eta_0,\Gamma^2\eta_1)) \\
&\leq F(\alpha(\eta_0,\eta_1)\mathcal{Q}^{\flat}(\Gamma^2\eta_0,\Gamma^2\eta_1)) \\
&\leq F(\mathfrak{p}^{\flat}(\eta_0,\eta_1)) - \mu \\
&= F(\max\{\mathcal{Q}^{\flat}(\eta_0,\eta_1), \mathcal{Q}^{\flat}(\eta_1,\eta_2), \mathcal{Q}^{\flat}(\eta_2,\eta_3)\}) - \mu \\
&\leq F(\max\{\mathfrak{v}, \mathcal{Q}^{\flat}(\eta_2,\eta_3)\}) - \mu.
\end{aligned} \tag{5}$$

If $\max\{\mathfrak{v}, \mathcal{Q}^{\flat}(\eta_2,\eta_3)\} = \mathcal{Q}^{\flat}(\eta_2,\eta_3)$, then (5) gives

$$F(\mathcal{Q}^{\flat}(\eta_2,\eta_3)) \leq F(\mathcal{Q}^{\flat}(\eta_2,\eta_3)) - \mu < F(\mathcal{Q}^{\flat}(\eta_2,\eta_3)).$$

This is a contradiction. It follows that

$$F(\mathcal{Q}^{\flat}(\eta_2,\eta_3)) \leq F(\mathfrak{v}) - \mu < F(\mathfrak{v}).$$

Since $\mu > 0$ and by (F_1), we have

$$\mathcal{Q}^{\flat}(\eta_2,\eta_3) < \mathfrak{v} = \max\{\mathcal{Q}^{\flat}(\eta_0,\eta_1), \mathcal{Q}^{\flat}(\eta_1,\eta_2)\}.$$

Again, by (3) with $\eta = \eta_1$ and $\mathfrak{m} = \eta_2$, we get

$$\begin{aligned}
\mathfrak{p}^{\flat}(\eta_1,\eta_2) &= \max\{\mathcal{Q}^{\flat}(\eta_1,\eta_2), \mathcal{Q}^{\flat}(\eta_1,\Gamma\eta_1), \mathcal{Q}^{\flat}(\Gamma\eta_1,\Gamma^2\eta_1), \mathcal{Q}^{\flat}(\eta_2,\Gamma\eta_2), \mathcal{Q}^{\flat}(\Gamma\eta_2,\Gamma^2\eta_2),\\
&\quad \frac{\mathcal{Q}^{\flat}(\eta_1,\Gamma\eta_2)+\mathcal{Q}^{\flat}(\eta_2,\Gamma\eta_1)}{2}, \frac{\mathcal{Q}^{\flat}(\Gamma\eta_1,\Gamma^2\eta_2)+\mathcal{Q}(\Gamma\eta_2,\Gamma^2\eta_1)}{2}\}\\
&= \max\{\mathcal{Q}^{\flat}(\eta_1,\eta_2), \mathcal{Q}^{\flat}(\eta_1,\eta_2), \mathcal{Q}^{\flat}(\eta_2,\eta_3), \mathcal{Q}^{\flat}(\eta_2,\eta_3), \mathcal{Q}^{\flat}(\eta_3,\eta_4),\\
&\quad \frac{\mathcal{Q}^{\flat}(\eta_1,\eta_3)+\mathcal{Q}^{\flat}(\eta_2,\eta_2)}{2}, \frac{\mathcal{Q}^{\flat}(\eta_2,\eta_4)+\mathcal{Q}(\eta_3,\eta_3)}{2}\}\\
&= \max\{\mathcal{Q}^{\flat}(\eta_1,\eta_2), \mathcal{Q}^{\flat}(\eta_2,\eta_3), \mathcal{Q}^{\flat}(\eta_3,\eta_4), \frac{\mathcal{Q}^{\flat}(\eta_1,\eta_3)}{2}, \frac{\mathcal{Q}^{\flat}(\eta_2,\eta_4)}{2}\}\\
&= \max\{\mathcal{Q}^{\flat}(\eta_1,\eta_2), \mathcal{Q}^{\flat}(\eta_2,\eta_3), \mathcal{Q}^{\flat}(\eta_3,\eta_4)\}. \qquad (6)
\end{aligned}$$

By (2) and (6), we obtain

$$\begin{aligned}
F(\mathcal{Q}^{\flat}(\eta_3,\eta_4)) &= F(\mathcal{Q}^{\flat}(\Gamma^2\eta_1,\Gamma^2\eta_2))\\
&\le F(\alpha(\eta_1,\eta_2)\mathcal{Q}^{\flat}(\Gamma^2\eta_1,\Gamma^2\eta_2))\\
&\le F(\mathfrak{p}^{\flat}(\eta_1,\eta_2)) - \mu\\
&= F(\max\{\mathcal{Q}^{\flat}(\eta_1,\eta_2), \mathcal{Q}^{\flat}(\eta_2,\eta_3), \mathcal{Q}^{\flat}(\eta_3,\eta_4)\}) - \mu.
\end{aligned}$$

If $\max\{\mathcal{Q}^{\flat}(\eta_1,\eta_2), \mathcal{Q}^{\flat}(\eta_2,\eta_3), \mathcal{Q}^{\flat}(\eta_3,\eta_4)\} = \mathcal{Q}^{\flat}(\eta_3,\eta_4)$, then we obtain

$$F(\mathcal{Q}^{\flat}(\eta_3,\eta_4)) \le F(\mathcal{Q}^{\flat}(\eta_3,\eta_4)) - \mu < F(\mathcal{Q}^{\flat}(\eta_3,\eta_4)),$$

which is a contradiction. We obtain

$$\max\{\mathcal{Q}^{\flat}(\eta_1,\eta_2), \mathcal{Q}^{\flat}(\eta_2,\eta_3)\} > \mathcal{Q}^{\flat}(\eta_3,\eta_4).$$

Therefore,

$$\mathfrak{v} > \mathcal{Q}^{\flat}(\eta_2,\eta_3) > \mathcal{Q}^{\flat}(\eta_3,\eta_4).$$

Inductively, continuing in this way, we prove that the sequence $\{\mathcal{Q}^{\flat}(\eta_\beta,\eta_{\beta+1})\}$ is strictly decreasing in Λ. □

Theorem 2. *Let $(\Lambda, \mathcal{Q})$ be a complete metric space, $\Gamma : \Lambda \to \Lambda$ a given map, and let $\alpha : \Lambda \times \Lambda \to [0,\infty)$ be a mapping. Suppose that the following affirmations hold:*
(i) There exists $\flat \in [1,\infty)$ and $\mu > 0$ such that for all $\eta, \mathfrak{m} \in \Lambda$,

$$\mathcal{Q}^{\flat}(\Gamma^2\eta,\Gamma^2\mathfrak{m}) > 0 \implies \mu + F(\alpha(\eta,\mathfrak{m})\mathcal{Q}^{\flat}(\Gamma^2\eta,\Gamma^2\mathfrak{m})) \le F(\mathfrak{p}^{\flat}(\eta,\mathfrak{m})),$$

where

$$\begin{aligned}
\mathfrak{p}^{\flat}(\eta,\mathfrak{m}) &= \max\{\mathcal{Q}^{\flat}(\eta,\mathfrak{m}), \mathcal{Q}^{\flat}(\eta,\Gamma\eta), \mathcal{Q}^{\flat}(\Gamma\eta,\Gamma^2\eta), \mathcal{Q}^{\flat}(\mathfrak{m},\Gamma\mathfrak{m}), \mathcal{Q}^{\flat}(\Gamma\mathfrak{m},\Gamma^2\mathfrak{m}),\\
&\quad \frac{\mathcal{Q}^{\flat}(\eta,\Gamma\mathfrak{m})+\mathcal{Q}^{\flat}(\mathfrak{m},\Gamma\eta)}{2}, \frac{\mathcal{Q}^{\flat}(\Gamma\eta,\Gamma^2\mathfrak{m})+\mathcal{Q}^{\flat}(\Gamma\mathfrak{m},\Gamma^2\eta)}{2}\}.
\end{aligned}$$

(ii) Γ is α-admissible;
(iii) There exists $\eta_0 \in \Lambda$ such that $\alpha(\eta_0,\Gamma\eta_0) \ge 1$;
(iv) Γ is continuous or orbitally continuous on Λ.

Then, Γ has a fixed point in Λ. Further, if Γ is α^*-admissible, then Γ has a unique fixed point $\mathfrak{o} \in \Lambda$. Moreover, for any $\eta_0 \in \Lambda$ if $\eta_{\beta+1} = \Gamma^{\beta+1}\eta_0 \neq \Gamma\eta_\beta$, for all $\beta \in \mathbb{N} \cup \{0\}$, then $\lim_{\beta\to\infty} \Gamma^\beta \eta_0 = \mathfrak{o}$.

Proof. Let $\eta_0 \in \Lambda$ be such that $\alpha(\Gamma\eta_0, \eta_0) \geq 1$ and construct a sequence $\{\eta_\beta\}$ by $\eta_{\beta+1} = \Gamma\eta_\beta$, for all $\beta \in \mathbb{N} \cup \{0\}$. If $\eta_{\beta_0} = \eta_{\beta_0+1}$, i.e., $\Gamma\eta_{\beta_0} = \eta_{\beta_0}$ for some $\beta_0 \in \mathbb{N} \cup \{0\}$, then η_{β_0} is a fixed point of Γ.

Now, we postulate that $\eta_\beta \neq \eta_{\beta+1}$ $\forall$ $\beta \geq 0$. Then, $\mathcal{Q}^\flat(\eta_\beta, \eta_{\beta+1}) > 0$, for all $\beta \geq 0$. By (ii), we have $\alpha(\eta_0, \Gamma\eta_0) \geq 1 \Rightarrow \alpha(\eta_1, \eta_2) = \alpha(\Gamma\eta_0, \Gamma^2\eta_0) \geq 1$. Therefore, inductively, we show that $\alpha(\eta_\beta, \eta_{\beta+1}) = \alpha(\Gamma^\beta\eta_0, \Gamma^{\beta+1}\eta_0) \geq 1$, for all $\beta \geq 0$. Letting $\mathfrak{v} = \max\{\mathcal{Q}^\flat(\eta_0, \eta_1), \mathcal{Q}^\flat(\eta_1, \eta_2)\}$.

Now, from (3), taking $\eta = \eta_{\beta-2}$ and $\mathfrak{m} = \eta_{\beta-1}$ with $\beta \geq 2$, we have

$$\begin{aligned}
\mathfrak{p}^\flat(\eta_{\beta-2}, \eta_{\beta-1}) = \max\{&\mathrm{d}^\flat(\eta_{\beta-2}, \eta_{\beta-1}), \mathrm{d}^\flat(\eta_{\beta-2}, \Gamma\eta_{\beta-2}), \mathrm{d}^\flat(\Gamma\eta_{\beta-2}, \Gamma^2\eta_{\beta-2}),\\
&\mathrm{d}^\flat(\eta_{\beta-1}, \Gamma\eta_{\beta-1}), \mathrm{d}^\flat(\Gamma\eta_{\beta-1}, \Gamma^2\eta_{\beta-1}),\\
&\frac{\mathrm{d}^\flat(\eta_{\beta-2}, \Gamma\eta_{\beta-1}) + \mathrm{d}^\flat(\eta_{\beta-1}, \Gamma\eta_{\beta-2})}{2}, \frac{\mathrm{d}^\flat(\Gamma\eta_{\beta-2}, \Gamma^2\eta_{\beta-1}) + \mathrm{d}^\flat(\Gamma\eta_{\beta-1}, \Gamma^2\eta_{\beta-2})}{2}\}\\
= \max\{&\mathrm{d}^\flat(\eta_{\beta-2}, \eta_{\beta-1}), \mathrm{d}^\flat(\eta_{\beta-2}, \eta_{\beta-1}), \mathrm{d}^\flat(\eta_{\beta-1}, \eta_\beta),\\
&\mathrm{d}^\flat(\eta_{\beta-1}, \eta_\beta), \mathrm{d}^\flat(\eta_\beta, \eta_{\beta+1}),\\
&\frac{\mathrm{d}^\flat(\eta_{\beta-2}, \eta_\beta) + \mathrm{d}(\eta_{\beta-1}, \eta_{\beta-1})}{2}, \frac{\mathrm{d}^\flat(\eta_{\beta-1}, \eta_{\beta+1}) + \mathrm{d}(\eta_\beta, \eta_\beta)}{2}\}\\
= \max\{&\mathrm{d}^\flat(\eta_{\beta-2}, \eta_{\beta-1}), \mathrm{d}^\flat(\eta_{\beta-2}, \eta_{\beta-1}), \mathrm{d}^\flat(\eta_{\beta-1}, \eta_\beta),\\
&\mathrm{d}^\flat(\eta_{\beta-1}, \eta_\beta), \mathrm{d}^\flat(\eta_\beta, \eta_{\beta+1}), \frac{\mathrm{d}^\flat(\eta_{\beta-2}, \eta_\beta)}{2}, \frac{\mathrm{d}^\flat(\eta_{\beta-1}, \eta_{\beta+1})}{2}\}\\
= \max\{&\mathrm{d}^\flat(\eta_{\beta-2}, \eta_{\beta-1}), \mathrm{d}^\flat(\eta_{\beta-1}, \eta_\beta), \mathrm{d}^\flat(\eta_\beta, \eta_{\beta+1})\}.
\end{aligned}$$

By (F_1), condition (ii), and Equation (2), we have

$$\begin{aligned}
F(\mathcal{Q}^\flat(\eta_\beta, \eta_{\beta+1})) &= F(\mathcal{Q}^\flat(\Gamma^2\eta_{\beta-2}, \Gamma^2\eta_{\beta-1}))\\
&\leq F(\alpha(\eta_{\beta-2}, \eta_{\beta-1})\mathcal{Q}^\flat(\Gamma^2\eta_{\beta-2}, \Gamma^2\eta_{\beta-1}))\\
&\leq F(\mathfrak{p}^\flat(\eta_{\beta-2}, \eta_{\beta-1})) - \mu\\
&\leq F(\max\{\mathcal{Q}^\flat(\eta_{\beta-2}, \eta_{\beta-1}), \mathcal{Q}^\flat(\eta_{\beta-1}, \eta_\beta), \mathcal{Q}^\flat(\eta_\beta, \eta_{\beta+1})\}) - \mu.
\end{aligned}$$

If $\max\{\mathcal{Q}^\flat(\eta_{\beta-2}, \eta_{\beta-1}), \mathcal{Q}^\flat(\eta_{\beta-1}, \eta_\beta), \mathcal{Q}^\flat(\eta_\beta, \eta_{\beta+1})\} = \mathcal{Q}^\flat(\eta_\beta, \eta_{\beta+1})$, then we obtain

$$F(\mathcal{Q}^\flat(\eta_\beta, \eta_{\beta+1})) \leq F(\mathcal{Q}^\flat(\eta_\beta, \eta_{\beta+1})) - \mu < F(\mathcal{Q}^\flat(\eta_\beta, \eta_{\beta+1})).$$

This is a contradiction. Therefore,

$$F(\mathcal{Q}^\flat(\eta_\beta, \eta_{\beta+1})) \leq F(\max\{\mathcal{Q}^\flat(\eta_{\beta-2}, \eta_{\beta-1}), \mathcal{Q}^\flat(\eta_{\beta-1}, \eta_\beta)\}) - \mu.$$

Since $\{\mathcal{Q}^\flat(\eta_\beta, \eta_{\beta+1})\}$ is a strictly nonincreasing sequence, we obtain

$$F(\mathcal{Q}^\flat(\eta_\beta, \eta_{\beta+1})) \leq F(\mathcal{Q}^\flat(\eta_{\beta-2}, \eta_{\beta-1})) - \mu \leq \ldots \leq F(\mathfrak{v}) - J\mu, \tag{7}$$

whenever $\beta = 2J$ or $\beta = 2J + 1$ for $J \geq 1$.

From (6), we obtain

$$\lim_{\beta\to\infty} F(\mathcal{Q}^\flat(\eta_\beta, \eta_{\beta+1})) = -\infty. \tag{8}$$

Therefore, by (F2) and by Equation (8), we have

$$\lim_{\beta\to\infty} \mathcal{Q}^{\flat}(\eta_\beta, \eta_{\beta+1}) = 0. \tag{9}$$

By (F3), there exists $0 < \mathbf{k} < 1$ such that

$$\lim_{\beta\to\infty} [\mathcal{Q}^{\flat}(\eta_\beta, \eta_{\beta+1})]^{\mathbf{k}} F(\mathcal{Q}^{\flat}(\eta_\beta, \eta_{\beta+1})) = 0. \tag{10}$$

Moreover, by Equation (7), we get

$$[\mathcal{Q}^{\flat}(\eta_\beta, \eta_{\beta+1})]^{\mathbf{k}}[F(\mathcal{Q}^{\flat}(\eta_\beta, \eta_{\beta+1})) - F(\mathfrak{v})] \leq -[\mathcal{Q}^{\flat}(\eta_\beta, \eta_{\beta+1})]^{\mathbf{k}}\, J\mu \leq 0, \tag{11}$$

where $\beta = 2\,J$ or $\beta = 2\,J + 1$ for $J \geq 1$. Setting $\beta \to \infty$ in (11) along with (9) and (10), we have

$$\lim_{\beta\to\infty} J[\mathcal{Q}^{\flat}(\eta_\beta, \eta_{\beta+1})]^{\mathbf{k}} = 0. \tag{12}$$

Now, two cases arise.
Case-(i): If β is even and $\beta \geq 2$, then by Equation (12), we have

$$\lim_{\beta\to\infty} \beta[\mathcal{Q}^{\flat}(\eta_\beta, \eta_{\beta+1})]^{\mathbf{k}} = 0. \tag{13}$$

Case-(ii): If β is odd and $\beta \geq 3$, then by Equation (12), we have

$$\lim_{\beta\to\infty} (\beta - 1)[\mathcal{Q}^{\flat}(\eta_\beta, \eta_{\beta+1})]^{\mathbf{k}} = 0. \tag{14}$$

Using (9), (14) gives

$$\lim_{\beta\to\infty} \beta[\mathcal{Q}^{\flat}(\eta_\beta, \eta_{\beta+1})]^{\mathbf{k}} = 0. \tag{15}$$

We conclude for the above cases that, $\exists\, \beta_1 \in \mathbb{N}$ such that

$$\beta[\mathcal{Q}^{\flat}(\eta_\beta, \eta_{\beta+1})]^{\mathbf{k}} \leq 1\; \forall\, \beta \geq \beta_1.$$

Therefore, we obtain

$$\mathcal{Q}^{\flat}(\eta_\beta, \eta_{\beta+1}) \leq \frac{1}{\beta^{\frac{1}{\mathbf{k}}}},\; \forall\, \beta \geq \beta_1.$$

Now, we prove the sequence $\{\eta_\beta\}$ is a Cauchy sequence. For all $\flat > \mathfrak{q} \geq \beta_1$, we have

$$\mathcal{Q}^{\flat}(\eta_\flat, \eta_\mathfrak{q}) \leq \mathcal{Q}^{\flat}(\eta_\flat, \eta_{\flat-1}) + \mathcal{Q}^{\flat}(\eta_{\flat-1}, \eta_{\flat-2}) + \ldots. + \mathcal{Q}^{\flat}(\eta_{\mathfrak{q}+1}, \eta_\mathfrak{q}) < \sum_{\mathfrak{k}=\mathfrak{q}}^{\infty} \mathcal{Q}^{\flat}(\eta_\mathfrak{k}, \eta_{\mathfrak{k}+1}) \leq \sum_{\mathfrak{k}=\mathfrak{q}}^{\infty} \frac{1}{\mathfrak{k}^{\frac{1}{\mathbf{k}}}}.$$

Taking $\mathfrak{q} \to \infty$, we get $\lim_{\flat,\mathfrak{q}\to\infty} \mathcal{Q}^{\flat}(\eta_\flat, \eta_\mathfrak{q}) = 0$, since $\sum_{\mathfrak{k}=\mathfrak{q}}^{\infty} \frac{1}{\mathfrak{k}^{\frac{1}{\mathbf{k}}}}$ is convergent. This proves that the sequence $\{\eta_\beta\}$ is a Cauchy sequence in Λ. By the completeness property, there exists $\mathfrak{o} \in \Lambda$ such that $\lim_{\beta\to\infty} \eta_\beta = \mathfrak{o}$. Now, we show that $\mathfrak{o}$ is a fixed point of Γ. Since Γ is continuous,

$$\mathcal{Q}^{\flat}(\mathfrak{o}, \Gamma\mathfrak{o}) = \lim_{\beta\to\infty} \mathcal{Q}^{\flat}(\eta_\beta, \Gamma\eta_\beta) = \lim_{\beta\to\infty} \mathcal{Q}^{\flat}(\eta_\beta, \eta_{\beta+1}) = 0.$$

This implies that $\mathfrak{o}$ is a fixed point of Γ.

Again, we postulate that Γ is orbitally continuous on Λ, then

$$\eta_{\beta+1} = \Gamma\eta_\beta = \Gamma(\Gamma^\beta \eta_0) \to \Gamma\mathfrak{o} \text{ as } \beta \to \infty.$$

By completeness, we obtain $\Gamma\mathfrak{o} = \mathfrak{o}$. Therefore, $Fix(\Gamma) \neq 0$.

Further, postulating that Γ is α^*-admissible, $\forall\ \mathfrak{o}, \mathfrak{o}^* \in Fix(\Gamma)$, we have $\alpha(\mathfrak{o}, \mathfrak{o}^*) \geq 1$. By Equations (2) and (3), we have

$$\begin{aligned}
\digamma(\mathcal{Q}^\flat(\mathfrak{o},\mathfrak{o}^*)) &= \digamma(\mathcal{Q}^\flat(\Gamma^2\mathfrak{o},\Gamma^2\mathfrak{o}^*)) \\
&= \digamma(\alpha(\mathfrak{o},\mathfrak{o}^*)\mathcal{Q}^\flat(\Gamma^2\mathfrak{o},\Gamma^2\mathfrak{o}^*)) \\
&\leq \digamma(\mathfrak{p}^\flat(\mathfrak{o},\mathfrak{o}^*)) - \mu \\
&= \digamma(\max\{\mathcal{Q}^\flat(\mathfrak{o},\mathfrak{o}^*), \mathcal{Q}^\flat(\mathfrak{o},\Gamma\mathfrak{o}), \mathcal{Q}^\flat(\Gamma\mathfrak{o},\Gamma^2\mathfrak{o}), \mathcal{Q}^\flat(\mathfrak{o}^*,\Gamma\mathfrak{o}^*), \mathcal{Q}^\flat(\Gamma\mathfrak{o}^*,\Gamma^2\mathfrak{o}^*), \\
&\quad \frac{\mathcal{Q}^\flat(\mathfrak{o},\Gamma\mathfrak{o}^*) + \mathcal{Q}^\flat(\mathfrak{o}^*,\Gamma\mathfrak{o})}{2}, \frac{\mathcal{Q}^\flat(\Gamma\mathfrak{o},\Gamma^2\mathfrak{o}^*) + \mathcal{Q}(\Gamma\mathfrak{o}^*,\Gamma^2\mathfrak{o})}{2}\}) - \mu \\
&= \digamma(\mathcal{Q}^\flat(\mathfrak{o},\mathfrak{o}^*)) - \mu.
\end{aligned}$$

Since $\mu > 0$ and using (F_1), we obtain

$$\digamma(\mathcal{Q}^\flat(\mathfrak{o},\mathfrak{o}^*)) < \digamma(\mathcal{Q}^\flat(\mathfrak{o},\mathfrak{o}^*)).$$

This is a contradiction. Therefore, Γ has a unique fixed point in Λ. $\square$

Example 10. *Let $\Lambda = [0,1]$ and $\mathcal{Q} : \Lambda \times \Lambda \to \mathbb{R}_+$ be given by*

$$\mathcal{Q}^\flat(\eta, \mathfrak{m}) = |\eta - \mathfrak{m}|,$$

for all $\eta, \mathfrak{m} \in \Lambda$. Then, $(\Lambda, \mathcal{Q})$ is a complete metric space. Define a mapping $\Gamma : \Lambda \to \Lambda$ by

$$\Gamma\eta = \frac{\eta^2}{2} + \frac{1}{8},$$

for all $\eta \in \Lambda$ with $\alpha(\eta, \mathfrak{m}) = 1$, for all $\eta, \mathfrak{m} \in \Lambda$. Then, Γ is α-admissible. Let $\digamma \in \Im$ be $\digamma(\mathfrak{r}) = \ln \mathfrak{r}, \mathfrak{r} > 0$. Since we have

$$|\Gamma\eta, \Gamma\mathfrak{m}| = \frac{1}{2}|\eta^2 - \mathfrak{m}^2| \leq |\eta - \mathfrak{m}|,$$

for all $\eta \in \Lambda$, we have

$$\begin{aligned}
\alpha(\eta,\mathfrak{m})(|\Gamma^2\eta, \Gamma^2\mathfrak{m}|^2) &= \frac{1}{256}|(2\eta^2 - \eta^4) - (2\mathfrak{m}^2 - \mathfrak{m}^4)|^2 \\
&\leq \frac{1}{64}(|\eta^4 - \mathfrak{m}^4 + \eta^2 - \mathfrak{m}^2|^2) \\
&\leq \frac{1}{64}(|\eta^4 - \mathfrak{m}^4|^2 + |\eta^2 - \mathfrak{m}^2|^2) \\
&= \frac{1}{64}|\eta^2 - \mathfrak{m}^2|^2 + \frac{1}{64}|\eta^4 - \mathfrak{m}^4|^2 \\
&\leq \frac{1}{2}(|\Gamma\eta - \Gamma\mathfrak{m}|^2 + \frac{1}{4}|\eta - \mathfrak{m}|^2) \\
&\leq \frac{5}{8}\max\{|\eta - \mathfrak{m}|^2, |\Gamma\eta - \Gamma\mathfrak{m}|^2\} \\
&\leq \frac{5}{8}\mathfrak{p}^2(\eta,\mathfrak{m}) \\
&= e^{-\mu}\mathfrak{p}^2(\eta,\mathfrak{m}).
\end{aligned}$$

where $-\mu = \ln(\frac{5}{8})$. *Applying the logarithm on both sides, we get*

$$\mu + \digamma(\alpha(\eta, \mathfrak{m})\mathcal{Q}^{\flat}(\Gamma^2\eta, \Gamma^2\mathfrak{m})) \leq \digamma(\mathfrak{p}^1(\eta, \mathfrak{m})).$$

This shows that Γ *is an* α-$\digamma$*-convex contraction mapping. We define a sequence* $\{\eta_\beta\}$ *by*

$$\eta_\beta = \frac{\beta}{\beta+1} - \frac{1}{\sqrt{2}},$$

then $\eta_\beta \to 1 - \frac{1}{\sqrt{2}}$, *as* $\beta \to \infty$.

Therefore,

$$\eta_{\beta+1} = \Gamma\eta_\beta = [\frac{1}{4}(\frac{\beta}{\beta+1} - \frac{1}{\sqrt{2}})^2 + \frac{1}{8}] \to 1 - \frac{1}{\sqrt{2}},$$

as $\beta \to \infty$. *Thus, all conditions of Theorem 2 are satisfied and* $\eta = 1 - \frac{1}{\sqrt{2}}$ *is the unique fixed point of* Γ *in* Λ.

Corollary 1. *Let* $(\Lambda, \mathcal{Q})$ *be a complete metric space and* $\alpha : \Lambda \times \Lambda \to [0, \infty)$ *a mapping. Postulating that* $\Gamma : \Lambda \to \Lambda$ *is a self-mapping, the following affirmations hold:*

(*i*) $\forall\, \eta, \mathfrak{m} \in \Lambda$,

$$\alpha(\eta, \mathfrak{m})\mathcal{Q}^{\flat}(\Gamma^2\eta, \Gamma^2\mathfrak{m}) \leq \Bbbk \max\{\mathcal{Q}^{\flat}(\eta, \mathfrak{m}), \mathcal{Q}^{\flat}(\eta, \Gamma\eta), \mathcal{Q}^{\flat}(\Gamma\eta, \Gamma^2\eta), \mathcal{Q}^{\flat}(\mathfrak{m}, \Gamma\mathfrak{m}), \mathcal{Q}^{\flat}(\Gamma\mathfrak{m}, \Gamma^2\mathfrak{m}), \frac{\mathcal{Q}^{\flat}(\eta, \Gamma\mathfrak{m}) + \mathcal{Q}^{\flat}(\mathfrak{m}, \Gamma\eta)}{2}, \frac{\mathcal{Q}^{\flat}(\Gamma\eta, \Gamma^2\mathfrak{m}) + \mathcal{Q}^{\flat}(\Gamma\mathfrak{m}, \Gamma^2\eta)}{2}\} \tag{16}$$

where $\Bbbk \in (0, 1)$;

(*ii*) Γ *is* α*-admissible;*

(*iii*) *There exists* $\eta_0 \in \Lambda$ *such that* $\alpha(\eta_0, \Gamma\eta_0) \geq 1$;

(*iv*) Γ *is continuous or orbitally continuous on* Λ.

Then, Γ *has a fixed point in* Λ. *Further, if* Γ *is an* α^**-admissible mapping, then* Γ *has a unique fixed point* $\mathfrak{o} \in \Lambda$. *Moreover, for any* $\eta_0 \in \Lambda$ *if* $\eta_{\beta+1} = \Gamma^{\beta+1}\eta_0 \neq \Gamma^\beta\eta_0$, *for all* $\beta \in \mathbb{N} \cup \{0\}$, *then* $\lim_{\beta\to\infty} \Gamma^\beta\eta_0 = \mathfrak{o}$.

Proof. Setting $\digamma(\mathfrak{r}) = \ln(\mathfrak{r}), \mathfrak{r} > 0$. Obviously, $\digamma \in \Im$. Applying the logarithm on both sides of (16), we get

$$-\ln\Bbbk + \ln\alpha(\eta, \mathfrak{m})\mathcal{Q}^{\flat}(\Gamma^2\eta, \Gamma^2\mathfrak{m}) \leq In(\max\{\mathcal{Q}^{\flat}(\eta, \mathfrak{m}), \mathcal{Q}^{\flat}(\eta, \Gamma\eta), \mathcal{Q}^{\flat}(\Gamma\eta, \Gamma^2\eta), \mathcal{Q}^{\flat}(\mathfrak{m}, \Gamma\mathfrak{m}), \mathcal{Q}^{\flat}(\Gamma\mathfrak{m}, \Gamma^2\mathfrak{m}), \frac{\mathcal{Q}^{\flat}(\eta, \Gamma\mathfrak{m}) + \mathcal{Q}^{\flat}(\mathfrak{m}, \Gamma\eta)}{2}, \frac{\mathcal{Q}^{\flat}(\Gamma\eta, \Gamma^2\mathfrak{m}) + \mathcal{Q}^{\flat}(\Gamma\mathfrak{m}, \Gamma^2\eta)}{2}\}),$$

which implies that

$$\mu + \digamma(\alpha(\eta, \mathfrak{m})\mathcal{Q}^{\flat}(\Gamma^2\eta, \Gamma^2\mathfrak{m})) \leq \digamma(\mathfrak{p}^1(\eta, \mathfrak{m})),$$

for all $\eta, \mathfrak{m} \in \Lambda$ with $\eta \neq \mathfrak{m}$ where $\mu = -\ln\Bbbk$. It follows that Γ is an α-$\digamma$-convex contraction with $\flat = 1$. Thus, all the affirmations of Theorem 2 are held and hence, Γ has a unique fixed point in Λ. $\square$

Corollary 2. *Let* $(\Lambda, \mathcal{Q})$ *be a complete metric space and* $\alpha : \Lambda \times \Lambda \to [0, \infty)$ *a mapping. Postulating that* $\Gamma : \Lambda \to \Lambda$ *is a self-mapping, the following affirmations hold:*

(*i*) $\forall\, \eta, \mathfrak{m} \in \Lambda$,

$$\alpha(\eta,\mathfrak{m})\mathcal{Q}^{\flat}(\Gamma^2\eta,\Gamma^2\mathfrak{m}) \leq \alpha_1\mathcal{Q}^{\flat}(\eta,\mathfrak{m}) + \alpha_2\mathcal{Q}^{\flat}(\eta,\Gamma\eta) + \alpha_3\mathcal{Q}^{\flat}(\Gamma\eta,\Gamma^2\eta)$$
$$+ \alpha_4\mathcal{Q}^{\flat}(\mathfrak{m},\Gamma\mathfrak{m}) + \alpha_5\mathcal{Q}^{\flat}(\Gamma\mathfrak{m},\Gamma^2\mathfrak{m}) + \alpha_6\left(\frac{\mathcal{Q}^{\flat}(\eta,\Gamma\mathfrak{m}) + \mathcal{Q}^{\flat}(\mathfrak{m},\Gamma\eta)}{2}\right)$$
$$+ \alpha_7\left(\frac{\mathcal{Q}^{\flat}(\Gamma\eta,\Gamma^2\mathfrak{m}) + \mathcal{Q}^{\flat}(\Gamma\mathfrak{m},\Gamma^2\eta)}{2}\right),$$

where $0 \leq \alpha_{\mathfrak{k}} < 1, \mathfrak{k} = 1,2,...,7$ *such that* $\sum_{\mathfrak{k}=1}^{7}\alpha_{\mathfrak{k}} < 1$;

(*ii*) Γ *is* α*-admissible;*

(*iii*) *There exists* $\eta_0 \in \Lambda$ *such that* $\alpha(\eta_0,\Gamma\eta_0) \geq 1$;

(*iv*) Γ *is continuous or orbitally continuous on* Λ.

Then, Γ *has a fixed point in* Λ*. Further, if* Γ *is an* α^**-admissible mapping, then* Γ *has a unique fixed point* $\mathfrak{o} \in \Lambda$*. Moreover, for any* $\eta_0 \in \Lambda$ *if* $\eta_{\beta+1} = \Gamma^{\beta+1}\eta_0 \neq \Gamma^{\beta}\eta_0$*, for all* $\beta \in \mathbb{N}\cup\{0\}$*, then* $\lim_{\beta\to\infty}\Gamma^{\beta}\eta_0 = \mathfrak{o}$.

Proof. Setting $F(\mathfrak{r}) = \ln(\mathfrak{r}), \mathfrak{r} > 0$. Obviously, $F \in \Im$. For all $\eta,\mathfrak{m} \in \Lambda$ with $\eta \neq \mathfrak{m}$, we obtain

$$\alpha(\eta,\mathfrak{m})\mathcal{Q}^{\flat}(\Gamma^2\eta,\Gamma^2\mathfrak{m}) = \mathcal{Q}^{\flat}(\Gamma^2\eta,\Gamma^2\mathfrak{m})$$
$$\leq \alpha_1\mathcal{Q}^{\flat}(\eta,\mathfrak{m}) + \alpha_2\mathcal{Q}^{\flat}(\eta,\Gamma\eta) + \alpha_3\mathcal{Q}^{\flat}(\Gamma\eta,\Gamma^2\eta)$$
$$+ \alpha_4\mathcal{Q}^{\flat}(\mathfrak{m},\Gamma\mathfrak{m}) + \alpha_5\mathcal{Q}^{\flat}(\Gamma\mathfrak{m},\Gamma^2\mathfrak{m}),$$
$$+ \alpha_6\left(\frac{\mathcal{Q}^{\flat}(\eta,\Gamma\mathfrak{m}) + \mathcal{Q}^{\flat}(\mathfrak{m},\Gamma\eta)}{2}\right) + \alpha_7\left(\frac{\mathcal{Q}^{\flat}(\Gamma\eta,\Gamma^2\mathfrak{m}) + \mathcal{Q}^{\flat}(\Gamma\mathfrak{m},\Gamma^2\eta)}{2}\right)$$
$$\leq \Bbbk\max\bigg\{\mathcal{Q}^{\flat}(\eta,\mathfrak{m}), \mathcal{Q}^{\flat}(\eta,\Gamma\eta), \mathcal{Q}^{\flat}(\Gamma\eta,\Gamma^2\eta), \mathcal{Q}^{\flat}(\mathfrak{m},\Gamma\mathfrak{m}), \mathcal{Q}^{\flat}(\Gamma\mathfrak{m},\Gamma^2\mathfrak{m}),$$
$$\frac{\mathcal{Q}^{\flat}(\eta,\Gamma\mathfrak{m}) + \mathcal{Q}^{\flat}(\mathfrak{m},\Gamma\eta)}{2}, \frac{\mathcal{Q}^{\flat}(\Gamma\eta,\Gamma^2\mathfrak{m}) + \mathcal{Q}^{\flat}(\Gamma\mathfrak{m},\Gamma^2\eta)}{2}\bigg\},$$

where $\Bbbk = \sum_{\mathfrak{k}=1}^{7}\alpha_{\mathfrak{k}} < 1$. By Corollary 1, Γ has a unique fixed point in Λ. □

Corollary 3. *Consider a continuous self-mapping* Γ *on a complete metric space* $(\Lambda,\mathcal{Q})$*. If there exists* $\Bbbk \in (0,1)$ *satisfying the following inequality*

$$\mathcal{Q}^{\flat}(\Gamma^2\eta,\Gamma^2\mathfrak{m})) \leq \Bbbk\max\bigg\{\mathcal{Q}^{\flat}(\eta,\mathfrak{m}), \mathcal{Q}^{\flat}(\eta,\Gamma\eta), \mathcal{Q}^{\flat}(\Gamma\eta,\Gamma^2\eta), \mathcal{Q}^{\flat}(\mathfrak{m},\Gamma\mathfrak{m}), \mathcal{Q}^{\flat}(\Gamma\mathfrak{m},\Gamma^2\mathfrak{m}),$$
$$\frac{\mathcal{Q}^{\flat}(\eta,\Gamma\mathfrak{m}) + \mathcal{Q}^{\flat}(\mathfrak{m},\Gamma\eta)}{2}, \frac{\mathcal{Q}^{\flat}(\Gamma\eta,\Gamma^2\mathfrak{m}) + \mathcal{Q}^{\flat}(\Gamma\mathfrak{m},\Gamma^2\eta)}{2}\bigg\}$$

for all $\eta,\mathfrak{m} \in \Lambda$*, then* Γ *has a unique fixed point in* Λ.

3. Application

In this application part, we provide a nonlinear integral equation application of our main results.

Consider a real-valued continuous function $\Lambda = \zeta[\mathtt{a},\mathtt{b}]$ defined on $[\mathtt{a},\mathtt{b}]$ with metric $\mathtt{d}(\varphi,\psi) = |\varphi-\psi| = \max_{\mathtt{s}\in[\mathtt{a},\mathtt{b}]}|\varphi(\mathtt{s})-\psi(\mathtt{s})|\ \forall\ \varphi,\psi \in \zeta[\mathtt{a},\mathtt{b}]$. Then, $(\Lambda,\mathtt{d})$ is a complete metric space.

Consider

$$\eta(\mathtt{s}) = \mathfrak{v}(\mathtt{s}) + \frac{1}{\mathtt{b}-\mathtt{a}} \int_{\mathtt{a}}^{\mathtt{b}} K(\mathtt{s},\mathtt{t},\eta(\mathtt{t}))\mathtt{dt}, \tag{17}$$

where $\mathtt{s},\mathtt{t} \in [\mathtt{a},\mathtt{b}]$, $\mathfrak{v}(\mathtt{s})$ is a given function in Λ and $K : [\mathtt{a},\mathtt{b}] \times [\mathtt{a},\mathtt{b}] \times \Lambda \to \mathbb{R}, \mathfrak{v} : [\mathtt{a},\mathtt{b}] \to \mathbb{R}$ are given continuous functions.

Theorem 3. *Let $(\Lambda,\mathtt{d})$ be a metric space with metric $\mathtt{d}(\varphi,\psi) = |\varphi-\psi| = \max_{\mathtt{s}\in[\mathtt{a},\mathtt{b}]} |\varphi(\mathtt{s}) - \psi(\mathtt{s})|\ \forall\ \varphi,\psi \in \Lambda$ and define a continuous operator $\Gamma : \Lambda \to \Lambda$ on Λ by*

$$\Gamma\eta(\mathtt{s}) = \mathfrak{v}(\mathtt{s}) + \frac{1}{\mathtt{b}-\mathtt{a}} \int_{\mathtt{a}}^{\mathtt{b}} K(\mathtt{s},\mathtt{t},\eta(\mathtt{t}))\mathtt{dt}. \tag{18}$$

If there exists $\Bbbk \in (0,1)$ such that $\forall\ \eta,\mathfrak{m} \in \Lambda$ with $\eta \neq \mathfrak{m}$ and $\mathtt{t},\mathtt{s} \in [\mathtt{a},\mathtt{b}]$ satisfying the following inequality

$$\begin{aligned}|K(\mathtt{s},\mathtt{t},\Gamma\eta(\mathtt{t})) - K(\mathtt{s},\mathtt{t},\Gamma\mathfrak{m}(\mathtt{t}))| \le \Bbbk \max\Big\{ & |\eta(\mathtt{t}) - \mathfrak{m}(\mathtt{t})|, |\Gamma\eta - \Gamma\mathfrak{m}|, |\eta - \Gamma\eta|, |\Gamma\eta - \Gamma^2\eta|, \\ & |\mathfrak{m} - \Gamma\mathfrak{m}|, |\Gamma\mathfrak{m} - \Gamma^2\mathfrak{m}|, \left(\frac{|\eta - \Gamma\mathfrak{m}| + |\mathfrak{m} - \Gamma\eta|}{2}\right), \\ & \left(\frac{|\Gamma\eta - \Gamma^2\mathfrak{m}| + |\Gamma\mathfrak{m} - \Gamma^2\eta|}{2}\right)\Big\},\end{aligned} \tag{19}$$

then, by (18), the integral operator has a unique solution $\mathfrak{o} \in \Lambda$ and for each $\eta_0 \in \Lambda, \Gamma\eta_\beta \neq \eta_\beta\ \forall\ \beta \in \mathbb{N} \cup \{0\}$, we have $\lim_{\beta\to\infty} \Gamma\eta_\beta = \mathfrak{o}$.

Proof. Define a mapping $\alpha : \Lambda \times \Lambda \to \mathbb{R}_+$ by $\alpha(\eta,\mathfrak{m}) = 1\ \forall\ \eta,\mathfrak{m} \in \Lambda$. Therefore, Γ is α-admissible. Let $\digamma \in \Im$ such that $\digamma(\mathfrak{x}) = In(\mathfrak{x}), \mathfrak{x} > 0$. Let $\eta_0 \in \Lambda$ and a sequence $\{\eta_\beta\}$ in Λ defined by $\eta_{\beta+1} = \Gamma\eta_\beta = \Gamma^{\beta+1}\eta_0\ \forall\ \beta \ge 0$. By Equation (18), we have

$$\eta_{\beta+1} = \Gamma\eta_\beta(\mathtt{s}) = \mathfrak{v}(\mathtt{s}) + \frac{1}{\mathtt{b}-\mathtt{a}} \int_{\mathtt{a}}^{\mathtt{b}} K(\mathtt{s},\mathtt{t},\eta_\beta(\mathtt{t}))\mathtt{dt}. \tag{20}$$

We prove that Γ is an α-$\digamma$-convex contraction on $\zeta[\mathtt{a},\mathtt{b}]$. By Equations (18) and (19), we obtain

$$\begin{aligned}|\Gamma^2\eta(\mathtt{s}) - \Gamma^2\mathfrak{m}(\mathtt{s})| &= \frac{1}{|\mathtt{b}-\mathtt{a}|} \left| \int_{\mathtt{a}}^{\mathtt{b}} K(\mathtt{s},\mathtt{t},\Gamma\eta(\mathtt{t}))\mathtt{dt} - K(\mathtt{s},\mathtt{t},\Gamma\mathfrak{m}(\mathtt{t}))\mathtt{dt} \right| \\ &\le \frac{1}{|\mathtt{b}-\mathtt{a}|} \int_{\mathtt{a}}^{\mathtt{b}} |K(\mathtt{s},\mathtt{t},\Gamma\eta(\mathtt{t})) - K(\mathtt{s},\mathtt{t},\Gamma\mathfrak{m}(\mathtt{t}))|\mathtt{dt} \\ &\le \frac{\Bbbk}{|\mathtt{b}-\mathtt{a}|} \int_{\mathtt{a}}^{\mathtt{b}} \max\Big\{ |\eta(\mathtt{t}) - \mathfrak{m}(\mathtt{t})|, |\Gamma\eta - \Gamma\mathfrak{m}|, |\eta - \Gamma\eta|, |\Gamma\eta - \Gamma^2\eta|, \\ &\quad |\mathfrak{m} - \Gamma\mathfrak{m}|, |\Gamma\mathfrak{m} - \Gamma^2\mathfrak{m}|, \left(\frac{|\eta - \Gamma\mathfrak{m}| + |\mathfrak{m} - \Gamma\eta|}{2}\right), \\ &\quad \left(\frac{|\Gamma\eta - \Gamma^2\mathfrak{m}| + |\Gamma\mathfrak{m} - \Gamma^2\eta|}{2}\right)\Big\}\mathtt{dt}.\end{aligned}$$

Taking the maximum on both sides, for all $\mathtt{s} \in [\mathtt{a},\mathtt{b}]$, we have

$$
\begin{aligned}
\mathtt{d}(\Gamma^2\eta,\Gamma^2\mathtt{m}) &= \max_{\mathtt{s}\in[\mathtt{a},\mathtt{b}]} |\Gamma^2\eta(\mathtt{s})-\Gamma^2\mathtt{m}(\mathtt{s})| \\
&\leq \frac{\Bbbk}{|\mathtt{b}-\mathtt{a}|}\max_{\mathtt{s}\in[\mathtt{a},\mathtt{b}]}\int_{\mathtt{a}}^{\mathtt{b}}\max\Big\{|\eta(\mathtt{t})-\mathtt{m}(\mathtt{t})|,|\Gamma\eta(\mathtt{t})-\Gamma\mathtt{m}(\mathtt{t})|,|\eta(\mathtt{t})-\Gamma\eta(\mathtt{t})|, \\
&\qquad |\Gamma\eta(\mathtt{t})-\Gamma^2\eta(\mathtt{t})|,|\mathtt{m}(\mathtt{t})-\Gamma\mathtt{m}(\mathtt{t})|,|\Gamma\mathtt{m}(\mathtt{t})-\Gamma^2\mathtt{m}(\mathtt{t})|, \\
&\qquad \left(\frac{|\eta(\mathtt{t})-\Gamma\mathtt{m}(\mathtt{t})|+|\mathtt{m}(\mathtt{t})-\Gamma\eta(\mathtt{t})|}{2}\right), \\
&\qquad \left(\frac{|\Gamma\eta(\mathtt{t})-\Gamma^2\mathtt{m}(\mathtt{t})|+|\Gamma\mathtt{m}(\mathtt{t})-\Gamma^2\eta(\mathtt{t})|}{2}\right)\Big\}\mathtt{dt}. \\
&\leq \frac{\Bbbk}{|\mathtt{b}-\mathtt{a}|}\max\Bigg[\max_{\vartheta\in[\mathtt{a},\mathtt{b}]}\Big\{|\eta(\vartheta)-\mathtt{m}(\vartheta)|,|\Gamma\eta(\vartheta)-\Gamma\mathtt{m}(\vartheta)|,|\eta(\vartheta)-\Gamma\eta(\vartheta)|, \\
&\qquad |\Gamma\eta(\vartheta)-\Gamma^2\eta(\vartheta)|,|\mathtt{m}(\vartheta)-\Gamma\mathtt{m}(\vartheta)|,|\Gamma\mathtt{m}(\vartheta)-\Gamma^2\mathtt{m}(\vartheta)|, \\
&\qquad \left(\frac{|\eta(\vartheta)-\Gamma\mathtt{m}(\vartheta)|+|\mathtt{m}(\vartheta)-\Gamma\eta(\vartheta)|}{2}\right), \\
&\qquad \left(\frac{|\Gamma\eta(\vartheta)-\Gamma^2\mathtt{m}(\vartheta)|+|\Gamma\mathtt{m}(\vartheta)-\Gamma^2\eta(\vartheta)|}{2}\right)\Big\}\Bigg]\int_{\mathtt{a}}^{\mathtt{b}}\mathtt{dt} \\
&= \Bbbk\max\Big\{\mathtt{d}(\eta,\mathtt{m}),\mathtt{d}(\Gamma\eta,\Gamma\mathtt{m}),\mathtt{d}(\eta,\Gamma\eta),\mathtt{d}(\Gamma\eta,\Gamma^2\eta),\mathtt{d}(\mathtt{m},\Gamma\mathtt{m}),\mathtt{d}(\Gamma\mathtt{m},\Gamma^2\mathtt{m}), \\
&\qquad \left(\frac{\mathtt{d}(\eta,\Gamma\mathtt{m})+\mathtt{d}(\mathtt{m},\Gamma\eta)}{2}\right),\left(\frac{\mathtt{d}(\Gamma\eta,\Gamma^2\mathtt{m})+\mathtt{d}(\Gamma\mathtt{m},\Gamma^2\eta)}{2}\right)\Big\} \\
&= \Bbbk\mathtt{p}^1(\eta,\mathtt{m}).
\end{aligned}
$$

Therefore, $\mathtt{d}(\Gamma^2\eta,\Gamma^2\mathtt{m}) \leq \Bbbk\mathtt{p}^1(\eta,\mathtt{m})$. Hence, we have

$$\alpha(\eta,\mathtt{m})\mathtt{d}(\Gamma^2\eta,\Gamma^2\mathtt{m}) \leq \Bbbk\mathtt{p}^1(\eta,\mathtt{m}).$$

Now, applying the logarithm on both sides, we get

$$-In\ \Bbbk + In[\alpha(\eta,\mathtt{m})\mathtt{d}(\Gamma^2\eta,\Gamma^2\mathtt{m})] \leq In\ \mathtt{p}^1(\eta,\mathtt{m}).$$

Therefore, we have

$$\Bbbk + \digamma(\alpha(\eta,\mathtt{m})\mathtt{d}(\Gamma^2\eta,\Gamma^2\mathtt{m}) \leq \digamma(\mathtt{p}^1(\eta,\mathtt{m})),$$

where $-\ln\ \Bbbk = \mu$. It follows that Γ is an α-$\digamma$-convex contraction with $\flat = 1\ \forall\ \eta,\mathtt{m} \in \Lambda$ with $\eta \neq \mathtt{m}$. Since Γ is α-admissible and $\Lambda = \zeta[\mathtt{a},\mathtt{b}]$ is a complete metric space, the iteration scheme converges to some point $\mathfrak{o} \in \Lambda$, i.e., $\lim_{\beta\to\infty}\eta_\beta \to \mathfrak{o}$. From the continuity, we show that $\mathfrak{o}$ is a fixed point of Γ. It follows that $\mathcal{T}\mathfrak{o} = \mathfrak{o}$. Clearly, $\mathrm{Fix}(\mathcal{T}) \neq \emptyset$. Now, $\forall\ \eta,\mathtt{m} \in Fix(\Gamma), \alpha(\mathfrak{o},\mathfrak{o}^*) = 1$. This shows that Γ is α^*-admissible. Thus, all the affirmations of Theorem 2 are held and hence, Γ has a unique fixed point solution $\mathfrak{o} \in \Lambda$. □

The example below demonstrates the existence of a singular integral operator solution meeting each of the conditions in Theorem 3.

Example 11. *Let $\Lambda = \zeta[0,1]$ be a set of all continuous function on [0, 1], $\mathfrak{v}(\mathtt{s}) = \frac{7}{15}\mathtt{s}^2$ and $K(\mathtt{s},\mathtt{t},\eta(\mathtt{t})) = \frac{1}{4}\mathtt{s}^2(1+\frac{\mathtt{t}}{2})(\eta(\mathtt{t})+1)$. Then, (18) becomes*

$$\Gamma\eta(\mathtt{s}) = \frac{7}{15}\mathtt{s}^2 + \int_0^1 \frac{1}{4}\mathtt{s}^2(1+\frac{\mathtt{t}}{2})(\eta(\mathtt{t})+1)\mathtt{dt}. \tag{21}$$

Now,

1. $\max|\frac{1}{4}\mathtt{s}^2(1+\frac{\mathtt{t}}{2})| \leq \frac{1}{2}$ *for all* $(\mathtt{s},\mathtt{t}) \in [0,1]\times[0,1]$;
2. *For all* $\eta, \mathfrak{m} \in \Lambda$ *with* $\eta \neq \mathfrak{m}$ *and* $(\mathtt{s},\mathtt{t}) \in [0,1]\times[0,1]$ *and using (18), we obtain*

$$|\Gamma\eta - \Gamma\mathfrak{m}| \leq |\eta - \mathfrak{m}|.$$

By the above inequality, we obtain Γ *is not an F-contraction. Now, we obtain*

$$\begin{aligned}\Big|\Gamma^2\eta(\mathtt{s}) - \Gamma^2\mathfrak{m}(\mathtt{s})\Big| &= \Big|\int_0^1 K\Big(\mathtt{s},\mathtt{t},\mathfrak{v}(\mathtt{s}) + \int_0^1 K\Big(\mathtt{s},\mathtt{t},\eta(\mathtt{s})\Big)d\mathtt{t}\Big)d\mathtt{t} - \int_0^1 K\Big(\mathtt{s},\mathtt{t},\mathfrak{v}(\mathtt{s}) \\ &\quad + \int_0^1 K\Big(\mathtt{s},\mathtt{t},\mathfrak{m}(\mathtt{s})\Big)d\mathtt{t}\Big)d\mathtt{t}\Big| \\ &\leq \int_0^1\int_0^1 \Big|\Big[\frac{\mathtt{s}^2(1+\frac{\mathtt{t}}{2})}{4}\Big]\Big(\eta(\mathtt{t}) - \mathfrak{m}(\mathtt{t})\Big)\Big| d\mathtt{t}d\mathtt{t} \\ &\leq \max_{\mathtt{s}\in[0,1]}\int_0^1\int_0^1 \Big|\Big[\frac{\mathtt{s}^2(1+\frac{\mathtt{t}}{2})}{4}\Big]\Big(\eta(\mathtt{t}) - \mathfrak{m}(\mathtt{t})\Big)\Big| d\mathtt{t}d\mathtt{t} \\ &\leq \frac{1}{2}\Big|\eta - \mathfrak{m}\Big| \\ &= \mathbf{e}^{-\mu}\mathfrak{p}^1(\eta,\mathfrak{m}).\end{aligned}$$

Therefore, $\Big|\Gamma^2\eta(\mathtt{s}) - \Gamma^2\mathfrak{m}(\mathtt{s})\Big| \leq \mathbf{e}^{-\mu}\mathfrak{p}^1(\eta,\mathfrak{m})$, *where* $In\,\frac{1}{2} = -\mu$. *Set* $\alpha : \Lambda\times\Lambda \to [0,\infty)$ *by* $\alpha(\eta,\mathfrak{m}) = 1$, *for all* $\eta,\mathfrak{m} \in \Lambda$ *and* $\digamma \in \Im$ *such that* $\digamma(\mathfrak{x}) = \ln(\mathfrak{x}), \mathfrak{x} > 0$. *Therefore, we obtain*

$$\alpha(\eta,\mathfrak{m})|\Gamma^2\eta - \Gamma^2\mathfrak{m}| \leq \mathfrak{p}^1(\eta,\mathfrak{m}).$$

Applying the logarithm on both sides, we get

$$\mu + \ln\alpha(\eta,\mathfrak{m})\mathtt{d}(\Gamma^2\eta,\Gamma^2\mathfrak{m}) \leq \ln\mathfrak{p}^1(\eta,\mathfrak{m}),$$

that is,

$$\mu + \digamma(\alpha(\eta,\mathfrak{m})\mathtt{d}(\Gamma^2\eta,\Gamma^2\mathfrak{m})) \leq \digamma(\mathfrak{p}^1(\eta,\mathfrak{m})).$$

We conclude that Γ *is an* α-$\digamma$*-convex contraction with* $\flat = 1\ \forall\ \eta,\mathfrak{m} \in \Lambda$. *Thus, all the affirmations of Theorem 2 are held and therefore, Equation (18) has a unique solution. It follows that* $\eta(\mathtt{s}) = \mathtt{s}^2$ *is the exact solution of Equation (18). Using Equations (20) and (21) becomes*

$$\eta_{\beta+1}(\mathtt{s}) = \Gamma\eta_\beta(\mathtt{s}) = \frac{7}{15}\mathtt{s}^2 + \int_0^1 \frac{1}{4}\mathtt{s}^2(1+\frac{\mathtt{t}}{2})(\eta_\beta(\mathtt{t})+1)d\mathtt{t}. \tag{22}$$

Letting $\eta_0(\mathtt{s}) = 0$ *be an initial solution. Letting* $\beta = 0,1,2,\ldots$, *respectively, in (22), we get*

$\eta_1(\mathtt{s}) = 0.7791666667\mathtt{s}^2$, $\eta_2(\mathtt{s}) = 0.8684461806\mathtt{s}^2$, $\eta_3(\mathtt{s}) = 0.8786761249\mathtt{s}^2$,
$\eta_4(\mathtt{s}) = 0.879848306\mathtt{s}^2$, $\eta_5(\mathtt{s}) = 0.8799826184\mathtt{s}^2$, $\eta_6(\mathtt{s}) = 0.8799980084\mathtt{s}^2$,
$\eta_7(\mathtt{s}) = 0.8799997718\mathtt{s}^2$, $\eta_8(\mathtt{s}) = 0.8799999739\mathtt{s}^2$, $\eta_9(\mathtt{s}) = 0.8799999959\mathtt{s}^2$,
$\eta_{10}(\mathtt{s}) = 0.8799999984\mathtt{s}^2$, $\eta_{11}(\mathtt{s}) = 0.8799999998\mathtt{s}^2$, $\eta_{12}(\mathtt{s}) = 0.88\mathtt{s}^2$,
$\eta_{13}(\mathtt{s}) = 0.88\mathtt{s}^2$.

Figure 1 discuss about the convergence criterion by using the $\eta(\mathtt{s})$ *numerical values.*

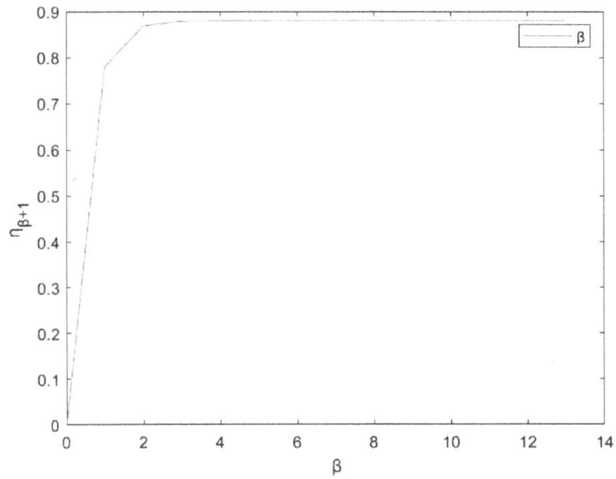

Figure 1. Convergence criterion.

Therefore, $\eta(\mathrm{s}) = 0.88\mathrm{s}^2$ *is the unique solution.*

4. Conclusions

This study introduced convexity conditions to α-F-contraction mappings with possible seven values. This research proved that the fixed point for α-F two-sided convex contraction mappings in a complete metric space was unique. The solution of a nonlinear integral equation was obtained via α-F-convex contraction mappings. This research work has many potential applications as the fixed point for these newly introduced convex contraction mappings can be established in different abstract spaces. Faraji and Radenovic provided some fixed-point results for convex contraction mappings on F-metric spaces. This will provide a structural method for finding a value of a fixed point. It is an interesting open problem to study the fixed-point results α-F-convex contraction mappings on complete F-metric spaces.

Author Contributions: Conceptualization, G.N., A.J.G., G.M. and O.E.; methodology, G.N., A.J.G., G.M. and O.E.; validation, O.E. and N.M.; formal analysis, G.N., A.J.G., G.M. and O.E.; investigation, G.N., A.J.G. and O.E.; writing—original draft preparation, G.N., A.J.G., G.M., O.E., D.S. and N.M.; writing—review and editing, O.E. and N.M.; supervision, O.E. and N.M.; project administration, O.E. and N.M.; funding acquisition, N.M. All authors have read and agreed to the published version of the manuscript.

Funding: This research received no external funding.

Data Availability Statement: Data is contained within the article.

Acknowledgments: The authors D. Santina and N. Mlaiki would like to thank Prince Sultan University for paying the publication fees for this work through TAS LAB.

Conflicts of Interest: The authors declare no conflict of interest.

References

1. Ćirić, L.B. Generalized contractions and fixed point theorems. *Publ. Inst. Math.* **1971**, *12*, 19–26.
2. Istrǎtescu, V.I. Some fixed point theorems for convex contraction mappings and convex non expansive mappings (I). *Liberta Math.* **1981**, *1*, 151–163.
3. Alghamdi, M.A.; Alnafei, S.H.; Radenovic, S.; Shahzad, N. Fixed point theorems for convex contraction mappings on cone metric spaces. *Math. Comput. Model.* **2011**, *54*, 2020–2026. [CrossRef]
4. Miculescu, R.; Mihail, A. A generalization of Istrǎtescu's fixed point theorem for convex contractions. *arXiv* **2015**. [CrossRef]

5. Miculescu, R.; Mihail, A. A generalization of Matkowski's fixed point theorem and Istrăţescu's fixed point theorem concerning convex contractions. *Fixed Point Theory Appl.* **2017**, *19*, 1525–1533. [CrossRef]
6. Latif, A.; Sintunavarat, W.; Ninsri, A. Approximate fixed point theorems for partial generalized convex contraction mappings in α-complete metric spaces. *Taiwanese J. Math.* **2015**, *19*, 315–333. [CrossRef]
7. Latif, A.; Al Subaie, R.F.; Alansari M.O. Fixed points of generalized multi-valued contractive mappings in metric type spaces. *J. Nonlinear Var. Anal.* **2022**, *6*, 123–138.
8. Miandaragh, M.A.; Postolache, M; Rezapour, S. Some approximate fixed point results for generalized α-contractive mapping. *Politehn. Univ. Bucharest Sci. Bull. Ser. A Appl. Math. Phys.* **2013**, *75*, 3–10.
9. Miandaragh, M.A.; Postolache, M.; Rezapour, S. Approximate fixed points of generalized convex contractions. *Fixed Point Theory Appl.* **2013**, *2013*, 255. [CrossRef]
10. Wardowski, D. Fixed points of a new type of contractive mappings in complete metric spaces. *Fixed Point Theory Appl.* **2012**, *2012*, 94. [CrossRef]
11. Samet, B.; Vetro, C.; Vetro, P. Fixed point theorems for (α, ψ)-contractive type mappings. *Nonlinear Anal.* **2012**, *75*, 2154–2165. [CrossRef]
12. Asem, V.; Singh, Y.M. On Meir-Keeler proximal contraction for non-self mappings. *J. Adv. Math. Stud.* **2022**, *15*, 250–261.
13. Karapinar, E.; Kumam, P.; Salimi, P. On $\alpha - \psi -$ Meir-Keeler contractive mappings. *Fixed Point Theory Appl.* **2013**, *2013*, 94. [CrossRef]
14. Karapinar, E. α-Geraghty contraction type mappings and some related fixed point results. *Filomat* **2014**, *28*, 37–48. [CrossRef]
15. Khan, M.S.; Singh, Y.M.; Maniu, G.; Postolache, M. On $(\alpha$, p)-convex contraction and asymptotic regularity. *J. Math. Comput. Sci.* **2018**, *18*, 132–145. [CrossRef]
16. Yildirim, I. Fixed point results for F-Hardy-Rogers contractions via Mann's iteration process in complete convex b-metric spaces. *Sahand Commun. Math. Anal.* **2022**, *19*, 15–32.
17. Singh, Y.M.; Khan, M.S.; Kang, S.M. F-convex contraction via admissible mapping and related fixed point theorems with an application. *Mathematics* **2018**, *6*, 105. [CrossRef]
18. Eke, K.S. Some approximate fixed point theorems for partial Chatterjea convex contractive maps in metric spaces. *Int. J. Math. Sci. J. Optim. Theory Appl.* **2022**, *8*, 1– 8.
19. Geleta, K.W.; Tola, K.K.; Teweldemedhin, S.G. Alpha-F-convex contraction mappings in b-metric space and a related fixed point theorem. *J. Function Spaces* **2021**, *2021*, 5720558. [CrossRef]
20. Alecsa, C.D. Some fixed point results regarding convex contractions of Presi'c type. *J. Fixed Point Theory Appl.* **2018**, *20*, 7. [CrossRef]
21. Chen, L.; Li, C.; Kaczmarek, R.; Zhao, Y. Several Fixed Point Theorems in Convex b-Metric Spaces and Applications. *Mathematics* **2020**, *8*, 2422. [CrossRef]
22. Karaca, N.; Yildirim, I. Fixed point theorem for Reich contraction mapping in convex b-metric spaces. *Aligarh Bull. Math.* **2021**, *40*, 29–39.
23. Arul Joseph, G.; Gunaseelan, M.; Lee, J.R.; Park, C. Solving a nonlinear integral equation via orthogonal metric space. *AIMS Math.* **2022**, *7*, 1198–1210.
24. Arul Joseph, G.; Gunasekaran, N.; Absar, U.H.; Gunaseelan, M.; Imran, A.B.; Kamsing, N. Common Fixed-Points Technique for the Existence of a Solution to Fractional Integro-Differential Equations via Orthogonal Branciari Metric Spaces. *Symmetry* **2022**, *14*, 1859.
25. Haokip, N. Convergence of an iteration scheme in convex metric spaces. *Proyecciones J. Math.* **2022**, *41*, 777–790. [CrossRef]
26. Khan, M.S.; Menaka, M.; Jacob, G.K.; Marudai, M. Proximity points for cyclic 2-convex contraction mappings. *Nonlinear Functional Anal. Appl.* **2020**, *25*, 1–12.
27. Gunasekaran, N.; Arul Joseph, G.; Gunaseelan, M.; Ozgur, E. Solving integral equations via admissible contraction mappings. *Filomat* **2022**, *36*, 4947–4961.
28. Khantwala, D.; Anejab, S.; Gairolac, U. A fixed point theorem for (ϕ, ψ)-convex contraction in metric spaces. *Adv. Theory Nonlinear Anal. Its Appl.* **2021**, *5*, 240–245.
29. Mitrovi'c, Z.D.; Aydi, H.; Mlaiki, N.; Gardaševi'c-Filipovi'c, M.; Kuki'c, K.; Radenovi'c, S.; De la Sen, M. Some new observations and results for convex contractions of Istratescu's type. *Symmetry* **2019**, *11*, 1457. [CrossRef]
30. Faraji, H.; Radenovi'c, S. Some fixed point results for convex contraction mappings on F-metric spaces. *Ser. Math. Inform.* **2020**, *35*, 939–948. [CrossRef]
31. Nallaselli, G.; Gnanaprakasam, A.J.; Mani, G.; Mitrović, Z.D.; Aloqaily, A.; Mlaiki, N. Integral equation via fixed point theorems on a new type of convex contraction in b-metric and 2-metric spaces. *Mathematics* **2023**, *11*, 344. [CrossRef]
32. Liu, Y.; Liu, Z.; Wen, C.F.; Yao, J.C.; Zeng, S. Existence of solutions for a class of noncoercive variational-hemivariational inequalities arising in contact problems. *Appl. Math. Optim.* **2021**, *84*, 2037–2059. [CrossRef]

33. Liu, Y.; Migórski, S.; Nguyen, V.T.; Zeng, S. Existence and convergence results for an elastic frictional contact problem with nonmonotone subdifferential boundary conditions. *Acta Math. Sci.* **2021**, *41*, 1151–1168. [CrossRef]
34. Zeng, S.; Migórski, S.; Khan, A.A. Nonlinear quasi-hemivariational inequalities: existence and optimal control. *SIAM J. Control Optim.* **2021**, *59*, 1246–1274. [CrossRef]

axioms

Article

The Design of State-Dependent Switching Rules for Second-Order Switched Linear Systems Revisited

Xiaolan Yuan and Yusheng Zhou *

School of Mathematics and Statistics, Guizhou University, Guiyang 550025, China
* Correspondence: yszhou@gzu.edu.cn

Abstract: This paper focuses on the asymptotic stability of second-order switched linear systems with positive real part conjugate complex roots for each subsystem. Compared with available studies, a more appropriate state-dependent switching rule is designed to stabilize a switched system with the phase trajectories of two subsystems rotating outward in the same direction or the opposite direction. Finally, several numerical examples are used to illustrate the effectiveness and superiority of the proposed method.

Keywords: switched system; unstable subsystem; asymptotic stability; state-dependent switching rule

MSC: 34A12; 93C23

Citation: Yuan, X.; Zhou, Y. The Design of State-Dependent Switching Rules for Second-Order Switched Linear Systems Revisited. *Axioms* **2022**, *11*, 566. https://doi.org/10.3390/axioms11100566

Academic Editors: Shengda Zeng, Stanisław Migórski and Yongjian Liu

Received: 9 September 2022
Accepted: 14 October 2022
Published: 19 October 2022

1. Introduction

For switched systems, differential equations are used to describe the dynamic behavior of the continuous characteristic, which are marked as subsystems. Meanwhile, a piecewise constant function is adopted to describe the discrete characteristic, which is referred to as a switching rule. As an important part of hybrid systems, switched systems have been exhibited in many practical fields, such as engine systems [1], network systems [2], stirred reactor systems [3], mobile robot systems [4], etc. Moreover, the expected performance of some complex controlled systems can be efficiently achieved by switching control strategies [5,6]. Taking the modern variable-speed wind turbine for example, it can switch back and forth between low and high wind speed modes according to the current wind speed, thus capturing as much wind energy as possible at rated power [7]. Meanwhile, considerable attention has been paid to investigations of switched systems over the last decades. Wu et al. [8] studied the stability of stochastic switched systems via probabilistic analysis. Tian et al. [9] considered the controllability and observability of multi-agent switched systems with continuous and discrete subsystems. Liu et al. [10] and Niu et al. [11,12] designed neural adaptive control strategies for nonlinear switched systems. However, in a practical controlled system, actuator or sensor failure would inevitably occur, thus destabilizing the original stable subsystem. Therefore, it would be very meaningful to conduct studies on switched systems with unstable subsystems, especially for switched systems with fully unstable subsystems, which in recent years has attracted the attention of many researchers and led to the development of numerous significant results. For instance, a fault detection observer was designed to address subsystem instability caused by unobservable factors [13]. A sufficient asymptotic stability condition was presented by a time-dependent strategy for a state-constrained switched system with multiple unstable subsystems [14]. However, to the best of the authors' knowledge, a switched system with the characteristic roots of each subsystem being positive has been rarely considered so far, and is thus the research subject of this paper.

The succesful design of a switching rule to render a switched system asymptotically stable presents an interesting problem that has attracted the attention of many scholars. As a robust closed-loop switching mechanism, state-dependent switching is relatively suitable for solving the above problem. Wu et al. [15] discussed the stability problem of stochastic switched systems via state-dependent switching rule. Liu and Long [16] designed a state-dependent switching rule with guaranteed dwell time to stabilize a class of nonlinear switched systems, with the help of a sum-of-squares constraint approach and an improved path-tracing method. Guo et al. [17] considered the multi-stability of switched neural networks with sinusoidal activation functions under state-dependent switching. Yang and Li [18] achieved the stability of stochastic switched neural networks with time-varying parameter uncertainty through a state-dependent switching approach. For a switched system where the characteristic roots of each subsystem are all positive real parts, the state-dependent switching rule would also be very applicable.

In practical problems, all subsystems may be unstable due to extreme operating environments, measurement failures, or actuator failures. In general, it could be difficult to make the switched system with fully unstable subsystems asymptotically stable via time-dependent switching rules. In particular, when the characteristic roots of each subsystem are all positive real parts, there are no stable factors in each subsystem. In this situation, it is impossible to compensate for the divergence of unstable subsystems through the stability factors of subsystems. That is, the time-dependent switching rule does not work, and only state-dependent switching rule can be applied to achieve asymptotic stability of such switched systems. In fact, for switched systems with the characteristic roots of each subsystem being all positive real parts, there has been little relevant research work, and no systematic universal method has been formed at present. To the best of the authors' knowledge, in the existing representative research literature, Pettersson investigated a special class of linear switched systems, in which the characteristic roots of each subsystem were all positive real parts [19]. A state-dependent switching rule was constructed by the largest region function strategy to achieve system asymptotic stability. However, the obtained results are somewhat conservative for adopting a linear matrix inequality approach. Furthermore, the calculation process is relatively complex. In order to fundamentally address the drawback of poor conservativeness, Ref. [20] constructed an energy function with practical physical meaning for each subsystem by introducing an invertible transformation. By analyzing the energy ratio functions of two subsystems, two switching lines with maximum and minimum energy loss were obtained to design a proper state-dependent switching rule. The obtained result is evidently simpler and less conservative than [19], and also demonstrates faster convergence of system states.

It is worth noting that the switching rule proposed in [20] is only applicable to switched systems where the phase trajectories of two subsystems rotate counter-clockwise. When the phase trajectories of both subsystems rotate clockwise, or one rotates counter-clockwise while the other clockwise, such a switching rule cannot guarantee system stability. Based on the above-mentioned discussions, two improved state-dependent switching rules are put forward in this paper. The main innovations are as follows:

(i) A more suitable state-dependent switching rule is designed to stabilize a switched system with the phase trajectories of both subsystems rotating in the same direction.

(ii) When the phase trajectories of two subsystems rotate outward in opposite directions, a novel state-dependent switching rule is proposed to guarantee system stability, by judging whether the system state satisfies a critical switching condition or not.

In addition to the introduction in Section 1, the remainder of the paper is organized as follows. Section 2 presents the knowledge of the second-order linear switched system. An improved switching rule is designed in Section 3 for the switched system with phase trajectories of subsystems rotating in the same direction. Section 4 designs a novel switching rule for switched systems in which the phase trajectories of subsystems rotate in opposite directions. Subsequently, two examples are given in Section 5 to illustrate the effectiveness of the proposed method. Finally, some conclusions of the paper are presented in Section 6.

2. System Description and Preliminaries

In general, the mathematical model of a linear switched system is described by

$$\begin{cases} \dot{\mathbf{x}}(t) = \mathbf{A}_{\sigma(t)}\mathbf{x}(t), \\ \mathbf{x}(0) = \mathbf{x}_0. \end{cases} \tag{1}$$

Here, $\sigma(t) : [0, \infty) \to \Lambda = \{1, 2, 3...N\}$ is a piecewise function that represents a switching rule. N is the number of subsystems in the switched system. $\mathbf{x}(t) \in \mathbb{R}^n$ denotes the state vector and $\mathbf{x}_0$ stands for the given initial value of the system. $\mathbf{A}_i \in \mathbb{R}^{n\times n}, i \in \Lambda$ is the state matrix of the ith subsystem. In this paper, a second-order switched system with two linear subsystems is considered, in which the eigenroots of each subsystem matrix are a pair of positive real part conjugate complex roots. That is to say, $N = 2$, $\mathbf{x}(t) \in \mathbb{R}^2$ and $\mathbf{A}_i \in \mathbb{R}^{2\times 2}$. Furthermore, $\mathbf{x}(t)$ and $\mathbf{A}_i$ are specifically depicted as

$$\mathbf{x}(t) = \begin{pmatrix} x_1(t) \\ x_2(t) \end{pmatrix}, \quad \mathbf{A}_i = \begin{pmatrix} a_i & b_i \\ c_i & d_i \end{pmatrix}, \quad i = 1, 2.$$

To elaborate the subsequent work in more clarity, some definitions, hypothesis and lemma should be distinctly provided.

Definition 1 ([21]). *Under the switching rule $\sigma(t)$, if the solution $\mathbf{x}(t)$ of the switched system* (1) *is bounded for all $t \in [0, \infty)$ and $\lim_{t\to\infty} \mathbf{x}(t) = \mathbf{0}$ holds for equilibrium point $\mathbf{x}_e = \mathbf{0}$, then the switched system* (1) *is said to be asymptotically stable at equilibrium point $\mathbf{x}_e = \mathbf{0}$.*

Definition 2 ([20]). *Consider the following second-order linear system*

$$\begin{pmatrix} \dot{x}_1 \\ \dot{x}_2 \end{pmatrix} = \begin{pmatrix} a & b \\ c & d \end{pmatrix} \begin{pmatrix} x_1 \\ x_2 \end{pmatrix}, \quad c \neq 0, \tag{2}$$

where its characteristic roots are a pair of conjugate complex roots with positive real parts. Then, the energy function presented by the sum of kinetic and potential energy, is defined as

$$E = \frac{1}{2}(ad - bc)x_1^2 + \frac{1}{2}(ax_1 + bx_2)^2. \tag{3}$$

Here, $ad - bc > 0$ denotes the equivalent stiffness coefficient and $a + d > 0$ stands for the equivalent damping coefficient.

Hypothesis 1. *Without loss of generality, $a_1d_1 - b_1c_1 > a_2d_2 - b_2c_2$ is assumed. Namely, the equivalent stiffness coefficient of the first subsystem is greater than that of the second subsystem.*

Lemma 1 ([20]). *When the phase trajectories of both second-order subsystems given in* (1) *rotate counter-clockwise, a state-dependent switching rule of the switched system* (1) *can be designed as*

$$\sigma(t) = \begin{cases} 1, & (x_2(t) - k_1x_1(t)) \cdot (x_2(t) - k_2x_1(t)) \geq 0, \\ 2, & (x_2(t) - k_1x_1(t)) \cdot (x_2(t) - k_2x_1(t)) < 0. \end{cases} \tag{4}$$

Here, k_1, k_2 are two constants with $k_1 < k_2$ and $x_2 = k_1x_1$, $x_2 = k_2x_1$ make the following energy ratio function

$$\frac{E_1}{E_2} = \frac{\frac{1}{2}(a_1d_1 - b_1c_1) + \frac{1}{2}(a_1 + b_1k)^2}{\frac{1}{2}(a_2d_2 - b_2c_2) + \frac{1}{2}(a_2 + b_2k)^2}, \quad k = \frac{x_2}{x_1} \tag{5}$$

take the maximum and minimum, respectively.

Remark 1. *According to Lemma 1, by using the switching rule* (4)*, the energy loss of the switched system* (1) *is the largest in a switching loop, so that the system state can converge to the equilibrium point as fast as possible.*

For the switched system (1) with characteristic roots of each subsystem being conjugate complex roots with positive real parts, the switching rule (4) is quite effective. However, ref. [20] only investigates the stability of a switched system with phase trajectories of both subsystems rotating counter-clockwise. The cases of two phase trajectories rotating clockwise or one rotating clockwise while the other rotates counter-clockwise are not considered. Motivated by the above discussion, the objectives of this paper are two-fold.

(i) One is to propose an improved state-dependent switching rule for stabilizing the switched system with the phase trajectories of two subsystems rotating outward in the same direction.

(ii) The other is to design an appropriate state-dependent switching rule to guarantee the asymptotic stability of the switched system with phase trajectories of two subsystems rotating in opposite directions.

3. The Case of Two Subsystems with Same Rotation Direction of Phase Trajectories

To address the stability problem of a switched system with phase trajectories of two subsystems rotating in the same direction, we first need to determine the rotation direction of phase trajectory for a second-order linear system. Thus, the following lemma is necessary.

Lemma 2. *The phase trajectory of system* (2) *rotates clockwise if and only if* $b - \frac{ad}{c} > 0$*. Furthermore, the phase trajectory of system* (2) *rotates counter-clockwise if and only if* $b - \frac{ad}{c} < 0$.

Proof of Lemma 2. We first show the sufficient proof. Since the characteristic roots of system (2) are positive real conjugate complex roots, the phase trajectory is spirally divergent and $c \neq 0$. Then, set a point on the phase trajectory as $(x_1, x_2)^{\mathrm{T}} = (-\frac{d}{c}, 1)^{\mathrm{T}}$. Substituting it into system (2) yields

$$\dot{x}_1 = b - \frac{ad}{c}, \quad \dot{x}_2 = 0.$$

When $b - \frac{ad}{c} > 0$, the tangent vector of phase trajectory is horizontal to the right. This implies that the phase trajectory rotates clockwise. Similarly, the tangent vector is horizontal to the left if $b - \frac{ad}{c} < 0$. Accordingly, the phase trajectory rotates counter-clockwise.

In the next step, we exhibit the necessary proof. Obviously, when the phase trajectory of system (2) rotates clockwise, the tangent vector at point $(x_1, x_2)^{\mathrm{T}}$ is horizontal to the right. This implies $b - \frac{ad}{c} > 0$. Conversely, when the phase trajectory of the system rotates counter-clockwise, the tangent vector at point $(x_1, x_2)^{\mathrm{T}}$ is horizontal to the left. Accordingly, it indicates $b - \frac{ad}{c} < 0$. This completes the proof. □

In fact, in order to stabilize the switched system (1) with same rotation direction of phase trajectories, we need to switch from the first (second) subsystem to the second (first) subsystem at the maximum (or minimum) value of energy ratio function $\frac{E_1}{E_2}$. Therefore, the increased energy from operation unstable subsystems can be compensated by the decreased energy from system switching. On this basis, an improved state-dependent switching rule is proposed as follows

$$\sigma(t) = \begin{cases} 1, & \phi \cdot (x_2(t) - k_1 x_1(t)) \cdot (x_2(t) - k_2 x_1(t)) \geq 0, \\ 2, & \phi \cdot (x_2(t) - k_1 x_1(t)) \cdot (x_2(t) - k_2 x_1(t)) < 0. \end{cases} \tag{6}$$

Here, the slope of $x_1 = 0$ is assumed to be negative infinity. ϕ is a sign function, described by

$$\phi = \begin{cases} 1, & k_1 - k_2 > 0 \text{ and } b_i - \frac{a_i d_i}{c_i} > 0, \\ -1, & k_1 - k_2 < 0 \text{ and } b_i - \frac{a_i d_i}{c_i} > 0, \\ -1, & k_1 - k_2 > 0 \text{ and } b_i - \frac{a_i d_i}{c_i} < 0, \\ 1, & k_1 - k_2 < 0 \text{ and } b_i - \frac{a_i d_i}{c_i} < 0. \end{cases} \quad (7)$$

The switching rule (6) includes rule (4) and is also applicable to the switched system with the phase trajectories of two subsystems rotating clockwise. That is, when two subsystems rotate in the same direction, either clockwise or counter-clockwise, the switching rule (6) can be adopted to guarantee the asymptotic stability of the switched system.

In order to better understand the above switching rule, we further present its geometric meaning. As shown in Figure 1a,d, when the system state goes from region Q_1 to Q_2 through the critical line $x_2 = k_1 x_1$, and the system switches from the first subsystem to the second subsystem, then the energy loss would be maximized under Hypothesis 1. On the contrary, when the system state goes from region Q_2 to Q_1 through the critical line $x_2 = k_2 x_1$, and the system switches from the second subsystem to the first subsystem, then the increased energy would be minimized. Thus, the first subsystem should be run in $(x_2 - k_1 x_1) \cdot (x_2 - k_2 x_1) \geq 0$ and the second subsystem should be run in $(x_2 - k_1 x_1) \cdot (x_2 - k_2 x_1) < 0$. Likewise, as reflected in Figure 1b,c, if the second subsystem is activated at $(x_2 - k_1 x_1) \cdot (x_2 - k_2 x_1) > 0$ and the first subsystem is activated at $(x_2 - k_1 x_1) \cdot (x_2 - k_2 x_1) \leq 0$, the total energy loss in the switching loop would be maximized. Based on the above analysis, the switching rule (6) is suitable for stabilizing the switched system (1) in which the phase trajectories of two subsystems rotate in the same direction.

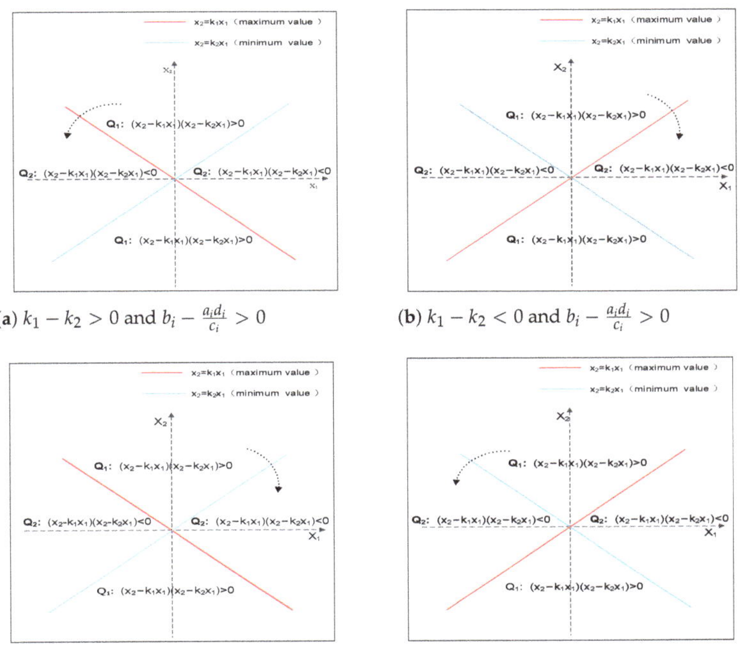

(**a**) $k_1 - k_2 > 0$ and $b_i - \frac{a_i d_i}{c_i} > 0$ (**b**) $k_1 - k_2 < 0$ and $b_i - \frac{a_i d_i}{c_i} > 0$

(**c**) $k_1 - k_2 > 0$ and $b_i - \frac{a_i d_i}{c_i} < 0$ (**d**) $k_1 - k_2 < 0$ and $b_i - \frac{a_i d_i}{c_i} < 0$

Figure 1. A diagram of system switching for different cases given in (7).

4. The Case of Two Subsystems with Opposite Rotation Directions of Phase Trajectories

In this section, we investigate the stability of switched systems with phase trajectories of two subsystems rotating outwards in opposite directions.

By means of the switching rule (6), the phase plane is divided into four switching regions, and only one subsystem can be operated in each switching region. When the phase trajectories of two subsystems rotate in opposite directions, the system state may switch back and forth on one of the two critical switching lines if switching rule (6) is adopted. In order to be more specific, an example is presented as below.

Example 1. *Consider a switched system consisting of the following two subsystem state matrices*

$$\mathbf{A}_1 = \begin{pmatrix} 1 & 4 \\ -80 & 2 \end{pmatrix}, \quad \mathbf{A}_2 = \begin{pmatrix} \frac{1}{2} & -6 \\ 10 & \frac{1}{2} \end{pmatrix}, \tag{8}$$

with the initial condition being $\mathbf{x}(0) = (-1, 2)^{\mathrm{T}}$.

By calculation, the eigenvalues of the first subsystem and the second subsystem are, respectively, given by $1.50 \pm 17.88i$ and $0.50 \pm 7.75i$. Since the characteristic roots of both subsystems are positive real parts, the two subsystems are unstable. According to Lemma 2, the phase trajectory of the first subsystem rotates clockwise, while the second one rotates counter-clockwise, as depicted in Figure 2. Clearly, the phase trajectories of the two subsystems rotate in opposite directions.

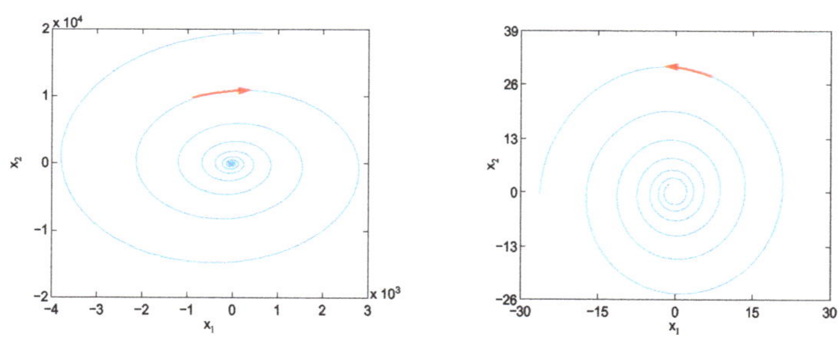

(**a**) The phase trajectory of the first subsystem (**b**) The phase trajectory of the second subsystem

Figure 2. The phase trajectories of the two subsystems.

In view of Equation (5), the energy ratio function between the first and second subsystems is obtained as

$$\frac{E_1}{E_2} = \frac{161 + \frac{(1+4k)^2}{2}}{\frac{241}{8} + \frac{(\frac{1}{2}-6k)^2}{2}}. \tag{9}$$

Taking the derivative of Equation (9) with respect to k yields the following two critical switching lines

$$x_2 = k_1 x_1 = 0.11 x_1, \quad x_2 = k_2 x_1 = -55.63 x_1. \tag{10}$$

Here, $x_2 = 0.11x_1$ and $x_2 = -55.63x_1$ make the energy ratio function (9) take the maximum and minimum values, respectively. As depicted in Figure 3, the switching rule (6) cannot stabilize the switched system (8) irrespective of whether $\phi = 1$ or $\phi = -1$. In particular, the system state switches back and forth on the critical switching line $x_2 = 0.11x_1$ when $\phi = 1$, as shown in Figure 4a. Similarly, in Figure 4b, the system state hovers around the critical switching line $x_2 = -55.63x_1$ when $\phi = -1$.

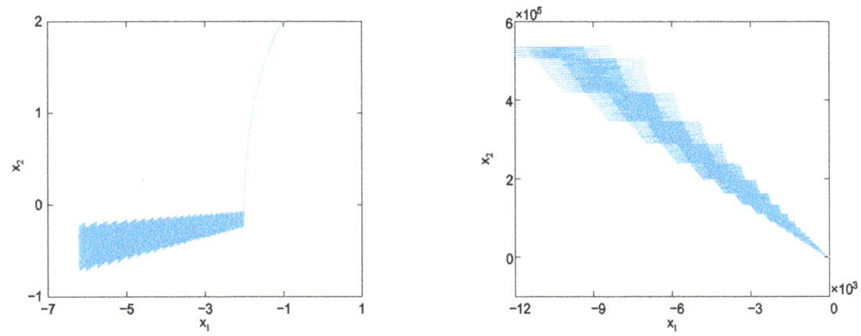

(**a**) $\phi = 1$ (**b**) $\phi = -1$

Figure 3. The phase diagrams of system (8) under the switching rule (6).

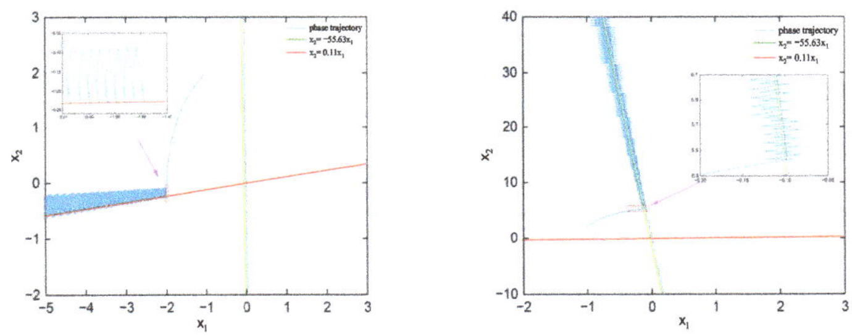

(**a**) $\phi = 1$ (**b**) $\phi = -1$

Figure 4. Phase diagrams and critical switching lines.

We can see from the above simulation that the switched system fails to switch from the first subsystem to the second subsystem at the maximum value of $\frac{E_1}{E_2}$, or from the second subsystem back to the first subsystem at the minimum value of $\frac{E_1}{E_2}$. In this situation, the energy reduced by system switching cannot offset the energy increased from the unstable subsystem operation. Naturally, the switching rule (6) cannot stabilize the switched system with phase trajectories of two subsystems rotating in opposite directions. In order to avoid the system switching occurring back and forth on one of the two critical switching lines, the switching rule (6) is improved as follows

$$\sigma(t+\triangle t) = \begin{cases} 1, & \sigma(t) = 1 \text{ and } (x_2(t) - k_1 x_1(t)) \cdot (x_2(t-\triangle t) - k_1 x_1(t-\triangle t)) > 0, \\ 2, & \sigma(t) = 1 \text{ and } (x_2(t) - k_1 x_1(t)) \cdot (x_2(t-\triangle t) - k_1 x_1(t-\triangle t)) \leq 0, \\ 1, & \sigma(t) = 2 \text{ and } (x_2(t) - k_2 x_1(t)) \cdot (x_2(t-\triangle t) - k_2 x_1(t-\triangle t)) \leq 0, \\ 2, & \sigma(t) = 2 \text{ and } (x_2(t) - k_2 x_1(t)) \cdot (x_2(t-\triangle t) - k_2 x_1(t-\triangle t)) > 0. \end{cases} \tag{11}$$

Here, $\triangle t$ is the step length of time in the numerical calculation, which is defined as 0.001 seconds in this paper.

In what follows, we will present a detailed explanation of the switching rule (11). For simplicity, we assume that the first subsystem is activated at the initial time, and the equivalent stiffness coefficients of two subsystems satisfy Hypothesis 1. In addition, $k_1$and k_2 are assumed to be the maximum and minimum points of $\frac{E_1}{E_2}$, respectively. To avoid switching back and forth on one critical switching line only, we need to make a restriction on the switching rule (6). That is, the system is required to switch from the first (or second) subsystem to the second (or first) one if and only if the system state crosses the switching line $x_2 = k_1x_1$ (or $x_2 = k_2x_1$). Moreover, whether the system state crosses the switching line $x_2 = k_1x_1$ can be judged by considering the inequation $(x_2(t) - k_1x_1(t)) \cdot (x_2(t - \triangle t) - k_1x_1(t - \triangle t)) > 0$. In other words, the system state crosses the switching line $x_2 = k_1x_1$ if and only if $(x_2(t) - k_1x_1(t)) \cdot (x_2(t - \triangle t) - k_1x_1(t - \triangle t)) < 0$ holds. Based on the above restriction, we can obtain the switching rule (11) and the system switching process is as follows. Starting from the first subsystem, we need to determine whether the inequation $(x_2(t) - k_1x_1(t)) \cdot (x_2(t - \triangle t) - k_1x_1(t - \triangle t)) > 0$ holds from time to time during its operation. If so, the first subsystem continues to run. Otherwise, the system state would cross the switching line $x_2 = k_1x_1$, and then the system needs to be switched from the first subsystem to the second subsystem. Similarly, it is necessary to judge whether the inequation $(x_2(t) - k_2x_1(t)) \cdot (x_2(t - \triangle t) - k_2x_1(t - \triangle t)) > 0$ holds in the operation of the second subsystem. Repeating the above switching steps, the energy loss from system switching in a switching loop could be maximized as much as possible, thereby rapidly achieving asymptotic stability.

Remark 2. *Although the switching mechanism proposed in this manuscript is suitable for a second-order switched system with three subsystems, the switching sequence of subsystems bears a significant impact on system stability. As such, constructing an optimal switching sequence that enables rapid convergence of the system presents a challenging problem under the proposed state-dependent switching rule.*

5. Simulation Results

Example 2. *To illustrate the effectiveness of the switching rule* (6)*, we consider a switched system with the following two state matrices*

$$\mathbf{A}_1 = \begin{pmatrix} \frac{1}{3} & -10 \\ 100 & \frac{1}{3} \end{pmatrix}, \quad \mathbf{A}_2 = \begin{pmatrix} 1 & -3 \\ 2 & \frac{1}{2} \end{pmatrix}, \tag{12}$$

where the initial condition is $\mathbf{x}(0) = (1, -1)^{\mathrm{T}}$.

By calculation, the eigenvalues of matrix $\mathbf{A}_1$ are $0.33 \pm 31.62i$ and the eigenvalues of matrix $\mathbf{A}_2$ are $0.75 \pm 2.44i$. It implies that both subsystems are unstable. Applying Lemma 2, phase trajectories of both subsystems rotate counter-clockwise. As can be seen in Figure 5, the phase trajectories of two subsystems rotate in the same direction, which indicates that the switching rule (6) is effective.

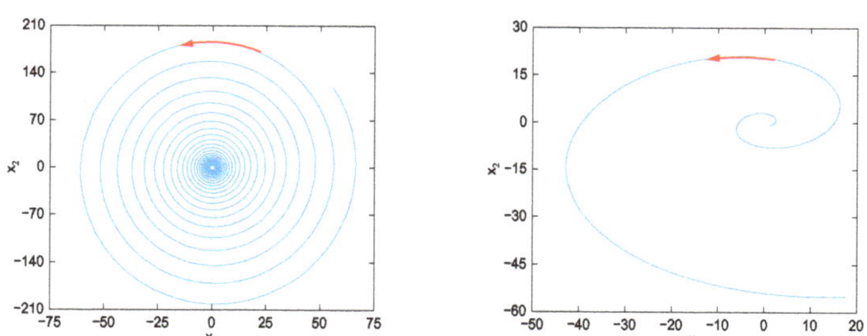

(**a**) The phase trajectory of the first subsystem (**b**) The phase trajectory of the second subsystem

Figure 5. The phase trajectories of the two subsystems.

According to Equation (5), the energy ratio function of two subsystems is calculated as

$$\frac{E_1}{E_2} = \frac{\frac{9001}{18} + \frac{(\frac{1}{3} - 10k)^2}{2}}{\frac{13}{4} + \frac{(1-3k)^2}{2}}. \tag{13}$$

By solving $\frac{d(\frac{E_1}{E_2})}{dk} = 0$, two critical switching lines are obtained as

$$x_2 = k_1 x_1 = 0.36x_1, \quad x_2 = k_2 x_1 = -30.92x_1. \tag{14}$$

Here, $x_2 = 0.36x_1$ and $x_2 = -30.92x_1$ make the energy ratio function (13) take the maximum and minimum values, respectively. For the two subsystems, since the rotation directions of their phase trajectories are counter-clockwise, $b_i - \frac{a_i d_i}{c_i} < 0$. Therefore, the switching rule of switched system (12) is finally derived as

$$\sigma(t) = \begin{cases} 1, & -(x_2(t) - 0.36x_1(t)) \cdot (x_2(t) + 30.92x_1(t)) \geq 0, \\ 2, & -(x_2(t) - 0.36x_1(t)) \cdot (x_2(t) + 30.92x_1(t)) < 0. \end{cases}$$

From Figure 6, we can see that the switched system (12) can be quickly stabilized to the equilibrium point under the switching rule (6). That is, the switching rule (6) can stabilize the switched system (1) with the phase trajectories of two subsystems rotating in the same direction.

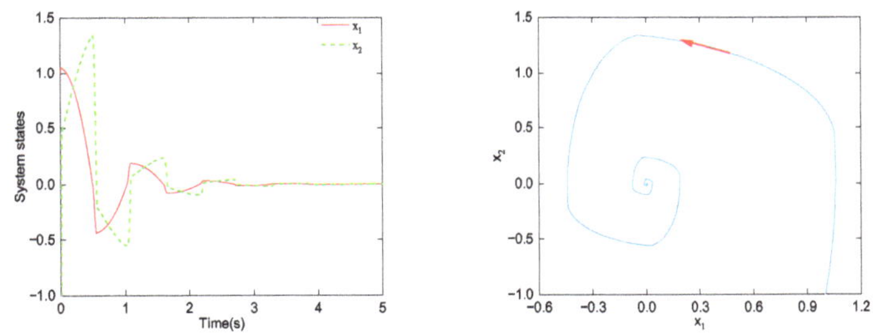

(**a**) The time history of system states (**b**) The phase diagram of switched system (12)

Figure 6. The switched system (12) is asymptotically stable under the switching rule (6).

Example 3. *The switched system* (8) *in Example 1 is used to clarify the validity of the switching rule* (11).

Since the phase trajectories of two subsystems rotate in opposite directions, the switching rule (11) is employed. Substituting Equation (10) into this state-dependent switching rule, one obtains

$$\sigma(t + \triangle t) = \begin{cases} 1, & \sigma(t) = 1 \text{ and } (x_2(t) - 0.11x_1(t)) \cdot (x_2(t - \triangle t) - 0.11x_1(t - \triangle t)) > 0, \\ 2, & \sigma(t) = 1 \text{ and } (x_2(t) - 0.11x_1(t)) \cdot (x_2(t - \triangle t) - 0.11x_1(t - \triangle t)) \leq 0, \\ 1, & \sigma(t) = 2 \text{ and } (x_2(t) + 55.63x_1(t)) \cdot (x_2(t - \triangle t) + 55.63x_1(t - \triangle t)) \leq 0, \\ 2, & \sigma(t) = 2 \text{ and } (x_2(t) + 55.63x_1(t)) \cdot (x_2(t - \triangle t) + 55.63x_1(t - \triangle t)) > 0. \end{cases}$$

As can be seen in Figure 7, the switching rule (11) makes the switched system (8) converge to the equilibrium point quickly. This indicates that the switching rule (11) is very effective when the phase trajectories of the two subsystems rotate in opposite directions.

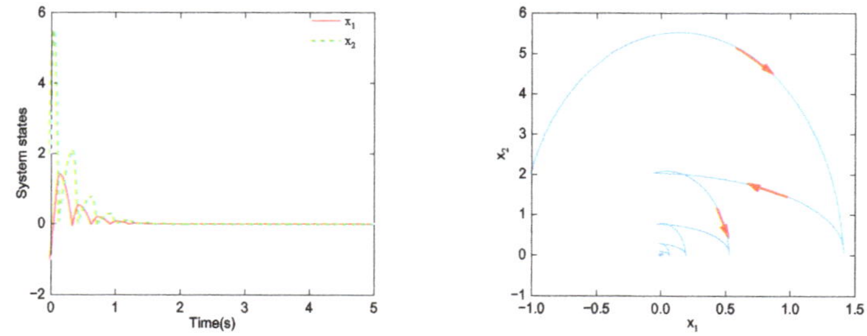

(**a**) The time histories of system states (**b**) The phase diagram of switched system (8)

Figure 7. The switched system (8) is asymptotically stable under the switching rule (11).

Example 4. *Consider a switched system* (1) *with the following three state matrices*

$$\mathbf{A}_1 = \begin{pmatrix} 1 & 100 \\ -100 & 1 \end{pmatrix}, \quad \mathbf{A}_2 = \begin{pmatrix} \frac{1}{3} & -10 \\ 30 & \frac{1}{2} \end{pmatrix}, \quad \mathbf{A}_3 = \begin{pmatrix} \frac{1}{4} & 1 \\ -9 & \frac{1}{4} \end{pmatrix}, \tag{15}$$

where the initial condition is $\mathbf{x}(0) = (2,4)^{\mathrm{T}}$.

The eigenvalues of matrices $\mathbf{A}_1$, $\mathbf{A}_2$, and $\mathbf{A}_3$ are calculated as $1 \pm 100i$, $0.42 \pm 17.32i$, and $0.25 + 3i$, respectively. Clearly, all subsystems are completely unstable. As shown in Figure 8, the phase trajectories of the first and third subsystems rotate clockwise outside, while the phase trajectory of the second subsystem rotates counter-clockwise outside.

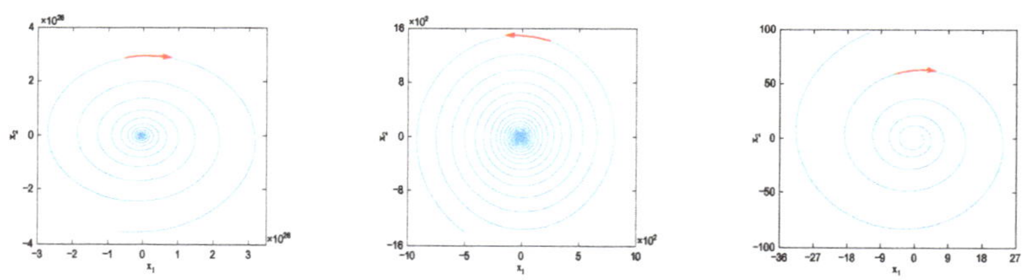

(**a**) The phase trajectory of the first subsystem (**b**) The phase trajectory of the second subsystem (**c**) The phase trajectory of the third subsystem

Figure 8. The phase trajectories of the three subsystems.

For a switched system (15) with three subsystems, there are six different switching sequences. Without loss of generality, the switching sequence is assumed to be $(i_1 \to i_2 \to i_3 \to i_4)$, where $i_4 = i_1$ and $i_s \in \{1,2,3\}, (s = 1,2,3)$ indicates that the i_sth subsystem is running.

If the phase trajectories of the i_sth subsystem and the i_{s+1}th subsystem rotate in the same direction, the switching rule (6) is adopted. Since the i_{s+1}th subsystem does not need to be switched back to the i_sth subsystem, the switching rule should be improved by adding the limited function $\sigma(t) = i_s$. As such, the switching rule is rewritten as

$$\sigma(t + \triangle t) = \begin{cases} i_s, & \sigma(t) = i_s \text{ and } \phi \cdot (x_2(t) - k_1 x_1(t)) \cdot (x_2(t) - k_2 x_1(t)) \geq 0, \\ i_{s+1}, & \sigma(t) = i_s \text{ and } \phi \cdot (x_2(t) - k_1 x_1(t)) \cdot (x_2(t) - k_2 x_1(t)) < 0. \end{cases}$$

Here, $x_2 = k_1 x_1$ and $x_2 = k_2 x_1$ make the energy ratio function $\frac{E_{i_s}}{E_{i_{s+1}}}$ take the maximum and minimum values, respectively. If the phase trajectories of the i_sth and the i_{s+1}th subsystems rotate in opposite directions, the switching rule (11) is used. Similarly, due to the unidirectional switching, the switching rule is formulated by

$$\sigma(t+\triangle t)=\begin{cases} i_s, & \sigma(t)=i_s \text{ and } (x_2(t)-k_1x_1(t))\cdot(x_2(t-\triangle t)-k_1x_1(t-\triangle t))>0, \\ i_{s+1}, & \sigma(t)=i_s \text{ and } (x_2(t)-k_1x_1(t))\cdot(x_2(t-\triangle t)-k_1x_1(t-\triangle t))\leq 0. \end{cases}$$

Here, $x_2=k_1x_1$ is the maximum point of the energy ratio function $\frac{E_{i_s}}{E_{i_{s+1}}}$.

Based on the above analysis, we only use switching sequences $(1\to3\to2\to1)$ and $(1\to2\to3\to1)$ as examples to illustrate the effect of switching sequences on system stability. As can be seen in Figure 9, the switched system (15) rapidly converges to the equilibrium point under the switching sequence $(1\to3\to2\to1)$. However, the switched system (15) diverges outward under the switching sequence $(1\to2\to3\to1)$, as depicted in Figure 10. From Figures 9 and 10, we can conclude that the switching sequence plays a crucial role in system stability. Moreover, constructing an appropriate switching sequence is both difficult and important for the switched system (1) with $N\geq3$.

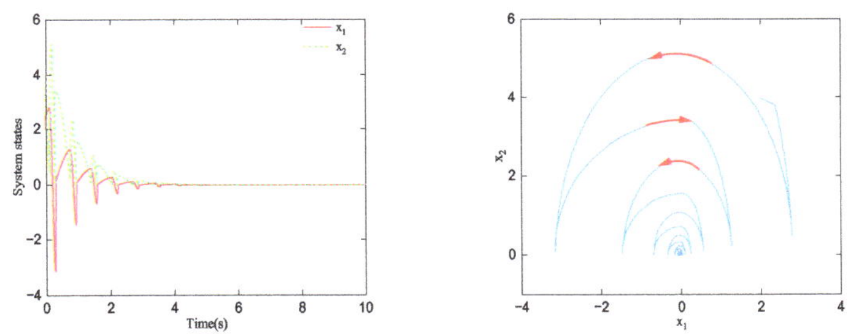

(**a**) The time histories of system states (**b**) The phase diagram of switched system (15)

Figure 9. The switched system (15) is asymptotically stable under the switching rule $(1\to3\to2\to1)$.

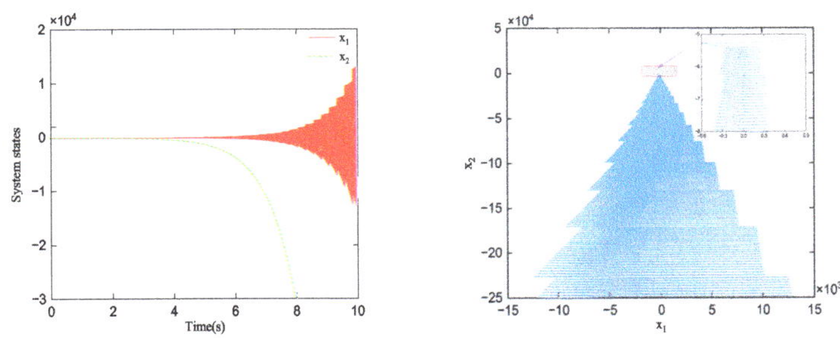

(**a**) The time histories of system states (**b**) The phase diagram of switched system (15)

Figure 10. The switched system (15) is not stable under the switching rule $(1\to2\to3\to1)$.

6. Conclusions

The asymptotic stability of a class of second-order switched linear systems, where the characteristic roots of each subsystem are a pair of complex conjugate roots with positive real parts, is investigated in this paper. For the switched systems with phase trajectories rotating in the same direction, a more appropriate state-dependent switching rule is formulated to guarantee system stability. In addition, a new switching rule is developed to stabilize the switched system in which the phase trajectories of two subsystems rotate in opposite directions.

Compared with previous findings, the proposed state-dependent switching rule has the advantages of fast convergence, simple computation and weak conservativeness. However, the limitation of the present method is that the considered switched system is overly simplistic. In view of this, we will try to extend the results to the case of higher-order subsystems in future, for which we need to find a matched mechanical model. Meanwhile, the proposed switching mechanism is expected in the case of multiple subsystems, in which the relationship between the switching sequence and subsystem characteristics warrant clarification. Both represent the focus of our future research work.

Author Contributions: The authors X.Y. and Y.Z. contributed equally to this work. All authors have read and agreed to the published version of the manuscript.

Funding: This work was supported by the National Natural Science Foundation under Grant (12162006), and the Cultivation Project of Guizhou University [2019] 63.

Institutional Review Board Statement: Not applicable.

Informed Consent Statement: Not applicable.

Data Availability Statement: Not applicable.

Acknowledgments: Not applicable.

Conflicts of Interest: The authors declare no conflict of interest.

References

1. Shi, Y.; Sun, X. Bumpless transfer control for switched linear systems and its application to aero-engines. *IEEE Trans. Circuits Syst. I Regul. Pap.* **2021**, *68*, 2171–2182. [CrossRef]
2. Wen, G.; Yu, X.; Yu, W.; Lu, J. Coordination and control of complex network systems with switching topologies: A survey. *IEEE Trans. Syst. Man Cybern. Syst.* **2021**, *51*, 6342–6357. [CrossRef]
3. Pang, H.; Liu, S. Robust exponential quasi-passivity and global stabilization for uncertain switched nonlinear systems. *Int. J. Robust Nonlinear Control* **2020**, *30*, 8117–8138. [CrossRef]
4. Tran, V.; Garratt, M.A.; Petersen, I.R. Switching formation strategy with the directed dynamic topology for collision avoidance of a multi-robot system in uncertain environments. *IET Control Theory Appl.* **2020**, *12*, 2948–2959. [CrossRef]
5. Han, S.; Zhong, Q.; Wang, Y.; Shi, K.; Zhong, S. Nonfragile consensus of nonlinear multiagent systems with intrinsic delays via aperiodic memory sampled-data control. *Int. J. Robust Nonlinear Control* **2022**, *32*, 5164–5183. [CrossRef]
6. Cai, X.; Shi, K.; She, K.; Zhong, S.; Soh, Y.; Yu, Y. Performance error estimation and elastic integral event triggering mechanism design for TS fuzzy networked control system under DoS attacks. *IEEE Trans. Fuzzy Syst.* **2022**, 1–12. [CrossRef]
7. Nouriani, A.; Moradi, H. Smooth switching in power control of wind turbines using a combination strategy of hysteresis and modified middle regions. *IET Control Theory Appl.* **2020**, *37*, 100585. [CrossRef]
8. Wu, X.; Tang, Y.; Cao, J.; Mao, X. Stability analysis for continuous-time switched systems with stochastic switching signals. *IEEE Trans. Automat. Contr.* **2018**, *63*, 3083–3090. [CrossRef]
9. Tian, L.; Guan, Y.; Wang, L. Controllability and observability of switched multi-agent systems. *Int. J. Control* **2019**, *92*, 1742–1752. [CrossRef]
10. Liu, Z.; Chen, B.; Lin, C. Adaptive neural quantized control for a class of switched nonlinear systems. *Inf. Sci.* **2020**, *537*, 313–333. [CrossRef]
11. Niu, B.; Wang, D.; Alotaibi, N.D.; Alsaadi, F.E. Adaptive neural state-feedback tracking control of stochastic nonlinear switched systems: An average dwell-time method. *IEEE Trans. Neural. Netw. Learn. Syst.* **2019**, *30*, 1076–1087. [CrossRef] [PubMed]
12. Niu, B.; Zhao, P.; Liu, J.D.; Ma, H.J.; Liu, Y.J. Global adaptive control of switched uncertain nonlinear systems: An improved MDADT method. *Automatica* **2020**, *116*, 108872. [CrossRef]
13. Su, Q.; Fan, Z.; Li, J. Finite-time fault detection filters design for switched systems with all subsystems unstable. *Int. J. Syst. Sci.* **2020**, *51*, 545–555. [CrossRef]
14. Cheng, L.; Xu, X.; Xue, Y.; Zhang, H. Stability analysis of switched systems with all subsystems unstable: A matrix polynomial approach. *ISA Trans.* **2021**, *114*, 99–105. [CrossRef]
15. Wu, Z.; Cui, M.; Shi, P.; Karimi, HR. Stability of stochastic nonlinear systems with state-dependent switching. *IEEE Trans. Automat. Contr.* **2013**, *58*, 1904–1918. [CrossRef]
16. Liu, Q.; Long, L. State-dependent switching law design with guaranteed dwell time for switched nonlinear systems. *Int. J. Robust Nonlinear Control* **2020**, *30*, 3314–3331. [CrossRef]
17. Guo, Z.; Ou, S.; Wang, J. Multistability of switched neural networks with sigmoidal activation functions under state-dependent switching. *Neural Netw.* **2020**, *122*, 239–252. [CrossRef] [PubMed]

18. Yang, D.; Li, X. Robust stability analysis of stochastic switched neural networks with parameter uncertainties via state-dependent switching law. *Neurocomputing* **2021**, *452*, 813–819. [CrossRef]
19. Pettersson, S. Synthesis of switched linear systems. In Proceedings of the 42nd IEEE International Conference on Decision and Control (IEEE Cat. No.03CH37475), Maui, HI, USA, 9–12 December 2003.
20. Chen, D.; Peng, Y. Energy analysis of a class of state-dependent switched systems with all unstable subsystems. *J. Frankl. Inst.* **2021**, *358*, 963–979. [CrossRef]
21. Lu, A.;Yang, G. Stabilization of switched systems with all modes unstable via periodical switching laws. *Automatica* **2020**, *122*, 109150. [CrossRef]

axioms

Article

Stability for a Class of Differential Set-Valued Inverse Variational Inequalities in Finite Dimensional Spaces

Xinyue Zhu [1], Wei Li [1,*] and Xueping Luo [2]

[1] Geomathematics Key Laboratory of Sichuan Province, College of Mathematics and Physics, Chengdu University of Technology, Chengdu 610059, China
[2] Department of Mathematics, Southwest Minzu University, Chengdu 610041, China
* Correspondence: lovelylw@126.com

Abstract: In this paper, we introduce and study a new class of differential set-valued inverse variational inequalities in finite dimensional spaces. By applying a result on differential inclusions involving an upper semicontinuous set-valued mapping with closed convex values, we first prove the existence of Carathéodory weak solutions for differential set-valued inverse variational inequalities. Then, by the existence result, we establish the stability for the differential set-valued inverse variational inequality problem when the constraint set and the mapping are perturbed by two different parameters. The closedness and continuity of Carathéodory weak solutions with respect to the two different parameters are obtained.

Keywords: differential set-valued inverse variational inequality; stability; Carathéodory weak solution

MSC: 49J40; 35B35; 49J53

Citation: Zhu, X.; Li, W.; Luo, X. Stability for a Class of Differential Set-Valued Inverse Variational Inequalities in Finite Dimensional Spaces. *Axioms* **2022**, *11*, 475. https://doi.org/10.3390/axioms11090475

Academic Editor: Simeon Reich

Received: 17 August 2022
Accepted: 13 September 2022
Published: 16 September 2022

1. Introduction

Let K be a nonempty closed convex set of R^n and $F : R^n \to 2^{R^n}$ be a set-valued mapping. A set-valued inverse variational inequality, denoted by SIVI(K, F), is to find $u \in R^n$ and $u^* \in F(u) \cap K$ such that

$$\langle y - u^*, u \rangle \geq 0, \quad \forall y \in K. \tag{1}$$

The solution to this problem is denoted by SOL(K, F). We write $\dot{x} := \frac{dx}{dt}$ for the time-derivative of function $x(t)$. In this paper, we study the following initial-value differential set-valued inverse variational inequality (denoted by DSIVI):

$$\begin{cases} \dot{x}(t) = f(t, x(t)) + B(t, x(t))u(t) \\ u(t) \in SOL(K, G(t, x(t)) + F(\cdot)) \\ x(0) = x_0, \end{cases} \tag{2}$$

where $\Omega := [0, T] \times R^m$, $(f, B, G) := \Omega \to R^m \times R^{m\times n} \times R^n$, $F := R^n \to 2^{R^n}$. Time-dependent functions $x(t)$ and $u(t)$ satisfy (2) in the weak sense of Carathéodory for $t \in [0, T]$ means that x is an absolutely continuous function on $[0, T]$, $x(t)$ satisfies the differential equation for almost all $t \in [0, T]$ and the initial-value condition. Moreover, u is an integrable function on $[0, T]$ and $u(t) \in SOL(K, G(t, x(t)) + F)$ for almost all $t \in [0, T]$.

Differential variational inequalities (DVIs) arise in some applied problems such as, for example, differential Nash games, operations research, physical sciences, and structural dynamics [1,2]. DVIs were first systematically studied in finite dimensional spaces by Pang and Stewart [1] in 2008 and gained much more attention to theoretical results, numerical algorithms, and applications. Stewart [3] investigated the uniqueness for a class of index-one DVIs in finite dimensional spaces. Li et al. [4,5] researched differential mixed variational inequalities and impulsive differential variational inequalities in finite dimensional spaces and obtained some existence results and numerical methods by using some results on differential inclusions and discrete Euler time-dependent procedures. Li et al. [6] proved the existence of the Carathéodory weak solutions for differential inverse variational inequalities in finite dimensional spaces and gave an application on the time-dependent price equilibrium problem. In [7], Liu et al. first explored partial differential variational inequalities in Banach spaces and proved the nonemptiness and compactness of the solution set. For more related work about DVIs, see [8–12].

The inverse variational inequality, like the variational inequality, has broad applications in optimization, engineering, economics, mechanics, and transportation [13–20]. Very recently, Luo [21] studied the stability for the set-valued inverse variational inequality (1) on Banach spaces. If F is single-valued, the set-valued inverse variational inequality (1) can be reduced to the singe-valued inverse variational inequality in [13]. Furthermore, if F is single-valued and inverse, the set-valued inverse variational inequality (1) can be transformed into the classical variational inequality. However, the above transforms both failed if F is set-valued.

The stability analysis of a DVI with perturbed data is very helpful in identifying sensitive parameters, predicting the coming changes of the equilibria as a result of the changes in the governing system, and providing helpful information for designing different equilibrium systems. Gwinner [22] researched stability of the solution set for a DVI and obtained a novel upper set convergence result with respect to perturbations in the data. When the mapping and the constraint set are perturbed by different parameters, Wang et al. [23] studied the stability for a class differential mixed variational inequality in finite dimensional spaces. To the best of our knowledge, there are some results about the existence of solutions for differential variational and inverse variational inequalities in finite dimensional spaces. However, there are very few results about the existence of solutions for differential set-valued inverse variational inequalities and the stability for differential single-valued or set-valued inverse variational inequalities in finite dimensional spaces. Motivated by the aforementioned work, in this paper we are devoted to stability analysis for the DSIVI (2) in finite dimensional spaces.

The goal of this paper is to study the existence of the Carathéodory weak solutions and the stability for DSIVI (2) in finite dimensional spaces with the constraint set K and the set-valued mapping F being perturbed by two different parameters. Our results about the existence of the Carathéodory weak solutions for DSIVI (2) generalize the corresponding results in [6]. Our stability results about the differential set-valued inverse variational inequality are very new. We also give an example of a time-dependent price equilibrium control problem influenced by the seasons to show that the realistic problem can be transformed into the stability for the differential inverse variational inequality.

The paper is organized as follows. Section 2 contains some useful definitions and lemmas. In Section 3, the existence and uniqueness results of Carathéodory solutions for DSIVI (2) are considered. Furthermore, the closedness and continuity of Carathéodory solution set with respect to the perturbed data in the constraint set K and the set-valued mapping F are obtained.

2. Preliminaries

In this section, we will introduce some basic notations and preliminary results.

Definition 1 ([24])**.** *Let X and Y be two metric spaces; Y^* is the dual space of Y. We say a set-valued mapping $F : X \to 2^Y$ is*

(i) Upper semicontinuous at $x \in X$ if and only if for any neighborhood U of $F(x)$, there exists the neighborhood $B(x, \eta)$ of x with $\eta > 0$ such that

$$\forall x' \in B(x,\eta), \quad F(x') \subset U;$$

(ii) *Lower semicontinuous at $x \in X$ if and only if for any $y \in F(x)$ and for any sequence of elements $x_n \in X$ converging to x, there exists a sequence of elements $y_n \in F(x_n)$ converging to y;*

(iii) *Upper hemicontinuous at $x \in X$ if and only if for any $r \in Y^*$, the function $x \mapsto \sup_{y \in F(x)} \langle r, y \rangle$ is upper semicontinuous at x.*

Definition 2 ([23,25]). *The set-valued mapping $F : R^n \to 2^{R^n}$ is said to be*

(i) *Strictly monotone on set $L \subset R^n$ iff for any $x, y \in L$, $x \neq y$, $x^* \in F(x)$, $y^* \in F(y)$, we have*

$$\langle x^* - y^*, x - y \rangle > 0;$$

(ii) *Strongly monotone with modulus $\mu > 0$, if for any $x, y \in R^n$ and $x^* \in F(x)$, $y^* \in F(y)$, we have*

$$\langle x^* - y^*, x - y \rangle \geq \mu \|x - y\|^2.$$

Definition 3. *A mapping $f : \Omega \to R^m$ (respectively, $B : \Omega \to R^{m \times n}$) is said to be Lipschitz continuous if there exists a constant $L_f > 0$ (respectively, $L_B > 0$) such that, for any $(t_1, x), (t_2, y) \in \Omega$, we have*

$$\|f(t_1, x) - f(t_2, y)\| \leq L_f(|t_1 - t_2| + \|x - y\|),$$

$$(respectively, \|B(t_1, x) - B(t_2, y)\| \leq L_B(|t_1 - t_2| + \|x - y\|)).$$

Lemma 1 ([26], Lemma 1). *Let X and Y be metric spaces. If a set-valued mapping $F : X \to P_f(Y) := \{D \subset Y : D \text{ is nonempty, closed}\}$ is upper semicontinuous, then F is closed.*

Lemma 2 ([27], Theorem 5.1). *Let $\mathbb{F} : \Omega \to 2^{R^m}$ be an upper semicontinuous set-valued mapping with nonempty closed convex values. Suppose that there exists a scalar $\rho^{\mathbb{F}} > 0$ satisfying*

$$\sup\{\|y\| : y \in \mathbb{F}(t, x)\} \leq \rho^{\mathbb{F}}(1 + \|x\|), \quad \forall (t, x) \in \Omega. \tag{3}$$

Then for every $x_0 \in R^m$, the DI:

$$\dot{x} \in \mathbb{F}(t, x), \quad x(0) = x_0$$

has a weak solution in the sense of Carathéodory.

Lemma 3 ([1], Lemma 6.3). *Let $h : \Omega \times R^n \to R^m$ be a continuous function and $U : \Omega \to 2^{R^n}$ be a closed set-valued map such that for some constant $\eta_U > 0$,*

$$\sup_{u \in U(t,x)} \|u\| \leq \eta_U(1 + \|x\|), \quad \forall (t, x) \in \Omega.$$

Let $v : [0, T] \to R^m$ be a measurable function and $x : [0, T] \to R^m$ be a continuous function satisfying $v(t) \in h(t, x(t), U(t, x(t)))$ for almost all $t \in [0, T]$. There exists a measurable function $u : [0, T] \to R^n$ such that $u(t) \in U(t, x(t))$ and $v(t) = h(t, x(t), U(t))$ for almost all $t \in [0, T]$.

Throughout the rest of this paper, let $K \subset R^n$ be a nonempty, closed, and convex subset. The symbols " $\rightharpoonup$" and " $\to$" are used to denote the weak convergence and strong convergence. Let the barrier cone of K be denoted by

$$barr(K) := \{y \in R^n : \sup_{x \in K} \langle y, x \rangle < \infty\}.$$

The recession cone of K, denoted by K_∞, is defined by

$$K_\infty := \{d \in R^n : \exists t_n \to 0, \exists x_n \in K, t_n x_n \rightharpoonup d\}.$$

The negative polar cone of the nonempty set $D \subset R^n$, denoted by D^-, is defined by

$$D^- := \{y \in R^n : \langle y, x\rangle \le 0, \forall x \in D\}.$$

Lemma 4 ([21], Theorem 4.2). *Let $L : Z_1 \to 2^{R^n}$ be a continuous set-valued mapping; $p_0 \in Z_1$, $\lambda_0 \in Z_2$ are given points; $F : R^n \times Z_2 \to 2^{R^n}$ is a set-valued mapping and lower semicontinuous on Z_2. Suppose that there exists a neighborhood of $P \times \Lambda$ of (p_0, λ_0), such that $L(p)$ has nonempty, closed, and convex values for any $p \in P$, and $F(x, \lambda)$ has nonempty closed values for every $x \in R^n$ and $\lambda \in \Lambda$. Moreover, for each $\lambda \in \Lambda$ and $q \in G(\Omega)$, the mapping $x \mapsto q + F(x, \lambda)$ is upper hemicontinuous and monotone. If*

$$(L(p_0))_\infty \cap \{x \in R^n : q + F(x, \lambda_0) \cap L(p_0) \neq \emptyset\}^- = \{0\},$$

then there exists a neighborhood $P' \times \Lambda'$ of (p_0, λ_0) with $P' \times \Lambda' \subset P \times \Lambda$, such that for every $(p, \lambda) \in P' \times \Lambda'$, the set $SOL(L(p), q + F(\cdot, \lambda))$ is nonempty and bounded.

In the rest of this paper, we assume (A) and (B) hold.

(A) f, B and G are Lipschitz continuous functions on Ω with Lipschitz constants $L_f > 0$, $L_B > 0$ and $L_G > 0$, respectively;

(B) B is bounded on Ω with $\text{ffi}_B := \sup_{(t,x)\in\Omega} \| B(t, x) \|$.

Remark 1. *If $f : \Omega \to R^m$ is a Lipschitz continuous function on Ω, we obtain that there exists a constant $\rho_f > 0$, for any $(t, x) \in \Omega$, such that*

$$\begin{aligned} \|f(t,x)\| &= \|f(t,x) - f(t_0,0) + f(t_0,0)\| \\ &\le \|f(t,x) - f(t_0,0)\| + \|f(t_0,0)\| \\ &\le L_f(|t - t_0| + \|x\|) + \|f(t_0,0)\| \\ &\le L_f(2T + \|x\|) + \|f(t_0,0)\| \\ &\le \rho_f(1 + \|x\|), \end{aligned}$$

where $t_0 \in [0, T], \rho_f = max\{L_f, 2L_f T + \|f(t_0, 0)\|\}$. Similarly, $G : \Omega \to R^n$ is a Lipschitz continuous function on Ω, so there exists a constant $\rho_G > 0$ such that $\|G(t, x)\| \le \rho_G(1 + \|x\|)$ for any $(t, x) \in \Omega$.

3. Existence and Uniqueness of Solutions for DSIVI (2)

In this section, we will show the existence and uniqueness of Carathéodory weak solutions for DSIVI (2) by applying Lemmas 2 and 3. For this purpose, we define a set-valued mapping $\mathbb{F} : \Omega \to 2^{R^n}$ as follows:

$$\mathbb{F}(t, x) := \{f(t, x) + B(t, x)u : u \in SOL(K, G(t, x) + F(\cdot))\}. \quad (4)$$

The following lemma presents some properties of the set-valued mapping $\mathbb{F}$ defined by (4) under the hypotheses (A) and (B).

In the following, $L^2([0, T]; R^n)$ is the set of all measurable functions $u : [0, T] \to R^n$, that satisfies $\int_0^T \|u(t)\|^2 dt < +\infty$. The norm of $\|u\|$ is defined by

$$\|u\| := (\int_0^T \|u(t)\|^2 dt)^{\frac{1}{2}}.$$

Lemma 5. *Let (f, G, B) satisfy conditions (A) and (B). Let $K \subset R^n$ be a nonempty, bounded, closed, and convex set and $F : R^n \to 2^{R^n}$ be an upper semicontinuous set-valued mapping with nonempty closed convex values. Suppose that there exists a constant $\rho > 0$ such that, for all $q \in G(\Omega)$,*

$$\sup\{\|u\| : u \in SOL(K, q + F(\cdot))\} \leq \rho(1 + \|q\|). \tag{5}$$

Then, there exists a constant $\rho^{\mathbb{F}} > 0$ such that (3) holds for the mapping $\mathbb{F}$. Hence, $\mathbb{F}$ is an upper semicontinuous closed-valued mapping on Ω.

Proof. We first prove that there is a constant $\rho^{\mathbb{F}} > 0$ such that (3) holds for the mapping $\mathbb{F}$. For any $y \in \mathbb{F}(t, x)$, from the definition of $\mathbb{F}$, we know there exists $u \in SOL(K, G(t, x) + F(\cdot))$ such that $y = f(t, x) + B(t, x)u$. From conditions (A) and (B), it is easy to see that there exists positive constants ρ_f and ρ_G such that

$$\|f(t, x)\| \leq \rho_f(1 + \|x\|), \tag{6}$$

and

$$\|G(t, x)\| \leq \rho_G(1 + \|x\|). \tag{7}$$

Applying (5), we obtain

$$\|y\| \leq \|f(t, x)\| + \|B(t, x)u\| \leq (\rho_f + \delta_B\rho + \delta_B\rho\rho_G)(1 + \|x\|).$$

If we let $\rho^{\mathbb{F}} = \rho_f + \delta_B\rho + \delta_B\rho\rho_G$, then (3) holds.

Next, we prove that $\mathbb{F}$ is upper semicontinuous. We note that under the linear growth condition (3), the upper semicontinuity of F holds if $\mathbb{F}$ is closed. Therefore, we need to prove $\mathbb{F}$ is closed on Ω. Let $\{(t_n, x_n)\} \subset \Omega$ be a sequence converging to some vector $(t_0, x_0) \in \Omega$ and $\{f(t_n, x_n) + B(t_n, x_n)u_n\} \subset \mathbb{F}(t_n, x_n)$ converging to z_0, where $u_n \in SOL(K, G(t_n, x_n) + F(\cdot))$. It follows that sequence $\{u_n\}$ is bounded by (5). Therefore, $\{u_n\}$ has a convergent subsequence, denoted again by $\{u_n\}$, with a limit point $u_0 \in R^n$. According to $u_n \in SOL(K, G(t_n, x_n) + F(\cdot))$, it is easy to see that there exists $u_n^* \in F(u_n)$ and $G(t_n, x_n) + u_n^* \in K$ such that

$$\langle y - G(t_n, x_n) - u_n^*, u_n \rangle \geq 0, \quad \forall y \in K.$$

By the boundedness of K, we get $\{u_n^*\}$ is bounded and has a convergent subsequence with a limit u_0^*, as the set-valued mapping F is upper semicontinuous with nonempty closed convex values. By Lemma 1, we obtain that F is closed, which means $Graph(F) := \{(x, y) \in R^n \times R^n : y \in F(x)\}$ is closed. We know $(u_n, u_n^*) \in Graph(F)$ since $u_n^* \in F(u_n)$. Therefore, $u_0^* \in F(u_0)$. Since G is Lipschitz continuous, it follows $\{G(t_n, x_n)\}$ converges to $G(t_0, x_0)$. Since K is closed, it follows that $G(t_0, x_0) + u_0^* \in (G(t_0, x_0) + F(u_0)) \cap K$ and

$$\langle y - G(t_0, x_0) - u_0^*, u_0 \rangle \geq 0, \quad \forall y \in K.$$

That means $u_0 \in SOL(K, G(t_0, x_0) + F(\cdot))$ and so

$$f(t_n, x_n) + B(t_n, x_n)u_n \to z_0 = f(t_0, x_0) + B(t_0, x_0)u_0 \in \mathbb{F}(t_0, x_0).$$

Therefore, $\mathbb{F}$ is closed. This completes the proof. □

Remark 2. *We would like to point out that Lemma 5 extends Lemma 2.5 in [6].*

Theorem 1. *Let (f, G, B) satisfy conditions (A) and (B). Let $K \subset R^n$ be a nonempty, bounded, closed, and convex set and $F : R^n \to 2^{R^n}$ be an upper semicontinuous set-valued mapping with nonempty closed convex values. Suppose for any $q \in G(\Omega)$, there exists a constant $\rho > 0$ such* *that* (5) *holds and the set* $SOL(K, q + F(\cdot))$ *is nonempty, closed, and convex. Then, DSIVI* (2) *has a Carathéodory weak solution.*

Proof. By Lemma 5, we obtain that there exists a constant $\rho^{\mathbb{F}} > 0$ such that (3) holds for the mapping $\mathbb{F}$ defined by (4) and $\mathbb{F}$ is an upper semicontinuous closed-valued mapping on Ω. Next, for any $(t, x) \in \Omega$, we prove $\mathbb{F}(t, x)$ is convex. Since for any $q \in G(\Omega)$, $SOL(K, q + F(\cdot))$ is nonempty, it is easy to see that $\mathbb{F}(t, x)$ is nonempty. However, for any $f(t, x) + B(t, x)u_1, f(t, x) + B(t, x)u_2 \in \mathbb{F}(t, x)$, where $u_1, u_2 \in SOL(K, G(t, x) + F(\cdot))$, by the convex of $SOL(K, G(t, x) + F(\cdot))$, we know that there exists a constant $\eta \in (0, 1)$ such that

$$\begin{aligned} &\eta(f(t,x) + B(t,x)u_1) + (1-\eta)(f(t,x) + B(t,x)u_2) \\ = \; & f(t,x) + B(t,x)(\eta u_1 + (1-\eta)u_2) \in \mathbb{F}(t,x), \end{aligned}$$

where $\eta u_1 + (1-\eta)u_2 \in SOL(K, G(t, x) + F(\cdot))$. This means $\mathbb{F}(t, x)$ is convex.

Because $\mathbb{F}$ is an upper semicontinuous set-valued mapping with nonempty closed convex values and there exists a constant $\rho^{\mathbb{F}} > 0$ such that (3) holds for the mapping $\mathbb{F}$, by Lemma 2, we obtain that the following differential inclusion $\dot{x} \in \mathbb{F}(t, x), x(0) = x_0$ has a Carathéodory weak solution $x(t)$. Thus, we have for any $t \in [0, T]$,

$$\int_0^t \dot{x}(s)ds = \int_0^t [f(s, x(s)) + B(s, x(s))u(s)]ds,$$

and

$$\|x(t)\| \le \|x_0\| + \int_0^t \rho^{\mathbb{F}}(1 + \|x(s)\|)ds.$$

Then, by the Gronwall inequality, we obtain

$$\|x(t)\| \le (\|x_0\| + \rho^{\mathbb{F}}T)e^{\rho^{\mathbb{F}}T}. \tag{8}$$

Therefore, from the above two inequalities we can obtain that $x(t)$ is absolutely continuous on $[0, T]$. Let $U(t, x) := SOL(K, G(t, x) + F(\cdot))$ and $h(t, x, u) := f(t, x) + B(t, x)u$. We conclude by Lemma 3 that there exists a measurable function $u(t)$ such that $u(t) \in SOL(K, G(t, x(t)) + F(\cdot))$ and $\dot{x}(t) = f(t, x) + B(t, x)u(t)$ for almost all t. By Lemma 6, it follows that for almost all $t \in [0, T]$, there exists $\rho > 0$ such that

$$\|u(t)\| \le \rho(1 + \|G(t, x(t))\|),$$

where $u(t) \in SOL(K, G(t, x(t)) + F(\cdot))$. From (6) and (8), it follows from the above inequality that for almost all $t \in [0, T]$,

$$\|u(t)\| \le \rho(1 + \rho_G(1 + (\|x_0\| + \rho^{\mathbb{F}}T)e^{\rho^{\mathbb{F}}T})).$$

Therefore, $u(t)$ is integrable on $[0, T]$. This completes the proof. □

Lemma 6. *Let* (f, G, B) *satisfy conditions* (A) *and* (B). *Let* $K \subset R^n$ *be a nonempty, bounded, closed, and convex set. Suppose the following statements hold:*

(i) $F : R^n \to 2^{R^n}$ *is strictly monotone and upper hemicontinuous on* R^n;

(ii) For any $q \in G(\Omega)$, $K_\infty \cap \{x \in R^n : q + F(x) \cap K \neq \emptyset\}^- = \{0\}$;

(iii) The interior of $barr(K)$ *is nonempty.*

Then, $SOL(K, q + F(\cdot))$ *is a singleton for any* $q \in G(\Omega)$. *Moreover, there exists a constant* $\rho > 0$ *such that* (5) *holds for any* $q \in G(\Omega)$.

Proof. Using conditions (i)–(iii) and according to Theorem 3.2 in [21], we can obtain that $SOL(K, q + F(\cdot)) \neq \emptyset$ for any $q \in G(\Omega)$. Next, we show $SOL(K, q + F(\cdot))$ is a singleton for any $q \in G(\Omega)$. We assume $u_1, u_2 \in SOL(K, q + F(\cdot))$ and $u_1 \neq u_2$, and we have

$$q + u_1^* \in (q + F(u_1)) \cap K, \quad \langle y - q - u_1^*, u_1 \rangle \geq 0, \quad \forall y \in K, \tag{9}$$

and

$$q + u_2^* \in (q + F(u_2)) \cap K, \quad \langle y - q - u_2^*, u_2 \rangle \geq 0, \quad \forall y \in K. \tag{10}$$

Letting $y = q + u_2^*$ in (9), we have

$$\langle u_2^* - u_1^*, u_1 \rangle \geq 0.$$

Letting $y = q + u_1^*$ in (10), we have

$$\langle u_1^* - u_2^*, u_2 \rangle \geq 0.$$

It follows from the above two inequalities that

$$\langle u_2^* - u_1^*, u_1 - u_2 \rangle \geq 0. \tag{11}$$

Since F is strictly monotone, $u_1 \neq u_2$, $u_1^* \in F(u_1)$, $u_2^* \in F(u_2)$, we obtain

$$\langle u_2^* - u_1^*, u_2 - u_1 \rangle > 0,$$

which contradicts (11). That means $SOL(K, q + F(\cdot))$ is a singleton for any $q \in G(\Omega)$ and so there exists a constant $\rho > 0$ such that (5) holds for any $q \in G(\Omega)$. This completes the proof. □

Theorem 2. *Let $K \subset R^n$ be a nonempty, bounded, closed, and convex set. Let (f, G, B) satisfy conditions* (A) *and* (B). *Suppose the following statements hold:*

(i) $F : R^n \to 2^{R^n}$ *is strictly monotone and upper hemicontinuous on* R^n;
(ii) $F : R^n \to 2^{R^n}$ *is an upper semicontinuous set-valued map with nonempty closed convex values;*
(iii) For any $q \in G(\Omega)$, $K_\infty \cap \{x \in R^n : q + F(x) \cap K \neq \emptyset\}^- = \{0\}$;
(iv) The interior of $barr(K)$ *is nonempty.*

Then, DSIVI (2) *has a Carathéodory weak solution.*

Proof. It follows from conditions (i), (iii), (iv), and Lemma 6 that (5) holds. By condition (ii) and Lemma 5, we know there exists a constant $\rho^{\mathbb{F}} > 0$ such that (3) holds, where $\mathbb{F}$ is defined by (4). Applying Theorem 1, we get DSIVI (2) has a Carathéodory weak solution. This completes the proof. □

Remark 3. *From the above proof, it is easy to see that* $u \in L^2([0, T]; R^n)$.

Theorem 3. *Assume conditions (ii)–(iv) in Theorem 2 hold and* $F : R^n \to 2^{R^n}$ *is strongly monotone and upper hemicontinuous on* R^n. *Then, DSIVI (2) has a unique Carathéodory weak solution* $(x, u) \in C([0, T]; R^m) \times L^2([0, T]; R^n)$.

Proof. By Theorem 2, we know DSIVI (2) has Carathéodory weak solutions. Now, we only need to prove the uniqueness of the Carathéodory weak solution for DSIVI (2). For this purpose, we let (x_1, u_1) and (x_2, u_2) be the Carathéodory weak solutions for DSIVI (2). Therefore,

$$\begin{cases} x_1(t) = x_0 + \int_0^t f(\tau, x_1(\tau)) + B(\tau, x_1(\tau))u_1(\tau)d\tau, & \text{for any } t \in [0,T] \\ u_1(t) \in SOL(K, G(t, x_1(t)) + F(\cdot)), & \text{for almost all } t \in [0,T] \\ x_1(0) = x_0, \end{cases} \tag{12}$$

and

$$\begin{cases} x_2(t) = x_0 + \int_0^t f(\tau, x_2(\tau)) + B(\tau, x_2(\tau))u_2(\tau)d\tau, & \text{for any } t \in [0,T] \\ u_2(t) \in SOL(K, G(t, x_2(t)) + F(\cdot)), & \text{for almost all } t \in [0,T] \\ x_2(0) = x_0. \end{cases} \tag{13}$$

For almost all $t \in [0,T]$, it is easy to see $u_1(t) \in SOL(K, G(t, x_1(t)) + F(\cdot))$ and $u_2(t) \in SOL(K, G(t, x_2(t)) + F(\cdot))$. Therefore, there exists a measurable E on $[0,T]$ with $mE = 0$ (mE denotes the Lebesgue measure of the set E on $[0,T]$) such that for any $t \in [0,T] \setminus E$, there exists $u_1^*(t) \in F(u_1(t))$ and $G(t, x_1(t)) + u_1^*(t) \in K$ such that

$$\langle y - G(t, x_1(t)) - u_1^*(t), u_1(t) \rangle \geq 0, \quad \forall y \in K \tag{14}$$

and there exists $u_2^*(t) \in F(u_2(t))$ and $G(t, x_2(t)) + u_2^*(t) \in K$ such that

$$\langle y - G(t, x_2(t)) - u_2^*(t), u_2(t) \rangle \geq 0, \quad \forall y \in K. \tag{15}$$

For $t \in [0,T] \setminus E$, letting $y = G(t, x_2(t)) + u_2^*(t)$ in (14), we get

$$\langle G(t, x_2(t)) + u_2^*(t) - G(t, x_1(t)) - u_1^*(t), u_1(t) \rangle \geq 0.$$

For $t \in [0,T] \setminus E$, letting $y = G(t, x_1(t)) + u_1^*(t)$ in (15), we get

$$\langle G(t, x_1(t)) + u_1^*(t) - G(t, x_2(t)) - u_2^*(t), u_2(t) \rangle \geq 0.$$

Therefore, for $t \in [0,T] \setminus E$, one has

$$\langle G(t, x_1(t)) + u_1^*(t) - G(t, x_2(t)) - u_2^*(t), u_2(t) - u_1(t) \rangle \geq 0,$$

and

$$\langle G(t, x_1(t)) - G(t, x_2(t)), u_2(t) - u_1(t) \rangle \geq \langle u_1^*(t) - u_2^*(t), u_1(t) - u_2(t) \rangle.$$

Since F is strongly monotone on R^n, it yields for almost all $t \in [0,T]$,

$$\langle u_1^*(t) - u_2^*(t), u_1(t) - u_2(t) \rangle \geq \mu \|u_1(t) - u_2(t)\|^2. \tag{16}$$

From the Cauchy–Schwarz inequality, we know that

$$\begin{aligned} & \langle G(t, x_1(t)) - G(t, x_2(t)), u_2(t) - u_1(t) \rangle \\ \leq \; & \|G(t, x_1(t)) - G(t, x_2(t))\| \|u_1(t) - u_2(t)\|. \end{aligned} \tag{17}$$

Therefore, combining (16) and (17), we get for almost all $t \in [0,T]$,

$$\begin{aligned} \mu \|u_1(t) - u_2(t)\| & \leq \|G(t, x_1(t)) - G(t, x_2(t))\| \\ & \leq L_G \|x_1(t) - x_2(t)\| \end{aligned} \tag{18}$$

and

$$\|u_1(t) - u_2(t)\| \leq \frac{L_G}{\mu} \|x_1(t) - x_2(t)\|. \tag{19}$$

Furthermore, from (12), (13), and (18), we infer that for any $t \in [0, T]$,

$$\begin{aligned} & \|x_1(t) - x_2(t)\| \\ = & \int_0^t \|f(\tau, x_1(\tau)) + B(\tau, x_1(\tau))u_1(\tau) - f(\tau, x_2(\tau)) + B(\tau, x_2(\tau))u_2(\tau)\|d\tau \\ \leq & \int_0^t \|f(\tau, x_1(\tau)) - f(\tau, x_2(\tau))\|d\tau + \delta_B \int_0^t \|u_1(\tau) - u_2(\tau)\|d\tau \\ \leq & L_f \int_0^t \|x_1(\tau) - x_2(\tau)\|d\tau + \delta_B \frac{L_G}{\mu} \int_0^t \|x_1(\tau) - x_2(\tau)\|d\tau \\ \leq & (L_f + \delta_B \frac{L_G}{\mu}) \int_0^t \|x_1(\tau) - x_2(\tau)\|d\tau. \end{aligned}$$

Apparently, there exists a constant $C = L_f + \delta_B \frac{L_G}{\mu} > 0$ such that

$$\|x_1(t) - x_2(t)\| \leq C \int_0^t \|x_1(\tau) - x_2(\tau)\|d\tau.$$

According to the Gronwall inequality, we get $x_1(t) = x_2(t)$ for all $t \in [0, T]$, so $x_1 = x_2$ in $C([0, T], R^m)$. From (18), we have $u_1(t) = u_2(t)$ in R^n for almost all $t \in [0, T]$. This means $u_1 = u_2$ in $L^2([0, T], R^n)$. This completes the proof. □

4. Stability for DSIVI (2)

In this section, we aim to study the stability for DSIVI (2) in finite dimensional spaces when both the mapping and the constraint set are perturbed by two different parameters. For this purpose, we consider the parametric DSIVI, denoted by DSIVI ($L(p)$, $G(t, x(t)) + F(\cdot, \lambda)$), as follows:

$$\begin{cases} \dot{x}(t) = f(t, x(t)) + B(t, x(t))u(t) \\ u(t) \in SOL(L(p), G(t, x(t)) + F(\cdot, \lambda)) \\ x(0) = x_0, \end{cases} \tag{20}$$

where (Z_1, d_1) and (Z_2, d_2) are two metric spaces. The nonempty closed convex subset K of R^n in DSIVI (2) is perturbed by a parameter p, which varies over (Z_1, d_1). Therefore, K is a perturbed set. That means $L : Z_1 \to 2^{R^n}$ is a set-valued mapping with nonempty closed convex values. The mapping $F : R^n \to 2^{R^n}$ is a set-valued mapping that is perturbed by a parameter λ, and λ varies over (Z_2, d_2). That is to say, $F : R^n \times Z_2 \to 2^{R^n}$. In what follows, to simplify notation, we let $S(p, \lambda)$ denote the Carathéodory weak solution for DSIVI (20). Next, we will establish the closedness and continuity of the mapping $(p, \lambda) \to S(p, \lambda)$.

Theorem 4. *Let (f, G, B) satisfy conditions (A) and (B), $p_0 \in Z_1$, $\lambda_0 \in Z_2$ be two given points. Assume the following conditions hold.*

(i) $L : Z_1 \to 2^{R^n}$ is a continuous set-valued mapping with nonempty bounded closed convex values and $\bigcup_{p \in U(p_0)} L(p)$ is compact, where $U(p_0)$ is a neighborhood of p_0;

(ii) $F : R^n \times Z_2 \to 2^{R^n}$ is an upper semicontinuous set-valued mapping with nonempty closed convex values on $R^n \times Z_2$ and lower semicontinuous on Z_2;

(iii) There exists a neighborhood Λ of λ_0, for each $\lambda \in \Lambda$, the mapping $x \mapsto q + F(x, \lambda)$ is upper hemicontinuous and monotone for any $q \in G(\Omega)$;

(iv) The set $SOL(L(p_0), q + F(\cdot, \lambda_0))$ is nonempty and bounded for any $q \in G(\Omega)$;

(v) $F : R^n \times Z_2 \to 2^{R^n}$ is strictly monotone and upper hemicontinuous on R^n.

Then, $S(p, \lambda)$ is closed at $(p_0, \lambda_0) \in Z_1 \times Z_2$.

Proof. From Theorem 3.2 in [21], we know that condition (iv) is equivalent to conditions (iii) and (iv) in Theorem 2. By conditions (i)–(iv), it follows from Lemma 4 that there exists a neighborhood $P' \times \Lambda'$ of (p_0, λ_0), $P' \times \Lambda' \subset P \times \Lambda$, such that for each $(p, \lambda) \in P' \times \Lambda'$, the set $SOL(L(p), q + F(\cdot, \lambda))$ is nonempty and bounded. It follows from Lemma 6 that there exists a constant $\rho > 0$ such that (5) holds for any $q \in G(\Omega)$. It is obvious that DSIVI (20) has solutions by Theorem 2.

Now, we prove $S(p, \lambda)$ is closed at (p_0, λ_0). Let $\{(p_n, \lambda_n)\} \subset P \times \Lambda$ be a given sequence with $(p_n, \lambda_n) \to (p_0, \lambda_0)$ and $(x_n, u_n) \in S(p_n, \lambda_n)$ with $(x_n, u_n) \to (x_0, u_0)$ in $C([0, T]; R^m) \times L^2([0, T], R^n)$. Therefore,

(a) For any $0 \le s \le t \le T$,

$$x_n(t) - x_n(s) = \int_s^t f(\tau, x_n(\tau)) + B(\tau, x_n(\tau))u_n(\tau)d\tau;$$

(b) For almost all $t \in [0, T]$, there exists $u_n^*(t) \in F(u_n(t), \lambda_n)$ and $G(t, x_n(t)) + u_n^*(t) \in L(p_n)$, for any $y_n \in L(p_n)$, such that

$$\langle y_n - G(t, x_n(t)) - u_n^*(t), u_n(t) \rangle \ge 0;$$

(c) The initial condition

$$x_n(0) = x_0.$$

From the convergence u_n converges to u_0 in $L^2([0, T], R^n)$, we obtain

$$\int_{[0,T]} \|u_n(t) - u_0(t)\|^2 dt < \infty$$

and

$$\begin{aligned} \lim_{n\to\infty} \|u_n - u_0\|_{L^2} &= \lim_{n\to\infty} (\int_{[0,T]} \|u_n(t) - u_0(t)\|^2 dt)^{\frac{1}{2}} \\ &= 0. \end{aligned}$$

Moreover, applying the Holder inequality, we know

$$\int_{[0,T]} \|u_n(t) - u_0(t)\| dt \le (\int_{[0,T]} \|u_n(t) - u_0(t)\|^2 dt)^{\frac{1}{2}} (\int_{[0,T]} 1^2 dt)^{\frac{1}{2}}$$

and

$$\lim_{n\to\infty} \int_{[0,T]} \|u_n(t) - u_0(t)\| dt \le \lim_{n\to\infty} (\int_{[0,T]} \|u_n(t) - u_0(t)\|^2 dt)^{\frac{1}{2}} = 0.$$

This means u_n converges to u_0 in $L^1([0, T], R^n)$, which is equivalent to $\|u_n - u_0\|_{L^1} \to 0$. By Theorem 4.9 in [28], there exists a sequence $u_n(t)$ and a function $h \in L^1$ such that

$$u_n(t) \to u_0(t), \text{ for almost all } t \in [0, T] \tag{21}$$

and

$$\|u_n(t)\| \le h(t), \text{ for almost all } t \in [0, T]. \tag{22}$$

Combining (21) and (22), by the Lebesgue control convergence theorem, we know

$$\lim_{n\to\infty} \int_{[0,T]} u_n(t) dt = \int_{[0,T]} u_0(t) dt.$$

However, from (b), it is easy to see that $G(t, x_n(t)) + u_n^*(t) \in L(p_n)$ for almost all $t \in [0, T]$. By condition (i), there exists a neighborhood $U(p_0)$ of p_0 such that $\bigcup_{p \in U(p_0)} L(p)$

is compact. Therefore, $\{u_n^*(t)\}$ has a subsequence, denoted again by $\{u_n^*(t)\}$, such that $u_n^*(t) \to u_0^*(t)$. Since $(u_n, \lambda_n) \to (u_0, \lambda_0)$, it follows from Lemma 1 and condition (ii) that $u_0^*(t) \in F(u_0(t), \lambda_0)$. Moreover, the lower semicontinuity of L implies that, for any $y \in L(p_0)$, there exists a sequence $\{y_n\}$ with $y_n \in L(p_n)$ such that $y_n \to y$.

Now, by (a), (b), and (c), we have

(a') For any $0 \le s \le t \le T$,

$$x_0(t) - x_0(s) = \int_s^t f(\tau, x_0(\tau)) + B(\tau, x_0(\tau))u_0(\tau)d\tau;$$

(b') For almost all $t \in [0, T]$, there exists $u_0^*(t) \in F(u_0(t), \lambda_0)$ and $G(t, x_0(t)) + u_0^*(t) \in L(p_0)$, for any $y \in L(p_0)$, such that

$$\langle y - G(t, x_0(t)) - u_0^*(t), u_0(t)\rangle \ge 0;$$

(c') The initial condition

$$x_0(0) = x_0.$$

Therefore, it deduces that $(x_0, u_0) \in S(p_0, \lambda_0)$. This completes the proof. □

Theorem 5. *Let (f, G, B) satisfy conditions (A) and (B); $p_0 \in Z_1$, $\lambda_0 \in Z_2$ are given points. Assume the following conditions hold.*

(i) $L : Z_1 \to 2^{R^n}$ is a continuous set-valued mapping with nonempty bounded closed convex values, and there exists a neighborhood $U(p_0)$ of p_0 such that $\bigcup_{p \in U(p_0)} L(p)$ is compact;

(ii) $F : R^n \times Z_2 \to 2^{R^n}$ is a upper semicontinuous set-valued mapping with nonempty closed convex values on $R^n \times Z_2$ and lower semicontinuous on Z_2;

(iii) For each $\lambda \in \Lambda$ and $q \in G(\Omega)$, the mapping $x \mapsto q + F(x, \lambda)$ is upper hemicontinuous and monotone, where Λ is a neighborhood of λ_0;

(iv) There exists a neighborhood $U(p_0, \lambda_0)$ of (p_0, λ_0) such that

$$\bigcup_{(p,\lambda) \in U(p_0,\lambda_0)} SOL(L(p), q + F(\cdot, \lambda))$$

is bounded for any $q \in G(\Omega)$;

(v) $F : R^n \times Z_2 \to 2^{R^n}$ is strongly monotone and upper hemicontinuous on R^n .

Then, $S(p, \lambda)$ is continuous at $(p_0, \lambda_0) \in Z_1 \times Z_2$.

Proof. From Theorem 3.2 in [21], we know that condition (iv) is equivalent to conditions (iii) and (iv) in Theorem 2. It follows from Theorem 3 that $S(p, \lambda)$ is a singleton by conditions $(i), (ii), (iv)$, and (v). Let $S(p_n, \lambda_n) = (x_n, u_n)$ with $(p_n, \lambda_n) \to (p_0, \lambda_0)$. Next, we need to prove sequence $\{x_n\}$ and $\{u_n\}$ have convergent subsequences, respectively.

Step 1. $\{x_n\}$ is uniformly bounded.

It is known that $(x_n, u_n) \in S(p_n, \lambda_n)$. Therefore, for almost all $t \in [0, T]$,

$$\dot{x}_n(t) = f(t, x_n(t)) + B(t, x_n(t))u_n(t), \quad n = 1, 2, \cdots. \tag{23}$$

Since $\mathbb{F}(t, x_n)$ defined by (4) satisfies (3), for any $t \in [0, T]$, we have

$$\|x_n(t)\| \le \|x_0\| + \int_0^t \rho^{\mathbb{F}}(1 + \|x_n(s)\|)ds.$$

Applying the Gronwall inequality, we know

$$\|x_n(t)\| \le (\|x_0\| + \rho^{\mathbb{F}} T)e^{\rho^{\mathbb{F}} T}.$$

Clearly, $\{x_n\}$ is uniformly bounded with $\|x\| = \sup_{t\in[0,T]} \|x(t)\|$.

Step 2. $\{x_n\}$ is an equicontinuous family of functions. Since $(x_n, u_n) \in S(p_n, \lambda_n)$, for almost all $t \in [0,T]$, $u_n(t) \in SOL(L(p_n), G(t, x_n(t)) + F(\cdot, \lambda_n))$. By condition (iv), for almost all $t \in [0,T]$ and $n = 1, 2, \cdots$, there exists a constant C such that $\|u_n(t)\| \leq C$.

In reality, (23) means for all $0 \leq s \leq t \leq T$,

$$x_n(t) - x_n(s) = \int_s^t f(\tau, x_n(\tau)) + B(\tau, x_n(\tau))u_n(\tau)d\tau, \quad n = 1, 2, \cdots.$$

We note that f is a Lipschitz continuous function on Ω, so for all $(t,x) \in \Omega$, there exists a constant $\rho_f > 0$ such that

$$\|f(t,x)\| \leq \rho_f(1 + \|x\|). \tag{24}$$

Since B is bounded on Ω and $\{u_n(t)\}$ is bounded for almost all $t \in [0,T]$, by (24), we have

$$\begin{aligned}
&\|x_n(t) - x_n(s)\| \\
= \;& \|\int_s^t f(\tau, x_n(\tau)) + B(\tau, x_n(\tau))u_n(\tau)d\tau\| \\
\leq \;& \int_s^t \|f(\tau, x_n(\tau))\|d\tau + \int_s^t \|B(\tau, x_n(\tau))u_n(\tau)\|d\tau \\
\leq \;& \int_s^t \|f(\tau, x_n(\tau))\|d\tau + \int_s^t \|B(\tau, x_n(\tau))\|\|u_n(\tau)\|d\tau \\
\leq \;& \int_s^t \rho_f(1 + \|x_n(\tau)\|)d\tau + \delta_B C|t-s| \\
\leq \;& \rho_f|t-s| + \rho_f(\|x_0\| + \rho^{\mathbb{F}}T)e^{\rho^{\mathbb{F}}T}|t-s| + \delta_B C|t-s| \\
\leq \;& (\rho_f(1 + (\|x_0\| + \rho^{\mathbb{F}}T)e^{\rho^{\mathbb{F}}T}) + \delta_B C)|t-s|.
\end{aligned}$$

Let $M = \rho_f(1 + (\|x_0\| + \rho^{\mathbb{F}}T)e^{\rho^{\mathbb{F}}T}) + \delta_B C$. Therefore, there exists a constant M such that, for any $n = 1, 2, \cdots$,

$$\|x_n(t) - x_n(s)\| \leq M|t-s|.$$

Then, sequence $\{x_n\}$ is equicontinuous. We can apply the Arzelà–Ascoli theorem to deduce that $\{x_n\}$ has a subsequence, denoted again by $\{x_n\}$, which converges to x_0.

Step 3. $S(p_n, \lambda_n) \to S(p_0, \lambda_0)$ in $C([0,T]; R^m) \times L^2([0,T]; R^n)$. We know that $u_n(t) \in SOL(L(p_n), G(t, x_n(t)) + F(\cdot, \lambda_n))$ for almost all $t \in [0,T]$. Then, there exists a measure E with $mE = 0$ such that $u_n(t) \in SOL(L(p_n), G(t, x_n(t)) + F(\cdot, \lambda_n))$ for any $t \in [0,T] \setminus E$. That is, for any $t \in [0,T] \setminus E$, there exists $u_n^*(t) \in F(u_n(t), \lambda_n)$ and $G(t, x_n(t)) + u_n^*(t) \in L(p_n)$ such that

$$\langle y - G(t, x_n(t)) - u_n^*(t), u_n(t)\rangle \geq 0, \quad \forall y \in L(p_n). \tag{25}$$

Take any small h such that $t + h \in [0,T] \setminus E$ and $u_n(t+h) \in SOL(L(p_n), G(t+h, x_n(t+h)) + F(\cdot, \lambda_n))$. Then, there exists $u_n^*(t+h) \in F(u_n(t+h), \lambda_n)$ and $G(t+h, x_n(t+h)) + u_n^*(t+h) \in L(p_n)$ such that, for any $t + h \in [0,T] \setminus E$,

$$\langle y - G(t+h, x_n(t+h)) - u_n^*(t+h), u_n(t+h)\rangle \geq 0, \quad \forall y \in L(p_n). \tag{26}$$

For any $t + h \in [0,T] \setminus E$, letting $y = G(t+h, x_n(t+h)) + u_n^*(t+h)$ in (25), we have

$$\langle G(t+h, x_n(t+h)) + u_n^*(t+h) - G(t, x_n(t)) - u_n^*(t), u_n(t)\rangle \geq 0.$$

For any $t \in [0,T] \setminus E$, letting $y = G(t, x_n(t)) + u_n^*(t)$ in (26), we have

$$\langle G(t, x_n(t)) + u_n^*(t) - G(t+h, x_n(t+h)) - u_n^*(t+h), u_n(t+h)\rangle \geq 0.$$

Therefore,

$$\begin{aligned} & \langle G(t+h, x_n(t+h)) - G(t, x_n(t)), u_n(t) - u_n(t+h) \rangle && (27) \\ \geq\ & \langle u_n^*(t) - u_n^*(t+h), u_n(t) - u_n(t+h) \rangle. && (28) \end{aligned}$$

By the monotonicity of F,

$$\langle u_n^*(t) - u_n^*(t+h), u_n(t) - u_n(t+h) \rangle \geq \mu \|u_n(t) - u_n(t+h)\|^2.$$

Applying the Cauchy–Schwarz inequality, we get

$$\begin{aligned} & \langle G(t+h, x_n(t+h)) - G(t, x_n(t)), u_n(t) - u_n(t+h) \rangle \\ \leq\ & \|G(t+h, x_n(t+h)) - G(t, x_n(t))\| \|u_n(t) - u_n(t+h)\|. \end{aligned}$$

Thus, combining the above two inequalities and applying the Lipschitz continuity of G, we obtain

$$\begin{aligned} \mu \|u_n(t) - u_n(t+h)\| &\leq \|G(t+h, x_n(t+h)) - G(t, x_n(t))\| \\ &\leq L_G(|h| + \|x_n(t+h) - x_n(t)\|), \end{aligned}$$

which means

$$\begin{aligned} \|u_n(t) - u_n(t+h)\| &\leq \frac{L_G}{\mu}(|h| + \|x_n(t+h) - x_n(t)\|) \\ &\leq \frac{L_G}{\mu}(|h| + M|h|) \\ &\leq \frac{L_G}{\mu}(M+1)|h|. \qquad (29) \end{aligned}$$

Let $l = \frac{L_G}{\mu}(M+1)$. Since $\{x_n\}$ is equicontinuous, it follows from (29) that for any $\epsilon > 0$, there exists $\delta = min\{T, \frac{\epsilon}{l\sqrt{2T}}\}$ such that, for all $n = 1, 2, \ldots$ and all $|h| \leq \delta$,

$$\begin{aligned} \int_0^{T-h} \|u_n(t+h) - u_n(h)\|^2 dt &\leq \int_0^{T-h} l^2 h^2 dt \\ &\leq l^2 h^2 (T-h) \\ &\leq l^2 \delta^2 (T+\delta) \\ &< \epsilon^2. \qquad (30) \end{aligned}$$

It is known that $\|u_n\|_{L^2} = (\int_{[0,T]} \|u_n(t)\|^2 dt)^{\frac{1}{2}} < \infty$, which means $\{u_n\}$ is bounded in $L^2[0,T]$. Applying inequality (30) and the boundedness of $\{u_n\}$, by Corollary 1.34 in [29], we get that the sequence $\{u_n\}$ is relatively compact in $L^2[0,T]$. We can obtain the closure of $\{u_n\}$ is compact. Therefore, $\{u_n\}$ exists a convergent subsequence, denoted again by $\{u_n\}$, which converges to u_0. Up to now, we get subsequence $(x_n, u_n) = S(p_n, \lambda_n)$ with $x_n \to x_0$ and $u_n \to u_0$. From Theorem 4, $S(p, \lambda)$ is closed at (p_0, λ_0). This means $(x_n, u_n) \to (x_0, u_0) = S(p_0, \lambda_0)$ and so $S(p, \lambda)$ is continuous at (p_0, λ_0). This completes the proof. □

5. An Example of a Time-Dependent Spatial Price Equilibrium Control Problem

In this section, we will give an example of the differential inverse variational inequality to the time-dependent spatial price equilibrium control problem. As discussed by Scrimali [15], assume that a single commodity is produced at m supply market, with typical supply market denoted by i, and is consumed at n demand markets, with typical demand market denoted by j, during the time interval $[0,T]$ with $T > 0$. Let (i,j) denote the typical pair of producers and consumers for $i = 1, 2, \cdots, m$ and $j = 1, 2, \cdots, n$. Let $S_i(t)$ be the supply of the commodity produced at supply market i at time $t \in [0, T]$ and group the supplies into a column vector

$$S(t) = (S_1(t), \cdots S_m(t)) \in R^m.$$

Let $D_j(t)$ be the demand of the commodity associated with demand market j at time $t \in [0, T]$ and group the demands into a column vector

$$D(t) = (D_1(t), \cdots D_n(t)) \in R^n.$$

Let $x_{ij}(t)$ be the commodity shipment from supply market i to demand market j at time $t \in [0, T]$ and group the commodity shipments into a column vector $x(t) \in R^{mn}$.

Li et al. [6] studied the time-dependent spatial price equilibrium control problem by establishing the relation between the problem and a differential inverse variational inequality. We restate it here with a concise version.

Assume that, for any $t \in [0, T]$,

$$S_i(t) = \sum_{j=1}^{n} x_{ij}(t), \qquad D_j(t) = \sum_{i=1}^{m} x_{ij}(t)$$

and resource exploitations $S(x(t), u(t))$ at supply market and consumption $D(x(t), u(t))$ at demands market can be controlled by adjusting the tax $u(t)$. Let

$$W(t, x(t), u(t)) = (S(x(t), u(t)), D(x(t), u(t))), \quad \forall t \in [0, T],$$

which can be written as

$$W(t, x(t), u(t)) = G(t, x(t)) + F(u(t)),$$

where $G(t, x)$ is a Carathéodory function with $\gamma(t) \in L^2[0, T]$ such that

$$\|G(t, x)\| \le \gamma(t) + \|x\|.$$

and F is a continuous mapping. Let

$$L = \{w \in L^2([0, T], R^{m+n}) : \underline{w}(t) \le w(t) \le \overline{w}(t) \text{ for almost all } t \in [0, T]\}$$

be the set of a feasible state influenced by the adjusted taxes $u(t)$, where $\underline{w}(t) = (\underline{S}(t), \underline{D}(t))$ and $\overline{w}(t) = (\overline{S}(t), \overline{D}(t))$ denote the lower and upper capacity constraints, respectively. Under some appropriate assumptions, finding the solution of a time-dependent optimal control equilibrium problem is equivalent to finding the Carathéodory solution $(x(t), u(t))$ for the following differential inverse variational inequality:

$$\begin{cases} \dot{x}(t) = f(t, x(t)) + B(t, x(t))u(t) \\ u(t) \in SOL(-L, -G(t, x(t)) - F(\cdot)) \\ x(0) = x_0, \end{cases}$$

For more details, we refer the reader to [6].

However, the total amount of supply for a commodity and the relevant tax adjustments policy on the markets always vary with the sales season and the off-season [21]. In real life, any minute change in the proportion of each strategy seen will lead to a change in strategy. Let 0 denote the off-season and 1 denote the sales season. During the off-season, policy-makers will motivate manufacturers to develop resources by lowering the taxes they need to bear. During the sales season, policy-makers resist more development resources by increasing taxes on manufacturers. That means the set L of a feasible state is influenced by a parameter p, where $p \in \{0, 1\}$. Because the supply and demand of the commodity are also influenced by the seasons, we assume the mapping F is influenced by a parameter λ, where $\lambda \in \{0,1\}$. Now, the time-dependent spatial price equilibrium control problem can be transformed into the following differential inverse variational inequality including parameters:

$$\begin{cases} \dot{x}(t) = f(t,x(t)) + B(t,x(t))u(t) \\ u(t) \in SOL(-L(p), -G(t,x(t)) - F(\cdot,\lambda)) \\ x(0) = x_0, \end{cases}$$

Therefore, the time-dependent spatial price equilibrium control problem influenced by seasons will lead to a stability problem for a class of differential inverse variational inequalities.

6. Conclusions

The paper is concerned with the stability analysis of differential set-valued inverse variational inequalities in finite dimensional spaces. First, we proved an important result about a set-valued mapping, Lemma 5, which extends Lemma 2.5 in [6] and plays an important role in proving the existence of Carathéodory weak solutions for DSIVI (2). Then we obtained the existence of Carathéodory weak solutions for DSIVI (2). Second, we established closedness and continuity for the differential set-valued inverse variational inequality problem when the constraint set and the mapping are perturbed by two different parameters. Finally, we gave an example of a time-dependent spatial price equilibrium control problem, which can be transformed into a differential inverse variational inequality in finite dimensional spaces.

For further research, we can note the following directions: First, to adapt the main methods to study the existence of Carathéodory weak solutions and stability for differential set-valued inverse mixed variational inequalities in finite dimensional spaces; second, to use the theory of semigroups, set-valued mappings, and variational inequality to study the partial differential set-valued inverse variational inequalities in Banach spaces.

Author Contributions: X.Z. and W.L. analyzed the existence and stability for the differential set-valued inverse variational inequality; X.Z. and X.L. analyzed the applications for the differential inverse variational inequality; X.Z. is the major contributor in writing the manuscript text. All authors have read and agreed to the published version of the manuscript.

Funding: This work was supported by Opening Fund of Geomathematics Key Laboratory of Sichuan Province (scsxdz2021yb06) and National Natural Science Foundation of China (Grant 11701480).

Data Availability Statement: Not applicable.

Acknowledgments: The authors thank the anonymous reviewers for their valuable comments and suggestions that helped us to improve the content of this paper.

Conflicts of Interest: The authors declare no conflict of interest.

References

1. Pang, J.S.; Stewart, D.E. Differential variational inequaliities. *Math. Program.* **2008**, *113*, 345–424. [CrossRef]
2. Chen, X.J.; Wang, Z.Y. Differential variational inequalitiy approach to dynamic games with shared constraints. *Math. Program.* **2014**, *146*, 379–408. [CrossRef]
3. Stewart, D.E. Uniqueness for index-one differential variational inequalities. *Nonlinear Anal. Hybrid Syst.* **2008**, *2*, 812–818. [CrossRef]
4. Li, X.S.; Huang, N.J.; O'Regan, D. Differential mixed variational inequalities in finite dimensional spaces. *Nonlinear Anal. Theory Methods Appl.* **2010**, *72*, 3875–3886. [CrossRef]
5. Li, X.S.; Huang, N.J. A class of impulsive differential variational inequalities in finite demensional space. *J. Frankl. Inst.* **2016**, *353*, 3151–3175. [CrossRef]
6. Li, W.; Wang, X.; Huang, N.J. Differential inverse variational inequalities in finite dimensional spaces. *Acta Math. Sci.* **2015**, *35*, 407–422. [CrossRef]
7. Liu, Z.H.; Zeng, S.D.; Motreanu, D. Evolutionary problems driven by variational inequalities. *J. Differ. Equ.* **2016**, *260*, 6787–6799. [CrossRef]
8. Liu, Z.H.; Sofonea, M. Differential quasivariational inequalities in contact machanics. *Acta Math. Sci.* **2017**, *37*, 26–32. [CrossRef]

9. Liu, Z.H.; Migrski, S.; Zeng, S.D. Partial differential variational inequalities involving nonlocal boundary conditions in Banach spaces. *J. Differ. Equ.* **2017**, *263*, 3989–4006. [CrossRef]
10. Chen, T.; Huang, N.J.; Li, X.S.; Zhou, Y.Z. A new class of differential ninliner system involving parabolic variational and history-dependent hemi-variational inequalities arising in contact mechanics. *Common. Nonliner Sci. Number. Simul.* **2021**, *101*, 24.
11. Li, W.; Wang, X.F. Stability analysis of partial differential set-valued variational inequalities on Banach spaces. *J. Convex Anal.* **2020**, *27*, 423–442.
12. Tang, G.J.; Cen, J.X.; Nguyen, V.T.; Zeng, S.D. Differential variational-hemivariational inequalities: Existence, uniqueness, stability, and convergence. *J. Fixed Point Theory Appl.* **2020**, *22*, 83. [CrossRef]
13. He, B.S.; Liu, X.H. Inverse variational inequalities in the economic field: Applications and algorithms. *Science Paper Online* 2006.
14. Yang, J.F. Dynamic power price problem: An inverse variational inequality approach. *J. Ind. Manag. Optim.* **2008**, *4*, 673–684. [CrossRef]
15. Scrimali, L. An inverse variational inequality approach to the evolutionary spatial price equilibrium problem. *Optim. Eng.* **2012**, *13*, 375–387. [CrossRef]
16. Xu, H.K.; Dey, S.; Vetrivel, V. Notes on a neural network approach to inverse variational inequalities. *Optimization* **2020**, *70*, 901–910. [CrossRef]
17. Jiang, Y.; Cai, X.G.; Han, D. Solving policy design problems: Alternating direction method of multipliers-based methods for structured inverse variational inequalities. *Eur. J. Oper. Res.* **2020**, *280*, 417–427. [CrossRef]
18. Yang, H.; Bell, M.G.H. Traffic restraint, road pricing and network equilibrium. *Transp. Res. Part B Methodol.* **1997**, *31*, 303–314. [CrossRef]
19. He, B.S.; Liu, H.X.; Li, M.; He, X.Z. PPA-based methods for monotone inverse variational inequalities. *Sci. Pap. Online* **2006**.
20. He, B.S.; He, X.Z.; Liu, H.X. Solving a class of constrained 'black-box' inverse variational inequalities. *Eur. J. Oper. Res.* **2010**, *204*, 391–401. [CrossRef]
21. Luo, X.P. Stability analysis of set-valued inverse variational inequalities in reflexive Banach spaces. *J. Fixed Point Theory Appl.* **2021**, *23*, 41. [CrossRef]
22. Gwinner, J. On a new class of differential variational inequalities and a stability result. *Math. Program.* **2013**, *139*, 205–221. [CrossRef]
23. Wang, X.; Li, W.; Li, X.S.; Huang, N.J. Stability for differential mixed variational inequalities. *Optim. Lett.* **2014**, *8*, 1873–1887. [CrossRef]
24. Aubin, J.P.; Frankowska, H. *Set-Valued Analysis*; Birkhauser: Boston, MA, USA, 1990.
25. Fan, J.H.; Wang, X.G. Gap functions and global error bounds for set-valued variational inequalities. *J. Comput. Appl. Math.* **2010**, *233*, 2956–2965. [CrossRef]
26. Guo, F.M.; Li, W.; Xiao, Y.B.; Migórski, S. Stability analysis of partial differential variational inequalities in Banach spaces. *Nonlinear Anal. Model. Control.* **2020**, *25*, 69–83. [CrossRef]
27. Deimling, K. *Multivalued Differential Equations*; Walter de Gruyter: Berlin, Germany, 1992.
28. Haim, B. *Functional Analysis, Sobolev Spaces and Partial Differential Equations*; Springer: New York, NY, USA, 2010; pp. 181–199. [CrossRef]
29. Hu, S.C.; Papageorgiou, N.S. *Handbook of Multivalued Analysis: Volume II: Applications*; Mathematics and Its Applications; Springer: New York, NY, USA, 1997.

axioms

MDPI

Article

Stability of Fractional-Order Quasi-Linear Impulsive Integro-Differential Systems with Multiple Delays

Mathiyalagan Kalidass [1,*], Shengda Zeng [2,*] and Mehmet Yavuz [3]

[1] Department of Mathematics, Bharathiar University, Coimbatore 641 046, India; kmathimath@gmail.com
[2] Guangxi Colleges and Universities Key Laboratory of Complex System Optimization and Big Data Processing, Yulin Normal University, Yulin 537000, China
[3] Department of Mathematics and Computer Sciences, Faculty of Science, Necmettin Erbakan University, Konya 42090, Türkiye; mehmetyavuz@erbakan.edu.tr
* Correspondence: kmathimath@gmail.com (M.K.); shengdazeng@ylu.edu.cn (S.Z.)

Abstract: In this paper, some novel conditions for the stability results for a class of fractional-order quasi-linear impulsive integro-differential systems with multiple delays is discussed. First, the existence and uniqueness of mild solutions for the considered system is discussed using contraction mapping theorem. Then, novel conditions for Mittag–Leffler stability (MLS) of the considered system are established by using well known mathematical techniques, and further, the two corollaries are deduced, which still gives some new results. Finally, an example is given to illustrate the applications of the results.

Keywords: fractional-order system; quasi-linear system; impulse; integro-differential equation; stability; multiple delays

Citation: Kalidass, M.; Zeng, S.; Yavuz, M. Stability of Fractional-Order Quasi-Linear Impulsive Integro-Differential Systems with Multiple Delays. *Axioms* **2022**, *11*, 308. https://doi.org/10.3390/axioms11070308

Academic Editor: Chris Goodrich

Received: 27 May 2022
Accepted: 17 June 2022
Published: 25 June 2022

1. Introduction

Differential equations involving an arbitrary non-integer order are often used as excellent tools for describing many dynamical processes because they have nonlocal properties and weakly singular kernels; for more details, see [1–3]. Most the investigations show that non-integer order calculus is more suitable and has accuracy when describing various physical systems in areas such as mechanical systems, electro-chemistry, biological systems and diffusion processes; see, for instance, [4–8]. Further, as pointed out in [9], the fractional-order derivative provides fundamental and general computation ability for efficient information processing and stimulus anticipation for real models. Usually, systems with nonlocal conditions are generalizations of local nonlinear boundary conditions, which gives better approximations in some physical problems [10]. Further, the quasi-linear integro-differential equations have occurred during the study of the nonlinear behavior of elastic strings and other areas of physics. Many interesting results on various forms of systems, including fractional-order, quasi-linear, integro-differential and non-local systems, are found in [11–15] and references therein.

On the other hand, impulses in differential equations reflect the dynamics of real world problems with unexpected discontinuities and rapid changes at certain instants, such as blood flows, heart beats and so on [16]. Impulsive behavior often exists in many real world systems. Fundamentally, the impulses are samples of state variables of a controlled system at discrete moments. These effects most often occur in pharmacokinetics, the radiation of electromagnetic waves, nanoelectronics, etc. [17]. There are number of interesting research papers on impulsive differential equations found in the literature; see [18–20] and references therein. The piecewise-continuous solutions for the impulsive Cauchy problem and impulsive boundary-value problem were studied in [21]. The existence and finite-time stability of an impulsive fractional-order system (FOS) using Gronwall inequality involving Hadamard-type singular kernel has been investigated in [20]. Wang et al. [19] derived the finite-time stability of impulsive fractional-order delayed systems using generalized Bellman-Gronwall's inequality.

The sufficient conditions for MLS and uniform asymptotic stability of nonlinear impulsive FOSs were obtained in [22]. The MLS of nonlinear FOSs with impulses has been analyzed in [23]. The MLS for impulsive FOSs with instantaneous and non-instantaneous impulses were studied in [24]. The MLS of a nonlinear FOS was studied in [25] by extending the Lyapunov direct method. The MLS for a coupled system of FOSs with impulses was investigated in [26]. The MLS for nonlinear fractional neutral singular systems were obtained in [27]. The finite time stability of delayed FOSs by Mittag–Leffler functions was analyzed in [28]. An MLS estimator for a nonlinear FOS using a linear quadratic regulator approach was studied in [29]. Many problems in viscoelasticity, acoustics, populations dynamics, electromagnetics, hydrology, chemical reactions and other areas can be modeled by fractional integro-differential equations; see [30–32] and references therein. For example, take the the nonlinear oscillation of earthquake model, fluid-dynamic traffic model, second-grade fluid model, circulant Halvorsen system, susceptible-infected-recovered epidemic model with a fractional derivative and many other recent developments in the description of anomalous by fractional dynamics; see [33–36].

The stability of dynamical systems is an essential one in the qualitative theory of dynamical systems, as it addresses the system trajectories under small perturbations of initial conditions. The stability analysis of FOS is more difficult than the classical ones because the fractional-order derivative is nonlocal and has infirm singular kernels [37,38]. In the literature, the concepts of the stability analysis of impulsive FOS are studied by various approaches. Among them, MLS is more useful in FOSs because the Mittag–Leffler functions are commonly used in fractional calculus, which generally features power-law convergence. Thus, in this paper we made an attempt to study MLS analysis for quasi-linear impulsive FOS with multiple time delays. Recently, many authors focused on the various types of stability analysis for FOS; for example, the q-MLS and direct Lyapunov method for q-FOS is discussed in [39]. The Mittag–Leffler input stability of FOSs with exogenous disturbances using the Lyapunov characterization is studied in [40]. Li et al. [41] proposed the MLS using the fractional Lyapunov direct method.

However, there are few results available for the MLS of FOS with impulse effects that could not be suitable for FOSs of quasi-linear type with multiple time delays. To the best of our knowledge, the Mittag–Leffler stability of FOSs has not been fully investigated, which motivated our present study. Thus, in this study the existence and uniqueness of solutions and MLS analysis of the impulsive quasi-linear FOS with multiple time delays are established using the well-known fixed point theorems and Mittag–Leffler approach. Further, the main contribution of this paper lies in deriving new stability conditions for the fractional-order quasi-linear system with nonlocal conditions, multiple time delays and impulses. Novel conditions for the Mittag–Leffler stability of FOSs is established. The existence and uniqueness of mild solutions for the FOS are discussed with help of the contraction mapping principle. Finally, an example is provided to show the applicability of the results.

2. Problem Description

Consider the fractional model given by

$$\begin{aligned} D^{\beta}\mathfrak{z}(t) + A(t,\mathfrak{z}(t))\mathfrak{z}(t) &= \mathfrak{f}(t,\mathfrak{z}(t),\mathfrak{z}(\tau(t))) + \int_0^t \mathfrak{g}(t,\alpha,\mathfrak{z}(\alpha),\mathfrak{z}(\delta(\alpha)))\mathrm{d}\alpha, \\ \mathfrak{z}(0) + \mathfrak{h}(\mathfrak{z}) &= \mathfrak{z}_0, \\ \Delta\mathfrak{z}(t_k) &= I_k(\mathfrak{z}(t_k)), \end{aligned} \tag{1}$$

in Banach space X, $0 < \beta \leq 1$, $t \in J = [0,T]$, $\mathfrak{z}_0 \in X$, $k = 1,2,\ldots,\mathfrak{m}$ and $0 < t_1 < t_2 < \ldots < t_{\mathfrak{m}} < T$. Assume $-A(t,\mathfrak{z}(t))$ is a closed linear operator defined on a dense domain $D(A)$ in X into X such that $D(A)$ is independent of t, and it generates an evolution operator in X.

Let $\mathfrak{z} \in PC(J, X)$ be continuous at $t \neq t_k$ and left continuous at $t = t_k$; in addition, right limit $\mathfrak{z}(t_k^+)$ exists for $k = 1, 2, \ldots, \mathfrak{m}$. Clearly $PC(J, X)$ is a Banach space with the norm $\|\mathfrak{z}\|_{PC} = \sup_{t \in J}\|\mathfrak{z}(t)\|$. Additionally, $\mathfrak{z}(\tau) = (\mathfrak{z}(\tau_1), \mathfrak{z}(\tau_2), \ldots, \mathfrak{z}(\tau_r))$ and $\mathfrak{z}(\delta) = (\mathfrak{z}(\delta_1), \mathfrak{z}(\delta_2), \ldots, \mathfrak{z}(\delta_\kappa))$ are multiple time-delays. The functions $\mathfrak{f}$, $\mathfrak{g}$ and $\mathfrak{h}$ are nonlinear in nature, satisfying:

(H_1) function $\mathfrak{f}$: $J \times X^{r+1} \to X$ is continuous, and there exist positive constants $\mathfrak{f}_1$, $\mathfrak{f}_2$ such that

$$\|\mathfrak{f}(t, \mathfrak{z}_1, \mathfrak{z}_2, \ldots, \mathfrak{z}_{r+1}) - \mathfrak{f}(t, \tilde{\mathfrak{z}}_1, \tilde{\mathfrak{z}}_2, \ldots, \tilde{\mathfrak{z}}_{r+1})\|_X \leq \mathfrak{f}_1 \sum_{p=1}^{r+1} \|\mathfrak{z}_p - \tilde{\mathfrak{z}}_p\|_X,$$

$\mathfrak{z}_p, \tilde{\mathfrak{z}}_p \in X$ and $\mathfrak{f}_2 = \max_{t \in J}\|\mathfrak{f}(t, 0, \ldots, 0)\|_X$.

(H_2) function $\mathfrak{g}$: $\Lambda \times X^{\kappa+1} \to X$ is continuous, and there exist positive constants $\mathfrak{g}_1$, $\mathfrak{g}_2$ such that

$$\begin{aligned} &\int_0^t \|\mathfrak{g}(t, \alpha, \mathfrak{z}_1, \mathfrak{z}_2, \ldots, \mathfrak{z}_{\kappa+1}) - \mathfrak{g}(t, \alpha, \tilde{\mathfrak{z}}_1, \tilde{\mathfrak{z}}_2, \ldots, \tilde{\mathfrak{z}}_{\kappa+1})\|_X d\alpha \\ &\qquad \leq \mathfrak{g}_1 \sum_{q=1}^{\kappa+1} \|\mathfrak{z}_q - \tilde{\mathfrak{z}}_q\|_X, \ \mathfrak{z}_q, \tilde{\mathfrak{z}}_q \in X, \\ &\mathfrak{g}_2 = \max\Big\{ \int_0^t \|\mathfrak{g}(t, \alpha, 0, \ldots, 0)\|_X d\alpha : (t, \alpha) \in \Lambda \Big\}. \end{aligned}$$

(H_3) τ_p and δ_q: $J \to J$ are bijective and absolutely continuous, and there exist constants c_p and b_q such that $\tau_p'(t) \geq c_p$ and $\delta_q'(t) \geq b_q$, respectively, for $t \in J$ and $\Lambda = \{(t, \theta), 0 \leq \theta \leq t \leq T\}$.

(H_4) Let Ω be a subset of X, and $\mathfrak{h}$: $PC(J, \Omega) \to Y$ is Lipschitz continuous in X and bounded in Y; i.e., there exist positive constants $\mathfrak{h}_1$, $\mathfrak{h}_2$ such that

$$\|\mathfrak{h}(\mathfrak{z})\|_Y \leq \mathfrak{h}_1 \text{ and } \|\mathfrak{h}(\mathfrak{z}) - \mathfrak{h}(\tilde{\mathfrak{z}})\|_Y \leq \mathfrak{h}_2 \max_{t \in J} \|\mathfrak{z} - \tilde{\mathfrak{z}}\|_{PC}, \ \mathfrak{z}, \tilde{\mathfrak{z}} \in PC(J, X).$$

(H_5) $\mathfrak{I}_k$: $X \to X$ are continuous and there exist constants $\mathfrak{l} > 0$, such that $\|\mathfrak{I}_k(\mathfrak{z}) - \mathfrak{I}_k(\tilde{\mathfrak{z}})\| \leq \mathfrak{l}\|\mathfrak{z} - \tilde{\mathfrak{z}}\|$, $\mathfrak{z}, \tilde{\mathfrak{z}} \in X$, where $k = 1, 2, 3, \ldots, \mathfrak{m}$.

2.1. Preliminaries

Let X and Y be two Banach spaces such that Y is densely and continuously embedded in X. For Banach space, the norm of X is denoted by $\|.\|_X$. The space of all bounded linear operators from X to Y is denoted by $\mathcal{B}(X, Y)$, and $\mathcal{B}(X, X)$ is written as $\mathcal{B}(X)$.

Now we recall some basic definitions and lemmas which will be useful in the main results.

Definition 1. *A two-parameter family of bounded linear operators $\mathfrak{U}(t, \Theta)$ and $0 \leq \Theta \leq t \leq T$, on X, is called an evolution system if the following two conditions are satisfied:*
(1) $\mathfrak{U}(t, t) = I$, $\mathfrak{U}(t, r)\mathfrak{U}(r, \Theta) = \mathfrak{U}(t, \Theta)$ *for* $0 \leq \Theta \leq r \leq t \leq T$,
(2) $(t, \Theta) \to \mathfrak{U}(t, \Theta)$ *is strongly continuous for* $0 \leq \Theta \leq t \leq T$.

Let E be the Banach space formed from domain $D(A)$ with the graph norm. Since $-A(t)$ is a closed operator, it follows that $-A(t)$ is in the set of bounded operators from E to X.

Definition 2. *A resolvent operator for* (1) *is a bounded operator-valued function $R_\mathfrak{z}(t, \Theta) \in \mathcal{B}(X)$, $0 \leq \Theta \leq t \leq T$, the space of bounded linear operator on X, having the following properties:*

- *$R_\mathfrak{z}(t, \Theta)$ is strongly continuous in Θ and t, $R_\mathfrak{z}(\Theta, \Theta) = I$, $0 \leq \Theta \leq T$, $\|R_\mathfrak{z}(t, \Theta)\| \leq \Upsilon e^{N(t-\Theta)}$ for some constants Υ and N.*
- *$R_\mathfrak{z}(t, \Theta)E \subset E$, $R_\mathfrak{z}(t, \Theta)$ is strongly continuous in Θ and t on E.*

- *For $x \in X$, $R_{\mathfrak{z}}(t,\Theta)x$ is continuously differentiable for $\Theta \in [0,T]$ and* $\frac{\partial R_{\mathfrak{z}}}{\partial \Theta}(t,\Theta)x = R_{\mathfrak{z}}(t,\Theta)A(\Theta,\mathfrak{z}(\Theta))x$.
- *For $x \in X$ and $\Theta \in [0,T]$, $R_{\mathfrak{z}}(t,\Theta)x$ is continuously differentiable for $t \in [\Theta,T]$ and* $\frac{\partial R_{\mathfrak{z}}}{\partial t}(t,\Theta)x = -A(t,\mathfrak{z}(t))R_{\mathfrak{z}}(t,\Theta)x$,

with $\frac{\partial R_{\mathfrak{z}}}{\partial \Theta}(t,\Theta)x$ and $\frac{\partial R_{\mathfrak{z}}}{\partial t}(t,\Theta)x$ are strongly continuous on $0 \le \Theta \le t \le T$. Further, $R_{\mathfrak{z}}(t,\Theta)$ can be extracted from the evolution operator of the generator $-A(t,\mathfrak{z})$. The resolvent operator is similar to the evolution operator for non-autonomous systems in a Banach space.

The Mittag–Leffler function (MLF) in one parameter is defined by $E_\beta(z) = \sum\limits_{n=0}^{\infty} \frac{z^n}{\Gamma(\beta n+1)}$ where $\beta > 0$ and MLF in two parameters is $E_{\beta_1,\beta_2}(z) = \sum\limits_{n=0}^{\infty} \frac{z^n}{\Gamma(\beta_1 n+\beta_2)}$ where $\beta_1 > 0$, $\beta_2 > 0$ and $z \in C$. Additionally, for $\beta_2 = 1$, $E_{\beta_1}(z) = E_{\beta_1,1}(z)$ and $E_{1,1}(z) = e^z$. Further, the Laplace transform of MLF in two parameters is $L\{t^{\beta_2-1}E_{\beta_1,\beta_2}(-\gamma t^\beta)\} = \frac{s^{\beta_1-\beta_2}}{s^{\beta_1}+\gamma}$ for $t \ge 0$, where $\gamma, s \in \mathbb{R}$.

Lemma 1 ([21]). *Let $\beta \in (0,1)$ and $\mathfrak{f}\colon J \to R$ be continuous. A function $\mathfrak{z}(t) \in C(J,R)$ given by*

$$\mathfrak{z}(t) = \mathfrak{z}_0 - \frac{1}{\Gamma(\beta)}\int_0^a (a-\alpha)^{\beta-1}\mathfrak{f}(\alpha)d\alpha + \frac{1}{\Gamma(\beta)}\int_0^t (t-\alpha)^{\beta-1}\mathfrak{f}(\alpha)d\alpha,$$

is the only solution of the fractional Cauchy problem ${}^cD_t^\beta = \mathfrak{f}(t)$ for all $t \in J$, $\mathfrak{z}(a) = \mathfrak{z}_0$, where $a > 0$.

Lemma 2 ([10]). *Let $R_{\mathfrak{z}}(t,\Theta)$ and $R_{\tilde{\mathfrak{z}}}(t,\Theta)$ be the resolvent operators for system* (1). *There exists a constant $c > 0$ such that*

$$\|R_{\mathfrak{z}}(t,\Theta)W - R_{\tilde{\mathfrak{z}}}(t,\Theta)W\| \le c\|W\|_Y \int_\Theta^t \|\mathfrak{z}(\sigma) - \tilde{\mathfrak{z}}(\sigma)\|d\sigma,$$

for every $\mathfrak{z}, \tilde{\mathfrak{z}} \in PC(J,X)$ and every $W \in Y$.

Let $S_\lambda = \{\mathfrak{z}\colon \mathfrak{z} \in PC(J,X), \mathfrak{z}(0) + \mathfrak{h}(\mathfrak{z}) = \mathfrak{z}_0, \Delta\mathfrak{z}(t_k) = \mathfrak{I}_k(\mathfrak{z}(t_k)), \|\mathfrak{z}\| \le \lambda\}$, for $t \in J$, $\lambda > 0$, $\mathfrak{z}_0 \in X$ and $k = 1,2,3,\ldots,\mathfrak{m}$.

Lemma 3 ([12]). *For*

$$\phi(t) = \frac{1}{\Gamma(\beta)}\int_0^t (t-\alpha)^{\beta-1}[\mathfrak{f}(\alpha,\mathfrak{z}(\alpha),\mathfrak{z}(\tau(\alpha))) + \int_0^\alpha \mathfrak{g}(\alpha,\eta,\mathfrak{z}(\eta),\mathfrak{z}(\delta(\eta)))d\eta]d\alpha,$$

there exists a constant θ such that $\|\phi(t)\|_Y \le \theta$ holds.

2.2. Existence and Uniqueness

Before presenting the stability results, we discuss the existence and uniqueness of mild solutions for the FOS (1).

Theorem 1. *Let $-A(t,\mathfrak{z}(t))$ generate the resolvent operator $\|R_{\mathfrak{z}}(t,\Theta)\| \le \Upsilon e^{N(t-\Theta)}$ with $\Upsilon_0 = \max\|R_{\mathfrak{z}}(t,\Theta)\|_Y$ for all $0 \le \Theta \le t \le T$, $\mathfrak{z} \in \Omega$, and the conditions (H_1)–(H_5) hold. If there exist positive constants $\lambda_1, \lambda_2, \lambda_3 \in (0, \frac{\lambda}{3}]$ and $\rho_1, \rho_2, \rho_3 \in [0, \frac{1}{3})$ such that*

$\lambda_1 = \Upsilon_0\|u_0\|_Y + \Upsilon_0\mathfrak{h}_1$, $\lambda_2 = \Upsilon_0\nu$, $\lambda_3 = \Upsilon_0\mathfrak{m}\mathfrak{l}\lambda$ *and*

$$\begin{aligned}
\rho_1 &= cT\|\mathfrak{z}_0\|_Y + \mathfrak{h}_1 cT + \Upsilon_0\mathfrak{h}_2, \\
\rho_2 &= cT\nu + \Upsilon_0\frac{T^\beta}{\Gamma(1+\beta)}\Big[\mathfrak{f}_1\Big(1+\frac{1}{c_1}+\ldots+\frac{1}{c_r}\Big) + \mathfrak{g}_1\Big(1+\frac{1}{b_1}+\ldots+\frac{1}{b_\kappa}\Big)\Big], \\
\rho_3 &= cT\mathfrak{m}\mathfrak{l}\lambda + \Upsilon_0\mathfrak{m}\mathfrak{l}, \text{ where } \sum_{k=1}^{\mathfrak{m}}\mathfrak{l} = \mathfrak{m}\mathfrak{l}, \\
\xi &= \frac{T^\beta}{\Gamma(1+\beta)}\Big[\mathfrak{f}_1\Big(\frac{1}{c_1}+\ldots+\frac{1}{c_r}\Big) + \mathfrak{g}_1\Big(\frac{1}{b_1}+\ldots+\frac{1}{b_\kappa}\Big)\Big], \\
\nu &= \frac{T^\beta}{\Gamma(1+\beta)}\lambda(\mathfrak{g}_1+\mathfrak{f}_1) + \xi\lambda + \frac{T^\beta}{\Gamma(1+\beta)}(\mathfrak{g}_2+\mathfrak{f}_2)
\end{aligned}$$

are satisfied, then the system (1) *has a unique mild solution*

$$\begin{aligned}
\mathfrak{z}(t) &= R_\mathfrak{z}(t,0)\mathfrak{z}_0 - R_\mathfrak{z}(t,0)\mathfrak{h}(\mathfrak{z}) + \frac{1}{\Gamma(\beta)}\int_0^t (t-\alpha)^{\beta-1}R_\mathfrak{z}(t,\Theta)[\mathfrak{f}(\alpha,\mathfrak{z}(\alpha),\mathfrak{z}(\tau(\alpha))) \\
&\quad + \int_0^\alpha \mathfrak{g}(\alpha,\eta,\mathfrak{z}(\eta),\mathfrak{z}(\delta(\eta)))d\eta]d\alpha + \sum_{0<t_k<t} R_\mathfrak{z}(t,t_k)\mathfrak{I}_k(\mathfrak{z}(t_k)) \qquad (2)
\end{aligned}$$

on J *for all* $\mathfrak{z}_0 \in X$.

By contraction mapping theorem, the unique mild solution of the form (2) for system (1) can be easily derived; for detailed proof, one can refer to [12].

Remark 1. *It is noted that in addition to the Assumptions* (H_1)–(H_5), *if* Y *is reflexive and the functions* $\mathfrak{f}$ *and* $\mathfrak{g}$ *are uniformly Hölder continuous, then the system* (1) *has a unique classical solution similar to* (2) *on* J.

3. Stability Results

In this section, we prove the Mittag–Leffler stability of the considered system.

Definition 3. *The mild solution of system* (1) *is said to be Mittag–Leffler stable if there exists a constant* $\beta \in (0,1)$ *and positive constants* a, b, M *and* μ *such that the solution* $\mathfrak{z}(t)$ *of system* (1) *satisfies*

$$\|\mathfrak{z}(t)\| \le M\|\mathfrak{z}_0\|^b\Big(E_\beta(-\mu(t-t_0)^\beta)\Big)^a, \quad t \ge 0.$$

Theorem 2. *Let* $-A(t,\mathfrak{z}(t))$ *generate the bounded resolvent operator* $\|R_\mathfrak{z}(t,\Theta)\| \le \Upsilon e^{N(t-\Theta)}$ *with* $\Upsilon_0 = \max\|R_\mathfrak{z}(t,\Theta)\|_Y$ *for all* $0 \le \Theta \le t \le T$, $\mathfrak{z} \in \Omega$, *and the conditions* (H_1)–(H_5) *hold. If there exist constants* $\mathfrak{f}_1$, $\mathfrak{g}_1$, $\mathfrak{h}_1$, *the mild solution of system* (1) *satisfies*

$$\|\mathfrak{z}(t)\| \le (1/\vartheta)\Upsilon_0(\|\mathfrak{z}_0\| + \mathfrak{h}_1)E_\beta\Big(\mu t^\beta\Big), \quad \forall t \in J, \qquad (3)$$

where $\vartheta = (1 - \Upsilon_0\mathfrak{m}\mathfrak{l})$ *and* $\mu = \frac{\Upsilon_0(\mathfrak{f}_1+\mathfrak{g}_1)}{\vartheta}$, *so the system* (1) *is Mittag–Leffler stable.*

Proof. Consider the mild solution of the system (1) of (2). Taking the norm on both sides, one can have

$$\begin{aligned}\|\mathfrak{z}(t)\| \leq\ & \|R_{\mathfrak{z}}(t,0)\|\|\mathfrak{z}_0\| + \|R_{\mathfrak{z}}(t,0)\|\|\mathfrak{h}(\mathfrak{z})\| \\ &+\frac{1}{\Gamma(\beta)}\int_0^t (t-\alpha)^{\beta-1}\|R_{\mathfrak{z}}(t,\Theta)\|\|\mathfrak{f}(\alpha,\mathfrak{z}(\alpha),\mathfrak{z}(\tau_1(\alpha)),\dots,\mathfrak{z}(\tau_r(\alpha)))\|d\alpha \\ &+\frac{1}{\Gamma(\beta)}\int_0^t (t-\alpha)^{\beta-1}\|R_{\mathfrak{z}}(t,\Theta)\| \\ &\times\Big(\int_0^\alpha \|\mathfrak{g}(\alpha,\eta,\mathfrak{z}(\eta),\mathfrak{z}(\delta_1(\eta)),\dots,\mathfrak{z}(\delta_\kappa(\eta)))\|d\eta\Big)d\alpha \\ &+\sum_{0<t_k<t}\|R_{\mathfrak{z}}(t,t_k)\|\|\mathfrak{I}_k(\mathfrak{z}(t_k))\|.\end{aligned}$$

Using the conditions (H_1), (H_2), (H_4) and (H_5), we get

$$\begin{aligned}\|\mathfrak{z}(t)\| \leq\ & \Upsilon_0\|\mathfrak{z}_0\| + \Upsilon_0\mathfrak{h}_1 + \Upsilon_0\mathfrak{m}\mathfrak{l}\|\mathfrak{z}(t)\| \\ &+\Upsilon_0\frac{1}{\Gamma(\beta)}\int_0^t (t-\alpha)^{\beta-1}\big(\mathfrak{f}_1(\|\mathfrak{z}(\alpha)\| + \|\mathfrak{z}(\tau_1(\alpha))\| + \dots \\ &+\|\mathfrak{z}(\tau_r(\alpha))\|)\big)d\alpha + \Upsilon_0\frac{1}{\Gamma(\beta)}\int_0^t (t-\alpha)^{\beta-1}\big(\mathfrak{g}_1(\|\mathfrak{z}(\alpha)\| \\ &+\|\mathfrak{z}(\delta_1(\alpha))\| + \dots + \|\mathfrak{z}(\delta_\kappa(\alpha))\|)\big)d\alpha, \\ \leq\ & \Upsilon_0\|\mathfrak{z}_0\| + \Upsilon_0\mathfrak{h}_1 + \Upsilon_0\mathfrak{m}\mathfrak{l}\|\mathfrak{z}(t)\| \\ &+{}_0D_t^{-\beta}[\mathfrak{f}_1(\|\mathfrak{z}(t)\| + \|\mathfrak{z}(\tau_1(t))\| + \dots + \|\mathfrak{z}(\tau_r(t))\|)]\Upsilon_0 \\ &+{}_0D_t^{-\beta}[\mathfrak{g}_1(\|\mathfrak{z}(t)\| + \|\mathfrak{z}(\delta_1(t))\| + \dots + \|\mathfrak{z}(\delta_\kappa(t))\|)]\Upsilon_0.\end{aligned}$$

There exists a non-negative function $M(t)$. We have

$$\begin{aligned}\|\mathfrak{z}(t)\| =\ & \Upsilon_0\|\mathfrak{z}_0\| + \Upsilon_0 k_5 + \Upsilon_0\mathfrak{m}\mathfrak{l}\|\mathfrak{z}(t)\| \\ &+{}_0D_t^{-\beta}(\mathfrak{f}_1(\|\mathfrak{z}(t)\| + \|\mathfrak{z}(\tau_1(t))\| + \dots + \|\mathfrak{z}(\tau_r(t))\|))\Upsilon_0 \\ &+{}_0D_t^{-\beta}(\mathfrak{g}_1(\|\mathfrak{z}(t)\| + \|\mathfrak{z}(\delta_1(t))\| + \dots + \|\mathfrak{z}(\delta_\kappa(t))\|))\Upsilon_0 - M(t).\end{aligned} \tag{4}$$

Taking Laplace transformations of both sides of (4), we get

$$\begin{aligned}\|\mathfrak{z}(s)\| =\ & \frac{\Upsilon_0\|\mathfrak{z}_0\|}{s} + \frac{\Upsilon_0\mathfrak{h}_1}{s} + \Upsilon_0\mathfrak{m}\mathfrak{l}\|\mathfrak{z}(s)\| + \Upsilon_0\mathfrak{f}_1 s^{-\beta}(\|\mathfrak{z}(s)\| + \|\mathfrak{z}(\tau_1(s))\| + \dots \\ &+\|\mathfrak{z}(\tau_r(s))\|) + \Upsilon_0\mathfrak{g}_1 s^{-\beta}(\|\mathfrak{z}(s)\| + \|\mathfrak{z}(\delta_1(s))\| + \dots + \|\mathfrak{z}(\delta_\kappa(s))\|) - M(s),\end{aligned}$$

$$\begin{aligned}\vartheta\Big[\frac{s^\beta-\mu}{s^\beta}\Big]\|\mathfrak{z}(s)\| =\ & \frac{1}{s}\Big[\Upsilon_0\|\mathfrak{z}_0\| + \Upsilon_0\mathfrak{h}_1 + \Upsilon_0\mathfrak{f}_1 s^{1-\beta}(\|\mathfrak{z}(\tau_1(s))\| + \dots + \|\mathfrak{z}(\tau_r(s))\|) \\ &+\Upsilon_0\mathfrak{g}_1 s^{1-\beta}(\|\mathfrak{z}(\delta_1(s))\| + \dots + \|\mathfrak{z}(\delta_\kappa(s))\|) - sM(s)\Big].\end{aligned}$$

Then,

$$\begin{aligned}\vartheta\|\mathfrak{z}(s)\| =\ & \frac{1}{s[s^\beta-\mu]}\Big[s^\beta\Upsilon_0\|\mathfrak{z}_0\| + \Upsilon_0\mathfrak{h}_1 s^\beta + \Upsilon_0\mathfrak{f}_1 s(\|\mathfrak{z}(\tau_1(s))\| + \dots + \|\mathfrak{z}(\tau_r(s))\|) \\ &+\Upsilon_0\mathfrak{g}_1 s[\|\mathfrak{z}(\delta_1(s))\| + \dots + \|\mathfrak{z}(\delta_\kappa(s))\|] - s^{\beta+1}M(s)\Big] \\ =\ & \frac{1}{s^\beta-\mu}\Big[s^{\beta-1}\Upsilon_0[\|\mathfrak{z}_0\| + \mathfrak{h}_1] - s^\beta M(s) \\ &+\Upsilon_0\mathfrak{f}_1 s^{\beta-\beta}(\|\mathfrak{z}(\tau_1(s))\| + \dots + \|\mathfrak{z}(\tau_r(s))\|) \\ &+\Upsilon_0\mathfrak{g}_1 s^{\beta-\beta}(\|\mathfrak{z}(\delta_1(s))\| + \dots + \|\mathfrak{z}(\delta_\kappa(s))\|)\Big].\end{aligned} \tag{5}$$

Taking Laplace inverse transformations on both sides of (5),

$$\begin{aligned}
\vartheta\|\mathfrak{z}(t)\| &= \Upsilon_0(\|\mathfrak{z}_0\| + \mathfrak{h}_1)E_{\beta,1}(\mu t^\beta) - M(t) * \left[t^{-1}E_{\beta,0}(\mu t^\beta)\right] \\
&\quad + \Upsilon_0\mathfrak{f}_1\left[t^{\beta-1}E_{\beta,\beta}(\mu t^\beta)\right] * [\|\mathfrak{z}(\tau_1(t))\| + \ldots + \|\mathfrak{z}(\tau_r(t))\|] \\
&\quad + \Upsilon_0\mathfrak{g}_1[t^{\beta-1}E_{\beta,\beta}(\mu t^\beta)] * [\|\mathfrak{z}(\delta_1(t))\| + \ldots + \|\mathfrak{z}(\delta_\kappa(t))\|], \\
&\leq \Upsilon_0(\|\mathfrak{z}_0\| + \mathfrak{h}_1)E_{\beta,1}\left(\mu t^\beta\right),
\end{aligned}$$

where * denotes the convolution operator; the terms involving with it are non-negative. Therefore, (3) has been achieved. Hence, from Definition 3, the solution of system (1) is Mittag–Leffler stable. □

In the case of the nonlocal term $\mathfrak{h}(\mathfrak{z}) = 0$, the initial condition of system (1) is reduced to $\mathfrak{z}(0) = \mathfrak{z}_0$, Then, the Mittag–Leffler stability results for this case can be achieved through the following corollary.

Corollary 1. *Let $-A(t, \mathfrak{z}(t))$ generate the bounded resolvent operator $\|R_\mathfrak{z}(t,\Theta)\| \leq \Upsilon e^{N(t-\Theta)}$ with $\Upsilon_0 = \max\|R_\mathfrak{z}(t,\Theta)\|_Y$ for all $0 \leq \Theta \leq t \leq T$, $\mathfrak{z} \in \Omega$, and the conditions (H_1)–(H_3), (H_5) hold. If there exist constants $\mathfrak{f}_1$, $\mathfrak{g}_1$, the mild solution of system (1) satisfies*

$$\|\mathfrak{z}(t)\| \leq (1/\vartheta)\Upsilon_0\|\mathfrak{z}_0\|E_\beta(\mu t^\beta), \quad \forall t \in J,$$

so the system (1) is Mittag–Leffler stable.

In the case $\int_0^t \mathfrak{g}(t, \alpha, \mathfrak{z}(\alpha), \mathfrak{z}(\delta(\alpha)))d\alpha = 0$ in (1), the system is reduced to an impulsive, fractional, nonlocal, quasilinear multi-delayed system of the form

$$\begin{aligned}
D^\beta\mathfrak{z}(t) + A(t, \mathfrak{z}(t))\mathfrak{z}(t) &= \mathfrak{f}(t, \mathfrak{z}(t), \mathfrak{z}(\tau(t))), \\
\mathfrak{z}(0) + \mathfrak{h}(\mathfrak{z}) &= \mathfrak{z}_0, \\
\Delta\mathfrak{z}(t_k) &= \mathfrak{I}_k(\mathfrak{z}(t_k)), \quad k = 1, 2, \ldots, \mathfrak{m},
\end{aligned} \tag{6}$$

where $t \in J$. Then, the stability of (6) can be stated as follows:

Corollary 2. *Let $-A(t, \mathfrak{z}(t))$ generate the bounded resolvent operator $\|R_\mathfrak{z}(t,\Theta)\| \leq \Upsilon e^{N(t-\Theta)}$ with $\Upsilon_0 = \max\|R_\mathfrak{z}(t,\Theta)\|_Y$ for all $0 \leq \Theta \leq t \leq T$, $\mathfrak{z} \in \Omega$, and the conditions (H_1), (H_3)–(H_5) hold. If there exist constants $\mathfrak{f}_1$, $\mathfrak{h}_1$, the mild solution of system (6) satisfies*

$$\|\mathfrak{z}(t)\| \leq (1/\vartheta)\Upsilon_0([\|\mathfrak{z}_0\| + \mathfrak{h}_1)E_\beta\left(\frac{\Upsilon_0\mathfrak{f}_1}{1 - \Upsilon_0\mathfrak{m}\mathfrak{l}}t^\beta\right), \quad \forall t \in J,$$

so the system (6) is Mittag–Leffler stable.

4. Application

Consider the fractional-order, nonlocal, impulsive, integro-differential systems with multiple delays of the form

$$\begin{aligned}
\frac{\partial^\beta\mathfrak{z}(x,t)}{\partial t^\beta} + a(x,t,\mathfrak{z}(x,t))\frac{\partial^2\mathfrak{z}(x,t)}{\partial x^2} &= x\arctan\varphi_p(x,t,\mathfrak{z}) + \int_0^t e^{-\varphi_q(x,s,\mathfrak{z})}ds, \qquad (7) \\
\mathfrak{z}(x,0) + \sum_{k=1}^{\mathfrak{m}} c_k\mathfrak{z}(x,t_k) &= \mathfrak{z}_0(x),\ x \in [0,\pi], \\
\mathfrak{z}(0,t) = \mathfrak{z}(\pi,t) &= 0,\ t \in J, \\
\Delta\mathfrak{z}(t_k,x) &= \frac{\mathfrak{z}(t_k,x)}{2 + \mathfrak{z}(t_k,x)},\ x \in (0,1),\ k = 1,\ldots,\mathfrak{m},
\end{aligned}$$

where $0 < \beta \leq 1$, $0 < t_1 < \ldots < t_m < T$. Let $X = L^2[0,\pi]$, $PC = PC(J, S_\delta)$, $S_\delta = \{y \in L^2[0,\pi]: \|y\| \leq \delta\}$. First, we prove that $-A(t,\mathfrak{z}(t))$ generates the bounded resolvent operator $R_\mathfrak{z}(t,\Theta)$ with the help of the following analysis. Let $a(x,t,\mathfrak{z}(x,t))$ be continuous; define $A(t,.) : X \longrightarrow X$ by $(A(t,.)w)(x) = a(x,t,\mathfrak{z}(x,t))w''$ with domain $D(A(t,.)) = \{w \in X\colon w, w'$ being absolutely continuous, $w'' \in X; w(0) = w(\pi) = 0\}$ is dense in the X and independent of t. Then,

$$A(t,\mathfrak{z})w = \sum_{n=1}^{\infty} n^2(w,w_n), w \in D(A), \tag{8}$$

where $(.,.)$ is the inner product in $L^2[0,\pi]$, $w_n = Z_n \circ \mathfrak{z}$ is the orthogonal set of eigenvectors in $A(t,\mathfrak{z})$ and $Z_n(t,s) = \sqrt{\frac{2}{\pi}} \sin n(t-s)^\beta$, $0 < \beta \leq 1$, $0 \leq s \leq t \leq a$, $n = 1,2,\ldots$

Then, the operator $[A(t,.) + \lambda^\beta I]^{-1}$ exits in $L(X)$ for any λ with $\mathrm{Re}\lambda \leq 0$ and

$$\|[A(t,.) + \lambda^\beta I]^{-1}\| \leq \frac{C_\alpha}{|\lambda| + 1}, \ t \in J. \tag{9}$$

Additionally, there exist constants $\nu \in (0,1]$ and C_β such that

$$\|[A(t_1,.) - A(t_2,.)]A^{-1}(s,.)\| \leq C_\beta |t_1 - t_2|^\eta, \ t_1, t_2, s \in J. \tag{10}$$

Under the conditions (8)–(10), each operator $-A(s,.)$, $s \in J$ generates an evolution operator $\exp(-t^\alpha A(s,.))$ for $t > 0$, and there exists a constant C_α such that

$$\|A^n(s,.)\exp(-t^\beta A(s,.))\| \leq \frac{C_\beta}{t^n}, \quad \forall\, n = 0,1,\ t > 0,\ s \in J.$$

Therefore, it can be concluded that the evolution operator of the $(\beta,\mathfrak{z})$ resolvent family has the form

$$R_{(\beta,\mathfrak{z})}(t,s)w = \sum_{n=1}^{\infty} \exp[-n^2(t-s)^\beta](w,w_n)w_n, \ w \in X.$$

From (7), the functions $\mathfrak{f}(\cdot)$, $\mathfrak{g}(\cdot)$ are given by $\mathfrak{f}(t,\mathfrak{z}(\beta(t))) = x\arctan \varphi_p(x,t,\mathfrak{z})$ and $\mathfrak{g}(t,s,\mathfrak{z}(\gamma(t))) = e^{-\varphi_q(x,s,\mathfrak{z})}$, which satisfies the assumptions (H_1)–(H_3) for $\varphi_\eta(x,s,\mathfrak{z}) = (\mathfrak{z}(x,\sin t), \mathfrak{z}(x,(\sin t)/2), \ldots, \mathfrak{z}(x,(\sin t)/\eta))$ and $\beta_\tau(t) = \gamma_\tau(t) = (\sin t)/\tau$, $\tau = 1,\ldots,\eta$, $\eta = \max(r,k)$.

Additionally, from the nonlocal (function) initial condition, $\mathfrak{h}(\mathfrak{z}(.,t)) = \sum_{k=1}^{\mathfrak{m}} c_k \mathfrak{z}(.,t_k)$ will satisfy Assumption (H_4) with $\sum_{k=1}^{\mathfrak{m}} c_k = \mathfrak{h}_1$. Further, the at impulse moments $\mathfrak{I}_k(\mathfrak{z}(t_k)) = \frac{\mathfrak{z}(t_k,x)}{2+\mathfrak{z}(t_k,x)}$ satisfies Assumption (H_5) with $\mathfrak{l} = \frac{1}{2}$.

Thus, Assumptions (H_1)–(H_5) (all) are satisfied, and it is possible to choose the constants in Theorem 2, which satisfy the required stability condition (3). Hence, by Definition 3, the considered system (7) is MLS on J.

5. Conclusions

The Mittag–Leffler stability results for a class of fractional-order, quasilinear, impulsive, integro-differential systems with multiple delays has been investigated. Based on the contraction mapping principle, the existence and uniqueness of a solution for the FOS was achieved. Then, novel conditions for MLS of the considered system were derived by using well known mathematical techniques, and further, some corollaries were proposed for the cases of initial conditions without a nonlocal term and an FOS in the absence of an integro-differential part. At last, the presented results were verified with an example, which illustrated the applications.

Author Contributions: All authors contributed equally to this article. All authors have read and agreed to the published version of the manuscript.

Funding: This research received no external funding.

Conflicts of Interest: The authors declare no conflict of interest.

References

1. Kilbas, A.A.; Srivastava, H.M.; Trujillo, J.J. *Theory and Applications of Fractional Differential Equations*; Elsevier: Amsterdam, The Netherlands, 2006.
2. Lakshmikantham, V. Theory of fractional functional differential equations. *Nonlinear Anal. Theory Methods Appl.* **2008**, *69*, 3337–3343. [CrossRef]
3. Podlubny, I. Fractional Differential Equation. *Math. Sci. Eng.* **1999**, *198*, 1–340.
4. Koeller, R.C. Application of fractional calculus to the theory of viscoelasticity. *J. Appl. Mech.* **1984**, *51*, 299–307. [CrossRef]
5. Akgun, R. Fractional order mixed difference operator and its applications in angular approximation. *Hacet. J. Math. Stat.* **2020**, *49*, 1594–1610. [CrossRef]
6. Aouiti, C.; Cao, J.; Jallouli, H.; Huang, C. Finite-time stabilization for fractional-order inertialneural networks with time-varying delays. *Nonlinear Anal. Model. Control* **2022**, *27*, 1–18. [CrossRef]
7. Debnath, L. Recent applications of fractional calculus to science and engineering. *Int. J. Math. Math. Sci.* **2003**, *54*, 3413–3442. [CrossRef]
8. Laskin, N. Fractional market dynamics. *Phys. A* **2000**, *287*, 482–492. [CrossRef]
9. Lundstrom, B.; Higgs, M.; Spain, W.; Fairhall, A. Fractional differentiation by neocortical pyramidal neurons. *Nat. Neurosci.* **2008**, *11*, 1335–1342. [CrossRef]
10. Debbouche, A.; Baleanu, D. Controllability of fractional evolution nonlocal impulsive quasilinear delay integro-differential systems. *Comput. Math. Appl.* **2011**, *62*, 1442–1450. [CrossRef]
11. Balachandran, K.; Park, J.Y.; Anandhi, E.R. Local controllability of quasilinear integrodifferential evolution systems in Banach spaces. *J. Math. Anal. Appl.* **2001**, *258*, 309–319. [CrossRef]
12. Debbouche, A. Fractional nonlocal impulsive quasilinear multi-delay integro-differential systems. *Adv. Differ. Equ.* **2011**, *2011*, art. no. 5 . [CrossRef]
13. Feckan, M.; Zhou, Y.; Wang, J. On the concept and existence of solution for impulsive fractional differential equations. *Commun. Nonlinear Sci. Numer. Simul.* **2012**, *17*, 3050–3060. [CrossRef]
14. Ugur, S.; Mufit, S. Some analysis on a fractional differential equation with a right-hand side which has a discontinuity at zero. *Hacet. J. Math. Stat.* **2020**, *49*, 1718–1725.
15. Zhao, D.; Mao, J. New controllability results of fractional nonlocal semilinear evolution systems with finite delay. *Complexity* **2020**, *2020*. [CrossRef]
16. Gou, T.L.; Jiang, W. Impulsive fractional functional differential equations. *Comput. Math. Appl.* **2012**, *64*, 3414–3424.
17. Lakshmikantham, V.; Bainov, D.D.; Simeonov, P.S. *Theory of Impulsive Differential Equations*; World Scientific: Singapore, 1989.
18. Fang, T.; Sun, J. Stability analysis of complex-valued impulsive system. *IET Control Theory Appl.* **2013**, *7*, 1152–1159. [CrossRef]
19. Wang, Q.; Lu, D.; Fang, Y. Stability analysis of impulsive fractional differential systems with delay. *Appl. Math. Lett.* **2015**, *40*, 1–6. [CrossRef]
20. Zhang, Y.; Wang, J. Existence and finite-time stability results for impulsive fractional differential equations with maxima. *J. Appl. Math. Comput.* **2016**, *51*, 67–79. [CrossRef]
21. Wang, J.; Zhou, Y.; Feckan, M. Nonlinear impulsive problems for fractional differential equations and Ulam stability. *Comput. Math. Appl.* **2012**, *64*, 3389–3405. [CrossRef]
22. Stamova, I.M. Mittag–Leffler stability of impulsive differential equations of fractional order. *Q. Appl. Math.* **2015**, *73*, 525–535. [CrossRef]
23. Yang, X.; Li, C.; Huang, T.; Song, Q. Mittag–Leffler stability analysis of nonlinear fractional-order systems with impulses. *Appl. Math. Comput.* **2017**, *293*, 416–422. [CrossRef]
24. Agarwal, R.; Hristova, S.; Regan, D.O. Mittag–Leffler stability for impulsive Caputo fractional differential equation. *Differ. Equ. Dyn. Syst.* **2021**, *29*, 689–705. [CrossRef]
25. Li, Y.; Chen, Y.; Podlubny, I.; Cao, Y. Mittag–Leffler stability of fractional order nonlinear dynamic systems. *Automatica* **2009**, *45*, 1965–1969. [CrossRef]
26. Li, H.L.; Jiang, Y.L.; Wang, Z.; Zhang, L.; Teng, Z. Global Mittag–Leffler stability of coupled system of fractional-order differential equations on network. *Appl. Math. Comput.* **2015**, *270*, 269–277. [CrossRef]
27. Li, X.; Liu, S.; Jiang, W.; Zhou, X. Mittag–Leffler stability of nonlinear fractional neutral singular systems. *Commun. Nonlinear Sci. Numer. Stimul.* **2012**, *17*, 3961–3966. [CrossRef]

28. Li, M.; Wang, J. Exploring delayed Mittag–Leffler type matrix functions to study finite time stability of fractional delay differential equations. *Appl. Math. Comput.* **2018**, *324*, 254–265. [CrossRef]
29. Martínez-Fuentes, O.; Martínez-Guerra, R. A novel Mittag–Leffler stable estimator for nonlinear fractional-order systems: a linear quadratic regulator approach. *Nonlinear Dyn.* **2018**, *94*, 1973–1986. [CrossRef]
30. Hammouch, Z.; Yavuz, M.; M; Ozdemir, N. Numerical solutions and synchronization of a variable-order fractional chaotic system. *Math. Model. Numer. Simul. Appl.* **2021**, *1*, 11–23. [CrossRef]
31. He, J.H. Some applications of nonlinear fractional differential equations and their approximations. *Bull. Sci. Technol.* **1999**, *15*, 86–90.
32. Ryabov, Y. E.; Puzenko, A. Damped oscillations in view of the fractional oscillator equation. *Phys. Rev. B* **2002**, *66*, 184201–184208. [CrossRef]
33. Dasbasi, B. Stability analysis of an incommensurate fractional-order SIR model. *Math. Model. Numer. Simul. Appl.* **2021**, *1*, 44–55.
34. Gholami, M.; Ghaziani, R.K.; Eskandari, Z. Three-dimensional fractional system with the stability condition and chaos control. *Math. Model. Numer. Simul. Appl.* **2022**, *2*, 41–47. [CrossRef]
35. Veeresha, P.; Yavuz, M.; Baishya, C. A computational approach for shallow water forced Korteweg–De Vries equation on critical flow over a hole with three fractional operators. *Int. J. Optim. Control Theor. Appl.* **2021**, *11*, 52–67. [CrossRef]
36. Yavuz, M.; Sene, N.; Yildiz, M. Analysis of the influences of parameters in the fractional second-grade fluid dynamics. *Mathematics* **2022**, *10*, 1125. [CrossRef]
37. Arthi, G.; Brindha, N. On finite-time stability of nonlinear fractional-order systems withimpulses and multi-state time delays. *Results Control Optim.* **2021**, *2*, 100010. [CrossRef]
38. Balachandran, K.; Park, J.Y.; Trujillo, J.J. Controllability of nonlinear fractional dynamical systems. *Nonlinear Anal.* **2012**, *75*, 1919–1926. [CrossRef]
39. Li, X.; Liu, S.; Jiang, W. q-Mittag–Leffler stability and Lyapunov direct method for differential systems with q-fractional order. *Adv. Differ. Equ.* **2018**, *2018*, 1–9. [CrossRef]
40. Sene, N. Mittag–Leffler input stability of fractional differential equations and its applications. *Am. Inst. Math. Sci.* **2020**, *13*, 867–880. [CrossRef]
41. Li, Y.; Chen, Y.; Podulbny, I. Stability of fractional-order nonlinear dynamic system: Lyapunov direct method and generalized Mittag–Leffler stability. *Comput. Math. Appl.* **2010**, *15*, 1810–1821. [CrossRef]

axiomsMDPI

Article

Nonlinear Eigenvalue Problems for the Dirichlet $(p,2)$-Laplacian

Yunru Bai [1], Leszek Gasiński [2,*] and Nikolaos S. Papageorgiou [3]

1 School of Science, Guangxi University of Science and Technology, Liuzhou 545006, China; yunrubai@163.com
2 Department of Mathematics, Pedagogical University of Cracow, Podchorazych 2, 30-084 Cracow, Poland
3 Department of Mathematics, National Technical University, Zografou Campus, 15780 Athens, Greece; npapg@math.ntua.gr
* Correspondence: leszek.gasinski@up.krakow.pl

Abstract: We consider a nonlinear eigenvalue problem driven by the Dirichlet $(p,2)$-Laplacian. The parametric reaction is a Carathéodory function which exhibits $(p-1)$-sublinear growth as $x \to +\infty$ and as $x \to 0^+$. Using variational tools and truncation and comparison techniques, we prove a bifurcation-type theorem describing the "spectrum" as $\lambda > 0$ varies. We also prove the existence of a smallest positive eigenfunction for every eigenvalue. Finally, we indicate how the result can be extended to (p,q)-equations ($q \neq 2$).

Keywords: $(p,2)$ and (p,q)-Laplacians; nonlinear regularity; positive solutions; strong comparison principle; sublinear reaction; bifurcation-type results

1. Introduction

Let $\Omega \subseteq \mathbb{R}^N$ be a bounded domain with C^2-boundary $\partial\Omega$. In this paper, we study the following nonlinear eigenvalue problem for the Dirichlet $(p,2)$-Laplacian

$$(P_\lambda) \qquad \begin{cases} -\Delta_p u(z) - \Delta u(z) = \lambda f(z,u(z)) & \text{in } \Omega, \\ u|_{\partial\Omega} = 0, \ u \geqslant 0, \ \lambda > 0, \ 2 < p. \end{cases}$$

For every $r \in (1,\infty)$ by Δ_r we denote the r-Laplacian differential operator defined by

$$\Delta_r u = \operatorname{div}\left(|Du|^{r-2}Du\right) \quad \forall u \in W_0^{1,p}(\Omega)$$

(Du stands for the gradient of u). When $r = 2$, we have the usual Laplacian denoted by Δ.

In the reaction, $\lambda > 0$ is a parameter and $f(z,x)$ is a Carathéodory function. Such a function is jointly measurable. We assume that for almost all $z \in \Omega$, $f(z,\cdot)$ is $(p-1)$-sublinear as $x \to +\infty$. We are looking for positive solutions as the parameter $\lambda > 0$ varies. Our work complements those by Gasiński and Papageorgiou [1] and Papageorgiou, Rădulescu and Repovš [2] where the reaction is $(p-1)$-superlinear in $x \in \mathbb{R}$. Moreover, in the aforementioned works, the equation is driven by the p-Laplacian differential operator which is homogeneous, a property used by the authors in the proof of their results. In contrast, here, the $(p,2)$-Laplace differential operator is not homogeneous.

We mention that equations driven by the sum of two differential operators of different structures (such as $(p,2)$-equations) arise in the mathematical models of many physical processes. We refer to the survey papers of Marano and Mosconi [3], Rădulescu [4] and the references therein.

2. Mathematical Background—Hypotheses

The main spaces in the analysis of problem (P_λ) are the Sobolev space $W_0^{1,p}(\Omega)$ and the Banach space

$$C_0^1(\overline{\Omega}) = \{u \in C^1(\overline{\Omega}) : u|_{\partial\Omega} = 0\}.$$

Citation: Bai, Y.; Gasiński, L.; Papageorgiou, N.S. Nonlinear Eigenvalue Problems for the Dirichlet $(p,2)$-Laplacian. *Axioms* **2022**, *11*, 58. https://doi.org/10.3390/axioms11020058

Academic Editor: Chris Goodrich

Received: 7 January 2022
Accepted: 28 January 2022
Published: 30 January 2022

By $\|\cdot\|$, we denote the norm of the Sobolev space $W_0^{1,p}(\Omega)$. On account of the Poincaré inequality, we have

$$\|u\| = \|Du\|_p \quad \forall u \in W_0^{1,p}(\Omega).$$

The Banach space $C_0^1(\overline{\Omega})$ is an ordered Banach space with positive (order) cone

$$C_+ = \{u \in C_0^1(\overline{\Omega}) : u(z) \geqslant 0 \text{ for all } z \in \overline{\Omega}\}.$$

This cone has a nonempty interior given by

$$\text{int}C_+ = \{u \in C_+ : u(z) > 0 \text{ for all } z \in \Omega, \ \frac{\partial u}{\partial n}|_{\partial\Omega} < 0\},$$

with n being the outward unit normal on $\partial\Omega$ and $\frac{\partial u}{\partial n} = (Du, n)_{\mathbb{R}^N}$.

We know that if $r \in (1, +\infty)$, then $W_0^{1,r}(\Omega)^* = W^{-1,r'}(\Omega)$ $(\frac{1}{r} + \frac{1}{r'} = 1)$. Let $A_r \colon W_0^{1,r}(\Omega) \longrightarrow W^{-1,r'}(\Omega)$ by the operator defined by

$$\langle A_r(u), h\rangle = \int_\Omega |Du|^{r-2}(Du, Dh)_{\mathbb{R}^N}\, dz \quad \text{for all } u, h \in W_0^{1,r}(\Omega).$$

The next proposition gathers the main properties of this operator (see Gasiński and Papageorgiou [5]).

Proposition 1. *The operator $A_r \colon W_0^{1,r}(\Omega) \longrightarrow W^{-1,r'}(\Omega)$ is bounded (that is, maps bounded sets to bounded sets), continuous, strictly monotone (thus maximal monotone too) and of type $(S)_+$, that is, A_r has the following property:*
if $u_n \longrightarrow u$ weakly in $W_0^{1,r}(\Omega)$ and $\limsup_{n\to\infty}\langle A_r(u_n), u_n - u\rangle \leqslant 0$, then $u_n \longrightarrow u$ in $W_0^{1,r}(\Omega)$.

If $r = 2$, then we write $A_2 = A \in \mathcal{L}(H_0^1(\Omega), H^{-1}(\Omega))$.

The Dirichlet r-Laplace differential operator has a principal eigenvalue denoted by $\widehat{\lambda}_1(r)$. Therefore, if we consider the nonlinear eigenvalue problem

$$\begin{cases} -\Delta_r u(z) = \widehat{\lambda}|u(z)|^{r-2}u(z) & \text{in } \Omega, \\ u|_{\partial\Omega} = 0, \end{cases}$$

then this problem has a smallest eigenvalue $\widehat{\lambda}_1(r) > 0$ which is isolated and simple. It has the following variational characterization:

$$\widehat{\lambda}_1(r) = \inf_{u \in W_0^{1,r}(\Omega), u \neq 0} \frac{\|Du\|_r^r}{\|u\|_r^r}. \tag{1}$$

For $x \in \mathbb{R}$, we define $x^\pm = \max\{\pm x, 0\}$. Then, for $u \in W_0^{1,p}(\Omega)$, we set $u^\pm(z) = u(z)^\pm$ for all $z \in \Omega$. We know that

$$u^\pm \in W_0^{1,p}(\Omega), \quad u = u^+ = u^-, \quad |u| = u^+ + u^-.$$

A set $S \subseteq W_0^{1,p}(\Omega)$ is said to be "downward directed", if given $u_1, u_2 \in S$, we can find $u \in S$ such that $u \leqslant u_1$, $u \leqslant u_2$.

If $u, v \colon \Omega \longrightarrow \mathbb{R}$ are measurable functions, then we write $u \prec v$ if and only if for all compact sets $K \subseteq \Omega$, we have

$$0 < c_K \leqslant v(z) - u(z) \quad \text{for a.a. } z \in K.$$

Evidently if $u, v \in C(\overline{\Omega})$ and $u(z) < v(z)$ for all $z \in \Omega$, then $u \prec v$.

Now, we introduce the hypotheses on the reaction $f(z, x)$.

H: $f\colon \Omega \times \mathbb{R} \longrightarrow \mathbb{R}$ is a Carathéodory function such that for a.a. $z \in \Omega$, $f(z,0) = 0$, $f(z,x) > 0$ for all $x > 0$ and

(i) For every $\varrho > 0$, there exists $a_\varrho \in L^\infty(\Omega)$ such that

$$f(z,x) \leqslant a_\varrho(z) \quad \text{for a.a. } z \in \Omega, \text{ all } 0 \leqslant x \leqslant \varrho;$$

(ii) $\lim_{x\to+\infty} \frac{f(z,x)}{x^{p-1}} = 0$ uniformly for a.a. $z \in \Omega$;

(iii) $\lim_{x\to 0^+} \frac{f(z,x)}{x^{p-1}} = 0$ uniformly for a.a. $z \in \Omega$;

(iv) for every $\varrho > 0$, there exists s$\widehat{\xi}_\varrho > 0$ such that for a.a. $z \in \Omega$, the function $x \longmapsto f(z,x) + \widehat{\xi}_\varrho x^{p-1}$ is nondecreasing on $[0,\varrho]$.

Remark 1. *Since we look for positive solutions and the above hypotheses concern the positive semiaxis $\mathbb{R}_+ = [0,+\infty)$, without any loss of generality we may assume that*

$$f(z,x) = 0 \quad \text{for a.a. } z \in \Omega, \text{ all } x \leqslant 0. \tag{2}$$

Hypothesis $H(ii)$ implies that $f(z,\cdot)$ is $(p-1)$-sublinear as $x \to +\infty$ while hypothesis $H(iii)$ says that $f(z,\cdot)$ is sublinear near 0^+. Hypothesis $H(iv)$ is essentially a one-sided local Lipschitz condition.

3. Positive Solutions

We introduce the following two sets:

$$\begin{aligned} \mathcal{L} &= \{\lambda > 0: \text{ problem } (P_\lambda) \text{ admits a positive solution}\}; \\ S_\lambda &= \text{the set of positive solutions for problem } (P_\lambda). \end{aligned}$$

We also set

$$\lambda_* = \inf \mathcal{L}.$$

First, we establish the existence of admissible parameters (eigenvalues) and determine the regularity properties of the corresponding solutions (eigenfunctions).

Proposition 2. *If hypotheses H hold, then $\mathcal{L} \neq \emptyset$ and $S_\lambda \subseteq \operatorname{int}C_+$ for all $\lambda > 0$.*

Proof. For every $\lambda > 0$, let $\varphi_\lambda\colon W_0^{1,p}(\Omega) \longrightarrow \mathbb{R}$ be the C^1-functional defined by

$$\varphi_\lambda(u) = \frac{1}{p}\|Du\|_p^p + \frac{1}{2}\|Du\|_2^2 - \int_\Omega F(z,u^+)\,dz \quad \forall u \in W_0^{1,p}(\Omega),$$

with $F(z,x) = \int_0^x f(z,s)\,ds$. From hypotheses $H(i),(ii)$, we see that given $\varepsilon > 0$, we can find $c_\varepsilon > 0$ such that

$$0 \leqslant F(z,x) \leqslant \frac{\varepsilon}{p}x^p + c_\varepsilon \quad \text{for a.a. } z \in \Omega, \text{ all } x \geqslant 0. \tag{3}$$

For $u \in W_0^{1,p}(\Omega)$, using (3) we have

$$\varphi_\lambda(u) \geqslant \frac{1}{p}\Big(\|Du\|_p^p - \lambda\varepsilon\|u\|_p^p\Big) + \frac{1}{2}\|Du\|_p^p - \lambda c_\varepsilon|\Omega|_N,$$

with $|\cdot|_N$ being the Lebesgue measure on $\mathbb{R}^N$. Using (1) with $r = p$, we obtain

$$\varphi_\lambda(u) \geqslant \frac{1}{p}\left(1 - \frac{\lambda\varepsilon}{\widehat{\lambda}_p(p)}\right)\|Du\|_p^p - \lambda c_\varepsilon|\Omega|_N.$$

Choosing $\varepsilon \in \left(0, \frac{\widehat{\lambda}_1(p)}{\lambda}\right)$, we infer that

$$\varphi_\lambda(u) \geqslant c_1 \|u\|^p - \lambda c_\varepsilon |\Omega|_N,$$

for some $c_1 > 0$ and thus φ_λ is coercive.

Additionally, using the Sobolev imbedding theorem, we see that φ_λ is sequentially weakly lower semicontinuous. So, by the Weierstrass–Tonelli theorem, we can find $u_0 \in W_0^{1,p}(\Omega)$ such that

$$\varphi_\lambda(u_0) = \min_{u \in W_0^{1,p}(\Omega)} \varphi_\lambda(u). \tag{4}$$

On account of the strict positivity of $f(z,\cdot)$, if $\overline{u} \in \operatorname{int}C_+$, then

$$\int_\Omega F(z,\overline{u})\,dz > 0. \tag{5}$$

Then, we have

$$\begin{aligned} \varphi_\lambda(\overline{u}) &= \frac{1}{p}\|D\overline{u}\|_p^p + \frac{1}{2}\|D\overline{u}\|_2^2 - \lambda \int_\Omega F(z,\overline{u})\,dz \\ &= c_2 - \lambda \int_\Omega F(z,\overline{u})\,dz, \end{aligned}$$

with $c_2 = c_2(\overline{u}) > 0$. From (5) and by choosing $\lambda > 0$ big, we have

$$\varphi_\lambda(\overline{u}) < 0,$$

so

$$\varphi_\lambda(u_0) < 0 = \varphi_\lambda(0)$$

(see (4)) and thus

$$u_0 \neq 0.$$

From (4), we have

$$\varphi'_\lambda(u_0) = 0,$$

so

$$\langle A_p(u_0), h\rangle + \langle A(u_0), h\rangle = \lambda \int_\Omega f(z,u_0^+)h\,dz \quad \forall h \in W_0^{1,p}(\Omega). \tag{6}$$

In (6), we choose $h = -u_0^- \in W_0^{1,p}(\Omega)$. We obtain

$$\|Du_0^-\|_p \leqslant 0,$$

thus $u_0 \geqslant 0$ and $u_0 \neq 0$.

Then, from (6), we have

$$\begin{cases} -\Delta_p u_0(z) - \Delta u_0(z) = \lambda f(z,u_0(z)) & \text{in } \Omega, \\ u_0|_{\partial\Omega} = 0, \end{cases} \tag{7}$$

for $\lambda > 0$ big and so $\mathcal{L} \neq \emptyset$.

From Theorem 7.1 of Ladyzhenskaya and Ural'tseva [6], we have that $u_0 \in L^\infty(\Omega)$. Then, the nonlinear regularity theory of Lieberman [7] implies that $u_0 \in C_+ \setminus \{0\}$. Let $\varrho = \|u_0\|_\infty$ and let $\widehat{\xi}_\varrho > 0$ be as postulated by hypothesis $H(iv)$. From (7), we have

$$-\Delta_p u_0(z) - \Delta u_0(z) + \lambda\widehat{\xi}_\varrho u_0(z)^{p-1} \geqslant 0 \quad \text{in } \Omega,$$

so
$$\Delta_p u_0(z) + \Delta u_0(z) \leqslant \lambda \widehat{\xi}_\varrho u_0(z)^{p-1} \quad \text{in } \Omega,$$

and thus $u_0 \in \text{int}C_+$ (see Pucci and Serrin [8] (pp. 111, 120)). Therefore, we conclude that $S_\lambda \subseteq \text{int}C_+$ for all $\lambda > 0$. $\square$

Next, we show that $\mathcal{L}$ is connected (more precisely, an upper half-line).

Proposition 3. *If hypotheses H hold, $\lambda \in \mathcal{L}$ and $\vartheta > \lambda$, then $\vartheta \in \mathcal{L}$.*

Proof. Since $\lambda \in \mathcal{L}$, we can find $u_\lambda \in S_\lambda \in \text{int}C_+$ (see Proposition 2). We introduce the Carathéodory function $k(z,x)$ defined by

$$k(z,x) = \begin{cases} f(z,u_\lambda(z)) & \text{if } x \leqslant u_\lambda(z) \\ f(z,x) & \text{if } u_\lambda(z) < x. \end{cases} \tag{8}$$

We set
$$K(z,x) = \int_0^x k(z,s)\,ds$$

and consider the C^1-functional $\psi_\vartheta\colon W_0^{1,p}(\Omega) \longrightarrow \mathbb{R}$ defined by

$$\psi_\vartheta(u) = \frac{1}{p}\|Du\|_p^p + \frac{1}{2}\|Du\|_2^2 - \int_\Omega \vartheta K(z,u)\,dz \quad \forall u \in W_0^{1,p}(\Omega).$$

Note that (8) and hypotheses $H(i), (ii)$ imply that, given $\varepsilon > 0$, we can find $\widehat{c}_\varepsilon > 0$ such that
$$K(z,x) \leqslant \frac{\varepsilon}{p}x^p + \widehat{c}_\varepsilon \quad \text{for a.a. } z \in \Omega, \text{ all } x \in \mathbb{R}. \tag{9}$$

Using (9) and choosing $\varepsilon > 0$ small, as in the proof of Proposition 2, we show that ψ_ϑ is coercive. In addition, it is sequentially weakly lower semicontinuous. Therefore, we can find $u_\vartheta \in W_0^{1,p}(\Omega)$ such that

$$\psi_\vartheta(u_\vartheta) = \min_{u \in W_0^{1,p}(\Omega)} \psi_\vartheta(u),$$

so $\psi'_\vartheta(u_\vartheta) = 0$ and thus

$$\langle A_p(u_\vartheta), h\rangle + \langle A(u_\vartheta), h\rangle = \int_\Omega \vartheta k(z,u_\vartheta)h\,dz \quad \forall h \in W_0^{1,p}(\Omega). \tag{10}$$

In (10), we choose $h = (u_\lambda - u_\vartheta)^+ \in W_0^{1,p}(\Omega)$. Then, using (8), we have

$$\begin{aligned} & \langle A_p(u_\vartheta), (u_\lambda - u_\vartheta)^+\rangle + \langle A(u_\vartheta), (u_\lambda - u_\vartheta)^+\rangle \\ = & \int_\Omega \vartheta f(z,u_\lambda)(u_\lambda - u_\vartheta)^+\,dz \\ \geqslant & \int_\Omega \lambda f(z,u_\lambda)(u_\lambda - u_\vartheta)^+\,dz \\ = & \langle A_p(u_\lambda), (u_\lambda - u_\vartheta)^+\rangle + \langle A(u_\lambda), (u_\lambda - u_\vartheta)^+\rangle \end{aligned}$$

since $f \geqslant 0$ and $u_\lambda \in S_\lambda$. Thus,
$$u_\lambda \leqslant u_\vartheta \tag{11}$$

(see Proposition 1).

From (8), (10) and (11), we infer that

$$\begin{cases} -\Delta_p u_\vartheta(z) - \Delta u_\vartheta(z) = \vartheta f(z,u_\vartheta(z)) & \text{in } \Omega, \\ u_\vartheta|_{\partial\Omega} = 0, \end{cases}$$

so $u_\vartheta \in S_\vartheta \subseteq C_+$ and thus $\vartheta \in \mathcal{L}$. $\square$

A byproduct of the above proof is the following corollary.

Corollary 1. *If hypotheses H hold, $\lambda \in \mathcal{L}$ and $u_\lambda \in S_\lambda \subseteq \mathrm{int}C_+$ and $\vartheta > \lambda$, then $\vartheta \in \mathcal{L}$ and we can find $u_\vartheta \in S_\vartheta \subseteq \mathrm{int}C_+$ such that $u_\lambda \leqslant u_\vartheta$.*

We can improve this corollary using the strong comparison principle of Gasiński and Papageorgiou [1] (Proposition 3.2).

Proposition 4. *If hypotheses H hold, $\lambda \in \mathcal{L}$ and $u_\lambda \in S_\lambda \subseteq \mathrm{int}C_+$ and $\vartheta > \lambda$, then $\vartheta \in \mathcal{L}$ and we can find $u_\vartheta \in S_\vartheta \subseteq \mathrm{int}C_+$ such that $u_\vartheta - u_\lambda \in \mathrm{int}C_+$.*

Proof. From Corollary 1, we already know that $\vartheta \in \mathcal{L}$ and there exists $u_\vartheta \in S_\vartheta \subseteq \mathrm{int}C_+$ such that

$$u_\lambda \leqslant u_\vartheta, \quad u_\lambda \neq u_\vartheta. \tag{12}$$

Consider the function $a\colon \mathbb{R}^N \longrightarrow \mathbb{R}^N$ defined by

$$a(y) = |y|^{p-2}y + y \quad \forall y \in \mathbb{R}^N.$$

Evidently, $a \in C^1(\mathbb{R}^N;\mathbb{R}^N)$ (recall that $2 < p$) and we have

$$\nabla a(y) = |y|^{p-2}\left(\mathrm{id} + (p-2)\frac{y \otimes y}{|y|^2}\right) + \mathrm{id} \quad \forall y \neq 0,$$

so

$$(\nabla a(y), \xi, \xi)_{\mathbb{R}^N} \geqslant |\xi|^2 \quad \forall y, \xi \in \mathbb{R}^N.$$

Then, the tangency principle of Pucci and Serrin [8] (Theorem 2.5.2, p. 35) implies that

$$u_\lambda(z) < u_\vartheta(z) \quad \forall z \in \Omega \tag{13}$$

(see (12)). Let $\varrho = \|u_\vartheta\|_\infty$ and let $\widehat{\xi}_\varrho > 0$ be as postulated by hypothesis $H(iv)$. We pick $\widetilde{\xi}_\varrho > \widehat{\xi}_\varrho$ and using (12), hypothesis $H(iv)$ and the facts that $f \geqslant 0$ and $u_\lambda \leqslant u_\vartheta$, we have

$$\begin{aligned}
&-\Delta_p u_\vartheta - \Delta u_\vartheta + \vartheta\widetilde{\xi}_\varrho u_\vartheta^{p-1} \\
= \;& \vartheta(f(z,u_\vartheta) + \widehat{\xi}_\varrho u_\vartheta^{p-1}) + \vartheta(\widetilde{\xi}_\varrho - \widehat{\xi}_\varrho)u_\vartheta^{p-1} \\
\geqslant \;& \vartheta(f(z,u_\lambda) + \widehat{\xi}_\varrho u_\lambda^{p-1}) + \vartheta(\widetilde{\xi}_\varrho - \widehat{\xi}_\varrho)u_\vartheta^{p-1} \\
\geqslant \;& \lambda f(z,u_\lambda) + \vartheta\widetilde{\xi}_\varrho u_\lambda^{p-1} \\
= \;& -\Delta_p u_\lambda - \Delta u_\lambda + \vartheta\widetilde{\xi}_\varrho u_\lambda^{p-1} \quad \text{in } \Omega.
\end{aligned} \tag{14}$$

Note that on account of (13), we have

$$0 \prec \vartheta(\widetilde{\xi}_\varrho - \widehat{\xi}_\varrho)(u_\vartheta^{p-1} - u_\lambda^{p-1}). \tag{15}$$

Then, (14), (15) and Proposition 3.2 of Gasiński and Papageorgiou [1] imply that $u_\vartheta - u_\lambda \in \mathrm{int}C_+$. $\square$

Proposition 5. *If hypotheses H hold, then $\lambda_* > 0$.*

Proof. We argue by contradiction. Suppose that $\lambda_* = 0$. Let $\{\lambda_n\}_{n\in\mathbb{N}} \subseteq \mathcal{L}$ be such that $\lambda_n \to 0^+$ and consider $u_n = u_{\lambda_n} \subseteq \mathrm{int}C_+$ for all $n \in \mathbb{N}$. We have

$$\langle A_p(u_n), h\rangle + \langle A(u_n), h\rangle = \int_\Omega \lambda_n f(z,u_n)h\,dz \quad \forall h \in W_0^{1,p}(\Omega),\ n \in \mathbb{N}. \tag{16}$$

On account of hypotheses $H(i), (ii)$, given $\varepsilon > 0$, we can find $c_\varepsilon > 0$ such that

$$0 \leqslant f(z, u_n(z)) \leqslant \varepsilon u_n(z)^{p-1} + c_\varepsilon \quad \text{for a.a. } z \in \Omega,\ n \in \mathbb{N}. \tag{17}$$

In (16), first, we choose $h = u_n \in W_0^{1,p}(\Omega)$ and then on the right hand side we use (17). We obtain

$$\|Du_n\|_p^p \leqslant \varepsilon \|u_n\|_p^p + c_3 \|u_n\| \quad \forall n \in \mathbb{N},$$

for some $c_3 = c_3(\varepsilon) > 0$, so

$$\left(1 - \frac{\varepsilon}{\widehat{\lambda}_1(p)}\right) \|u_n\|^{p-1} \leqslant c_3 \quad \forall n \in \mathbb{N}$$

(see (1) with $r = p$). Choosing $\varepsilon \in (0, \widehat{\lambda}_1(p))$, we see that the sequence $\{u_n\}_{n \in \mathbb{N}} \subseteq W_0^{1,p}(\Omega)$ is bounded. We may assume that

$$u_n \longrightarrow u_* \quad \text{weakly in } W_0^{1,p}(\Omega) \quad \text{and} \quad u_n \longrightarrow u_* \quad \text{in } L^p(\Omega). \tag{18}$$

In (16), we choose $h = u_n - u_* \in W_0^{1,p}(\Omega)$, pass to the limit as $n \to +\infty$ and use (18). We obtain

$$\lim_{n \to +\infty} \left(\langle A_p(u_n), u_n - u_* \rangle + \langle A(u_n), u_n - u_* \rangle\right) = 0,$$

so, using the monotonicity of A, we obtain

$$\limsup_{n \to +\infty} \left(\langle A_p(u_n), u_n - u_* \rangle + \langle A(u), u_n - u_* \rangle\right) = 0,$$

thus

$$\limsup_{n \to +\infty} \left(\langle A_p(u_n), u_n - u_* \rangle\right) \leqslant 0$$

and hence

$$u_n \longrightarrow u_* \quad \text{in } W_0^{1,p}(\Omega) \tag{19}$$

(see Proposition 1). Hypotheses $H(i), (ii), (iii)$ imply that given $\varepsilon > 0$, we can find $c_4 = c_4(\varepsilon) > 0$ such that

$$0 \leqslant f(z, x) \leqslant \varepsilon x + c_4 x^{p-1} \quad \text{for a.a. } z \in \Omega,\ x \geqslant 0, \tag{20}$$

so

$$0 \leqslant f(z, u_n(z)) \leqslant \varepsilon u_n(z) + c_4 u_n(z)^{p-1} \quad \text{for a.a. } z \in \Omega,\ n \in \mathbb{N},$$

thus the sequence $\{f(\cdot, u_n(\cdot)) \subseteq L^{p'}(\Omega)$ is bounded (see (19) and recall that $p' < 2 < p$). Therefore, if in (16) we pass to the limit as $n \to +\infty$, we obtain

$$\langle A_p(u_*), h \rangle + \langle A(u_*), h \rangle = 0 \quad \forall h \in W_0^{1,p}(\Omega).$$

Choosing $h = u_* \in W_0^{1,p}(\Omega)$, we obtain

$$\|Du_*\|_p \leqslant 0,$$

so

$$u_* = 0. \tag{21}$$

From (19) and the nonlinear regularity theory of Lieberman [7], we know that there exist $\alpha \in (0,1)$ and $c_5 > 0$ such that

$$u_n \in C_0^{1,\alpha}(\overline{\Omega}) \quad \text{and} \quad \|u_n\|_{C_0^{1,\alpha}(\overline{\Omega})} \leqslant c_5 \quad \forall n \in \mathbb{N}. \tag{22}$$

Since the embedding $C_0^{1,\alpha}(\overline{\Omega}) \subseteq C_0^1(\overline{\Omega})$ is compact, from (19), (21) and (22), we infer that

$$u_n \longrightarrow 0 \quad \text{in } C_0^1(\overline{\Omega}) \quad \text{as } n \to +\infty. \tag{23}$$

Let $y_n = \frac{u_n}{\|u_n\|_{1,2}}$, for $n \in \mathbb{N}$, with $\|\cdot\|_{1,2}$ denoting the norm of $H_0^1(\Omega)$. We have

$$\|y_n\|_{1,2} = 0, \quad y_n \geqslant 0 \quad \forall n \in \mathbb{N}.$$

We may assume that

$$y_n \longrightarrow y \quad \text{weakly in } H_0^1(\Omega), \quad y_n \longrightarrow y \quad \text{in } L^2(\Omega), \quad y \geqslant 0. \tag{24}$$

From (16), we have

$$\|u_n\|_{1,2}^{p-2}\langle A_p(y_n), h\rangle + \langle A(y_n), h\rangle = \lambda_n \int_\Omega \frac{f(z,u_n)}{\|u_n\|_{1,2}} h\,dz \quad \forall h \in W_0^{1,p}(\Omega). \tag{25}$$

On account of (20), we have

$$0 \leqslant \frac{f(z,u_n(z))}{\|u_n\|_{1,2}} \leqslant \varepsilon y_n(z) + u_n(z)^{p-2} y_n(z) \leqslant c_6 y_n(z) \quad \text{for a.a. } z \in \Omega,\ n \in \mathbb{N},$$

for some $c_6 > 0$ and thus

$$\text{the sequence } \left\{\frac{f(\cdot,u_n(\cdot))}{\|u_n\|}\right\}_{n\in\mathbb{N}} \subseteq L^p(\Omega) \text{ is bounded} \tag{26}$$

(recall that, if $2 < p$, then $p' < 2$). Therefore, if in (25) we pass to the limit as $n \to +\infty$ and use (23), (24) and (26), we obtain

$$\langle A(y), h\rangle \leqslant 0 \quad \forall h \in W_0^{1,p}(\Omega),$$

so $y = 0$ and hence $\|Dy_n\|_2 \longrightarrow 0$ and $n \to +\infty$ (see (25)), a contradiction since $\|y_n\|_{1,2} = 1$ for all $n \in \mathbb{N}$. Therefore, we conclude that $\lambda_* > 0$. □

Next, we prove a multiplicity result when $\lambda > \lambda_*$.

Proposition 6. *If hypotheses H hold and $\lambda > \lambda_*$, then problem (P_λ) has at least two positive solutions*

$$u_0, \widehat{u} \in \operatorname{int}C_+, \quad u_0 \neq \widehat{u}.$$

Proof. Let $\mu \in (\lambda_*, \lambda)$. We have $\mu, \lambda \in \mathcal{L}$ and then, according to Proposition 4, we can find $u_0 \in S_\lambda \subseteq \operatorname{int}C_+$ and $u_\mu \in S_\mu \subseteq \operatorname{int}C_+$ such that

$$u_0 - u_\mu \in \operatorname{int}C_+. \tag{27}$$

We truncate $f(z,\cdot)$ from below at $u_\mu(z)$ and introduce the Carathéodory function $e(z,x)$ defined by

$$e(z,x) = \begin{cases} f(z,u_\mu(z)) & \text{if } x \leqslant u_\mu(z), \\ f(z,x) & \text{if } u_\mu(z) < x. \end{cases} \tag{28}$$

We set

$$E(z,x) = \int_0^x e(z,s)\,ds$$

and consider the C^1-functional $\widehat{\varphi}_\lambda : W_0^{1,p}(\Omega) \longrightarrow \mathbb{R}$ defined by

$$\widehat{\varphi}_\lambda(u) = \frac{1}{p}\|Du\|_p^p + \frac{1}{2}\|Du\|_2^2 - \int_\Omega \lambda E(z,u)\,dz \quad \forall u \in W_0^{1,p}(\Omega).$$

Let

$$[u_\mu) = \{u \in W_0^{1,p}(\Omega) : \; u_\mu(z) \leqslant u(z) \text{ for a.a. } z \in \Omega\}.$$

Then, from (28), we see that

$$\widehat{\varphi}_\lambda|_{[u_\mu)} = \varphi_\lambda|_{[u_\mu)} + \xi, \tag{29}$$

with $\xi \in \mathbb{R}$. From the proof of Proposition 2, we know that φ_λ is coercive. Hence φ_λ is coercive. Additionally, φ_λ is sequentially weakly lower semicontinuous. Therefore, we can find $\widehat{u}_0 \in W_0^{1,p}(\Omega)$ such that

$$\widehat{\varphi}_\lambda(\widehat{u}_0) = \min_{u \in W_0^{1,p}(\Omega)} \widehat{\varphi}_\lambda(u), \tag{30}$$

so

$$\widehat{\varphi}'_\lambda(\widehat{u}_0) = 0,$$

and hence

$$\langle A_p(\widehat{u}_0), h\rangle + \langle A(\widehat{u}_0), h\rangle = \int_\Omega \lambda e(z, \widehat{u}_0) h\,dz \quad \forall h \in W_0^{1,p}(\Omega). \tag{31}$$

Choose $h \in (u_\mu - \widehat{u}_0)^+ \in W_0^{1,p}(\Omega)$. Using (28), we have

$$\begin{aligned} & \langle A_p(\widehat{u}_0), (u_\mu - \widehat{u}_0)^+\rangle + \langle A(\widehat{u}_0), (u_\mu - \widehat{u}_0)^+\rangle \\ = & \int_\Omega \lambda f(z, u_\mu)(u_\mu - \widehat{u}_0)^+\,dz \\ \geqslant & \int_\Omega \mu f(z, u_\mu)(u_\mu - \widehat{u}_0)^+\,dz \\ = & \langle A_p(u_\mu), (u_\mu - \widehat{u}_0)^+\rangle + \langle A(u_\mu), (u_\mu - \widehat{u}_0)^+\rangle \end{aligned}$$

(since $f \geqslant 0$, $\mu < \lambda$ and $u_\mu \in S_\mu$), so

$$u_\mu \leqslant \widehat{u}_0$$

(see Proposition 1).

Then, from (28) and (31), we infer that $\widehat{u}_0 \in S_\lambda \subseteq \text{int}C_+$.

If $\widehat{u}_0 \neq u_0$, then this is the second positive solution of (P_λ). Therefore, we assume that

$$\widehat{u}_0 = u_0.$$

From (27), (29) and (30), it follows that

$$u_0 \in \text{int}C_+ \text{ is a local } C_0^1(\overline{\Omega})\text{-minimizer of } \varphi_\lambda$$

and so

$$u_0 \in \text{int}C_+ \text{ is a local } W_0^{1,p}(\Omega)\text{-minimizer of } \varphi_\lambda \tag{32}$$

(see Gasiński and Papageorgiou [9]).

Hypothesis $H(iii)$ implies that given $\varepsilon > 0$, we can find $\delta = \delta(\varepsilon) > 0$ such that

$$F(z,x) \leqslant \frac{\varepsilon}{2}x^2 \quad \text{for a.a. } z \in \Omega, \text{ all } |x| \leqslant \delta \tag{33}$$

(see (2)). Let $u \in C_0^1(\overline{\Omega})$ with $\|u\|_{C_0^1(\overline{\Omega})} \leqslant \delta$. We have

$$\varphi_\lambda(u) \;\geqslant\; \frac{1}{p}\|Du\|_p^p + \frac{1}{2}\|Du\|_2^2 - \frac{\lambda\varepsilon}{2}\|u\|_2^2$$

$$\geqslant \frac{1}{p}\|Du\|_p^p + \frac{1}{2}\left(1 - \frac{\lambda\varepsilon}{\widehat{\lambda}_1(2)}\right)\|Du\|_2^2$$

(see (1) with $r = 2$). Choosing $\varepsilon \in (0, \frac{\widehat{\lambda}_1(2)}{\lambda})$, we obtain

$$\varphi_\lambda(u) \geqslant \frac{1}{p}\|u\|^p \quad \forall u \in C_0^1(\overline{\Omega}),\ \|u\|_{C_0^1(\overline{\Omega})} \leqslant \delta,$$

so

$$u = 0 \text{ is a local } C_0^1(\overline{\Omega})\text{-minimizer of } \varphi_\lambda$$

and thus

$$u = 0 \text{ is a local } W_0^{1,p}(\Omega)\text{-minimizer of } \varphi_\lambda \tag{34}$$

(see Gasiński and Papageorgiou [9]).

We assume that $\varphi_\lambda(0) = 0 \leqslant \varphi_\lambda(u_0)$. The reasoning is similar if the opposite inequality holds, using (34) instead of (32).

We also assume that

$$K_{\varphi_\lambda} = \{u \in W_0^{1,p}(\Omega) :\ \varphi'_\lambda(u) = 0\}$$

(the critical set of φ_λ) is finite. Otherwise, we already have an infinity of distinct positive solutions of (P_λ). On account of (32) and using Theorem 5.7.6 of Papageorgiou, Rădulescu and Repovš [2] (p. 449), we can find $\varrho \in (0,1)$ small such that

$$\varphi_\lambda(0) = 0 \leqslant \varphi_\lambda(u_0) < \inf_{\|u-u_0\|=\varrho} \varphi_\lambda(u) = m_\lambda,\ 0 < \varphi < \|u_0\|. \tag{35}$$

Recall that φ_λ is coercive (see the proof of Proposition 2). Therefore, from Proposition 5.1.15 of Papageorgiou, Rădulescu and Repovš [2] (p. 449), we have that

$$\varphi_\lambda \text{ satisfies the PS-condition.} \tag{36}$$

Then, (35) and (36) permit the use of the mountain pass theorem. Therefore, we can find

$\widehat{u} \in W_0^{1,p}(\Omega)$ such that

$$\varphi'_\lambda(\widehat{u}) = 0 \quad \text{and} \quad m_\lambda \leqslant \varphi_\lambda(\widehat{u}). \tag{37}$$

From (35) and (37), we conclude that

$$\widehat{u} \in S_\lambda \subseteq \text{int}C_+ \quad \text{and} \quad \widehat{u} \neq u_0.$$

□

It remains to be decided what we can say for the critical parameter value λ_*. We show that $\lambda_* > 0$ is admissible too.

Proposition 7. *If hypotheses H hold, then* $\lambda_* \in \mathcal{L}$.

Proof. Let $\{\lambda_n\}_{n\in\mathbb{N}} \subseteq \mathcal{L}$ be such that $\lambda_n \longrightarrow \lambda_*^+$. We can find $u_n \in S_{\lambda_n} \subseteq \text{int}C_+$ such that

$$\langle A_p(u_n), h\rangle + \langle A(u_n), h\rangle = \lambda_n \int_\Omega f(z, u_n) h\, dz \quad \forall h \in W_0^{1,p}(\Omega),\ n \in \mathbb{N}. \tag{38}$$

In (38), we use $h = u_n \in W_0^{1,p}(\Omega)$. Then,

$$\|u_n\|^p \leqslant \lambda_1 \int_\Omega f(z, u_n) u_n\, dz \quad \forall n \in \mathbb{N}. \tag{39}$$

On account of hypotheses $H(i), (ii)$, given $\varepsilon > 0$, we can find $c_\varepsilon > 0$ such that

$$0 \leqslant f(z,x)x \leqslant \varepsilon x^p + c_\varepsilon \quad \text{for a.a. } z \in \Omega, \text{ all } x \geqslant 0. \tag{40}$$

We use (40) in (39) and have

$$\|u_n\|^p \leqslant \lambda_1 \frac{\varepsilon}{\widehat{\lambda}_1(p)} \|u_n\|^p + c_\varepsilon |\Omega|_N$$

(see (1) with $r = p$ and recall that $|\cdot|_N$ is the Lebesgue measure on $\mathbb{R}^N$), so

$$\left(1 - \frac{\lambda_1}{\widehat{\lambda}_1(p)}\varepsilon\right)\|u_n\|^p \leqslant c_\varepsilon |\Omega|_N \quad \forall n \in \mathbb{N}.$$

We choose $\varepsilon \in (0, \frac{\widehat{\lambda}_1(p)}{\lambda_1})$ and infer that the sequence $\{u_n\}_{n\in\mathbb{N}} \subseteq W_0^{1,p}(\Omega)$ is bounded. Therefore, we may assume that

$$u_n \longrightarrow u_* \quad \text{weakly in } W_0^{1,p}(\Omega) \quad \text{and} \quad u_n \longrightarrow u_* \quad \text{in } L^p(\Omega).$$

Then, reasoning as in the proof of Proposition 5 (see the part of the proof after (18)), we show that

$$u_n \longrightarrow u_* \quad \text{in } W_0^{1,p}(\Omega),\ u_* \neq 0.$$

Therefore, if in (38) we pass to the limit as $n \to +\infty$, then

$$\langle A_p(u_*), h\rangle + \langle A(u_*), h\rangle = \lambda_* \int_\Omega f(f, u_*) h \, dz \quad \forall h \in W_0^{1,p}(\Omega),$$

so $u_* \in S_{\lambda_*} \subseteq \mathrm{int}C_+$ and so $\lambda_* \in \mathcal{L}$. □

We have proved that

$$\mathcal{L} = [\lambda_*, \infty).$$

Next, we show that for every $\lambda \in \mathcal{L}$, problem (P_λ) admits a smallest positive solution (minimal positive solution).

Proposition 8. *If hypotheses H hold and $\lambda \in \mathcal{L}$, then problem (P_λ) admits a smallest solution $u_\lambda^* \in S_\lambda \subseteq \mathrm{int}C_+$ (that is, $u_\lambda^* \leqslant u$ for all $u \in S_\lambda$).*

Proof. From Proposition 7 of Papageorgiou, Rădulescu and Repovš [10], we know that S_λ is downward directed. Using Lemma 3.10 of Hu and Papageorgiou [11] (p. 178), we can find a decreasing sequence $\{u_n\}_{n\in\mathbb{N}} \subseteq S_\lambda$ such that

$$\inf_{n\in\mathbb{N}} u_n = \inf S_\lambda.$$

We have

$$\langle A_p(u_n), h\rangle + \langle A(u_n), h\rangle = \int_\Omega \lambda f(z, u_n) h \, dz \quad \forall h \in W_0^{1,p}(\Omega),\ n \in \mathbb{N} \tag{41}$$

and

$$0 \leqslant u_n \leqslant u_1 \quad \forall n \in \mathbb{N}. \tag{42}$$

In (41), we choose $h = u_n \in W_0^{1,p}(\Omega)$ and then use (42) and hypothesis $H(i)$ to establish that $\{u_n\}_{n\in\mathbb{N}} \subseteq W_0^{1,p}(\Omega)$ is bounded. Therefore, we may assume that

$$u_n \longrightarrow u_\lambda^* \quad \text{weakly in } W_0^{1,p}(\Omega) \quad \text{and} \quad u_n \longrightarrow u_\lambda^* \quad \text{in } L^p(\Omega). \tag{43}$$

Then, as before (see the proof of Proposition 5 after (18)), using (43) we obtain

$$u_n \longrightarrow u_\lambda^* \quad \text{in } W_0^{1,p}(\Omega) \quad \text{and} \quad u_\lambda^* \neq 0. \tag{44}$$

If in (41) we pass to the limit as $n \to +\infty$ and use (44), then

$$\langle A_p(u_\lambda^*), h\rangle + \langle A(u_\lambda^*), h\rangle = \int_\Omega \lambda f(z, u_\lambda^*) h\, dz \quad \forall h \in W_0^{1,p}(\Omega),$$

so $u_\lambda^* \in S_\lambda \subseteq \text{int}C_+$, $u_\lambda^* = \inf S_\lambda$. □

The theorem that follows summarizes our findings concerning the changes in the set of positive solutions of (P_λ) as $\lambda > 0$ moves.

Theorem 1. *If hypotheses H hold, then there exists $\lambda_* > 0$ such that*
(a) *for all $\lambda > \lambda_*$ problem (P_λ) has at least two positive solutions $u_0, \widehat{u} \in \text{int}C_+$, $u_0 \neq \widehat{u}$;*
(b) *for $\lambda = \lambda_*$, problem (P_λ) has at least one positive solution $u_* \in \text{int}C_+$;*
(c) *for every $\lambda \in (0, \lambda_*)$ problem (P_λ) has no positive solution;*
(d) *for every $\lambda \in \mathcal{L} = [\lambda_*, \infty)$, problem (P_λ) has a smallest positive solution $u_\lambda^* \in \text{int}C_+$.*

Remark 2. From Proposition 4, we know that the minimal solution map $\widehat{k}\colon \mathcal{L} \longrightarrow C_0^1(\overline{\Omega})$ defined by $\widehat{k}(\lambda) = u_\lambda^*$ is strictly increasing in the sense that

$$\text{if } \lambda_* \leqslant \mu \leqslant \lambda, \text{ then } u_\lambda^* - u_\mu^* \in \text{int}C_+.$$

It is worth mentioning that when the reaction $f(z, \cdot)$ is $(p-1)$-superlinear, then we have the "bifurcation" in $\lambda > 0$, for small values of the parameter (see [1], [2]). Here, $f(z, \cdot)$ is $(p-1)$-sublinear, and the "bifurcation" in $\lambda > 0$ occurs for large values of the parameter.

4. (p,q)-Equations

In this section, we briefly mention the situation for the more general (p,q)-equations, $q \neq 2$. We now deal with the following nonlinear Dirichlet eigenvalue problem:

$$(P_\lambda)' \qquad \left\{ \begin{array}{l} -\Delta_p u(z) - \Delta_q u(z) = \lambda f(z, u(z)) \quad \text{in } \Omega, \\ u|_{\partial\Omega} = 0,\ u \geqslant 0,\ \lambda > 0, 1 < q < p. \end{array} \right.$$

If we strengthen the conditions on $f(z, \cdot)$, we can have a similar "bifurcation-type" result for problem $(P_\lambda)'$.

The new conditions on $f(z,x)$ are the following:
<u>H′:</u> $f\colon \Omega \times \mathbb{R} \longrightarrow \mathbb{R}$ is a Carathéodory function, $f(z,0) = 0$ for a.a. $z \in \Omega$, hypotheses $H'(i), (ii), (iii)$ are the same as the corresponding hypotheses $H(i), (ii), (iii)$ and (iv) for a.a. $z \in \Omega$, $f(z, \cdot)$ is strictly increasing on $\mathbb{R}^+$.

Remark 3. According to hypothesis $H'(iv)$, we have

$$0 < f(z,x) \quad \text{for a.a. } z \in \Omega, \text{ all } x > 0.$$

The function $f(z,x) = a(z)x^{\tau-1}$ for a.a. $z \in \Omega$, all $x \geqslant 0$ with $a \in L^\infty(\Omega)$ and $1 < \tau < q < p$ satisfies hypotheses H'.

For the (p,q)-equation ($q \neq 2$), we cannot use the tangency principle of Pucci and Serrin [8] (p. 35) (see the proof of Proposition 4). Instead, on account of the stronger condition $H'(iv)$, we can use Proposition 3.4 of Gasiński and Papageorgiou [1] (strong comparison principle) and have that $u_\vartheta - u_\lambda \in \text{int}C_+$. Then, all the other results remain valid and so we can have the following bifurcation-type result for problem $(P_\lambda)'$.

Theorem 2. *If hypotheses H' hold, then there exists $\lambda'_* > 0$ such that*
(a) *for all $\lambda > \lambda'_*$, problem $(P_\lambda)'$ has at least two positive solutions $u_0, \hat{u} \in \text{int}C_+$, $u_0 \neq \hat{u}$;*
(b) *for $\lambda = \lambda'_*$, problem $(P_\lambda)'$ has at least one positive solution $u_* \in \text{int}C_+$;*
(c) *for every $\lambda \in (0, \lambda_*)'$, problem $(P_\lambda)'$ has no positive solution;*
(d) *for every $\lambda \in \mathcal{L}' = [\lambda'_*, \infty)$, problem $(P_\lambda)'$ has a smallest positive solution $u^*_\lambda \in \text{int}C_+$.*

Remark 4. *The function $f(z,x)$ defined by*

$$f(z,x) = \begin{cases} a(z)\left((x^+)^{r-1} + (x^+)^{\eta-1}\right) & \text{if} \quad |x| \leqslant 1, \\ a(z)\ln(x^+) & \text{if} \quad 1 < |x|, \end{cases}$$

with $a \in L^\infty(\Omega)$, $p < r < \eta$ satisfies hypotheses H but not hypotheses H'.

Author Contributions: Conceptualization, L.G. and N.S.P.; formal analysis, Y.B. and L.G.; investigation, Y.B., L.G. and N.S.P.; methodology, L.G. and N.S.P.; resources, L.G. and N.S.P.; supervision, N.S.P.; validation, Y.B., L.G. and N.S.P.; visualization, L.G. and N.S.P.; writing—original draft preparation, L.G. and N.S.P.; writing—review and editing, Y.B. and L.G. All authors have read and agreed to the published version of the manuscript.

Funding: This research received no external funding.

Conflicts of Interest: The authors declare no conflict of interest.

References

1. Gasiński, L.; Papageorgiou, N.S. Constant sign and nodal solutions for superlinear double phase problems. *Adv. Calc. Var.* **2021**, *14*, 613–626. [CrossRef]
2. Papageorgiou, N.S.; Rădulescu, V.D.; Repovš, D.D. Positive solutions for nonlinear nonhomogeneous parametric Robin problems. *Forum Math.* **2018**, *30*, 553–580. [CrossRef]
3. Marano, S.A.; Mosconi, S.J.N. Some recent results on the Dirichlet problem for (p,q)-Laplace equations. *Discrete Contin. Dyn. Syst. Ser. S* **2018**, *11*, 279–291. [CrossRef]
4. Rădulescu, V.D. Isotropic and anistropic double-phase problems: Old and new. *Opuscula Math.* **2019**, *39*, 259–279. [CrossRef]
5. Gasiński, L.; Papageorgiou, N.S. *Nonlinear Analysis*; Chapman & Hall/CRC: Boca Raton, FL, USA, 2006.
6. Ladyzhenskaya, O.A.; Ural'tseva, N.N. *Linear and Quasilinear Elliptic Equations*; Academic Press: New York, NY, USA; London, UK, 1968.
7. Lieberman, G.M. The natural generalization of the natural conditions of Ladyzhenskaya and Ural'tseva for elliptic equations. *Comm. Partial. Differ. Equ.* **1991**, *16*, 311–361. [CrossRef]
8. Pucci, P.; Serrin, J. *The Maximum Principle*; Birkhäuser: Basel, Switzerland, 2007.
9. Gasiński, L.; Papageorgiou, N.S. Multiple solutions for nonlinear coercive problems with a nonhomogeneous differential operator and a nonsmooth potential. *Set-Valued Var. Anal.* **2012**, *3*, 417–443. [CrossRef]
10. Papageorgiou, N.S.; Rădulescu, V.D.; Repovš, D.D. Positive solutions for perturbations of the Robin eigenvalue problem plus an indefinite potential. *Discrete Contin. Dyn. Syst.* **2017**, *37*, 2589–2618. [CrossRef]
11. Hu, S.; Papageorgiou, N.S. *Handbook of Multivalued Analysis: Volume I: Theory (Mathematics and Its Applications, 419)*; Kluwer Academic Publishers: Dordrecht, The Netherlands, 1997.

axioms

Article

Hopf Bifurcation Analysis of a Diffusive Nutrient–Phytoplankton Model with Time Delay

Ruizhi Yang, Liye Wang and Dan Jin *

Department of Mathematics, Northeast Forestry University, Harbin 150040, China; yangrz@nefu.edu.cn (R.Y.); wangliye8991@163.com (L.W.)
* Correspondence: jindan720@163.com

Abstract: In this paper, we studied a nutrient–phytoplankton model with time delay and diffusion term. We studied the Turing instability, local stability, and the existence of Hopf bifurcation. Some formulas are obtained to determine the direction of the bifurcation and the stability of periodic solutions by the central manifold theory and normal form method. Finally, we verify the above conclusion through numerical simulation.

Keywords: delay; diffusion; hopf bifurcation; nutrient-phytoplankton model

Citation: Yang, R.; Wang, L.; Jin, D. Hopf Bifurcation Analysis of a Diffusive Nutrient–Phytoplankton Model with Time Delay. *Axioms* **2022**, *11*, 56. https://doi.org/10.3390/axioms11020056

Academic Editors: Shengda Zeng, Stanisław Migórski and Yongjian Liu

Received: 21 December 2021
Accepted: 27 January 2022
Published: 29 January 2022

1. Introduction

One of the most complex and difficult problems in water pollution treatment is the prevention and control of algal bloom. Due to the complexity of the pollution source and the difficulty factor of material removal, it takes a lot of energy, but it is not very effective. Therefore, scientists search for better methods to prevent and cure algal bloom, especially using mathematical models, in order to find reasonable prevention and cure measures [1–7]. In addition, many scholars further study the dynamics of the N-P model by considering factors such as time delay and diffusion [8–12]. M. Rehim et al. studied a nutrient–plankton–zooplankton system with toxic phytoplankton and three delays, and showed the phenomenon of stability switches [8]. Y. Wang and W. Jiang considered a differential algebraic phytoplankton–zooplankton system with delay and harvesting, and indicated that the toxic liberation delay of phytoplankton may affect the stability of the coexisting equilibrium [10]. In particular, Huppert et al. [13] considered the following N-P model

$$\begin{cases} \frac{dN(t)}{dt} = a - bNP - eN, \\ \frac{dP(t)}{dt} = cNP - dP, \end{cases} \tag{1}$$

where N is the nutrient level and P is the density of phytoplankton. a denotes the constant external nutrient inflow. b represents the maximal nutrient uptake rate. c represents the maximal conversion rate of nutrients into phytoplankton. d stands for the per capita mortality rate of phytoplankton. e denotes the per capita loss rate of nutrients. Relevant research work has analyzed the reasonable, deterministic, and empirical relationship between the abundance of toxin-producing phytoplankton and the diversity of plankton communities with large amounts of plankton but no toxins (called nontoxic plankton plants, NTP) [14]. In the case of toxic substances released by toxic phytoplankton (TPP), a simple model of vegetative phytoplankton was proposed and analyzed to understand the dynamic changes of the phenomenon of the seasonal mass reproductive cycle. The presence of chemical and toxic substances helps explain this phenomenon [15–17]. In [18], Chakraborty et al.

considered the effect of toxins produced by toxic phytoplankton on the death of nontoxic phytoplankton, and produced the following equation

$$\begin{cases} \frac{dN}{dt} = a - bNP - eN, \\ \frac{dP}{dt} = cNP - dP - \frac{\theta P^2}{\mu^2+P^2}. \end{cases} \tag{2}$$

where θ is the release rate of toxic chemicals by the TPP population, and μ denotes the half-saturation constant.

Since the spatial distribution of nutrients and phytoplankton is inhomogeneous, there is diffusion. In addition, there is a time delay in the conversion from nutrients to phytoplankton. So, we incorporate reaction diffusion and time delay into the model (2), that is

$$\begin{cases} \frac{\partial N}{\partial t} = d_1 \triangle N + a - bNP - eN, \\ \frac{\partial P}{\partial t} = d_2 \triangle P + cPN(t-\tau) - dP - \frac{\theta P^2}{\mu^2+P^2}, \end{cases} \tag{3}$$

where d_1 and d_2 are diffusion coefficients for N and P, respectively. $\triangle$ is the Laplace operator. This is based on the assumption that the prey and predator are not stationary and will spread randomly . τ is the time delay that occurs for nutrients to be converted to phytoplankton. For analysis convenience, we have denoted

$$h = \frac{b}{a}, \quad s = \frac{e}{a}, \quad \alpha = \frac{d}{c}, \quad \beta = \frac{\theta}{c}.$$

The corresponding problem has the following form

$$\begin{cases} \frac{\partial N}{\partial t} = d_1 \triangle N + a(-hNP - Ns + 1), & x \in (0, l\pi),\ t > 0, \\ \frac{\partial P}{\partial t} = d_2 \triangle P + cP\left(-\alpha + N(t-\tau) - \frac{\beta P}{\mu^2+P^2}\right), & x \in (0, l\pi),\ t > 0, \\ N_x(0,t) = P_x(0,t) = 0, N_x(l\pi,t) = P_x(l\pi,t) = 0, & t > 0, \\ N(x,t) = N_0(x,t) \geq 0, P(x,t) = P_0(x,t) \geq 0, & x \in [0, l\pi], t \in [-\tau, 0]. \end{cases} \tag{4}$$

The content of the paper is arranged as follows. In Section 2, we study the stability and the existence of the Hopf bifurcation. In Section 3, we analyze the property of Hopf bifurcation. In Section 4, we provide a numerical simulation to verify the previous conclusions. Finally, we conclude this paper.

2. Stability Analysis

In [18], Chakraborty et al. studied the existence of equilibria. We cite the following result. The equilibrium points satisfy the following equation

$$\begin{cases} 1 - hNP - sN = 0, \\ -\alpha + N - \frac{\beta P}{\mu^2+P^2} = 0, \end{cases} \tag{5}$$

It can be calculated that trivial equilibrium $\left(\frac{1}{s}, 0\right)$ and interior equilibrium (N_*, P_*), where $N_* = \frac{1}{hP_*+s}$, and P_* is a root of the equation

$$h\alpha P^3 + (h\beta + s\alpha - 1)P^2 + \left(h\alpha\mu^2 + s\alpha\right)P - \mu^2(1 - s\alpha) = 0.$$

We provide the result from [18] as follows.

Lemma 1. *The existence of a positive equilibrium for the model* (4) *can be divided into the following cases.*

(1) *If* $1 - s\alpha \leq 0$, *system* (2) *has no positive equilibrium.*
(2) *If* $0 < 1 - s\alpha \leq h\beta$, *system* (2) *has one unique positive equilibrium.*
(3) *If* $1 - s\alpha > h\beta$, *then system* (2) *has either three or one positive equilibrium.*

In what follows, we always assume that $0 < 1 - s\alpha \leq h\beta$, and we study the stability of problem (4) for (N_*, P_*). Denote

$$N_1(t) = N(\cdot, t) \quad N_2(t) = P(\cdot, t), \quad N = (N_1, N_2)^T,$$

$$X = C([0, l\pi], \mathbb{R}^2), \text{ and } \mathscr{C}_\tau := C([-\tau, 0], X).$$

The linearized system of (4) at (N^*, P^*) is

$$\dot{N} = (\mathbb{D}\Delta + L)N, \tag{6}$$

where

$$\mathbb{D} = \begin{pmatrix} d_1 & 0 \\ 0 & d_2 \end{pmatrix}, \quad \mathrm{dom}(\mathbb{D}\Delta) = \{(N, P)^T : N, P \in C^2([0, l\pi], \mathbb{R}^2), N_x, P_x = 0, x = 0, l\pi\},$$

and $L : \mathscr{C}_\tau \mapsto X$ is defined by

$$L\phi(\cdot) = L_1\phi(\cdot) + L_2\phi(\cdot - \tau),$$

for $\phi = (\phi_1, \phi_2)^T \in \mathscr{C}_\tau$ with

$$L_1 = \begin{pmatrix} -aA & -aB \\ 0 & D \end{pmatrix}, \qquad L_2 = \begin{pmatrix} 0 & 0 \\ \widetilde{C} & 0 \end{pmatrix},$$

$$A = hP_* + s, \quad B = \frac{h}{hP_* + s}, \quad \widetilde{C} = cP_*, \quad D = \frac{c\beta P_*(P_*^2 - \mu^2)}{(\mu^2 + P_*^2)^2}. \tag{7}$$

The characteristic equations are

$$\lambda^2 + \lambda A_n + B_n + C_n e^{-\lambda\tau} = 0, \quad n \in \mathcal{N}_0, \tag{8}$$

where $A_n = (d_1 + d_2)\frac{n^2}{l^2} + aA - D$, $B_n = d_1 d_2 \frac{n^4}{l^4} + (aAd_2 - Dd_1)\frac{n^2}{l^2} - aAD$, $C = aB\widetilde{C}$.

2.1. Non-Delay Model

When $\tau = 0$, the characteristic becomes

$$\lambda^2 - T_n\lambda + D_n = 0, \quad n \in \mathcal{N}_0, \tag{9}$$

where

$$\begin{cases} T_n = -(d_1 + d_2)\frac{n^2}{l^2} + D - aA, \\ D_n = d_1 d_2 \frac{n^4}{l^4} + (aAd_2 - Dd_1)\frac{n^2}{l^2} + a(B\widetilde{C} - AD), \end{cases}$$

and the eigenvalues are given by

$$\lambda_n = \frac{T_n \pm \sqrt{T_n^2 - 4D_n}}{2}, \quad n \in \mathcal{N}_0. \tag{10}$$

Then, make hypothesis

$$a > a_0 := \frac{D}{A}, \qquad B\widetilde{C} - AD > 0. \tag{11}$$

Theorem 1. *Suppose $d_1 = d_2 = 0$, $\tau = 0$, and hypothesis (11) hold, then the equilibrium (N_*, P_*) is locally asymptotically stable.*

Proof. Suppose $d_1 = d_2 = 0$, $\tau = 0$, and hypothesis (11) hold, we can obtain $T_0 < 0$, $D_0 > 0$, so the real part of the roots of the characteristic equation is negative, then the equilibrium (N_*, P_*) is locally asymptotically stable. □

It is calculated that the discriminant of D_n is $\Gamma = a^2A^2d_2^2 + 2ad_1d_2\left(AD - 2B\widetilde{C}\right) + D^2d_1^2$, and

$$a_{\pm} = \frac{d_1(2B\widetilde{C} - AD) \pm d_1\sqrt{4B\widetilde{C}(B\widetilde{C} - AD)}}{A^2d_2} \tag{12}$$

$$\sigma_{\pm} = \frac{-(aAd_2 - Dd_1) \pm \sqrt{(aAd_2 - Dd_1)^2 - 4d_1d_2a(B\widetilde{C} - AD)}}{2d_1d_2}. \tag{13}$$

It is easy to verify that $a_- < \frac{d_1}{d_2}a_0 < a_+$ under the hypothesis (11).

Theorem 2. *Suppose $d_1 > 0$, $d_2 > 0$, $\tau = 0$, and hypothesis* (11) *hold. For the system* (4)*, we have the following conclusion.*

(1) *If $a \geq \frac{d_1}{d_2}a_0$, then the equilibrium (N_*, P_*) is locally asymptotically stable.*
(2) *If $a_- < a < \frac{d_1}{d_2}a_0$, then the equilibrium (N_*, P_*) is locally asymptotically stable.*
(3) *If $a_0 < a < a_-$, and there is no $k \in \mathcal{N}$ such that $\frac{k^2}{l^2} \in (\sigma_-, \sigma_+)$, then the equilibrium (N_*, P_*) is locally asymptotically stable.*
(4) *If $a_0 < a < a_-$, and there is a $k \in \mathcal{N}$ such that $\frac{k^2}{l^2} \in (\sigma_-, \sigma_+)$, then the equilibrium (N_*, P_*) is Turing unstable.*

Proof. We can obtain $T_n < 0$ and $D_n > 0$ for $a \geq \frac{d_1}{d_2}a_0$. It can be concluded that all the characteristic roots have a negative real part. Then, the equilibrium (N_*, P_*) is locally asymptotically stable (so, statement (1) is true). In the same way, statements (1)–(3) are also correct. Suppose the conditions in statement (4) are true, then at least there is a positive real part of eigenvalue root. Then, the equilibrium (N_*, P_*) is Turing unstable. □

2.2. Delay Model

Now, suppose $\tau > 0$, one of the conditions (1)–(3) in Theorem 2 and hypothesis (11) hold. Assume $i\omega(\omega > 0)$ is a solution of Equation (8), we can obtain

$$-w^2 + iA_nw + B_n + Ccosw\tau - iCsinw\tau = 0.$$

Then we have

$$\begin{cases} -w^2 + B_n + Ccosw\tau = 0, \\ wA_n - Csinw\tau = 0, \end{cases} \tag{14}$$

which leads to

$$w^4 + (A_n^2 - 2B_n)w^2 + B_n^2 - C^2 = 0. \tag{15}$$

Let $z = \omega^2$, Equation (15) is

$$z^2 + (A_n^2 - 2B_n)z + B_n^2 - C^2 = 0. \tag{16}$$

By direct computation, we have

$$\begin{aligned} A_n^2 - 2B_n &= \left(aA + d_1\frac{n^2}{l^2}\right)^2 + \left(D - d_2\frac{n^2}{l^2}\right)^2 > 0, \\ B_n + C &= D_n > 0, \\ B_n - C &= d_1d_2\frac{n^4}{l^4} + (aAd_2 - Dd_1)\frac{n^2}{l^2} - a(AD + B\widetilde{C}). \end{aligned} \tag{17}$$

Define
$$\mathbb{M} = \{ m \in \mathbb{N}_0 \mid B_n - C < 0 \; with \; n = m\}. \tag{18}$$

Lemma 2. *Suppose one of the conditions (1)–(3) in Theorem 2 and hypothesis* (11) *hold. If* $\mathbb{M} = \emptyset$, *then Equation* (16) *has no positive root. If* $\mathbb{M} \neq \emptyset$, *then the equation has positive roots.*

Proof. The roots of Equation (16) are
$$z_n^{\pm} = \frac{1}{2}[-(A_n^2 - 2B_n) \pm \sqrt{(A_n^2 - 2B_n)^2 - 4(B_n^2 - C^2)}] \tag{19}$$

It is easy to verify that $z_n^+ > 0$ if and only if $n \in \mathbb{M}$, and z_n^- is always negative or a non real number. □

Suppose one of the conditions (1)–(3) in Theorem 2 and hypothesis (11) hold, from Equation (14), we can obtain
$$\sin \omega\tau = \frac{\omega A_n}{C} > 0, \qquad \cos \omega\tau = \frac{\omega^2 - B_n}{C}.$$

For $n \in \mathbb{M}$, then Equation (8) has a pair of purely imaginary roots $\pm i\omega_n$ at τ_n^j, $j \in \mathbb{N}_0$,
$$\omega_n = \sqrt{z_n}, \quad \tau_n^j = \tau_n^0 + \frac{2j\pi}{\omega_n}, \quad \tau_n^0 = \frac{1}{\omega_n} \arccos \frac{\omega_n^2 - B_n}{C}. \tag{20}$$

Lemma 3. *Suppose one of the conditions (1)–(3) in Theorem 2 and hypothesis* (11) *hold. Then*
$$Re[\frac{d\lambda}{d\tau}]|_{\tau=\tau_n^j} > 0 \;\; for \;\; n \in \mathbb{M} \;\; and \;\; j \in \mathbb{N}_0.$$

Proof. From (8), we can obtain
$$(\frac{d\lambda}{d\tau})^{-1} = \frac{A_n + 2\lambda}{\lambda C e^{-\lambda\tau}} - \frac{\tau}{\lambda}.$$

Then
$$Re(\frac{d\lambda}{d\tau})^{-1}_{\tau=\tau_n^j} = \frac{A_n^2 w^2 + 2w^2(w^2 - B_n)}{A_n^2 w^4 + (w^3 - B_n w)^2} = \frac{\sqrt{(A_n^2 - 2B_n)^2 - 4(B_n^2 - C^2)}}{w^4 + B_n^2 + (A_n^2 - 2B_n)w^2} > 0.$$

□

Denote $\mathcal{D} := \{\tau_n^j : \tau_m^j \neq \tau_n^k, \; m \neq n, \; m,n \in \mathbb{M}, \; j,k \in \mathbb{N}_0\}$, and $\tau_* = \min\{\tau \in \mathcal{D}\}$.

Theorem 3. *For system* (4), *assume one of the conditions (1)–(3) in Theorem 2 and hypothesis* (11) *hold, then we have the following conclusion.*

(1) *If* $\mathbb{M} = \emptyset$, (N_*, P_*) *is locally asymptotically stable for* $\tau \geq 0$.
(2) *If* $\mathbb{M} \neq \emptyset$, (N_*, P_*) *is locally asymptotically stable for* $\tau \in [0, \tau_*)$ *and unstable for* $\tau > \tau_*$.
(3) *Hopf bifurcation occurs when* $\tau = \tau_0^j$ $(j \in \mathbb{N}_0, \;\; n \in \mathbb{M})$.

Proof. If $\mathbb{M} = \emptyset$, then $B_n - C > 0$ and $B_n^2 - C^2 > 0$, so Equation (16) has no positive root; then, the roots of Equation (8) all have negative real parts. Therefore, (N_*, P_*) is locally asymptotically stable. Similarly, statement (2) is also correct. When $\tau = \tau_0^j$ $(j \in \mathbb{N}_0, \; n \in \mathbb{M})$ implying that $T_n = 0$, then Hopf bifurcation occurs near (N_*, P_*). □

3. Property of Hopf Bifurcation

By the method [19–21], we study the property of Hopf bifurcation. For fixed $j \in \mathbb{N}_0$ and $n \in \mathbb{M}$, denote $\tilde{\tau} = \tau_n^j$. Let $\tilde{N}(x,t) = N(x,\tau t) - N_*$, and $\tilde{P}(x,t) = P(x,\tau t) - P_*$. The system (4) (drop the tilde) is

$$\begin{cases} \frac{\partial N}{\partial t} = \tau(d_1 \triangle N + a(1 - h(N+N_*)(P+P_*) - s(N+N_*)), \\ \frac{\partial P}{\partial t} = \tau(d_2 \triangle P + c(N(t-1) - N_*)(P+P_*) - \alpha(P+P_*) - \frac{\beta(P+P_*)^2}{\mu^2+(P+P_*)^2}. \end{cases} \tag{21}$$

Let

$$\tau = \tilde{\tau} + \mu, \;\; N_1(t) = N(\cdot,t), \;\; N_2(t) = P(\cdot,t) \text{ and } N = (N_1, N_2)^T.$$

Then (21) is written as

$$\frac{dN(t)}{dt} = \tilde{\tau} D \Delta N(t) + L_{\tilde{\tau}}(N_t) + F(N_t, \mu), \tag{22}$$

where

$$L_\mu(\phi) = \mu \begin{pmatrix} -aA\phi_1(0) - aB\phi_2(0) \\ C\phi_1(-1) + D\phi_2(0) \end{pmatrix}, \tag{23}$$

$$F(\phi,\mu) = \mu D \Delta \phi + L_\mu(\phi) + f(\phi,\mu), \tag{24}$$

with

$$\begin{aligned} f(\phi,\mu) &= (\tilde{\tau}+\mu)(F_1(\phi,\mu), F_2(\phi,\mu))^T, \\ F_1(\phi,\mu) &= a(1 - h(\phi_1(0)+N_*)(\phi_2(0)+P_*) - s(\phi_1(0)+N_*) + A\phi_1(0) + B\phi_2(0)), \\ F_2(\phi,\mu) &= c((\phi_1(-1)+N_*)(\phi_2(0)+P_*) - \alpha(\phi_2(0)+P_*) - \frac{\beta(P_*+\phi_2(0))^2}{\mu^2+(P_*+\phi_2(0))^2}). \end{aligned}$$

Then

$$\frac{dN(t)}{dt} = \tilde{\tau} D \Delta N(t) + L_{\tilde{\tau}}(N_t) \tag{25}$$

has characteristic roots $\Lambda_n := \{i\omega_n\tilde{\tau}, -i\omega_n\tilde{\tau}\}$. Its linear functional differential equation is

$$\frac{dz(t)}{dt} = -\tilde{\tau} D \frac{n^2}{l^2} z(t) + L_{\tilde{\tau}}(z_t). \tag{26}$$

There exists a 2×2 matrix function $\eta^n(\sigma, \tilde{\tau})$ $-1 \leq \sigma \leq 0$, such that

$$-\tilde{\tau} D \frac{n^2}{l^2} \phi(0) + L_{\tilde{\tau}}(\phi) = \int_{-1}^{0} d\eta^n(\sigma,\tau)\phi(\sigma).$$

Choose

$$\eta^n(\sigma,\tau) = \begin{cases} \tau E & \sigma = 0, \\ 0 & \sigma \in (-1,0), \\ -\tau F & \sigma = -1, \end{cases} \quad E = \begin{pmatrix} -aA - d_1\frac{n^2}{l^2} & -aB \\ 0 & D - d_2\frac{n^2}{l^2} \end{pmatrix}, \; F = \begin{pmatrix} 0 & 0 \\ C & 0 \end{pmatrix}. \tag{27}$$

Define

$$\begin{aligned} (\psi,\phi) &= \psi(0)\phi(0) - \int_{-1}^{0}\int_{\xi=0}^{\sigma} \psi(\xi-\sigma) d\eta^n(\sigma,\tilde{\tau})\phi(\xi)d\xi \\ &= \psi(0)\phi(0) + \tilde{\tau}\int_{-1}^{0} \psi(\xi+1)F\phi(\xi)d\xi, \end{aligned} \tag{28}$$

for $\phi \in C([-1,0],\mathbb{R}^2)$, $\psi \in C([-1,0],\mathbb{R}^2)$. Choose $p_1(\theta) = (1,\xi)^T e^{i\omega_n\tilde{\tau}\sigma}$ $(\sigma \in [-1,0])$, $p_2(\sigma) = \overline{p_1(\sigma)}$ is a basis of $A(\tilde{\tau})$ with Λ_n and $q_1(r) = (1,\eta)e^{-i\omega_n\tilde{\tau}r}$ $(r \in [0,1])$, $q_2(r) = \overline{q_1(r)}$ is a basis of A^* with Λ_n, where

$$\xi = \frac{Ce^{-i\tilde{\tau}\omega_n}}{i\omega_n + \frac{d_2n^2}{l^2} - D}, \quad \eta = \frac{B}{i\omega_n + D - \frac{d_2n^2}{l^2}}.$$

Let $\Phi = (\Phi_1, \Phi_2)$ and $\Psi^* = (\Psi_1^*, \Psi_2^*)^T$ with

$$\Phi_1(\sigma) = \frac{p_1(\sigma) + p_2(\sigma)}{2}, \quad \Phi_2(\sigma) = \frac{p_1(\sigma) - p_2(\sigma)}{2i}, \quad \text{for } \theta \in [-1,0].$$

In addition,

$$\Psi_1^*(r) = \frac{q_1(r) + q_2(r)}{2}, \quad \Psi_2^*(r) = \frac{q_1(r) - q_2(r)}{2i}, \quad \text{for } r \in [0,1].$$

Then we can compute by (28)

$$D_1^* := (\Psi_1^*, \Phi_1),\ D_2^* := (\Psi_1^*, \Phi_2),\ D_3^* := (\Psi_2^*, \Phi_1),\ D_4^* := (\Psi_2^*, \Phi_2).$$

Define $(\Psi^*, \Phi) = (\Psi_j^*, \Phi_k) = \begin{pmatrix} D_1^* & D_2^* \\ D_3^* & D_4^* \end{pmatrix}$ and construct a new basis Ψ for P_* by

$$\Psi = (\Psi_1, \Psi_2)^T = (\Psi^*, \Phi)^{-1}\Psi^*.$$

Then $(\Psi, \Phi) = I_2$. In addition, define $f_n := (\beta_n^1, \beta_n^2)$, where

$$\beta_n^1 = \begin{pmatrix} \cos\frac{n}{l}x \\ 0 \end{pmatrix}, \quad \beta_n^2 = \begin{pmatrix} 0 \\ \cos\frac{n}{l}x \end{pmatrix}.$$

We also define

$$d \cdot f_n = d_1\beta_n^1 + d_2\beta_n^2, \quad \text{for } d = (d_1, d_2)^T \in \mathscr{D}_1,$$

and

$$< N, P > := \frac{1}{l\pi}\int_0^{l\pi} N_1\overline{P_1}dx + \frac{1}{l\pi}\int_0^{l\pi} N_2\overline{P_2}dx$$

for $N = (N_1, N_2)$, $P = (P_1, P_2)$, $N, P \in X$, and $< \phi, f_0 >= (< \phi, f_0^1 >, < \phi, f_0^2 >)^T$. Equation (21) can be rewritten as

$$\frac{dN(t)}{dt} = A_{\tilde{\tau}}N_t + R(N_t, \mu), \tag{29}$$

where

$$R(N_t, \mu) = \begin{cases} 0, & \theta \in [-1, 0), \\ F(N_t, \mu), & \theta = 0. \end{cases} \tag{30}$$

By the decomposition of $\mathscr{C}_1$, the above solution is

$$N_t = \Phi\begin{pmatrix} x_1 \\ x_2 \end{pmatrix} f_n + h(x_1, x_2, \mu), \tag{31}$$

with

$$\begin{pmatrix} x_1 \\ x_2 \end{pmatrix} = (\Psi, < N_t, f_n >),$$

and

$$h(x_1, x_2, \mu) \in P_S\mathscr{C}_1, \ h(0,0,0) = 0, \ Dh(0,0,0) = 0.$$

The solution of (22) is

$$N_t = \Phi\begin{pmatrix} x_1(t) \\ x_2(t) \end{pmatrix} f_n + h(x_1, x_2, 0). \tag{32}$$

Let $z = x_1 - ix_2$, and notice that $p_1 = \Phi_1 + i\Phi_2$. Then, we can obtain

$$\Phi\begin{pmatrix} x_1 \\ x_2 \end{pmatrix} f_n = (\Phi_1, \Phi_2)\begin{pmatrix} \frac{z+\bar{z}}{2} \\ \frac{i(z-\bar{z})}{2} \end{pmatrix} f_n = \frac{1}{2}(p_1 z + \overline{p_1 z}) f_n,$$

and

$$h(x_1, x_2, 0) = h(\frac{z+\bar{z}}{2}, \frac{i(z-\bar{z})}{2}, 0).$$

Hence, (32) is

$$\begin{aligned} N_t &= \frac{1}{2}(p_1 z + \overline{p_1 z}) f_n + h(\frac{z+\bar{z}}{2}, \frac{i(z-\bar{z})}{2}, 0) \\ &= \frac{1}{2}(p_1 z + \overline{p_1 z}) f_n + W(z, \bar{z}), \end{aligned} \tag{33}$$

where

$$W(z, \bar{z}) = h(\frac{z+\bar{z}}{2}, \frac{i(z-\bar{z})}{2}, 0).$$

From [19], z meets

$$\dot{z} = i\omega_n \tilde{\tau} z + g(z, \bar{z}), \tag{34}$$

among them

$$g(z, \bar{z}) = (\Psi_1(0) - i\Psi_2(0)) < F(N_t, 0), f_n > . \tag{35}$$

Let

$$W(z, \bar{z}) = W_{20}\frac{z^2}{2} + W_{11} z\bar{z} + W_{02}\frac{\bar{z}^2}{2} + \cdots, \tag{36}$$

$$g(z, \bar{z}) = g_{20}\frac{z^2}{2} + g_{11} z\bar{z} + g_{02}\frac{\bar{z}^2}{2} + \cdots; \tag{37}$$

from Equations (33) and (36), we can obtain

$$N_t(0) = \frac{1}{2}(z + \bar{z})\cos\left(\frac{nx}{l}\right) + W_{20}^{(1)}(0)\frac{z^2}{2} + W_{11}^{(1)}(0) z\bar{z} + W_{02}^{(1)}(0)\frac{\bar{z}^2}{2} + \cdots,$$

$$P_t(0) = \frac{1}{2}(\xi + \bar{\xi}\bar{z})\cos\left(\frac{nx}{l}\right) + W_{20}^{(2)}(0)\frac{z^2}{2} + W_{11}^{(2)}(0) z\bar{z} + W_{02}^{(2)}(0)\frac{\bar{z}^2}{2} + \cdots,$$

$$N_t(-1) = \frac{1}{2}(z e^{-i\omega_n \tilde{\tau}} + \bar{z} e^{i\omega_n \tilde{\tau}})\cos(\frac{nx}{l}) + W_{20}^{(1)}(-1)\frac{z^2}{2} + W_{11}^{(1)}(-1) z\bar{z} + W_{02}^{(1)}(-1)\frac{\bar{z}^2}{2} + \cdots,$$

and

$$\overline{F}_1(N_t, 0) = \frac{1}{\tilde{\tau}} F_1 = \alpha_1 N_t(0) P_t(0) + O(4), \tag{38}$$

$$\overline{F}_2(N_t, 0) = \frac{1}{\tilde{\tau}} F_2 = c N_t(-1) P_t(0) + \beta_1 P_t^2(0) + \beta_2 P_t^3(0) + O(4), \tag{39}$$

with

$$\alpha_1 = -ah,\ \ \beta_1 = \frac{\beta c(3\mu^2 P_*^2 - \mu^4)}{(\mu^2 + P_*^2)^2},\ \ \beta_2 = -\frac{4\beta c\mu^2 P_*(P_*^2 - \mu^2)}{(\mu^2 + P_*^2)^4}.$$

Hence,

$$\overline{F}_1(N_t, 0) = \cos^2(\frac{nx}{l})(\frac{z^2}{2}\chi_{20} + z\overline{z}\chi_{11} + \frac{\overline{z}^2}{2}\overline{\chi}_{20}) + \frac{z^2\overline{z}}{2}\cos\frac{nx}{l}\varsigma_{11} + \frac{z^2\overline{z}}{2}\cos^3\frac{nx}{l}\varsigma_{12} + \cdots, \quad (40)$$

$$\overline{F}_2(N_t, 0) = \cos^2(\frac{nx}{l})(\frac{z^2}{2}\varrho_{20} + z\overline{z}\varrho_{11} + \frac{\overline{z}^2}{2}\overline{\varrho}_{20}) + \frac{z^2\overline{z}}{2}\cos\frac{nx}{l}\varsigma_{21} + \frac{z^2\overline{z}}{2}\cos^3\frac{nx}{l}\varsigma_{22} + \cdots, \quad (41)$$

$$\begin{aligned} < F(N_t, 0), f_n > &= \tilde{\tau}(\overline{F}_1(N_t, 0) f_n^1 + \overline{F}_2(N_t, 0) f_n^2) \\ &= \frac{z^2}{2}\tilde{\tau}\begin{pmatrix} \chi_{20} \\ \varsigma_{20} \end{pmatrix}\Gamma + z\overline{z}\tilde{\tau}\begin{pmatrix} \chi_{11} \\ \varsigma_{11} \end{pmatrix}\Gamma + \frac{\overline{z}^2}{2}\tilde{\tau}\begin{pmatrix} \overline{\chi}_{20} \\ \overline{\varsigma}_{20} \end{pmatrix}\Gamma + \frac{z^2\overline{z}}{2}\tilde{\tau}\begin{pmatrix} \kappa_1 \\ \kappa_2 \end{pmatrix} + \cdots \end{aligned} \quad (42)$$

with

$$\Gamma = \frac{1}{l\pi}\int_0^{l\pi}\cos^3(\frac{nx}{l})dx,$$

$$\begin{aligned} \chi_{20} &= \frac{\alpha_1\xi}{2},\ \ \chi_{11} = \alpha_1\left(\frac{\eta}{4} + \frac{\xi}{4}\right),\ \ \varsigma_{12} = 0, \\ \varsigma_{11} &= \alpha_1(\xi W_{11}^1(0) + W_{11}^2(0) + \frac{W_{20}^1(0)}{2}\eta + \frac{W_{20}^2(0)}{2}), \\ \varrho_{20} &= \frac{1}{2}\xi e^{-i\tau\omega_n}\left(c + \beta_1\xi e^{i\tau\omega_n}\right), \\ \varrho_{11} &= \frac{1}{4}e^{-i\tau\omega_n}\left(c\left(\eta + \xi e^{2i\tau\omega_n}\right) + 2\beta_1\eta\xi e^{i\tau\omega_n}\right), \\ \varsigma_{21} &= W_{11}^2(0)\left(2\beta_1\xi + ce^{-i\tau\omega_n}\right) + W_{20}^2(0)\left(\beta_1\eta + \frac{1}{2}ce^{i\tau\omega_n}\right) + c\xi W_{11}^1(-1) + \frac{c\eta W_{02}^1(-1)}{2}, \\ \varsigma_{22} &= \frac{3}{4}\beta_2\eta\xi^2. \end{aligned} \quad (43)$$

$$\kappa_1 = \varsigma_{11}\frac{1}{l\pi}\int_0^{l\pi}\cos^2(\frac{nx}{l})dx + \varsigma_{12}\frac{1}{l\pi}\int_0^{l\pi}\cos^4(\frac{nx}{l})dx,$$

$$\begin{aligned} \kappa_2 = {} & \varsigma_{21}\frac{1}{l\pi}\int_0^{l\pi}\cos^2(\frac{nx}{l})dx \\ & + \varsigma_{22}\frac{1}{l\pi}\int_0^{l\pi}\cos^4(\frac{nx}{l})dx. \end{aligned}$$

Denote

$$\Psi_1(0) - i\Psi_2(0) := (\gamma_1\ \ \gamma_2).$$

Notice that

$$\frac{1}{l\pi}\int_0^{l\pi}\cos^3(\frac{nx}{l})dx = 0,\ \ n \in \mathbb{N},$$

and we have

$$\begin{aligned} &(\Psi_1(0) - i\Psi_2(0)) < F(N_t, 0), f_n >= \\ &\quad \frac{z^2}{2}(\gamma_1\chi_{20} + \gamma_2\varsigma_{20})\Gamma\tilde{\tau} + z\overline{z}(\gamma_1\chi_{11} + \gamma_2\varsigma_{11})\Gamma\tilde{\tau} + \frac{\overline{z}^2}{2}(\gamma_1\overline{\chi}_{20} + \gamma_2\overline{\varsigma}_{20})\Gamma\tilde{\tau} \\ &\quad + \frac{z^2\overline{z}}{2}\tilde{\tau}[\gamma_1\kappa_1 + \gamma_2\kappa_2] + \cdots, \end{aligned} \quad (44)$$

From (35), (37) and (44), we have $g_{20} = g_{11} = g_{02} = 0$, for $n \in \mathbb{N}$. If $n = 0$, we obtain

$$g_{20} = \gamma_1\tilde{\tau}\chi_{20} + \gamma_2\tilde{\tau}\varrho_{20},\quad g_{11} = \gamma_1\tilde{\tau}\chi_{11} + \gamma_2\tilde{\tau}\varrho_{11},\quad g_{02} = \gamma_1\tilde{\tau}\overline{\chi}_{20} + \gamma_2\tilde{\tau}\overline{\varrho}_{20}.$$

Furthermore, for $n \in \mathbb{N}_0$, $g_{21} = \tilde{\tau}(\gamma_1\kappa_1 + \gamma_2\kappa_2)$. Now, we compute $W_{20}(\theta)$ and $W_{11}(\theta)$ for $\theta \in [-1, 0]$. From [19], we obtain

$$\dot{W}(z,\overline{z}) = W_{20}z\dot{z} + W_{11}\dot{z}\overline{z} + W_{11}z\dot{\overline{z}} + W_{02}\overline{z}\dot{\overline{z}} + \cdots,$$

$$A_{\tilde{\tau}}W(z,\overline{z}) = A_{\tilde{\tau}}W_{20}\frac{z^2}{2} + A_{\tilde{\tau}}W_{11}z\overline{z} + A_{\tilde{\tau}}W_{02}\frac{\overline{z}^2}{2} + \cdots,$$

$$\dot{W}(z,\overline{z}) = A_{\tilde{\tau}}W + H(z,\overline{z}),$$

where

$$\begin{aligned} H(z,\overline{z}) &= H_{20}\frac{z^2}{2} + W_{11}z\overline{z} + H_{02}\frac{\overline{z}^2}{2} + \cdots \\ &= X_0F(N_t,0) - \Phi(\Psi, < X_0F(N_t,0), f_n > \cdot f_n). \end{aligned} \tag{45}$$

Hence, we have

$$(2i\omega_n\tilde{\tau} - A_{\tilde{\tau}})W_{20} = H_{20}, \quad -A_{\tilde{\tau}}W_{11} = H_{11}, \quad (-2i\omega_n\tilde{\tau} - A_{\tilde{\tau}})W_{02} = H_{02}, \tag{46}$$

that is,

$$W_{20} = (2i\omega_n\tilde{\tau} - A_{\tilde{\tau}})^{-1}H_{20}, \quad W_{11} = -A_{\tilde{\tau}}^{-1}H_{11}, \quad W_{02} = (-2i\omega_n\tilde{\tau} - A_{\tilde{\tau}})^{-1}H_{02}. \tag{47}$$

By (44), we have

$$\begin{aligned} H(z,\overline{z}) &= -\Phi(0)\Psi(0) < F(N_t,0), f_n > \cdot f_n \\ &= -\left(\frac{p_1(\theta)+p_2(\theta)}{2}, \frac{p_1(\theta)-p_2(\theta)}{2i}\right)\begin{pmatrix} \Phi_1(0) \\ \Phi_2(0) \end{pmatrix} < F(N_t,0), f_n > \cdot f_n \\ &= -\frac{1}{2}[p_1(\theta)(\Phi_1(0) - i\Phi_2(0)) + p_2(\theta)(\Phi_1(0) + i\Phi_2(0))] < F(N_t,0), f_n > \cdot f_n \\ &= -\frac{1}{2}[(p_1(\theta)g_{20} + p_2(\theta)\overline{g}_{02})\frac{z^2}{2} + (p_1(\theta)g_{11} + p_2(\theta)\overline{g}_{11})z\overline{z} + (p_1(\theta)g_{02} + p_2(\theta)\overline{g}_{20})\frac{\overline{z}^2}{2}] + \cdots. \end{aligned}$$

Therefore by (45), for $\theta \in [-1, 0)$,

$$H_{20}(\theta) = \begin{cases} 0 & n \in \mathbb{N}, \\ -\frac{1}{2}(p_1(\theta)g_{20} + p_2(\theta)\overline{g}_{02}) \cdot f_0 & n = 0, \end{cases}$$

$$H_{11}(\theta) = \begin{cases} 0 & n \in \mathbb{N}, \\ -\frac{1}{2}(p_1(\theta)g_{11} + p_2(\theta)\overline{g}_{11}) \cdot f_0 & n = 0, \end{cases}$$

$$H_{02}(\theta) = \begin{cases} 0 & n \in \mathbb{N}, \\ -\frac{1}{2}(p_1(\theta)g_{02} + p_2(\theta)\overline{g}_{20}) \cdot f_0 & n = 0, \end{cases}$$

and

$$H(z,\overline{z})(0) = F(N_t,0) - \Phi(\Psi, < F(N_t,0), f_n >) \cdot f_n,$$

where

$$H_{20}(0) = \begin{cases} \tilde{\tau}\begin{pmatrix} \chi_{20} \\ \varrho_{20} \end{pmatrix}\cos^2(\frac{nx}{l}), & n \in \mathbb{N}, \\ \tilde{\tau}\begin{pmatrix} \chi_{20} \\ \varrho_{20} \end{pmatrix} - \frac{1}{2}(p_1(0)g_{20} + p_2(0)\overline{g}_{02}) \cdot f_0, & n = 0. \end{cases} \tag{48}$$

$$H_{11}(0) = \begin{cases} \tilde{\tau}\begin{pmatrix} \chi_{11} \\ \varrho_{11} \end{pmatrix}\cos^2(\frac{nx}{l}), & n \in \mathbb{N}, \\ \tilde{\tau}\begin{pmatrix} \chi_{11} \\ \varrho_{11} \end{pmatrix} - \frac{1}{2}(p_1(0)g_{11} + p_2(0)\overline{g}_{11}) \cdot f_0, & n = 0. \end{cases} \tag{49}$$

Then, we can obtain

$$\dot{W}_{20} = A_{\tilde{\tau}}W_{20} = 2i\omega_n\tilde{\tau}W_{20} + \frac{1}{2}(p_1(\theta)g_{20} + p_2(\theta)\overline{g}_{02}) \cdot f_n, \quad -1 \le \theta < 0.$$

That is,

$$W_{20}(\theta) = \frac{i}{2i\omega_n\tilde{\tau}}(g_{20}p_1(\theta) + \frac{\overline{g}_{02}}{3}p_2(\theta)) \cdot f_n + E_1e^{2i\omega_n\tilde{\tau}\theta},$$

where

$$E_1 = \begin{cases} W_{20}(0) & n \in \mathbb{N}, \\ W_{20}(0) - \frac{i}{2i\omega_n\tilde{\tau}}(g_{20}p_1(\theta) + \frac{\overline{g}_{02}}{3}p_2(\theta)) \cdot f_0 & n = 0. \end{cases}$$

Using the definition of $A_{\tilde{\tau}}$ and (46), we have that for $-1 \le \theta < 0$

$$\begin{aligned} &-(g_{20}p_1(0) + \frac{\overline{g}_{02}}{3}p_2(0)) \cdot f_0 + 2i\omega_n\tilde{\tau}E_1 - A_{\tilde{\tau}}(\frac{i}{2\omega_n\tilde{\tau}}(g_{20}p_1(0) + \frac{\overline{g}_{02}}{3}p_2(0)) \cdot f_0) \\ &- A_{\tilde{\tau}}E_1 - L_{\tilde{\tau}}(\frac{i}{2\omega_n\tilde{\tau}}(g_{20}p_1(0) + \frac{\overline{g}_{02}}{3}p_2(0)) \cdot f_n + E_1e^{2i\omega_n\tilde{\tau}\theta}) \\ &= \tilde{\tau}\begin{pmatrix} \chi_{20} \\ \varrho_{20} \end{pmatrix} - \frac{1}{2}(p_1(0)g_{20} + p_2(0)\overline{g}_{02}) \cdot f_0. \end{aligned}$$

As

$$A_{\tilde{\tau}}p_1(0) + L_{\tilde{\tau}}(p_1 \cdot f_0) = i\omega_0p_1(0) \cdot f_0,$$

and

$$A_{\tilde{\tau}}p_2(0) + L_{\tilde{\tau}}(p_2 \cdot f_0) = -i\omega_0p_2(0) \cdot f_0,$$

we have

$$2i\omega_nE_1 - A_{\tilde{\tau}}E_1 - L_{\tilde{\tau}}E_1e^{2i\omega_n} = \tilde{\tau}\begin{pmatrix} \chi_{20} \\ \varrho_{20} \end{pmatrix}\cos^2(\frac{nx}{l}), \quad n \in \mathbb{N}_0.$$

That is,

$$E_1 = \tilde{\tau}E\begin{pmatrix} \chi_{20} \\ \varrho_{20} \end{pmatrix}\cos^2(\frac{nx}{l})$$

where

$$E = \begin{pmatrix} 2i\omega_n\tilde{\tau} + d_1\frac{n^2}{l^2} + aA & aB \\ -Ce^{-2i\omega_n\tilde{\tau}} & -D + 2i\omega_n\tilde{\tau} + d_2\frac{n^2}{l^2} \end{pmatrix}^{-1}.$$

Similarly, we have

$$-\dot{W}_{11} = \frac{i}{2\omega_n\tilde{\tau}}(p_1(\theta)g_{11} + p_2(\theta)\overline{g}_{11}) \cdot f_n, \quad -1 \le \theta < 0.$$

That is,

$$W_{11}(\theta) = \frac{i}{2i\omega_n\tilde{\tau}}(p_1(\theta)\overline{g}_{11} - p_1(\theta)g_{11}) + E_2.$$

Then,

$$E_2 = \tilde{\tau}E^*\begin{pmatrix} \chi_{11} \\ \varrho_{11} \end{pmatrix}\cos^2(\frac{nx}{l}),$$

where

$$E^* = \begin{pmatrix} d_1\frac{n^2}{l^2} + aA & aB \\ -C & -D + d_2\frac{n^2}{l^2} \end{pmatrix}^{-1}.$$

Therefore, we have

$$\begin{cases} c_1(0) = \frac{i}{2\omega_n \tilde{\tau}}(g_{20}g_{11} - 2|g_{11}|^2 - \frac{|g_{02}|^2}{3}) + \frac{1}{2}g_{21}, & \mu_2 = -\frac{Re(c_1(0))}{Re(\lambda'(\tau_n^j))}, \\ T_2 = -\frac{1}{\omega_n \tilde{\tau}}[Im(c_1(0)) + \mu_2 Im(\lambda'(\tau_n^j))], & \beta_2 = 2Re(c_1(0)). \end{cases} \tag{50}$$

By [19], we have the following theorem.

Theorem 4. *For any critical value τ_n^j, we have the Hopf bifurcation is forward ($\mu_2 > 0$) or backward ($\mu_2 < 0$). The bifurcating periodic solutions are orbitally asymptotically stable ($\beta_2 < 0$) or unstable ($\beta_2 > 0$). The period increases ($T_2 > 0$) or decreases ($T_2 < 0$).*

4. Numerical Simulations

In order to verify the previous conclusion, we provide some numerical simulations by Matlab. In particular, the numerical simulation of the systems with $\tau = 0$ is implemented by the pdepe function in Matlab, and $\tau > 0$ is implemented by the finite-difference methods. Choose the following parameters.

$$d_1 = 2,\ h = 1.667,\ s = 0.267,\ \alpha = 0.1,\ a = 1,\ \beta = 0.48,\ \mu = 0.18,\ c = 0.5,\ l = 4. \tag{51}$$

By direct computation, we have $(N_*, P_*) \approx (1.2130, 0.3344)$ is the unique positive equilibrium, and $A \approx 0.8244$, $B \approx 2.0220$, $C \approx 0.1672$, $D \approx 0.3064$, $BC - AD \approx 0.0854 > 0$, and $a_0 \approx 0.3717$. Hence, hypothesis (11) holds. Now, we give the curves of a_- and $\frac{d_1}{d_2}a_0$ with the predator's diffusion coefficient d_2 (Figure 1). We can see that $a_0 < a < a_-$ holds when $d_2 < d_2^*$, then the Turing instability of (N_*, P_*) may occur. When $d_2 > d_2^*$, then $a > a_-$ holds, which implies (N_*, P_*) is locally asymptotically stable. Choose $d_2 = 0.1$, we have $a_- = 2.4603$, $\sigma_- = 0.1723$, $\sigma_+ = 2.4800$, and $k \in \{2, 3, 4, 5, 6\}$ such that $\frac{k^2}{l^2} \in (\sigma_-, \sigma_+)$. Then (N_*, P_*) is Turing unstable (Figure 2).

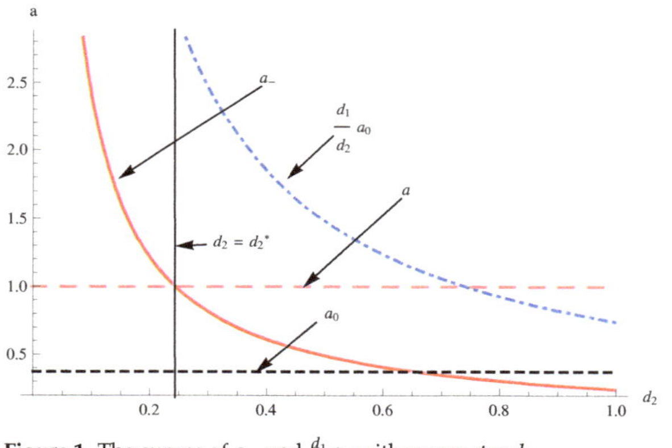

Figure 1. The curves of a_- and $\frac{d_1}{d_2}a_0$ with parameter d_2.

We choose $d_2 = 0.4$, and change the parameter β, which represents the release rate of toxic chemicals by the TPP population. The bifurcation diagram of system (4) with parameter β is given in Figure 3. We can see that the increasing parameter β is not beneficial to the stability of (N_*, P_*) initially. However, when β crosses some critical value, increasing parameter β is of benefit to the stability of (N_*, P_*). In particular, when the parameter β is sufficiently large, (N_*, P_*) will always be stable.

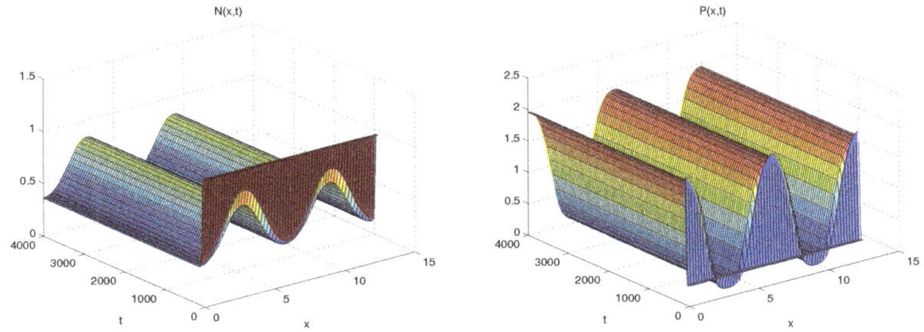

Figure 2. Numerical simulations for (4) with $\tau = 0$ and $d_2 = 0.1$.

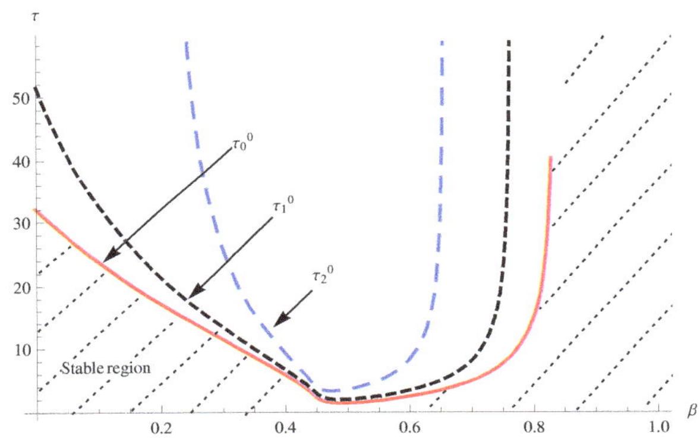

Figure 3. Bifurcation diagram of system (4) with parameter *beta*.

If we choose $\beta = 0.48$, we have $\tau_* = \tau_0^0 \approx 1.5710$ and $\omega_0 \approx 0.2460$. Then (P_*, N_*) is locally asymptotically stable for $\tau \in [0, \tau_*)$ (Figure 4), and Hopf bifurcation occurs when $\tau = \tau_*$. We obtain

$$\mu_2 \approx 0.5391 > 0, \quad \beta_2 \approx -0.1217 < 0, \quad \text{and} \quad T_2 \approx 12.3699 > 0.$$

Hence, the stable bifurcating periodic solutions exist for $\tau > \tau_*$ (Figure 5). However, if we choose $\beta = 0.6$ and $\tau = 2.3$, (P_*, N_*) is locally asymptotically stable (Figure 6).

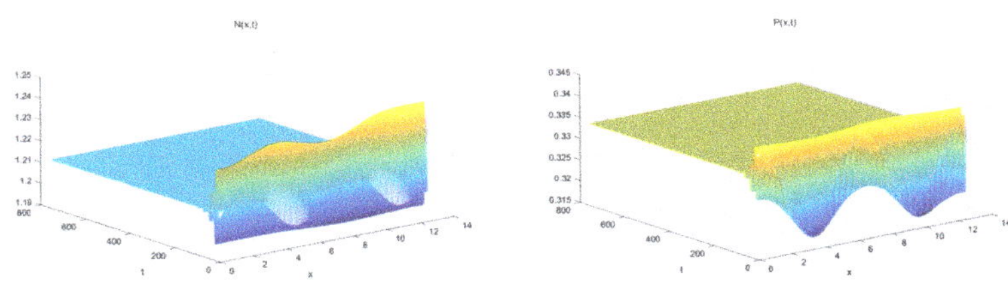

Figure 4. Numerical simulations for (4) with $\tau = 1.2$ and $\beta = 0.48$.

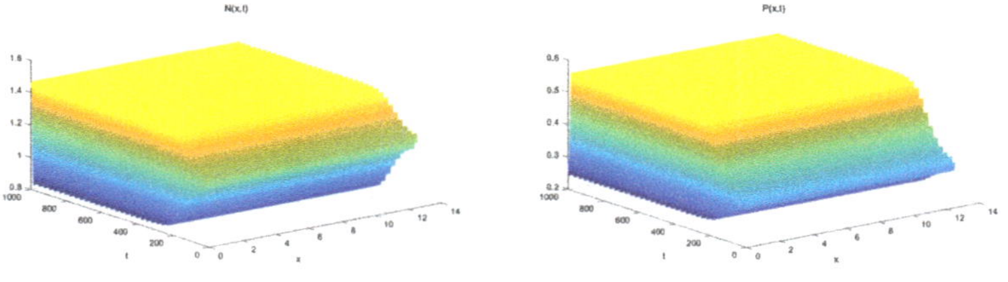

Figure 5. Numerical simulations for (4) with $\tau = 1.7$ and $\beta = 0.48$.

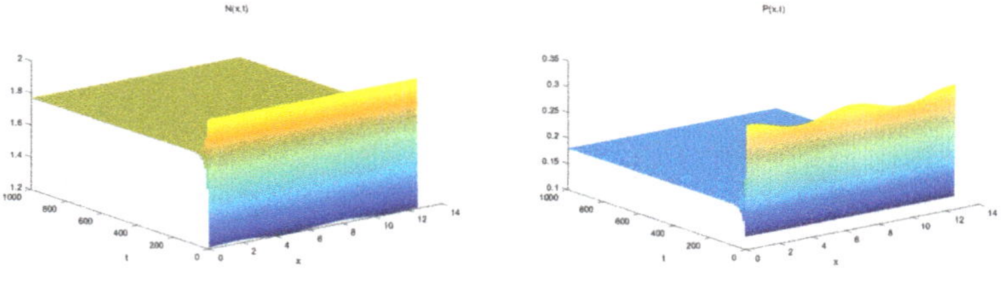

Figure 6. Numerical simulations for (4) with $\tau = 1.7$ and $\beta = 0.6$.

5. Conclusions

Diffusion and time delay was incorporated into a nutrient–phytoplankton model. The instability and Hopf bifurcation induced by the time delay was studied. Through the central manifold theory and normal form method, some parameters were given to determine the property of bifurcating periodic solutions. The results indicate diffusion may induce Turing unstable. The release rate β of toxic chemicals by the TPP population has a stabilizing and destabilizing effect on the stability of the positive equilibrium. In addition, the time delay can also affect the stability of the positive equilibrium, and it can induce periodic oscillation of prey and predator population density.

Author Contributions: Conceptualization, R.Y. and D.J.; methodology, R.Y.; software, L.W.; Investigation, R.Y. and L.W.; writing—original draft preparation, L.W.; writing—review and editing, R.Y. and D.J.; Project administration, D.J.; Funding acquisition, R.Y. All authors have read and agreed to the published version of the manuscript.

Funding: This research was funded by Fundamental Research Funds for the Central Universities (Grant No. 2572019BC01) and Postdoctoral Program of Heilongjiang Province (Grant No. LBH-Q21060).

Data Availability Statement: Not applicable.

Acknowledgments: The authors wish to express their gratitude to the editors and the reviewers for the helpful comments.

Conflicts of Interest: The authors declare no conflict of interest.

References

1. Luo, J. Phytoplankton-zooplankton dynamics in periodic environments taking into account eutrophication. *Math. Biosci.* **2013**, *245*, 126–136. [CrossRef] [PubMed]
2. Dai, C.; Zhao, M. Nonlinear Analysis in a Nutrient-Algae-Zooplankton System with Sinking of Algae. *Abstr. Appl. Anal.* **2014**, *2014*, 278457. [CrossRef]
3. Rehim, M.; Wu, W.; Muhammadhaji, A. On the Dynamical Behavior of Toxic-Phytoplankton-Zooplankton Model with Delay. *Discret. Dyn. Nat. Soc.* **2015**, *2015*, 756315. [CrossRef]
4. Chakraborty, K.; Jana, S.; Kar, T.K. Global dynamics and bifurcation in a stage structured prey-predator fishery model with harvesting. *Appl. Math. Comput.* **2012**, *218*, 9271–9290. [CrossRef]
5. Rehim, M.; Imran, M. Dynamical analysis of a delay model of phytoplankton-zooplankton interaction. *Appl. Math. Model.* **2012**, *36*, 638–647. [CrossRef]
6. Chakrabarti, S. Eutrophication global aquatic environmental problem: A review. *Res. Rev. J. Ecol. Environ. Sci.* **2018**, *6*, 1–6.

7. Sharma, A.K.; Sharma, A.; Agnihotri, K. Bifurcation behaviors analysis of a plankton model with multiple delays. *Int. J. Biomath.* **2016**, *9*, 1650086. [CrossRef]
8. Rehim, M.; Zhang, Z.; Muhammadhaji, A. Mathematical analysis of a nutrient-plankton system with delay. *SpringerPlus* **2016**, *5*, 1–22. [CrossRef] [PubMed]
9. Meng, X.Y.; Wang, J.G.; Huo, H.F. Dynamical Behaviour of a Nutrient-Plankton Model with Holling Type IV, Delay, and Harvesting. *Discret. Dyn. Nat. Soc.* **2018**, *2018*, 9232590. [CrossRef]
10. Wang, Y.; Jiang, W. Bifurcations in a delayed differential-algebraic plankton economic system. *J. Appl. Anal. Comput.* **2017**, *7*, 1431–1447. [CrossRef]
11. Guo, Q.; Dai, C.; Yu, H.; Liu, H.; Sun, X.; Li, J.; Zhao, M. Stability and bifurcation analysis of a nutrient hytoplankton model with time delay. *Math. Methods Appl. Sci.* **2020**, *43*, 3018–3039. [CrossRef]
12. Thakur, N.K.; Ojha, A.; Tiwari, P.K.; Upadhyay, R.K. An investigation of delay induced stability transition in nutrient-plankton systems. *Chaos Solitons Fractals* **2021**, *142*, 110474. [CrossRef]
13. Huppert, A.; Blasius, B.; Stone, L. A Model of Phytoplankton Blooms. *Am. Nat.* **2002**, *159*, 156-171. [CrossRef] [PubMed]
14. Roy, S. Do phytoplankton communities evolve through a self-regulatory abundance-diversity relationship? *Bio Syst.* **2009**, *95*, 160–165. [CrossRef] [PubMed]
15. Pal, S.; Chatterjee, S.; Chattopadhyay, J. Role of toxin and nutrient for the occurrence and termination of plankton bloom Results drawn from field observations and a mathematical model. *Biosystems* **2007**, *90*, 87–100. [CrossRef] [PubMed]
16. Roy, S.; Alam, S.; Chattopadhyay, J. Competing Effects of Toxin-Producing Phytoplankton on Overall Plankton Populations in the Bay of Bengal. *Bull. Math. Biol.* **2006**, *68*, 2303. [CrossRef] [PubMed]
17. Sarkar, R.R.; Chattopadhayay, J. Occurrence of planktonic blooms under environmental fluctuations and its possible control mechanism–mathematical models and experimental observations. *J. Theor. Biol.* **2003**, *224*, 501–516. [CrossRef]
18. Chakraborty, S.; Chatterjee, S.; Venturino, E.; Chattopadhyay, J. Recurring Plankton Bloom Dynamics Modeled via Toxin-Producing Phytoplankton. *J. Biol. Phys.* **2007**, *33*, 271–290. [CrossRef]
19. Wu, J. *Theory and Applications of Partial Functional-Differential Equations*; Springer: New York, NY, USA, 1996.
20. Ruan, S.; Wei, J. On the zeros of transcendental functions with applications to stability of delay differential equations with two delays. *Dyn. Contin. Discrete Impuls. Syst. Ser. A Math. Anal.* **2003**, *10*, 863–874.
21. Hassard, B.D.; Kazarinoff, N.D.; Wan, Y.H. *Theory and Applications of Hopf Bifurcation*; Cambridge University Press: Cambridge, UK, 1981.

axioms

Article

The Darboux Transformation and *N*-Soliton Solutions of Gerdjikov–Ivanov Equation on a Time–Space Scale

Huanhe Dong, Xiaoqian Huang, Yong Zhang, Mingshuo Liu and Yong Fang *

College of Mathematics and Systems Science, Shandong University of Science and Technology, Qingdao 266590, China; mathsdong@126.com (H.D.); huangxiaoqian1998@163.com (X.H.); yzhang19900402@163.com (Y.Z.); liumingshuo2010@126.com (M.L.)
* Correspondence: fangyong@sdust.edu.cn

Abstract: The Gerdjikov–Ivanov (GI) equation is one type of derivative nonlinear Schrödinger equation used widely in quantum field theory, nonlinear optics, weakly nonlinear dispersion water waves and other fields. In this paper, the coupled GI equation on a time–space scale is deduced from Lax pairs and the zero curvature equation on a time–space scale, which can be reduced to the classical and the semi-discrete GI equation by considering different time–space scales. Furthermore, the Darboux transformation (DT) of the GI equation on a time–space scale is constructed via a gauge transformation. Finally, *N*-soliton solutions of the GI equation are given through applying its DT, which are expressed by the Cayley exponential function. At the same time, one-solition solutions are obtained on three different time–space scales ($\mathbb{X} = \mathbb{R}$, $\mathbb{X} = \mathbb{C}$ and $\mathbb{X} = \mathbb{K}p$).

Keywords: Gerdjikov-Ivanov equation; time–space scales; Darboux transformation; *N*-soliton solution

MSC: 35Q51; 35K05; 34N05

Citation: Dong H.H.; Huang X.Q.; Zhang Y.; Liu M.S.; Fang Y. The Darboux Transformation and *N*-Soliton Solutions of Gerdjikov–Ivanov Equation on a Time–Space Scale. *Axioms* **2021**, *10*, 294. https://doi.org/10.3390/axioms10040294

Academic Editors: Shengda Zeng, Stanisław Migórski and Yongjian Liu

Received: 12 September 2021
Accepted: 3 November 2021
Published: 5 November 2021

1. Introduction

There are some practical problems that cannot be solved accurately by using only continuous or discrete analysis. In order to unify continuous and discrete analysis, a time scale was initiated by Stefan Hilger in 1988, which is an arbitrary nonempty closed subset of the real numbers [1–3]. In recent years, extensive research about time scales has been conducted, particularly in stability, oscillation and initial-boundary value problems [4–8]. In addition, time scale dynamic equations have wide application prospects in many areas, such as population dynamic models [9], epidemic models [10,11] and models of the financial consumption process [12,13].

Toda's lattice, Hirota's network and nonlinear Schrödinger dynamic equations were derived on a time–space scale by extending an Ablowitz–Ladik hierarchy of integrable dynamic systems on a time–space scale [14]. This extension facilitates a variety of modeling applications of Ablowitz–Ladik hierarchies, including optics and chaos in dispersion numerical schemes [15]. The formulas for solutions of boundary value problem of Burgers equation and heat equation were derived on a time–space scale by using the Cole–Hopf transformation. These formulas may be used to study the wave motion on a time–space scale. Sine-Gordon equation was obtained on a time–space scale and its solution expressed by the Cayley exponential function was given [16–18]. However, the development of time–space scales is relatively slow in nonlinear dynamical systems compared to other fields.

There are important applications regarding the derivative nonlinear Schrödinger (DNLS) equation in many fields [19]. In particular, in situations where higher order nonlinear effects need to be restored, a family of DNLS equations was investigated [20]. There are three famous DNLS equations, which are the DNLS I equation [21,22], DNLS

II equation [23,24] and DNLS III equation [25]. The forms of these three equations are as follows

$$iq_t + q_{xx} + i\left(q^2 q^*\right)_x = 0,$$

$$iq_t + q_{xx} + iqq^* q_x = 0,$$

$$iq_t + q_{xx} + \frac{1}{2}q^3 q^{*2} - iq^2 q_x^* = 0,$$

where $q*$ represents the complex conjugate of q. They can be transformed into each other by a gauge transformation [26]. Specifically, the last equation is also known as the Gerdjikov–Ivanov (GI) equation, which was discovered by Gerdjikov and Ivanov [27]. In recent years, several useful methods have been proposed for obtaining solutions of the GI equation, such as the Darboux transformation (DT) [28,29], algebra-geometric solution [30–33], Wronskian type solution [29,34] and Hamiltonian structures [35,36].

The advantage of DT is that new solutions can be obtained successively through iteration. The explicit soliton-like solution of the GI equation was obtained by its DT [26]. The explicit N-fold DT with multiparameters for the GI equation was constructed with the help of a gauge transformation [28]. The dark soliton, bright soliton, breather solution and periodic solution are given explicitly from different seed solutions. In this paper, the coupled GI equation on a time–space scale is deduced by the Lax matrix equation extended on a time–space scale. This extension will provide a wider range of nonlinear integrable dynamic models and promote solutions to practical problems.

This paper is organized as follows. In Section 2, the coupled GI equation on a time–space scale is obtained, which can be reduced to the classical and the semi-discrete GI equation. In Section 3, N-fold DT and N-soliton solutions of the GI equation on a time–space scale are constructed with the help of a gauge transformation. In particular, one-soliton solutions of the GI equation on three different time–space scales are obtained from seed solution. The last section is our conclusions.

2. GI Equation on a Time–Space Scale

For constructing the GI equation on a time–space scale, jump operators, graininess functions and the $\nabla-$derivative are introduced as follows [1–3].

Definition 1. *For $(t,x) \in \mathbb{T} \times \mathbb{X}$, backward jump operators are defined as*

$$\sigma : \mathbb{T} \to \mathbb{T},\ \rho : \mathbb{X} \to \mathbb{X},$$

$$\sigma(t) = \sup\{s \in \mathbb{T} : s < t\},\ \rho(x) = \sup\{y \in \mathbb{X} : y < x\}. \tag{1}$$

For $x \in \mathbb{X}$, the forward jump operator $\beta(x) : \mathbb{X} \to \mathbb{X}$ is defined as $\beta(x) = \rho^{-1}(x) = \inf\{y \in \mathbb{X} : y > x\}$.

Definition 2. *The $\nabla-$derivative associated with t (time) and x (space) variables is defined as*

$$\nabla_t f(t,x) = \lim_{p \to \mu(t)} \frac{f(t,x) - f^{\sigma}(t,x)}{p}, \tag{2}$$

$$\nabla_x f(t,x) = \lim_{q \to \nu(x)} \frac{f(t,x) - f^{\rho}(t,x)}{q}, \tag{3}$$

where the graininess functions $\mu : \mathbb{T} \to [0,+\infty)$, $\nu : \mathbb{X} \to [0,+\infty)$ are defined as

$$\mu(t) = t - \sigma(t),\ \nu(x) = x - \rho(x). \tag{4}$$

Note that,

$$f^{\sigma}(t,x) := f(\sigma(t),x) = f(t,x) - \mu(t)\nabla_t f(t,x), \tag{5}$$

$$f^{\rho}(t,x) := f(t,\rho(x)) = f(t,x) - \nu(x)\nabla_x f(t,x). \tag{6}$$

Definition 3. *The Cayley exponential function on a time scale is defined by*

$$e_\alpha(x, x_0) := \exp\left(\int_{t_0}^{x} \zeta_{\mu(s)}(\alpha(s))\Delta s\right),\ e_\alpha(x) := e_\alpha(x, 0),$$

where $\alpha = \alpha(x)$ is a given rd-continuous regressive function and

$$\zeta_h(z) := \frac{1}{h}\log\frac{1+\frac{1}{2}zh}{1-\frac{1}{2}zh},\ h > 0,\ \zeta_0(z) := z.$$

When $\mathbb{X} = \mathbb{R}$ and $\mathbb{X} = h\mathbb{Z}$, the Cayley exponential function becomes

$$e_\alpha(x) = e^{\int_0^x \alpha(s)ds} \text{and}$$
$$e_\alpha(x) = \left(\frac{1+\frac{1}{2}\alpha h}{1-\frac{1}{2}\alpha h}\right)^{\frac{x}{h}},$$

respectively.

Lemma 1. *Take $\mathbb{T} \times \mathbb{X} = \mathbb{R} \times \mathbb{R}$. The backward jump operators*

$$\sigma(t) = \sup(-\infty, t) = t,\ \rho(x) = \sup(-\infty, x) = x, \tag{7}$$

and the graininess functions

$$\mu(t) = t - \sigma(t) = 0,\ \nu(x) = x - \rho(x) = 0. \tag{8}$$

Lemma 2. *Take $\mathbb{T} \times \mathbb{X} = \mathbb{R} \times \mathbb{Z}$. The backward jump operators*

$$\sigma(t) = \sup(-\infty, t) = t,\ \rho(x) = \sup\{x-1, x-2, \cdots\} = x - 1, \tag{9}$$

and the graininess functions

$$\mu(t) = t - \sigma(t) = 0,\ \nu(x) = x - \rho(x) = 1. \tag{10}$$

Lemma 3. *When $\mathbb{X} = \mathbb{R}$, $\mathbb{X} = \hbar\mathbb{Z}$ and $\mathbb{X} = \mathbb{K}_p$, the $\nabla-$derivative becomes*

$$\nabla_x f(x) = f_x(x),$$
$$\nabla_x f(x) = \frac{f(x) - f(x-\hbar)}{\hbar} \text{and}$$
$$\nabla_x f(x) = \frac{f(x) - f(p^{-1}x)}{(1-p^{-1})x},$$

respectively.

In what follows, based on Lax pairs of DNLS equation from the generalized Kaup–Newell spectrum problem [32], a ∇-dynamical system is introduced

$$\begin{cases} \nabla_x \psi(t,x) = U(t,x)\psi(t,x), \\ \nabla_t \psi(t,x) = V(t,x)\psi(t,x), \end{cases} \tag{11}$$

where

$$\begin{cases} U = \begin{pmatrix} -i\lambda^2 - \frac{1}{2}iqr & \lambda q \\ \lambda r & i\lambda^2 + \frac{1}{2}iqr \end{pmatrix}, \\ V = \begin{pmatrix} A(t,x) & B(t,x) \\ C(t,x) & -A(t,x) \end{pmatrix}, \end{cases} \tag{12}$$

with $\psi = \begin{pmatrix} \psi_1(t,x) \\ \psi_2(t,x) \end{pmatrix}$, q and r are potential functions, and λ is a spectral parameter.

According to the compatibility condition $\nabla_{xt}\psi = \nabla_{tx}\psi$ and ∇−derivative product rules [15], the zero curvature equation on a time–space scale is obtained

$$\nabla_t U - \nabla_x V + U^\sigma V - V^\rho U = 0. \tag{13}$$

Then, substituting Equation (12) into Equation (13), we find

$$\begin{cases} -i(C+C^\rho)\lambda^2 - (r^\sigma A + rA^\rho + \nabla_t r)\lambda - \frac{1}{2}i(qr)^\sigma C - \frac{1}{2}iqrC^\rho + \nabla_x C = 0, \\ -i(B+B^\rho)\lambda^2 - (q^\sigma A + qA^\rho + \nabla_t q)\lambda - \frac{1}{2}i(qr)^\sigma B - \frac{1}{2}iqrB^\rho - \nabla_x B = 0, \\ -i(A-A^\rho)\lambda^2 + (q^\sigma C - rB^\rho)\lambda - \frac{1}{2}i(qr)^\sigma A + \frac{1}{2}iqrA^\rho - \frac{1}{2}i\nabla_t(qr) - \nabla_x A = 0, \\ -i(A-A^\rho)\lambda^2 + \lambda(r^\sigma B - qC^\rho) - \frac{1}{2}i(qr)^\sigma A + \frac{1}{2}iqrA^\rho - \frac{1}{2}i\nabla_t(qr) + \nabla_x A = 0. \end{cases} \tag{14}$$

Take $A,\ B$ and C as quaternary polynomials of λ,

$$A = \sum_{j=0}^{4} a_j\lambda^j,\ B = \sum_{j=0}^{4} b_j\lambda^j,\ C = \sum_{j=0}^{4} c_j\lambda^j. \tag{15}$$

Then, by substituting Equation (15) into Equation (14), these relations are obtained

$$\begin{cases} a_4 = -2i,\ a_1 = a_3 = b_0 = b_2 = b_4 = c_0 = c_2 = c_4 = 0, \\ b_3 = -b_3^\rho + 2(q^\sigma + q),\ c_3 = -c_3^\rho + 2(r^\sigma + r) = 0, \\ b_1 = -b_1^\rho + iqa_2^\rho + iq^\sigma a_2 - \frac{1}{2}qrb_3^\rho - \frac{1}{2}(qr)^\sigma b_3 + i\nabla_x b_3, \\ c_1 = -c_1^\rho + ira_2^\rho + ir^\sigma a_2 - \frac{1}{2}qrc_3^\rho - \frac{1}{2}(qr)^\sigma c_3 - i\nabla_x c_3, \\ a_2 = \nabla_x^{-1}(\frac{1}{2}q^\sigma c_1 - \frac{1}{2}r^\sigma b_1 - \frac{1}{2}rb_1^\rho + \frac{1}{2}qc_1^\rho), \\ a_0 = \nabla_x^{-1}(-\frac{1}{2}iqr^\sigma a_0^\rho + \frac{1}{4}qrr^\sigma b_1^\rho - \frac{1}{2}ir^\sigma b_1^x - \frac{1}{2}iq^\sigma r^\sigma a_0 + \frac{1}{4}(qr)^\sigma b_1 r^\sigma \\ \qquad + \frac{1}{2}iqra_0^\rho - \frac{1}{4}q^2rc_1^\rho + \frac{1}{2}ir^\sigma qa_0 - \frac{1}{4}(qr)^\sigma qc_1 - \frac{1}{2}ic_{1x}q), \end{cases} \tag{16}$$

and evolution equations on a time–space scale are obtained

$$\nabla_t q = qa_0^\rho + q^\sigma a_0 + \frac{1}{2}iqrb_1^\rho + \frac{1}{2}i(qr)^\sigma b_1 + \nabla_x b_1, \tag{17}$$

$$\nabla_t r = -ra_0^\rho - r^\sigma a_0 - \frac{1}{2}iqrc_1^\rho - \frac{1}{2}i(qr)^\sigma c_1 + \nabla_x c_1. \tag{18}$$

According to Equations (5) and (6), Equation (16) is reduced to

$$b_3 = 2(2 - \nu(x)\nabla_x)^{-1}(q + q^\sigma), \tag{19}$$

$$c_3 = 2(2 - \nu(x)\nabla_x)^{-1}(r + r^\sigma), \tag{20}$$

$$b_1 = 2i(2 - \nu(x)\nabla_x)^{-1}m_1 a_2 + \frac{1}{2}(2 - \nu(x)\nabla_x)^{-1}m_4(q + q^\sigma), \tag{21}$$

$$c_1 = 2i(2 - \nu(x)\nabla_x)^{-1}m_2 a_2 + \frac{1}{2}(2 - \nu(x)\nabla_x)^{-1}m_3(r + r^\sigma), \tag{22}$$

$$\nabla_x a_0 = \frac{1}{2}im_5 a_0 + \frac{1}{2}i(r^\sigma m_4 m_1 - qm_4 m_2)a_2 + \frac{1}{8}r^\sigma m_4^2(q + q^\sigma) - \frac{1}{8}qm_4 m_3(r + r^\sigma), \tag{23}$$

$$\nabla_x a_2 = \frac{1}{2} i(m_1 m_2 - m_2 m_1)(2 - \nu(x)\nabla_x) a_2 + \frac{1}{2} m_1 m_3 (r + r^\sigma) + \frac{1}{2} m_2 m_4 (q + q^\sigma), \tag{24}$$

with

$$\begin{aligned}
m_1 &= [q^\sigma + q(1 - \nu(x)\nabla_x)](2 - \nu(x)\nabla_x)^{-1}, \\
m_2 &= [r^\sigma + r(1 - \nu(x)\nabla_x)](2 - \nu(x)\nabla_x)^{-1}, \\
m_3 &= [(qr)^\sigma + (qr)(1 - \nu(x)\nabla_x) + 2i\nabla_x](2 - \nu(x)\nabla_x)^{-1}, \\
m_4 &= [(qr)^\sigma + (qr)(1 - \nu(x)\nabla_x) - 2i\nabla_x](2 - \nu(x)\nabla_x)^{-1}, \\
m_5 &= (qr - qr^\sigma)(1 - \nu(x)\nabla_x) + qr^\sigma - q^\sigma r^\sigma.
\end{aligned}$$

Then, the coupled GI equation on a time–space scale is obtained

$$\begin{cases} \nabla_t q = q(1 - \nu(x)\nabla_x) a_0 + q^\sigma a_0 + \frac{1}{2} iqr(1 - \nu(x)\nabla_x) b_1 + \frac{1}{2} i(qr)^\sigma b_1 + \nabla_x b_1, \\ \nabla_t r = -r(1 - \nu(x)\nabla_x) a_0 - r^\sigma a_0 - \frac{1}{2} iqr(1 - \nu(x)\nabla_x) c_1 - \frac{1}{2} i(qr)^\sigma c_1 + \nabla_x c_1, \end{cases} \tag{25}$$

where a_0, b_1, c_1 are defined by Equations (21)–(23), respectively.

In the following, two special kinds of equations are given as follows.

Case I: Taking $\mathbb{T} \times \mathbb{X} = \mathbb{R} \times \mathbb{R}$, we find $\mu(t) = 0, \nu(x) = 0$. Equations (21)–(23) are reduced to

$$\begin{aligned}
b_1 &= iq_x, \\
c_1 &= -ir_x, \\
a_0 &= \frac{1}{2}(rq_x - qr_x) + \frac{1}{4} iq^2 r^2.
\end{aligned}$$

Then, Equation (25) is reduced to the coupled GI equation

$$\begin{cases} iq_t + q_{xx} + iq^2 r_x + \frac{1}{2} q^3 r^2 = 0, \\ ir_t - r_{xx} + ir^2 q_x - \frac{1}{2} q^2 r^3 = 0. \end{cases} \tag{26}$$

When $r = -q^*$, the classical GI equation is obtained

$$iq_t + q_{xx} + \frac{1}{2} q^3 q^{*2} - iq^2 q_x^* = 0. \tag{27}$$

Case II: Taking $\mathbb{T} \times \mathbb{X} = \mathbb{R} \times \mathbb{Z}$, we find $\mu(t) = 0,\ \nu(x) = 1$.

$$\begin{aligned}
f^\sigma(x,t) &= f(x,t), \\
f^\rho(x,t) &= Ef(x,t) = f(x,t) - (1 - E) f(x,t),
\end{aligned} \tag{28}$$

where E is the shift operator. Then, Equations (19)–(24) are reduced to

$$b_3 = 4(1 + E)^{-1} q, \tag{29}$$

$$c_3 = 4(1 + E)^{-1} r, \tag{30}$$

$$a_2 = (1 - E)^{-1}\left(qr^2 + rm_7 q\right), \tag{31}$$

$$b_1 = 2i(1 + E)^{-1} q(1 - E)^{-1}\left(qr^2 + rm_7 q\right) + (1 + E)^{-1} m_7 q, \tag{32}$$

$$c_1 = 2i(1 + E)^{-1} r(1 - E)^{-1}\left(qr^2 + rm_7 q\right) + (1 + E)^{-1} m_6 q, \tag{33}$$

$$a_0 = \frac{1}{2}i(1-E)^{-1}(rm_7q - qm_7r)(1-E)^{-1}\left(qr^2 + rm_7q\right) + \frac{1}{4}(1-E)^{-1}\left(rm_7^2q - qm_7m_6r\right), \tag{34}$$

with

$$m_6 = qr + 2i(1-E)(1+E)^{-1},$$
$$m_7 = qr - 2i(1-E)(1+E)^{-1}.$$

Therefore, the semi-discrete coupled GI equation is obtained

$$\begin{aligned} q_t &= q(1+E)a_0 + \frac{1}{2}iqr(1+E)b_1 + (1-E)b_1, \\ r_t &= -r(1+E)a_0 - \frac{1}{2}iqr(1+E)c_1 + (1-E)c_1, \end{aligned} \tag{35}$$

where a_0, b_1, and c_1 are defined by Equations (32)–(34), respectively.

3. DT of GI Equation on a Time–Space Scale

In this section, we construct a DT for GI equation and give its N-soliton solutions on a time–space scale.

3.1. Construction of DT on a Time–Space Scale

First, it can be shown by long calculations that Equation (12) is transformed to

$$\begin{cases} U = -i\lambda^2\sigma_3 + \lambda Q - \frac{1}{2}iQ^2\sigma_3, \\ V = -2i\sigma_3\lambda^4 + B_3\lambda^3 + a_2\sigma_3\lambda^2 + B_1\lambda + a_0\sigma_3, \end{cases} \tag{36}$$

with σ_3 is a Pauli matrix where $Q = \begin{pmatrix} 0 & q \\ -q^* & 0 \end{pmatrix}$, $B_1 = \begin{pmatrix} 0 & b_1 \\ c_1 & 0 \end{pmatrix}$, $B_3 = \begin{pmatrix} 0 & b_3 \\ c_3 & 0 \end{pmatrix}$, $a_j(j=0,2), b_j, c_j(j=1,3)$ are defined by Equations (19)–(24), respectively.

Then, the ∇-dynamical system Equation (11) is transformed into

$$\begin{cases} \nabla_x\psi[1] = U[1]\psi[1], \\ \nabla_t\psi[1] = V[1]\psi[1], \end{cases} \tag{37}$$

under a gauge transformation

$$\psi[1] = T[1]\psi. \tag{38}$$

Substituting Equation (38) into Equation (37), we find

$$U[1]T[1] = \nabla_x T[1] + T[1]^\rho U, \tag{39}$$

$$V[1]T[1] = \nabla_t T[1] + T[1]^\sigma V, \tag{40}$$

where

$$\begin{cases} U[1] = -i\lambda^2\sigma_3 + \lambda Q[1] - \frac{1}{2}iQ[1]^2\sigma_3, \\ V[1] = -2i\sigma_3\lambda^4 + B_3[1]\lambda^3 + a_2[1]\sigma_3\lambda^2 + B_1[1]\lambda + a_0[1]\sigma_3, \end{cases} \tag{41}$$

with $Q[1] = \begin{pmatrix} 0 & q[1] \\ -q[1]^* & 0 \end{pmatrix}$, $B_1[1] = \begin{pmatrix} 0 & b_1[1] \\ c_1[1] & 0 \end{pmatrix}$, $B_3[1] = \begin{pmatrix} 0 & b_3[1] \\ c_3[1] & 0 \end{pmatrix}$.

Assume

$$T[1] = T_0 + T_1\lambda \tag{42}$$

where $T_0 = \begin{pmatrix} a & b \\ c & d \end{pmatrix}$, $T_1 = \begin{pmatrix} a_{11} & b_{12} \\ c_{21} & d_{22} \end{pmatrix}$.

Substituting Equation (42) into Equation (39) and comparing the coefficients in the terms of the same powers $\lambda^j (j = 0, \cdots, 5)$ on both sides of equation, we find

$$\begin{cases} c_{21} = b_{12} = 0, \\ a_{11} = d_{22} = 1, \\ q[1] = q + ib + ib^{\rho}, \\ q[1]^* = q^* + ic + ic^{\rho}. \end{cases} \tag{43}$$

Setting $S = -T_0 = \begin{pmatrix} s_{11} & s_{12} \\ s_{21} & s_{22} \end{pmatrix}$, we obtain

$$T[1] = \lambda I - S, \tag{44}$$

$$q[1] = q - is_{12} - is_{12}^{\rho}. \tag{45}$$

Substituting Equation (44) into Equation (39), we obtain

$$\nabla_x S = \frac{1}{2} i S^{\rho} Q^2 \sigma_3 + \frac{1}{2} i S Q^2 \sigma_3 + Q S^2 - S^{\rho} Q S + i S^{\rho} S^2 \sigma_3 + i S^3 \sigma_3. \tag{46}$$

Assume

$$S = H \Lambda H^{-1} \tag{47}$$

with $\Lambda = \begin{pmatrix} \lambda & 0 \\ 0 & \lambda^* \end{pmatrix}$ is an eigenvalue matrix, $H = \begin{pmatrix} \psi_1 & \psi_2^* \\ \psi_2 & -\psi_1^* \end{pmatrix}$ is a fundamental solution matrix and satisfies

$$\begin{cases} \nabla_x H = -i\sigma_3 H \Lambda^2 + Q H \Lambda - \frac{1}{2} i Q^2 \sigma_3 H, \\ \nabla_t H = -2i\sigma_3 H \Lambda^4 + B_3 \Lambda^3 + a_2 \sigma_3 H \Lambda^2 + B_1 H \Lambda + a_0 \sigma_3 H. \end{cases} \tag{48}$$

It is easy to obtain

$$\begin{aligned} \nabla_x S &= \nabla_x \left(H \Lambda H^{-1} \right) \\ &= \frac{1}{2} i S^{\rho} Q^2 \sigma_3 + \frac{1}{2} i S Q^2 \sigma_3 + Q S^2 - S^{\rho} Q S + i S^{\rho} S^2 \sigma_3 + i S^3 \sigma_3, \end{aligned} \tag{49}$$

which means that Equation (47) yields Equation (46). From $T[1]_t + T[1]^{\sigma} V = V[1] T[1]$, we find

$$\begin{aligned} & - \nabla_t S + (\lambda I - S^{\sigma}) \left(-2i\sigma_3 \lambda^4 + B_3 \lambda^3 + a_2 \sigma_3 \lambda^2 + B_1 \lambda + a_0 \sigma_3 \right) \\ = & \left(-2i\sigma_3 \lambda^4 + B_3[1] \lambda^3 + a_2[1] \sigma_3 \lambda^2 + B_1[1] \lambda + a_0[1] \sigma_3 \right) (\lambda I - S). \end{aligned} \tag{50}$$

Comparing the coefficients in terms of the same powers $\lambda^j (j = 0, \cdots, 5)$ on both sides of Equation (50), we obtain

$$\begin{aligned} &\lambda^0 : -\nabla_t S - a_0 S^{\sigma} \sigma_3 = -a_0[1] \sigma_3 S, \\ &\lambda^1 : a_0 \sigma_3 - S^{\sigma} B_1 = -B_1[1] S + a_0[1] \sigma_3, \\ &\lambda^2 : B_1 - a_2 S^{\sigma} \sigma_3 = B_1[1] - a_2[1] \sigma_3 S, \\ &\lambda^3 : a_2 \sigma_3 - S^{\sigma} B_3 = a_2[1] \sigma_3 - B_3[1] S, \\ &\lambda^4 : B_3 + 2i S^{\sigma} \sigma_3 = B_3[1] + 2i\sigma_3 S, \\ &\lambda^5 : -2i\sigma_3 = -2i\sigma_3. \end{aligned} \tag{51}$$

Then, the gauge transformations Equations (44) and (45) are proven to be DT of the GI equation on a time–space scale.

3.2. Soliton Solutions of the GI Equation on a Time–Space Scale

Soliton solutions of the GI equation on a time–space scale are constructed by applying its DT. First, Equation (11) is transformed to

$$\begin{cases} \nabla_x \psi[0] = U[0]\psi[0] = \begin{pmatrix} -i\lambda^2 + \frac{1}{2}iq[0]q[0]^* & \lambda q[0] \\ -\lambda q[0]^* & i\lambda^2 - \frac{1}{2}iq[0]q[0]^* \end{pmatrix}\psi[0], \\ \nabla_t \psi[0] = V[0]\psi[0] = \begin{pmatrix} -2i\lambda^4 + a_2[0]\lambda^2 + a_0[0] & b_3[0]\lambda^3 + b_1[0]\lambda \\ c_3[0]\lambda^3 + c_1[0]\lambda & 2i\lambda^4 - a_2[0]\lambda^2 - a_0[0] \end{pmatrix}\psi[0], \end{cases} \tag{52}$$

where $\psi[0]=\begin{pmatrix} \psi_1[0] \\ \psi_2[0] \end{pmatrix}$.

Let us set the spectral parameter $\lambda = \lambda_1$. A one-fold DT of the GI equation on a time–space scale is constructed

$$\begin{aligned} \psi[1] &= T[1]\psi[0] \\ &= (\lambda I - S[0])\psi[0] \\ &= \begin{pmatrix} \lambda - s_{11}[0] & -s_{12}[0] \\ -s_{21}[0] & \lambda - s_{22}[0] \end{pmatrix}\psi[0], \\ q[1] &= q[0] - is_{12}[0] - is_{12}[0]^\rho \\ &= q[0] - i\frac{(\lambda_1 - \lambda_1^*)\psi_1[0]\psi_2^*[0]}{\Delta_0} - i\frac{(\lambda_1 - \lambda_1^*)\psi_1^\rho[0]\psi_2^{*\rho}[0]}{\Delta_0^\rho}, \end{aligned} \tag{53}$$

where

$$S = \frac{1}{\Delta_0}\begin{pmatrix} -\lambda_1|\psi_1[0]|^2 + \lambda_1^*|\psi_2[0]|^2 & (\lambda_1^* - \lambda_1)\psi_1[0]\psi_2^*[0] \\ (-\lambda_1^* - \lambda_1)\psi_1^*[0]\psi_2[0] & -\lambda_1^*|\psi_1[0]|^2 - \lambda_1|\psi_2[0]|^2 \end{pmatrix}, \tag{54}$$

with $\Delta_0 = -|\psi_1[0]|^2 - |\psi_2[0]|^2$.

Under the DT (53), the ∇-dynamical system (52) is transformed into

$$\begin{cases} \nabla_x \psi[1] = U[1]\psi[1] = \begin{pmatrix} -i\lambda^2 + \frac{1}{2}iq[1]q[1]^* & \lambda q[1] \\ -\lambda q[1]^* & i\lambda^2 - \frac{1}{2}iq[1]q[1]^* \end{pmatrix}\psi[1], \\ \nabla_t \psi[1] = V[1]\psi[1] = \begin{pmatrix} -2i\lambda^4 + a_2[1]\lambda^2 + a_0[1] & b_3[1]\lambda^3 + b_1[1]\lambda \\ c_3[1]\lambda^3 + c_1[1]\lambda & 2i\lambda^4 - a_2[1]\lambda^2 - a_0[1] \end{pmatrix}\psi[1]. \end{cases} \tag{55}$$

In what follows, taking the "seed solution" $q[0] = 0$, we obtain eigenvectors $\psi[0]$ of Equation (52) with $\lambda = \lambda_1$

$$\psi[0]=\begin{pmatrix} \psi_1[0] \\ \psi_2[0] \end{pmatrix}=\begin{pmatrix} e_{-i\lambda_1^2}(x,0)e_{-2i\lambda_1^4}(t,0) \\ e_{i\lambda_1^2}(x,0)e_{2i\lambda_1^4}(t,0) \end{pmatrix}, \tag{56}$$

$$\psi^\rho[0]=\begin{pmatrix} \psi_1^\rho[0] \\ \psi_2^\rho[0] \end{pmatrix}=\begin{pmatrix} [1 - i\lambda_1^2\nu(x)]e_{-i\lambda_1^2}(x,0)e_{-2i\lambda_1^4}(t,0) \\ [1 + i\lambda_1^2\nu(x)]e_{i\lambda_1^2}(x,0)e_{2i\lambda_1^4}(t,0) \end{pmatrix}, \tag{57}$$

where $e_{\pm i\lambda_1^2}(x,0)$ and $e_{\pm 2i\lambda_1^4}(t,0)$ are Cayley exponential functions [18]. Then, a one-soliton solution of the GI equation on a time–space scale is obtained

$$q[1] = \frac{i(\lambda_1 - \lambda_1^*)E_3}{E_1 + E_2} + \frac{i(\lambda_1 - \lambda_1^*)(1 - i\lambda_1^{*2}\nu(x))E_3}{(1 + i\lambda_1^{*2}\nu(x))E_1 + (1 - i\lambda_1^{*2}\nu(x))E_2}, \tag{58}$$

where

$$E_1 = -e_{-i(\lambda_1^2-\lambda_1^{*2})}(x,0)e_{-2i(\lambda_1^4-\lambda_1^{*4})}(t,0),$$
$$E_2 = -e_{i(\lambda_1^2-\lambda_1^{*2})}(x,0)e_{2i(\lambda_1^4-\lambda_1^{*4})}(t,0),$$
$$E_3 = -e_{-i(\lambda_1^2+\lambda_1^{*2})}(x,0)e_{-2i(\lambda_1^4+\lambda_1^{*4})}(t,0).$$

Similarly, we take the spectral parameter $\lambda = \lambda_2$. A two-fold DT of the GI equation on a time–space scale is constructed

$$\begin{aligned}
\psi[2] &= T[2]\psi[1] \\
&= (\lambda I - S[1])\psi[1] \\
&= \begin{pmatrix} \lambda - s_{11}[1] & -s_{12}[1] \\ -s_{21}[1] & \lambda - s_{22}[1] \end{pmatrix}\psi[1] \\
&= T[2]T[1]\psi[0], \\
q[2] &= q[1] - is_{12}[1] - is_{12}[1]^{\rho} \\
&= q[1] - i\frac{(\lambda_2-\lambda_2^*)\psi_1[1]\psi_2^*[1]}{\Delta_1} - i\frac{(\lambda_2-\lambda_2^*)\psi_1^{\rho}[1]\psi_2^{*\rho}[1]}{\Delta_1^{\rho}},
\end{aligned} \tag{59}$$

where

$$S[1] = \frac{1}{\Delta_1}\begin{pmatrix} -\lambda_2|\psi_1[1]|^2 + \lambda_2^*|\psi_2[1]|^2 & (\lambda_2^*-\lambda_2)\psi_1[1]\psi_2[1]^* \\ (-\lambda_2^*-\lambda_2)\psi_1[1]^*\psi_2[1] & -\lambda_2^*|\psi_1[1]|^2 - \lambda_2|\psi_2[1]|^2 \end{pmatrix}, \tag{60}$$

with $\Delta_1 = -|\psi_1[1]|^2 - |\psi_2[1]|^2$.

When the spectral parameter $\lambda = \lambda_N$, N-fold DT is constructed as follows

$$\begin{aligned}
\psi[N] &= T[N]\psi[N-1] \\
&= (\lambda I - S[N-1])\psi[N-1] \\
&= \begin{pmatrix} \lambda - s_{11}[N-1] & -s_{12}[N-1] \\ -s_{21}[N-1] & \lambda - s_{22}[N-1] \end{pmatrix}\psi[N-1] \\
&= T[N]\cdots T[3]T[2]T[1]\psi[0], \\
q[N] &= q[N-1] - is_{12}[N-1] - is_{12}^{\rho}[N-1] \\
&= q[0] + i\sum_{j=1}^{N}\frac{\left(\lambda_j-\lambda_j^*\right)\psi_1[j-1]\psi_2^*[j-1]}{|\psi_1[j-1]|^2+|\psi_2[j-1]|^2} + i\sum_{j=1}^{N}\frac{\left(\lambda_j-\lambda_j^*\right)\psi_1^{\rho}[j-1]\psi_2^{*\rho}[j-1]}{\left|\psi_1^{\rho}[j-1]\right|^2+\left|\psi_2^{\rho}[j-1]\right|^2}.
\end{aligned} \tag{61}$$

An N-soliton solution of the GI equation on a time–space scale is obtained

$$q[N] = i\sum_{j=1}^{N}\frac{\left(\lambda_j-\lambda_j^*\right)\psi_1[j-1]\psi_2^*[j-1]}{|\psi_1[j-1]|^2+|\psi_2[j-1]|^2} + i\sum_{j=1}^{N}\frac{\left(\lambda_j-\lambda_j^*\right)\psi_1^{\rho}[j-1]\psi_2^{*\rho}[j-1]}{\left|\psi_1^{\rho}[j-1]\right|^2+\left|\psi_2^{\rho}[j-1]\right|^2}. \tag{62}$$

In what follows, N-fold DT and N-soliton solutions of the GI equation on three special time–space scales are obtained as follows.

Case I: Taking $\mathbb{T}\times\mathbb{X}=\mathbb{R}\times\mathbb{R}$, we obtain an N-fold DT of the classical GI equation

$$\begin{aligned}\psi[N] &= T[N]\psi[N-1]\\ &= (\lambda I - S[N-1])\psi[N-1]\\ &= \begin{pmatrix}\lambda - s_{11}[N-1] & -s_{12}[N-1]\\ -s_{21}[N-1] & \lambda - s_{22}[N-1]\end{pmatrix}\psi[N-1]\\ &= T[N]\cdots T[3]T[2]T[1]\psi[0],\\ q[N] &= q[N-1]-2is_{12}[N-1]\\ &= q[0]+2i\sum_{j=1}^{N}\frac{\left(\lambda_j-\lambda_j^*\right)\psi_1[j-1]\psi_2^*[j-1]}{|\psi_1[j-1]|^2+|\psi_2[j-1]|^2}.\end{aligned} \tag{63}$$

When $N=1$, $q[0]$=0 and the spectral parameter $\lambda_1=\alpha_1+i\eta_1$, we obtain a one-soliton solution of Equation (27)

$$q[1] = -2\eta_1 e^{2iY_1}\operatorname{sech}(2X_1), \tag{64}$$

where

$$\begin{aligned}X_1 &= 4\alpha_1\eta_1 x + 16\left(\alpha_1^3\eta_1-\alpha_1\eta_1^3\right)t,\\ Y_1 &= -2\left(\alpha_1^2-\eta_1^2\right)x - 4\left(\alpha_1^2-6\alpha_1^2\eta_1^2\right)t.\end{aligned}$$

The profile of the one-soliton in Figure 1.

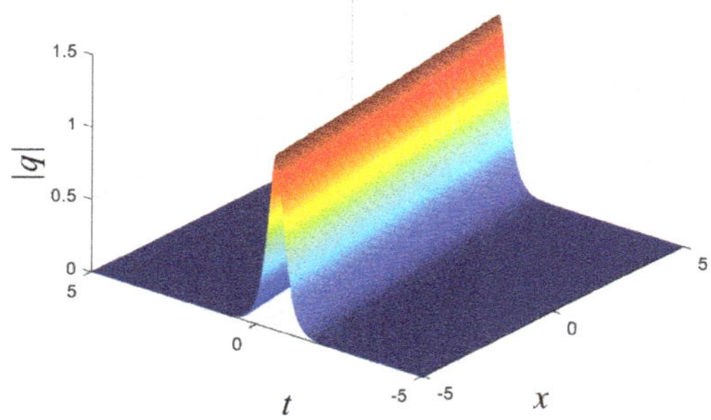

Figure 1. One-soliton solution (64) with $\alpha_1=0.7$, $\eta_1=0.6$.

When $N=2$, $q[0]$=0 and the spectral parameter $\lambda_2=\alpha_2+i\eta_2$, we obtain a two-soliton solution of Equation (27)

$$\begin{aligned}q[2] =& -2\eta_1 e^{2iY_1}\operatorname{sech}(2X_1) - 4\eta_2\frac{M_1M_2e^{-2iY_2}-\alpha_1M_1\operatorname{sech}(2X_1)e^{2X_2-2iY_1}}{|M_1|^2e^{2X_2}+|M_2|^2e^{-2X_2}+M_4+M_5+M_6}\\ &+4\eta_2\frac{i\eta_1M_2\operatorname{sech}(2X_1)e^{-2X_2-2iY_1}-M_3}{|M_1|^2e^{2X_2}+|M_2|^2e^{-2X_2}+M_4+M_5+M_6},\end{aligned} \tag{65}$$

where

$$\begin{aligned}
M_1 &= \alpha_2 - \alpha_1 \tanh(2X_1) + (\eta_2 - \eta_1)i, \\
M_2 &= \alpha_2 - \alpha_1 + (\eta_2 - \eta_1 \tanh(2X_1))i, \\
M_3 &= i\alpha_1\eta_1 \operatorname{sech}^2(2X_1)e^{-4iY_1+2iY_2}, \\
M_4 &= 2i \operatorname{sech}(2X_1) \sinh(2iY_1 - 2iY_2)(\eta_1\alpha_2 + \alpha_1\eta_2), \\
M_5 &= 2 \operatorname{sech}(2X_1) \cosh(2iY_1 - 2iY_2)\left(\eta_1\eta_2 - \eta_1^2 + \alpha_1\alpha_2 - \alpha_1^2\right), \\
M_6 &= \operatorname{sech}^2(2X_1)\left(\eta_1^2 e^{-2X_2} + \alpha_1^2 e^{2X_2}\right), \\
X_2 &= 4\alpha_2\eta_2 x + 16\left(\alpha_2^3\eta_2 - \alpha_2\eta_2^3\right)t, \\
Y_2 &= -2\left(\alpha_2^2 - \eta_2^2\right)x - 4\left(\alpha_2^2 - 6\alpha_2^2\eta_2^2\right)t.
\end{aligned}$$

Case II: Taking $\mathbb{T} \times \mathbb{X} = \mathbb{R} \times \mathbb{C}$, we find

$$\mu(t) = 0, \quad \nu(x) = \begin{cases} \frac{1}{3^{m+1}}, & x \in \mathbb{L}, \\ 0, & x \in \mathbb{C}\backslash\mathbb{L}, \end{cases} \tag{66}$$

where $\mathbb{C}$ is a Cantor set. $\mathbb{L}$ contains left discrete elements of $\mathbb{C}$,

$$\mathbb{L} = \left\{ \sum_{k=1}^{m} \frac{a_k}{3^k} + \frac{1}{3^{m+1}} : m \in N,\ a_k \in \{0,2\}, 1 \le k \le m \right\}.$$

Then, an N-fold DT of the GI equation is constructed

$$\begin{aligned}
\psi[N] &= T[N]\psi[N-1] \\
&= (\lambda I - S[N-1])\psi[N-1] \\
&= \begin{pmatrix} \lambda - s_{11}[N-1] & -s_{12}[N-1] \\ -s_{21}[N-1] & \lambda - s_{22}[N-1] \end{pmatrix}\psi[N-1] \\
&= T[N]\cdots T[3]T[2]T[1]\psi[0],
\end{aligned}$$

$$q[N] = \begin{cases} q[0] + i\sum\limits_{j=1}^{N} \frac{\left(\lambda_j - \lambda_j^*\right)\psi_1[j-1]\psi_2^*[j-1]}{|\psi_1[j-1]|^2 + |\psi_2[j-1]|^2} + i\sum\limits_{j=1}^{N} \frac{\left(\lambda_j - \lambda_j^*\right)\psi_1^\rho[j-1]\psi_2^{*\rho}[j-1]}{|\psi_1^\rho[j-1]|^2 + |\psi_2^\rho[j-1]|^2}, & x \in \mathbb{L},\ t \in \mathbb{R}, \\ q[0] + 2i\sum\limits_{j=1}^{N} \frac{\left(\lambda_j - \lambda_j^*\right)\psi_1[j-1]\psi_2^*[j-1]}{|\psi_1[j-1]|^2 + |\psi_2[j-1]|^2}, & x \in \mathbb{C}\backslash\mathbb{L},\ t \in \mathbb{R}. \end{cases} \tag{67}$$

According to Definition 3, we have

$$e_{\pm 2i\lambda_1^4}(x,0) = \left[\frac{1 \pm \frac{i\lambda_1^4}{3^{m+1}}}{1 \mp \frac{i\lambda_1^4}{3^{m+1}}}\right]^{\frac{x}{3^{m+1}}}, \quad e_{\pm i\lambda_1^2}(x,0) = \left[\frac{1 \pm \frac{i\lambda_1^2}{2\times 3^{m+1}}}{1 \mp \frac{i\lambda_1^2}{2\times 3^{m+1}}}\right]^{\frac{x}{3^{m+1}}}.$$

When $N = 1$, $q[0] = 0$ and the spectral parameter $\lambda_1 = \alpha_1 + i\eta_1$, a one-soliton solution is obtained

$$q[1] = \begin{cases} \frac{1}{N_1} - \frac{(3^{m+1} - i\alpha_1^2)^2 M_7 - (i\eta_1^2 - 2\alpha_1\eta_1)^2 M_7}{(i\alpha_1^2 - i\eta_1^2)N_2}, & x \in \mathbb{L},\ t \in \mathbb{R}, \\ -2\eta_1 e^{2iY_1} \operatorname{sech}(2X_1), & x \in \mathbb{C}\backslash\mathbb{L},\ t \in \mathbb{R}, \end{cases} \tag{68}$$

where

$$N_1 = E_1|_{\lambda_1=\alpha_1+i\eta_1} + E_2|_{\lambda_1=\alpha_1+i\eta_1},$$
$$N_2 = E_1|_{\lambda_1=\alpha_1+i\eta_1} - E_2|_{\lambda_1=\alpha_1+i\eta_1},$$
$$M_7 = 2\eta_1\left[1+\frac{i\alpha_1^2}{3^{m+1}}\left(2i\eta_1^2-2i\alpha_1^2\right)\right]^{3^{m+1}x} e^{\left(24i\alpha_1^2\eta_1^2-4i\alpha_1^4\right)t}.$$

Case III: Taking $\mathbb{T}\times\mathbb{X}=\mathbb{R}\times\mathbb{K}_p$, we find

$$\mu(t)=0,\qquad \nu(x)=\begin{cases}(1-p^{-1})x,\ x=p^k\in p^{\mathbb{Z}},\\ 0,\ x=0,\end{cases} \tag{69}$$

where $p>1$, $p^{\mathbb{Z}}=\left\{p^k: k\in\mathbb{Z}\right\}$ and $\mathbb{K}_p=p^{\mathbb{Z}}\bigcup\{0\}$.

Then, an N-fold DT is constructed

$$\begin{aligned}\psi[N]&=T[N]\psi[N-1]\\&=(\lambda I-S[N-1])\psi[N-1]\\&=\begin{pmatrix}\lambda-s_{11}[N-1] & -s_{12}[N-1]\\ -s_{21}[N-1] & \lambda-s_{22}[N-1]\end{pmatrix}\psi[N-1]\\&=T[N]\cdots T[3]T[2]T[1]\psi[0],\end{aligned}$$

$$q[N]=\begin{cases}q[0]+i\sum\limits_{j=1}^{N}\frac{\left(\lambda_j-\lambda_j^*\right)\psi_1[j-1]\psi_2^*[j-1]}{|\psi_1[j-1]|^2+|\psi_2[j-1]|^2}+i\sum\limits_{j=1}^{N}\frac{\left(\lambda_j-\lambda_j^*\right)\psi_1^\rho[j-1]\psi_2^{*\rho}[j-1]}{\left|\psi_1^\rho[j-1]\right|^2+\left|\psi_2^\rho[j-1]\right|^2},\ x\in p^{\mathbb{Z}},\ t\in\mathbb{R},\\ q[0]+2i\sum\limits_{j=1}^{N}\frac{\left(\lambda_j-\lambda_j^*\right)\psi_1[j-1]\psi_2^*[j-1]}{|\psi_1[j-1]|^2+|\psi_2[j-1]|^2},\ x=0,\ t\in\mathbb{R}.\end{cases} \tag{70}$$

According to

$$\int_a^b f(x)\nabla x=\left(1-p^{-1}\right)\sum_{x=a}^{b}xf(x),$$
$$\int_a^b f(\rho(x))\nabla x=(p-1)\sum_{x=a}^{b}xf(x),$$

we have

$$e_{\pm i\lambda_1^2}(x,0)=e^{\left(1-p^{-1}\right)\sum\limits_{x=0}^{p^k}\pm i\lambda_1^2},$$
$$e_{\pm i\lambda_1^2}(\rho(x),0)=e^{(p-1)\sum\limits_{x=0}^{p^k}\pm i\lambda_1^2}.$$

When $N=1$, $q[0]$=0 and the spectral parameter $\lambda_1=\alpha_1+i\eta_1$, a one-soliton solution is obtained

$$q[1]=\begin{cases}-\eta_1 e^{\left(16\alpha_1\eta_1^3-16\alpha_1^3\eta_1-4i\alpha_1^4+24i\alpha_1^2\eta_1^2\right)t}M_8,\ x\in p^{\mathbb{Z}},\ t\in\mathbb{R},\\ -2\eta_1 e^{2iY_1}\operatorname{sech}(2X_1),\ x=0,\ t\in\mathbb{R},\end{cases} \tag{71}$$

where

$$\begin{aligned}M_8=&e^{\left(1-p^{-1}\right)\sum\limits_{x=0}^{p^k}\left(-2i\alpha_1^2+2i\eta_1^2\right)x}\operatorname{sech}\left(1-p^{-1}\right)\sum_{x=0}^{p^k}4\alpha_1\eta_1x\\&+e^{(p-1)\sum\limits_{k=0}^{p^k}\left(-2i\alpha_1^2+2i\eta_1^2\right)x}\operatorname{sech}(p-1)\sum_{x=0}^{p^k}4\alpha_1\eta_1x.\end{aligned}$$

4. Conclusions

In this paper, the coupled GI equation on a time–space scale was obtained by extending the Lax matrix equation on a time–space scale, which can be reduced to the classical GI equation. In particular, the semi-discrete GI equation was given by providing parallel computations for the discrete and continuous case. The standard DT of the GI equation was extended on a time–space scale. On this basis, its N-soliton solutions on a time–space scale were obtained, which were expressed using Cayley exponential functions.

The extension provides a wider range of nonlinear integrable dynamic models and promotes the study of nonlinear dynamic systems. By taking the "seed solution" $q = 0$ and $\lambda = \alpha + i\beta$, one-solition solutions of the GI equation were obtained on three different time–space scales ($\mathbb{X} = \mathbb{R}$, $\mathbb{X} = \mathbb{C}$ and $\mathbb{X} = \mathbb{K}p$). In one case, the exact solution (64) and its dynamic figure were obtained when $x \in \mathbb{R}$. In the other cases, when $x \in \mathbb{C}\backslash\mathbb{L}$ and $x = 0$, exact solutions (68) and (71) were obtained and were similar to Equation (64). However, when $x \in \mathbb{L}$ and $x \in p^{\mathbb{Z}}$, the structures of solutions (68) and (71) were more complicated and their values were different from those of Equation (64) at those discontinuity points.

Due to the limitations of the computer, it was difficult to obtain their dynamic figures at this stage. Furthermore, there is another well-known equation, the Eckhaus equation, which possesses a very similar structure. The Eckhaus equation is also integrable and has soliton-like solutions expressed in terms of the hyperbolic functions [37,38]. Therefore, we will find the most effective way to reduce structures of solutions (68) and (71) on $\mathbb{C}$ and $\mathbb{K}p$, and study the Eckhaus equation on a time–space scale in our future work.

Author Contributions: Conceptualization, H.D., Y.Z. and X.H.; methodology, H.D.; software, Y.Z.; validation, H.D., Y.Z. and Y.F.; formal analysis, M.L.; investigation, Y.Z. and M.L.; writing—original draft preparation, Y.Z. and X.H.; project administration, H.D.. All authors have read and agreed to the published version of the manuscript.

Funding: This work was supported by the National Natural Science Foundation of China (Grant No. 11975143, 12105161, 61602188), Natural Science Foundation of Shandong Province (Grant No. ZR2019QD018), CAS Key Laboratory of Science and Technology on Operational Oceanography (Grant No. OOST2021-05), Scientific Research Foundation of Shandong University of Science and Technology for Recruited Talents (Grant No. 2017RCJJ068, 2017RCJJ069).

Institutional Review Board Statement: Not applicable.

Informed Consent Statement: Not applicable.

Data Availability Statement: Not applicable.

Acknowledgments: The authors would like to express their thanks to the editors and the reviewers for their kind comments to improve our paper.

Conflicts of Interest: The authors declare no conflict of interest.

References

1. Hilger, S. Analysis on Measure Chains-A Unified Approach to Continuous and Discrete Calculus. *Results Math.* **1990**, *18*, 18–56. [CrossRef]
2. Bohner, M.; Peterson, A. *Advances in Dynamic Equations on a Time Scale*; Birkhauser: Boston, MA, USA, 2003.
3. Bohner, M.; Peterson, A. *Dynamic Equations on a Time Scale: An Introduction with Applications*; Springer Science and Business Media: Berlin, Germany, 2012.
4. Meng, H.; Wang, L. Multiple periodic solutions in shifts δ ± for an impulsive functional dynamic equation on time scales. *Adv. Differ. Equ.* **2014**, *152*, 1–52.
5. Agarwal, R.P.; Bohner, M.; Peterson, A. Dynamic equations on time scales: A survey. *J. Comput. Appl. Math.* **2002**, *141*, 1–26. [CrossRef]
6. Saker, S.H. Oscillation of nonlinear dynamic equations on time scales. *Appl. Math. Comput.* **2004**, *148*, 81–91. [CrossRef]
7. Kosmatov, N. Multi-point boundary value problems on time scales at resonance. *J. Math. Anal. Appl.* **2006**, *323*, 253–266. [CrossRef]
8. Anderson, D.R. Eigenvalue intervals for a two-point boundary value problem on a measure chain. *J. Comput. Appl. Math.* **2002**, *141*, 57–64. [CrossRef]

9. Christiansen, F.B.; Fenchel, T.M. *Theories of Populations in Biological Communities, volume 20 of Lecture Notes in Ecological Studies*; Springer: Berlin, Germany, 1997.
10. Andreasen, V. *Multiple Time Scales in the Dynamics of Infectious Diseases*; Springer: Berlin/Heidelberg, Germany, 1978.
11. Bowman, C.; Gumel, A.B.; Dricssche, P. A mathematical model for assessing control strategies against West Nile virus. *Bull. Math. Biol.* **2005**, *67*, 1107–1133. [CrossRef] [PubMed]
12. Atici, F.M.; Biles, D.C.; Lebedinsky, A. An application of time scales to economics. *Math. Comput. Model.* **2006**, *43*, 718–726. [CrossRef]
13. Dryl, M.; Torres, D. A General Delta-Nabla Calculus of Variations on Time Scales with Application to Economics. *Int. J. Dyn. Syst. Differ.* **2014**, *5*, 42–71. [CrossRef]
14. Hovhannisyan, G. Ablowitz–Ladik hierarchy of integrable equations on a time–space scale. *J. Appl. Phys.* **2014**, *55*, 102701. [CrossRef]
15. Hovhannisyan, G.; Bonecutter, L.; Mizer, A. On Burgers equation on a time–space scale. *Adv. Differ. Equ.* **2015**, *289*, 1–19. [CrossRef]
16. Cieslinski, J.L.; Nikiciuk, T.; Wakiewicz, K. The sine-Gordon equation on time scales. *J. Math. Anal. Appl.* **2015**, *423*, 1219–1230. [CrossRef]
17. Cieslinski, J.L. Pseudospherical surfaces on time scales: A geometric definition and the spectral approach. *J. Phys. A-Math. Theor.* **2007**, *40*, 12525–12538. [CrossRef]
18. Cieslinski, J.L. New definitions of exponential, hyperbolic and trigonometric functions on time scales. *J. Math. Anal. Appl.* **2012**, *388*, 8–22. [CrossRef]
19. Clarkson, P.A.; Tuszynski, J.A. Exact solutions of the multidimensional derivative nonlinear Schrodinger equation for many-body systems of criticality. *J. Phys. A* **1990**, *23*, 4269. [CrossRef]
20. Hisakado, M.; Wadati, M. Integrable MultiComponent Hybrid Nonlinear Schrödinger Equations. *J. Phys. Soc. Jap.* **1995**, *64*, 408–413. [CrossRef]
21. Kaup, D.J.; Newell, A.C. An exact solution for a derivative nonlinear Schrödinger equation. *J. Math. Phys.* **1978**, *19*, 798–801. [CrossRef]
22. Xu, S.; He, J.; Wang, L. The Darboux transformation of the derivative nonlinear Schrödinger equation. *J. Phys. A* **2011**, *44*, 6629–6636. [CrossRef]
23. Chen, H.H.; Lee, Y.C.; Liu, C.S. Integrability of Nonlinear Hamiltonian Systems by Inverse Scattering Method. *Phys. Scr.* **2007**, *20*, 490. [CrossRef]
24. Ren, H.Y.; Li, D.S. Self-adjointness and Conservation Laws of Chen-Lee-Liu Equation. *J. Pingdingshan Univ.* **2013**, *28*, 14–17.
25. Gerdjikov, V.S.; Ivanov, M.I. The quadratic bundle of general form and the nonlinear evolution equations. *Bulg. J. Phys.* **1983**, *10*, 35.
26. Fan, E.G. Darboux transformation and soliton-like solutions for the Gerdjikov–Ivanov equation. *J. Phys. A* **2000**, *33*, 6925. [CrossRef]
27. Gerdjikov, V.S.; Ivanov, M.I. A quadratic pencil of general type and nonlinear evolution equations. II. Hierarchies of Hamiltonian structures. *Bulg. J. Phys.* **1983**, *10*, 130–143.
28. Pei, L.; Li, B. The Darboux transformation of the Gerdjikov–Ivanov equation from non-zero seed. In Proceedings of the 2011 International Conference on Consumer Electronics, Communications and Networks (CECNet), Xianning, China, 16–18 April 2011; pp. 5320–5323.
29. Guo, L.; Zhang, Y.; Xu, S. The higher order Rogu'e Wave solutions of the Gerdjikov–Ivanov equation. *Phys. Scr.* **2014**, *89*, 240. [CrossRef]
30. Dai, H.H.; Fan, E.G. Variable separation and algebro-geometric solutions of the Gerdjikov–Ivanov equation. *Chaos Soliton. Fract.* **2004**, *22*, 93–101. [CrossRef]
31. Arshed, S. Two Reliable Techniques for the Soliton Solutions of Perturbed Gerdjikov–Ivanov Equation. *Optik* **2018**, *33*, 6925. [CrossRef]
32. Nematollah, K.; Hossein, J. Analytical solutions of the Gerdjikov–Ivanov equation by using $\exp(\phi(\xi))$-expansion method. *Optik* **2017**, *139*, 72–76.
33. Cao, C.; Geng, X.; Wang, H. Algebro-geometric solution of the 2+1 dimensional Burgers equation with a discrete variable. *J. Math. Phys.* **2002**, *43*, 621–643. [CrossRef]
34. Saburo, K.; Tetsuya, K. Solutions of a derivative nonlinear schrödinger hierarchy and its similarity reduction. *Glasgow Math. J.* **2005**, *47*, 99–107. [CrossRef]
35. Fan, E.G. Integrable evolution systems based on Gerdjikov–Ivanov equations, bi-Hamiltonian structure, finite-dimensional integrable systems and N-fold Darboux transformation. *J. Math. Phys.* **2000**, *41*, 7769–7782. [CrossRef]
36. Fan, E.G. Bi-Hamiltonian Structure and Liouville Integrability for a Gerdjikov–Ivanov Equation Hierarchy. *Chinese Phys. Lett.* **2001**, *18*, 1.
37. Cherniha, R. Galilean-invariant Nonlinear PDEs and their Exact Solutions. *J. Nonlinear Math. Phys.* **1995**, *2*, 374–383. [CrossRef]
38. Calogero, F.; Lillo, S.D. The Eckhaus PDE $i\psi_t + \psi_{xx} + 2(|\psi|^2)_x\psi + |\psi|^4\psi = 0$. *Inverse Probl.* **1999**, 3, 633. [CrossRef]

axioms

MDPI

Article

Degenerated and Competing Dirichlet Problems with Weights and Convection

Dumitru Motreanu

D. Motreanu Département de Mathématiques, Université de Perpignan, 66860 Perpignan, France; motreanu@univ-perp.fr

Abstract: This paper focuses on two Dirichlet boundary value problems whose differential operators in the principal part exhibit a lack of ellipticity and contain a convection term (depending on the solution and its gradient). They are driven by a degenerated (p,q)-Laplacian with weights and a competing (p,q)-Laplacian with weights, respectively. The notion of competing (p,q)-Laplacians with weights is considered for the first time. We present existence and approximation results that hold under the same set of hypotheses on the convection term for both problems. The proofs are based on weighted Sobolev spaces, Nemytskij operators, a fixed point argument and finite dimensional approximation. A detailed example illustrates the effective applicability of our results.

Keywords: degenerated (p,q)-Laplacian; competing (p,q)-Laplacian; weighted Sobolev space; convection; finite dimensional approximation; weak solution; generalized solution

MSC: 35J70; 35J92; 47H30

Citation: Motreanu, D. Degenerated and Competing Dirichlet Problems with Weights and Convection. *Axioms* **2021**, *10*, 271. https://doi.org/10.3390/axioms10040271

Academic Editor: Tatiana Odzijewicz

Received: 21 September 2021
Accepted: 15 October 2021
Published: 22 October 2021

1. Introduction

Consider a bounded domain Ω in $\mathbb{R}^N$ ($N \geq 1$) with a Lipschitz boundary $\partial\Omega$, numbers $1 < q < p < \infty$, functions $a, b \in L^1(\Omega)$ with $a(x), b(x) > 0$ for a.e. $x \in \Omega$ and a Carathéodory function $f : \Omega \times \mathbb{R} \times \mathbb{R}^N \to \mathbb{R}$ (i.e., $f(\cdot, t, \xi)$ is measurable on Ω for each $(t,\xi) \in \mathbb{R} \times \mathbb{R}^N$ and $f(x,\cdot,\cdot)$ is continuous on $\mathbb{R} \times \mathbb{R}^N$ for a.e. $x \in \Omega$). The aim of this paper is to investigate the quasilinear Dirichlet problems

$$\begin{cases} -\mathrm{div}(a(x)|\nabla u|^{p-2}\nabla u + b(x)|\nabla u|^{q-2}\nabla u) = f(x,u,\nabla u) & \text{in } \Omega \\ u = 0 & \text{on } \partial\Omega \end{cases} \tag{1}$$

and

$$\begin{cases} -\mathrm{div}(a(x)|\nabla u|^{p-2}\nabla u - b(x)|\nabla u|^{q-2}\nabla u) = f(x,u,\nabla u) & \text{in } \Omega \\ u = 0 & \text{on } \partial\Omega. \end{cases} \tag{2}$$

Notice that problem (1) is driven by a sum of weighted p-Laplacians, whereas problem (2) by a difference of weighted p-Laplacians. The weights $a \in L^1(\Omega)$ and $b \in L^1(\Omega)$ are strongly related to the ellipticity property, but act in a fundamentally different way in these problems. The celebrated p-Laplacian and q-Laplacian are used instead of more general operators in the above formulations just to highlight the main ideas.

The differential operator in the principal part of Equation (1) is the sum

$$u \mapsto \mathrm{div}(a(x)|\nabla u|^{p-2}\nabla u) + \mathrm{div}(b(x)|\nabla u|^{p-2}\nabla u)$$

of the degenerated p-Laplacian with weight $a \in L^1(\Omega)$ and the degenerated q-Laplacian with weight $b \in L^1(\Omega)$ that should be consistent. This operator was introduced in [1] where it was called the degenerated (p,q)-Laplacian with weights $a, b \in L^1(\Omega)$. Its construction is reviewed in Section 2. The characteristic property of this operator is the degeneracy, meaning that one cannot guarantee the existence of a constant $k > 0$ to have

$$\langle -\mathrm{div}(a(x)|\nabla u|^{p-2} + b(x)|\nabla u|^{q-2})\nabla u), u\rangle \geq k \int_\Omega (|\nabla u(x)|^p + |\nabla u(x)|^q)dx.$$

Due to this, one cannot apply the classical elliptic theory.

The differential operator in the principal part of Equation (2) is the difference

$$u \mapsto \mathrm{div}(a(x)|\nabla u|^{p-2}\nabla u) - \mathrm{div}(b(x)|\nabla u|^{p-2}\nabla u)$$

of the degenerated p-Laplacian with weight $a \in L^1(\Omega)$ and of the degenerated q-Laplacian with weight $b \in L^1(\Omega)$. Such a nonlinear operator with weights is considered for the first time. We call it the competing (p,q)-Laplacian with weights $a, b \in L^1(\Omega)$. In this case, we go beyond the degeneracy, actually completely dropping the ellipticity because the quantity

$$\langle -\mathrm{div}(a(x)|\nabla u|^{p-2}\nabla u - b(x)|\nabla u|^{q-2}\nabla u), u\rangle = \int_\Omega (a(x)|\nabla u(x)|^p - b(x)|\nabla u(x)|^q)dx$$

can have an arbitrary sign (note that $a(x)$ and $b(x)$ are positive). For problem (2), any method of monotone type, including the use of pseudomonotone operators, fails to apply.

The right-hand side $f(x,u,\nabla u)$ of the equations in (1) and (2) is a convection term; that is, it depends on the solution u and on its gradient ∇u. The dependence on the gradient ∇u generally prevents having a variational structure for problems (1) and (2), so the variational methods are not applicable. In order to find the needed estimates, an essential part of our development is devoted to the Nemytskij operator associated with the convection term $f(x,u,\nabla u)$ under an appropriate growth condition for the function $f(x,t,\xi)$ on $\Omega \times \mathbb{R} \times \mathbb{R}^N$. Different results regarding unweighted problems involving (p,q)-Laplacian and convection terms can be found in [2].

The problems (1) and (2) have only recently been regarded in their generality. To the best of our knowledge, there is solely the existence theorem for problem (1), obtained in [1] through the theory of pseudomonotone operators. For the particular case of (1) where the equation is governed by a degenerated p-Laplacian (i.e., $b = 0$ in (1)), existence results based on minimization and degree theoretic methods can be found in [3] and a method to create a sub-supersolution was developed in [4]. Concerning problem (2) driven by competing operators, there is no available result except for the most particular situation where $a(x) = b(x) \equiv 1$ in Ω (i.e., the problem without weights), whose study was initiated in [5] and continued in [6,7].

In the present paper, we overcome the lack of ellipticity, monotonicity and variational structure in problems (1) and (2) by means of a passing to limit process involving approximate solutions generated through fixed point arguments on finite dimensional spaces. This approach was implemented in [6,7] for unweighted problems (i.e., $a(x) = b(x) \equiv 1$ in Ω). Here, the development is substantially modified due to the completely different functional setting under the weights $a \in L^1(\Omega)$ and $b \in L^1(\Omega)$.

For problem (1), we are able to establish the existence of a solution in a weak sense, whereas for problem (2), we prove the existence of a solution in a generalized sense. It is worth noting that in the case of problem (1) any generalized solution is a weak solution. Moreover, our results can be viewed as providing approximations in the sense of strong convergence for solutions to problems (1) and (2) by finite dimensional approximate solutions.

Inspired by [3], a major step in our treatment is a reduction within the framework of classical Sobolev spaces. We impose a suitable growth condition for the convection term $f(x,u,\nabla u)$ to match this reduction. The growth condition is expressed using a positive quantity (p_s in the text) described by the weights $a \in L^1(\Omega)$ and $b \in L^1(\Omega)$, which provide the best integrability rate.

We plan to use the present work for studying evolutionary counterparts for problems (1) and (2).

The rest of the paper is organized as follows. Section 2 presents the degenerated and competing (p,q)-Laplacians with weights. Section 3 sets forth the associated Nemytskij operator. Section 4 contains our main result on the solvability and approximation for problem (1). Section 5 focuses on the solvability of problem (2). Section 6 illustrates by an example the effective applicability of our theorems.

2. Degenerated and Competing (P, Q)-Laplacians with Weights

Throughout the text, we denote by $\to$ the strong convergence and by $\rightharpoonup$ the weak convergence in any normed space X under consideration. The norm on X is denoted by $\|\cdot\|_X$, while the notation $\langle\cdot,\cdot\rangle_X$ stands for the duality pairing between X and its dual X^*. For the rest of the paper, by a bounded map we understand a map between normed spaces that maps bounded sets to bounded sets.

We fix the framework for the underlying weighted Sobolev spaces related to problems (1) and (2). For a systematic study of weighted Sobolev spaces, we refer to [3,8]. The completeness property for such spaces is discussed in [9]. This functional setting was also discussed in [1].

Given a real number $p \in (1,+\infty)$ and a positive function $a \in L^1(\Omega)$, the weighted space

$$W^{1,p}(a,\Omega) := \{u \in L^p(\Omega) : \int_\Omega a(x)|\nabla u(x)|^p dx < \infty\},$$

is endowed with the norm

$$\|u\|_{W^{1,p}(a,\Omega)} := \left(\|u\|^p_{L^p(\Omega)} + \int_\Omega a(x)|\nabla u(x)|^p dx\right)^{\frac{1}{p}}, \quad \forall u \in W^{1,p}(a,\Omega).$$

We note that $C_0^\infty(\Omega) \subset W^{1,p}(a,\Omega)$. The closure of $C_0^\infty(\Omega)$ in $W^{1,p}(a,\Omega)$ with respect to the norm $\|\cdot\|_{W^{1,p}(a,\Omega)}$ is the space $W_0^{1,p}(a,\Omega)$. The dual spaces of $W^{1,p}(a,\Omega)$ and $W_0^{1,p}(a,\Omega)$ are denoted by $W^{1,p}(a,\Omega)^*$ and $W_0^{1,p}(a,\Omega)^*$, respectively.

A reduction in the setting of classical Sobolev spaces is based on the following condition from [3] (p. 26):

(H1). $a^{-s} \in L^1(\Omega)$ for some $s \in \left(\max\left\{\frac{N}{p}, \frac{1}{p-1}\right\}, +\infty\right)$.

Proposition 1. *Under condition (H1), there are the continuous embeddings*

$$W^{1,p}(a,\Omega) \hookrightarrow W^{1,p_s}(\Omega) \hookrightarrow L^p(\Omega), \tag{3}$$

where

$$p_s = \frac{ps}{s+1}. \tag{4}$$

In addition, the embedding $W^{1,p_s}(\Omega) \hookrightarrow L^p(\Omega)$ is compact. Furthermore,

$$\|u\|_{W_0^{1,p}(a,\Omega)} := \left(\int_\Omega a(x)|\nabla u(x)|^p dx\right)^{\frac{1}{p}}, \quad \forall u \in W_0^{1,p}(a,\Omega),$$

is an equivalent norm on $W_0^{1,p}(a,\Omega)$ for which $W_0^{1,p}(a,\Omega)$ becomes a uniformly convex Banach space.

Proof. The proof is essentially completed in [3]. For the sake of clarity, we highlight aspects relevant for problems (1) and (2).

It can be seen from (4) that $p_s > 1$ if and only if $s > 1/(p-1)$, which by assumption (H1) is true. In order to prove the first inclusion in (3), let $u \in W^{1,p}(a,\Omega)$. Using Hölder's inequality, hypothesis (H1) and (4) (note $p_s < p$), we infer that

$$\int_\Omega |\nabla u(x)|^{p_s} dx = \int_\Omega (a(x)^{\frac{p_s}{p}} |\nabla u(x)|^{p_s}) a(x)^{-\frac{p_s}{p}} dx$$
$$\leq \left(\int_\Omega a(x)|\nabla u(x)|^p dx\right)^{\frac{p_s}{p}} \left(\int_\Omega a(x)^{-\frac{p_s}{p-p_s}} dx\right)^{\frac{p-p_s}{p}}$$
$$\leq \|a^{-s}\|_{L^1(\Omega)}^{\frac{1}{s+1}} \|u\|_{W^{1,p}(a,\Omega)}^{p_s}, \quad \forall u \in W_0^{1,p}(a,\Omega).$$

The continuous inclusion $W^{1,p}(a,\Omega) \hookrightarrow W^{1,p_s}(\Omega)$ is proven.

The Rellich–Kondrachov embedding theorem ensures the compact embedding $W^{1,p_s}(\Omega) \hookrightarrow L^r(\Omega)$, with $1 \leq r < p_s^*$, where p_s^* is the critical exponent corresponding to p_s, that is,

$$p_s^* := \begin{cases} \frac{Np_s}{N-p_s} & \text{if } N > p_s (\Leftrightarrow ps < N(s+1)) \\ +\infty & \text{if } N \leq p_s (\Leftrightarrow ps \geq N(s+1)). \end{cases}$$

We have that $p_s^* > p$ if and only if $s > N/p$. Since the latter holds by assumption (H1), the compactness of the second inclusion in (3) follows.

The desired equivalence of norms is a consequence of (3) and the Poincaré inequality on $W_0^{1,p_s}(\Omega)$ because with a positive constant C,

$$\|u\|_{L^p(\Omega)} \leq C\|u\|_{W^{1,p}(a,\Omega)}, \quad \forall u \in W_0^{1,p}(a,\Omega).$$

It remains to show that $W_0^{1,p}(a,\Omega)$ is a uniformly convex Banach space. It suffices to have $a^{-\frac{1}{p-1}} \in L^1(\Omega)$ (see [3] Theorem 1.3). From hypothesis (H1), it is known that $a^{-s} \in L^1(\Omega)$ with $s > 1/(p-1)$, which results in

$$\int_\Omega a(x)^{-\frac{1}{p-1}} dx = \int_{\{a(x)<1\}} a(x)^{-\frac{1}{p-1}} dx + \int_{\{a(x)\geq 1\}} a(x)^{-\frac{1}{p-1}} dx$$
$$\leq \int_\Omega a(x)^{-s} dx + \text{meas}(\Omega) < \infty,$$

thus completing the proof. □

The degenerated p-Laplacian with the weight $a \in L^1(\Omega)$ is defined as the map $\Delta_p^a : W_0^{1,p}(a,\Omega) \to W_0^{1,p}(a,\Omega)^*$ given by $\Delta_p^a(u) = \text{div}(a(x)|\nabla u|^{p-2}\nabla u)$ for all $u \in W_0^{1,p}(a,\Omega)$, i.e.,

$$\langle -\Delta_p^a(u), v\rangle_{W_0^{1,p}(a,\Omega)} = \int_\Omega a(x)|\nabla u(x)|^{p-2}\nabla u(x)\nabla v(x) dx, \quad \forall u,v \in W_0^{1,p}(a,\Omega).$$

The definition makes sense as can be seen through Hölder's inequality

$$\left|\int_\Omega a(x)|\nabla u(x)|^{p-2}\nabla u(x)\nabla v(x) dx\right|$$
$$\leq \int_\Omega (a(x)^{\frac{p-1}{p}} |\nabla u(x)|^{p-1})(a(x)|^{\frac{1}{p}} |\nabla v(x)|) dx$$
$$\leq \left(\int_\Omega a(x)|\nabla u(x)|^p dx\right)^{\frac{p-1}{p}} \left(\int_\Omega a(x)|\nabla v(x)|^p dx\right)^{\frac{1}{p}} < \infty, \quad \forall u,v \in W_0^{1,p}(a,\Omega).$$

The ordinary p-Laplacian is recovered when $a(x) \equiv 1$ in Ω.

The degenerated p-Laplacian $\Delta_p^a : W_0^{1,p}(a,\Omega) \to W_0^{1,p}(a,\Omega)^*$ is continuous and bounded. We denote by λ_1 the first eigenvalue of $-\Delta_p^a : W_0^{1,p}(a,\Omega) \to W_0^{1,p}(a,\Omega)^*$ corresponding to the weight $a \in L^1(\Omega)$ with $a^{-\frac{1}{p-1}} \in L^1(\Omega)$. Specifically, λ_1 is the least $\lambda > 0$ for which the problem

$$\begin{cases} -\mathrm{div}(a(x)|\nabla u|^{p-2}\nabla u) = \lambda |u|^{p-2}u & \text{in } \Omega \\ u = 0 & \text{on } \partial\Omega \end{cases}$$

possesses a nontrivial solution. It can be variationally characterized as

$$\lambda_1 = \inf_{u \in W_0^{1,p}(a,\Omega)\setminus\{0\}} \frac{\int_\Omega a(x)|\nabla u(x)|^p dx}{\|u\|_{L^p(\Omega)}^p}. \tag{5}$$

More details on the degenerated p-Laplacian with weight can be seen in [3].

For the positive weights $a \in L^1(\Omega)$ and $b \in L^1(\Omega)$ entering problems (1) and (2), we have the degenerated p-Laplacian $\Delta_p^a : W_0^{1,p}(a,\Omega) \to W_0^{1,p}(a,\Omega)^*$ with weight $a \in L^1(\Omega)$ and the degenerated q-Laplacian $\Delta_q^b : W_0^{1,2}(b,\Omega) \to W_0^{1,2}(b,\Omega)^*$ with weight $b \in L^1(\Omega)$. The two operators need to be consistent, which is achieved under the following compatibility condition for the weights:

(H2). $1 < q < p < +\infty$ and $a^{-\frac{q}{p-q}} b^{\frac{p}{p-q}} \in L^1(\Omega)$.

Proposition 2. *Assume that condition (H2) holds. Then, one has the continuous embedding* $W_0^{1,p}(a,\Omega) \hookrightarrow W_0^{1,q}(b,\Omega)$.

Proof. By hypothesis (H2) and Hölder's inequality, we infer that

$$\begin{aligned} \int_\Omega b(x)|\nabla u(x)|^q dx &= \int_\Omega (a(x)^{-\frac{q}{p}} b(x))(a(x)^{\frac{q}{p}}|\nabla u(x)|^q) dx \\ &\le \left(\int_\Omega a(x)^{-\frac{q}{p-q}} b(x)^{\frac{p}{p-q}} dx\right)^{\frac{p-q}{p}} \left(\int_\Omega a(x)|\nabla u(x)|^p dx\right)^{\frac{q}{p}} \\ &\le \|a^{-\frac{q}{p-q}} b^{\frac{p}{p-q}}\|_{L^1(\Omega)}^{\frac{p-q}{p}} \|u\|_{W^{1,p}(a,\Omega)}^q, \quad \forall u,v \in W_0^{1,p}(a,\Omega), \end{aligned}$$

which proves the result. □

Under condition (H2), on the basis of Proposition 2, the map $\Delta_p^a + \Delta_q^b : W_0^{1,p}(a,\Omega) \to W_0^{1,p}(a,\Omega)^*$ called the degenerated (p,q)-Laplacian with weights $a,b \in L^1(\Omega)$ is well-defined. It is given by

$$\begin{aligned} &\langle -(\Delta_p^a + \Delta_q^b)u, v\rangle_{W_0^{1,p}(a,\Omega)} \\ &= \int_\Omega (a(x)|\nabla u(x)|^{p-2}\nabla u(x) + b(x)|\nabla u(x)|^{q-2}\nabla u(x))\nabla v(x) dx, \quad \forall u,v \in W_0^{1,p}(a,\Omega). \end{aligned} \tag{6}$$

The degenerated (p,q)-Laplacian with weights $a,b \in L^1(\Omega)$ was introduced in [1].

Again on the basis of Proposition 2, the map $\Delta_p^a - \Delta_q^b : W_0^{1,p}(a,\Omega) \to W_0^{1,p}(a,\Omega)^*$ given by

$$\begin{aligned} &\langle -(\Delta_p^a - \Delta_q^b)u, v\rangle_{W_0^{1,p}(a,\Omega)} \\ &= \int_\Omega (a(x)|\nabla u(x)|^{p-2}\nabla u(x) + b(x)|\nabla u(x)|^{q-2}\nabla u(x))\nabla v(x) dx, \quad \forall u,v \in W_0^{1,p}(a,\Omega), \end{aligned} \tag{7}$$

is well-defined provided condition (H2) is satisfied. We call it the competing (p,q)-Laplacian with weights $a,b \in L^1(\Omega)$ and is introduced here for the first time.

Proposition 3. *Under assumption (H2), the maps* $\Delta_p^a + \Delta_q^b : W_0^{1,p}(a,\Omega) \to W_0^{1,p}(a,\Omega)^*$ *and* $\Delta_p^a - \Delta_q^b : W_0^{1,p}(a,\Omega) \to W_0^{1,p}(a,\Omega)^*$ *are continuous and bounded. In addition, under (H1) and (H2), the* $(S)_+$ *property holds for the map* $-(\Delta_p^a + \Delta_q^b) : W_0^{1,p}(a,\Omega) \to W_0^{1,p}(a,\Omega)^*$*; that is, any sequence* $\{u_n\} \subset W_0^{1,p}(a,\Omega)$ *satisfying* $u_n \rightharpoonup u$ *in* $W_0^{1,p}(a,\Omega)$ *and*

$$\limsup_{n\to\infty} \langle -(\Delta_p^a + \Delta_q^b)u_n, u_n - u\rangle_{W_0^{1,p}(a,\Omega)} \le 0 \tag{8}$$

is strongly convergent. Thus, $u_n \to u$ *in* $W_0^{1,p}(a,\Omega)$.

Proof. Due to the continuous embedding $W^{1,p}(a,\Omega) \hookrightarrow W^{1,q}(b,\Omega)$ in Proposition 2, $\Delta_p^a + \Delta_q^b$ and $\Delta_p^a - \Delta_q^b$ inherit the continuity and boundedness from Δ_p^a and Δ_p^b.

For the second part of the statement, let a sequence $\{u_n\} \subset W_0^{1,p}(a,\Omega)$ with the required properties. By (6), the monotonicity of $-\Delta_q^b$ and Hölder's inequality, we obtain

$$\begin{aligned}
&\langle -(\Delta_p^a + \Delta_q^b)(u_n) + (\Delta_p^a + \Delta_q^b)(u), u_n - u\rangle_{W_0^{1,p}(a,\Omega)} \\
&\ge \langle -\Delta_p^a(u_n) + \Delta_p^a(u), u_n - u\rangle_{W_0^{1,p}(a,\Omega)} \\
&\ge (\|u_n\|_{W_0^{1,p}(a,\Omega)} - \|u\|_{W_0^{1,p}(a,\Omega)})(\|u_n\|^{p-1}_{W_0^{1,p}(a,\Omega)} - \|u\|^{p-1}_{W_0^{1,p}(a,\Omega)}) \ge 0.
\end{aligned}$$

It follows from the above estimate, (8) and $u_n \rightharpoonup u$ in $W_0^{1,p}(a,\Omega)$ that there holds $\lim_{n\to+\infty} \|u_n\|_{W_0^{1,p}(a,\Omega)} = \|u\|_{W_0^{1,p}(a,\Omega)}$. From Proposition 1, we know that the space $W_0^{1,p}(a,\Omega)$ is uniformly convex. Therefore, we can conclude that $u_n \to u$ in $W_0^{1,p}(a,\Omega)$. □

3. An Associated Nemytskij Operator

In this section we focus on the right-hand side of the equations in (1) and (2), i.e., the convection term $f(x,u,\nabla u)$. Our goal is to identify the growth condition for the function $f(x,t,\xi)$ to match the reduction in Proposition 1 to the unweighted Sobolev space $W_0^{1,p_s}(\Omega)$. The appropriate growth for $f(x,t,\xi)$ is the one used in [1].

In order to simplify the presentation, for any real number $r > 1$, we denote $r' := r/(r-1)$ (the Hölder conjugate of r). This convention will be preserved for the rest of the paper.

Lemma 1. *Assume (H1) and (H2) and in addition that the Carathéodory function* $f : \Omega \times \mathbb{R} \times \mathbb{R}^N \to \mathbb{R}$ *satisfies the growth condition:*
(***H3***).

$$|f(x,t,\xi)| \le \sigma(x) + c_1|t|^\alpha + c_2|\xi|^\beta \text{ for a.e } x \in \Omega, \ \forall (t,\xi) \in \mathbb{R}\times\mathbb{R}^N, \tag{9}$$

with $\sigma \in L^{\gamma'}(\Omega)$ *for* $\gamma \in (1, p_s^*)$ *and constants* $c_1 > 0, c_2 > 0, \alpha \in [0, p_s^* - 1), \beta \in [0, \frac{p_s}{(p_s^*)'})$.
Set

$$\theta := \min\left\{\gamma', \frac{p_s^*}{\alpha}, \frac{p_s}{\beta}\right\}. \tag{10}$$

Then, the Nemytskij operator $\mathcal{N}_f : L^{p_s^*}(\Omega) \times (L^{p_s}(\Omega))^N \to L^\theta(\Omega)$ *associated with the function* f *which is given by*

$$\mathcal{N}_f(v,z) = f(\cdot, v(\cdot), z(\cdot)), \quad \forall v,z \in L^{p_s^*}(\Omega) \times (L^{p_s}(\Omega))^N \tag{11}$$

is well-defined, continuous and bounded.

Proof. The requirements in (H3) postulate $\gamma' > 1$ (note $\gamma > 1$),

$$\frac{p_s^*}{\alpha} > \frac{p_s^*}{p_s^* - 1} = (p_s^*)' > 1, \; \frac{p_s}{\beta} > (p_s^*)' > 1$$

(note that $p_s^* > p > 1$). Then, a consequence of (10) is that $\theta > 1$.

We observe that (9) yields

$$|f(x,t,\xi)| \leq \tilde{\sigma}(x) + c_1|t|^{\frac{p_s^*}{\theta}} + c_2|\xi|^{\frac{p_s}{\theta}} \text{ for a.e } x \in \Omega, \; \forall(t,\xi) \in \mathbb{R} \times \mathbb{R}^N, \tag{12}$$

with $\tilde{\sigma} \in L^\theta(\Omega)$. Indeed, (10) gives

$$\alpha \leq \frac{p_s^*}{\theta} \text{ and } \beta \leq \frac{p_s}{\theta}.$$

Hence (12) is derived from (9) with $\tilde{\sigma}(x) = \sigma(x) + c_1 + c_2$ for a.e. $x \in \Omega$ obtaining $\tilde{\sigma} \in L^{\gamma'}(\Omega) \subset L^\theta(\Omega)$.

Using Krasnoselskij's theorem, we infer from (12) that $\mathcal{N}_f$ introduced in (11) has the required properties, thus proving the result. □

Let $N_f : W^{1,p}(a,\Omega) \to W^{1,p}(a,\Omega)^*$ be defined by

$$\langle N_f(u), v\rangle_{W^{1,p}(a,\Omega)} = \int_\Omega f(x,u(x),\nabla u(x))v(x)dx, \quad \forall u,v \in W_0^{1,p}(a,\Omega).$$

Due to the first inclusion in (3), it holds that $(u,\nabla u) \in L^{p_s^*}(\Omega) \times (L^{p_s}(\Omega))^N$ whenever $u \in W_0^{1,p}(a,\Omega)$. It turns out

$$\langle N_f(u), v\rangle_{W^{1,p}(a,\Omega)} = \langle \mathcal{N}_f(u,\nabla u), v\rangle_{L^\theta(\Omega)'}, \quad \forall u,v \in W_0^{1,p}(a,\Omega). \tag{13}$$

The assertion below provides a key tool for investigating problems (1) and (2).

Proposition 4. *Assume (H1)–(H3). If $u_n \rightharpoonup u$ in $W_0^{1,p}(a,\Omega)$, it holds that*

$$\lim_{n\to\infty} \langle N_f(u_n), u_n - u\rangle_{W_0^{1,p}(a,\Omega)} = 0. \tag{14}$$

Proof. Recalling the convention made in the beginning of this section, (10) entails

$$\theta' = \max\left\{\gamma, \left(\frac{p_s^*}{\alpha}\right)', \left(\frac{p_s}{\beta}\right)'\right\}. \tag{15}$$

By (H3) we have $\gamma < p_s^*$,

$$\left(\frac{p_s^*}{\alpha}\right)' = \frac{\frac{p_s^*}{\alpha}}{\frac{p_s^*}{\alpha} - 1} = \frac{p_s^*}{p_s^* - \alpha} < p_s^*,$$

$$\left(\frac{p_s}{\beta}\right)' = \frac{\frac{p_s}{\beta}}{\frac{p_s}{\beta} - 1} = \frac{p_s}{p_s - \beta} < \frac{p_s}{p_s - \frac{p_s}{(p_s^*)'}} = \frac{(p_s^*)'}{(p_s^*)' - 1} = p_s^*.$$

Hence, (15) yields $1 < \theta' < p_s^*$ and we can apply the Rellich–Kondrachov compact embedding theorem to deduce that the embedding $W^{1,p_s}(\Omega) \hookrightarrow L^{\theta'}(\Omega)$ is compact, which results in $u_n \to u$ in $L^{\theta'}(\Omega)$.

Since (13) implies that

$$|\langle N_f(u_n), u_n - u\rangle_{W^{1,p}(a,\Omega)}| \leq \|\mathcal{N}_f(u_n,\nabla u_n)\|_{L^\theta(\Omega)}\|u_n - u\|_{L^{\theta'}(\Omega)}. \tag{16}$$

and Lemma 1 ensures that $\{\mathcal{N}_f(u_n, \nabla u_n)\}$ is bounded in $L^{\theta}(\Omega)$, from (16) we arrive at (14), as desired. □

4. Solvability and Approximation for the Degenerate Elliptic Problem (1)

The object of this section is to develop an approach based on finite dimensional approximations for problem (1).

Since the Banach space $W_0^{1,p}(a,\Omega)$ is separable (see Section 2), there exists a Galerkin basis for it. This amounts to saying that there is a sequence $\{X_n\}$ of vector subspaces of $W_0^{1,p}(a,\Omega)$ such that

(i) $\dim(X_n) < \infty, \quad \forall n;$
(ii) $X_n \subset X_{n+1}, \quad \forall n;$
(iii)

$$\overline{\bigcup_n X_n} = W_0^{1,p}(a,\Omega).$$

We fix such a sequence of subspaces $\{X_n\}$. Each approximate problem on X_n will be resolved by means of a consequence of Brouwer's fixed point theorem.

Proposition 5. *Assume the conditions (H1)–(H3) and in addition*
(H4). *there exists $\rho \in L^1(\Omega)$ and constants $d_1 > 0$ and $d_2 > 0$ provided $\lambda_1^{-1}d_1 + d_2 < 1$, where λ_1 denotes the first eigenvalue of $-\Delta_p^a$ on $W_0^{1,p}(a,\Omega)$, such that*

$$f(x,t,\xi)t \le \rho(x) + d_1|t|^p + d_2 a(x)|\xi|^p \tag{17}$$

for a.e $x \in \Omega$ and all $(t,\xi) \in \mathbb{R} \times \mathbb{R}^N$.
Then for each n there exists $u_n \in X_n$ such that

$$\langle -(\Delta_p^a + \Delta_q^b)(u_n), v\rangle_{W_0^{1,p}(a,\Omega)} = \int_\Omega f(x,u_n(x),\nabla u_n(x))v(x)dx, \quad \forall v \in X_n. \tag{18}$$

Proof. For each n, consider the continuous map $A_n : X_n \to X_n^*$ defined by

$$\langle A_n(u), v\rangle_{X_n} = \langle -(\Delta_p^a + \Delta_q^b)(u), v\rangle_{W_0^{1,p}(a,\Omega)} - \int_\Omega f(x,u(x),\nabla u(x))v(x)dx, \quad \forall v \in X_n.$$

The definition of the operator A_n, (17) and (5) lead to

$$\begin{aligned}\langle A_n(v), v\rangle_{X_n} &= \int_\Omega (a(x)|\nabla v|^p + b(x)|\nabla v|^q - f(x,v,\nabla v)v)dx \\ &\ge \|v\|^p_{W_0^{1,p}(a,\Omega)} - \|\rho\|_{L^1(\Omega)} - d_1\|v\|^p_{L^p(\Omega)} - d_2\|v\|^p_{W_0^{1,p}(a,\Omega)} \\ &\ge (1 - d_1\lambda_1^{-1} - d_2)\|v\|^p_{W_0^{1,p}(a,\Omega)} - \|\rho\|_{L^1(\Omega)}, \quad \forall v \in X_n.\end{aligned}$$

Thanks to the assumption $1 - d_1\lambda_1^{-1} - d_2 > 0$ in (H4), it follows that

$$\langle A_n(v), v\rangle_{X_n} \ge 0 \text{ whenever } v \in X_n \text{ with } \|v\|_{W_0^{1,p}(a,\Omega)} = R$$

provided $R = R(n) > 0$ is sufficiently large. In view of the fact that X_n is a finite dimensional space, by a well-known consequence of Brouwer's fixed point theorem (see, e.g., [10] (p. 37)) there exists $u_n \in X_n$ solving the equation $A_n(u_n) = 0$. This means exactly that $u_n \in X_n$ is a solution for problem (18), which completes the proof. □

We are in a position to state our main result on problem (1).

Theorem 1. *Assume that the conditions (H1)–(H4) are fulfilled. Then, the sequence $\{u_n\}$, with $u_n \in X_n$ constructed in Proposition 5, contains a subsequence which is strongly convergent in $W_0^{1,p}(a,\Omega)$ to a weak solution of problem (1) meaning that*

$$\int_\Omega (a(x)|\nabla u|^{p-2}\nabla u + b(x)|\nabla u|^{q-2}\nabla u)\nabla v dx = \int_\Omega f(x,u,\nabla u)v dx \tag{19}$$

for all $v \in W_0^{1,p}(a,\Omega)$.

Proof. We claim that the sequence $\{u_n\}$ built in Proposition 5 is bounded in $W_0^{1,p}(a,\Omega)$. Acting with $v = u_n$ in (18) gives

$$\|u_n\|^p_{W_0^{1,p}(a,\Omega)} + \|u_n\|^q_{W_0^{1,q}(a,\Omega)} = \int_\Omega f(x,u_n,\nabla u_n)u_n dx.$$

Then, through (17) and (5) we obtain

$$\begin{aligned}\|u_n\|^p_{W_0^{1,p}(a,\Omega)} &\le \|\rho\|_{L^1(\Omega)} + d_1\|u\|^p_{L^p(\Omega)} + d_2\|u\|^p_{W_0^{1,p}(a,\Omega)} \\ &\le \|\rho\|_{L^1(\Omega)} + (d_1\lambda_1^{-1} + d_2)\|u\|^p_{W_0^{1,p}(a,\Omega)}.\end{aligned}$$

Thanks to $\lambda_1^{-1}d_1 + d_2 < 1$, as known from hypothesis (H4), the claim is verified.

Recall from Proposition 1 that $W_0^{1,p}(a,\Omega)$ is a uniformly convex Banach space, so it is reflexive. Hence, the bounded sequence $\{u_n\}$ possesses a subsequence denoted again $\{u_n\}$ such that for some $u \in W_0^{1,p}(a,\Omega)$ it holds $u_n \rightharpoonup u$ in $W_0^{1,p}(a,\Omega)$.

Proposition 3 and Lemma 1 ensure that the operators $\Delta_p^a + \Delta_q^b : W_0^{1,p}(a,\Omega) \to W_0^{1,p}(a,\Omega)^*$ and $N_f : W_0^{1,p}(a,\Omega) \to W_0^{1,p}(a,\Omega)^*$ are bounded. Then, in view of the reflexivity of $W_0^{1,p}(a,\Omega)$ along a relabeled subsequence, one has

$$-(\Delta_p^a + \Delta_q^b)(u_n) - N_f(u_n) \rightharpoonup \eta \text{ in } W_0^{1,p}(a,\Omega)^* \tag{20}$$

for some $\eta \in W_0^{1,p}(a,\Omega)^*$.

Let us prove that $\eta = 0$. For $v \in \bigcup_n X_n$ choose m with $v \in X_m$. According to Proposition 5 and property (ii) in the definition of Galerkin basis, we may apply (18) for all $n \ge m$, which reads as

$$\langle -(\Delta_p^a + \Delta_q^b)(u_n) - N_f(u_n), v\rangle_{W_0^{1,p}(a,\Omega)} = 0 \text{ for all } n \ge m.$$

Letting $n \to \infty$ enables us to derive from (20) that

$$\langle \eta, v\rangle_{W_0^{1,p}(a,\Omega)} = 0, \quad \forall v \in \bigcup_n X_n.$$

The property (iii) in the definition of Galerkin basis $\{X_n\}$ highlights the density of the set $\bigcup_n X_n$ in $W_0^{1,p}(a,\Omega)$. As η vanishes on $\bigcup_n X_n$, it follows that $\eta = 0$.

Therefore, (20) becomes

$$-(\Delta_p^a + \Delta_q^b)(u_n) - N_f(u_n) \rightharpoonup 0 \text{ in } W_0^{1,p}(a,\Omega)^*. \tag{21}$$

In particular, we have

$$\lim_{n\to\infty} \langle -(\Delta_p^a + \Delta_q^b)(u_n) - N_f(u_n), u\rangle_{W_0^{1,p}(a,\Omega)} = 0. \tag{22}$$

Now, we return to (18) and insert $v = u_n$, obtaining

$$\langle -(\Delta_p^a + \Delta_q^b)(u_n) - N_f(u_n), u_n \rangle_{W_0^{1,p}(a,\Omega)} = 0, \quad \forall n,$$

which in conjunction with (22) yields

$$\lim_{n\to\infty} \langle -(\Delta_p^a + \Delta_q^b)(u_n) - N_f(u_n), u_n - u \rangle_{W_0^{1,p}(a,\Omega)} = 0.$$

Taking into account Proposition 4, this amounts to saying that

$$\lim_{n\to\infty} \langle -(\Delta_p^a + \Delta_q^b)(u_n), u_n - u \rangle_{W_0^{1,p}(a,\Omega)} = 0.$$

Consequently, the sequence $\{u_n\}$ satisfies (8). We are thus allowed to apply Proposition 3 which provides the strong convergence $u_n \to u$ in $W_0^{1,p}(a,\Omega)$.

Using the continuity of the nonlinear operators $\Delta_p^a + \Delta_q^b : W_0^{1,p}(a,\Omega) \to W_0^{1,p}(a,\Omega)^*$ and $N_f : W_0^{1,p}(a,\Omega) \to W_0^{1,p}(a,\Omega)^*$ as known by Proposition 2 and Lemma 1, we infer from the strong convergence $u_n \to u$ in $W_0^{1,p}(a,\Omega)$ that

$$-(\Delta_p^a + \Delta_q^b)(u_n) - N_f(u_n) \to -(\Delta_p^a + \Delta_q^b)(u) - N_f(u) \text{ in } W_0^{1,p}(a,\Omega)^*.$$

A simple comparison with (21) confirms that

$$-(\Delta_p^a + \Delta_q^b)(u) - N_f(u) = 0,$$

which is just (19). The proof is complete. □

5. Resolving the Non-Elliptic Problem (2)

Due to the total lack of ellipticity of the competing (p,q)-Laplacian $\Delta_p^a - \Delta_q^b$ with weights $a \in L^1(\Omega)$ and $b \in L^1(\Omega)$ as introduced in (7), i.e., the differential operator $\operatorname{div}(a(x)|\nabla u|^{p-2}\nabla u - b(x)|\nabla u|^{q-2}\nabla u)$, when the weights $a(x)$ and $b(x)$ are positive, we are not able to prove the existence of a weak solution for problem (2) in the weak sense. For this reason, we seek a solution in the following generalized sense.

Definition 1. *An element $u \in W_0^{1,p}(a,\Omega)$ is called a generalized solution to problem* (2) *if there exists a sequence $\{u_n\} \subset W_0^{1,p}(a,\Omega)$ such that*

(j) $u_n \rightharpoonup u$ *in* $W_0^{1,p}(\Omega)$;

(jj) for every $v \in W_0^{1,p}(a,\Omega)$, it holds that

$$\lim_{n\to\infty} \int_\Omega ((a(x)|\nabla u_n|^{p-2}\nabla u_n - b(x)|\nabla u_n|^{q-2}\nabla u_n)\nabla v - f(x,u_n,\nabla u_n)v)dx = 0;$$

(jjj)

$$\lim_{n\to\infty} \int_\Omega ((a(x)|\nabla u_n|^{p-2}\nabla u_n - b(x)|\nabla u_n|^{q-2}\nabla u_n)\nabla(u_n - u)dx = 0.$$

Our result for the non-elliptic problem (2) is as follows.

Theorem 2. *Assume for $1 < q < p < +\infty$ that the positive weights $a \in L^1(\Omega)$ and $b \in L^1(\Omega)$ and the Carathéodory function $f : \Omega \times \mathbb{R} \times \mathbb{R}^N \to \mathbb{R}$ that the conditions (H1)–(H4) hold. Then, there exists at least a generalized solution $u \in W_0^{1,p}(a,\Omega)$ of problem* (2) *in the sense of Definition 1.*

Proof. The proof is carried over along the pattern of Theorem 1. Fix a Galerkin basis $\{X_n\}$ of $W_0^{1,p}(a,\Omega)$, i.e., a sequence of finite dimensional vector subspaces of $W_0^{1,p}(a,\Omega)$ such that the properties (i)–(iii) in Section 4 hold.

We claim that for each n there exists $u_n \in X_n$ such that

$$\int_\Omega ((a(x)|\nabla u_n|^{p-2}\nabla u_n - b(x)|\nabla u_n|^{q-2}\nabla u_n)\nabla v - f(x,u_n,\nabla u_n)v)dx = 0, \quad \forall v \in X_n. \tag{23}$$

To this end, define the continuous map $B_n : X_n \to X_n^*$ by

$$\langle B_n(u), v\rangle_{X_n} = \int_\Omega ((a(x)|\nabla u|^{p-2}\nabla u - b(x)|\nabla u|^{q-2}\nabla u)\nabla v - f(x,u,\nabla u)v)dx$$

for all $u, v \in X_n$. The continuous embedding $W^{1,p}(a,\Omega) \hookrightarrow W^{1,q}(b,\Omega)$ (see Proposition 2), (17) and (5) imply that

$$\langle B_n(v), v\rangle_{X_n} \geq (1 - d_1\lambda_1^{-1} - d_2)\|v\|^p_{W_0^{1,p}(a,\Omega)} - C\|v\|^q_{W_0^{1,p}(a,\Omega)} - \|\rho\|_{L^1(\Omega)}, \quad \forall v \in X_n.$$

with a constant $C > 0$. By the assumption $1 - d_1\lambda_1^{-1} - d_2 > 0$ in (H4) and the fact that $p > q$, it turns out

$$\langle B_n(v), v\rangle_{X_n} \geq 0 \text{ for all } v \in X_n \text{ with } \|v\|_{W_0^{1,p}(a,\Omega)} = R$$

if $R = R(n) > 0$ is sufficiently large. According to condition (i) in the definition of Galerkin basis, the space X_n is finite dimensional. This enables us to apply a well-known consequence of Brouwer's fixed point theorem (see, e.g., [10] (p. 37)) obtaining a $u_n \in X_n$ with $B_n(u_n) = 0$. Therefore, we obtain (23), thus proving the claim.

Next, we show that the sequence $\{u_n\}$ is bounded in $W_0^{1,p}(a,\Omega)$. Since $u_n \in X_n$, we can take $v = u_n$ as a test function in (23), where

$$\|u_n\|^p_{W_0^{1,p}(a,\Omega)} = \|u_n\|^q_{W_0^{1,q}(a,\Omega)} + \int_\Omega f(x,u_n,\nabla u_n)u_n dx. \tag{24}$$

The continuous embedding $W^{1,p}(a,\Omega) \hookrightarrow W^{1,q}(b,\Omega)$ in Proposition 2, in conjunction with (17) and (5), ensures the estimate

$$\begin{aligned}\|u_n\|^p_{W_0^{1,p}(a,\Omega)} &\leq C\|u_n\|^q_{W_0^{1,p}(a,\Omega)} + \|\rho\|_{L^1(\Omega)} + d_1\|u\|^p_{L^p(\Omega)} + d_2\|u\|^p_{W_0^{1,p}(a,\Omega)} \\ &\leq C\|u_n\|^q_{W_0^{1,p}(a,\Omega)} + \|\rho\|_{L^1(\Omega)} + (d_1\lambda_1^{-1} + d_2)\|u\|^p_{W_0^{1,p}(a,\Omega)},\end{aligned}$$

with a constant $C > 0$. On account of $p > q$ and assumption $\lambda_1^{-1}d_1 + d_2 < 1$ in (H4), we conclude that the sequence $\{u_n\}$ is bounded in $W_0^{1,p}(a,\Omega)$.

Proposition 1 guarantees the reflexivity of the space $W_0^{1,p}(a,\Omega)$. We are thus allowed to extract a subsequence still denoted as $\{u_n\}$ such that $u_n \rightharpoonup u$ in $W_0^{1,p}(\Omega)$ for some $u \in W_0^{1,p}(a,\Omega)$. The requirement (j) in Definition 1 is fulfilled.

Equality (23) expresses that

$$\langle -\Delta_p^a(u_n) + \Delta_q^b(u_n) - N_f(u_n), v\rangle_{W_0^{1,p}(a,\Omega)} = 0, \quad \forall v \in X_n. \tag{25}$$

Inserting $v = u_n$ in (25) leads to

$$\langle -\Delta_p^a(u_n) + \Delta_q^b(u_n) - N_f(u_n), u_n\rangle_{W_0^{1,p}(a,\Omega)} = 0, \quad \forall n. \tag{26}$$

The sequence $\{(-\Delta_p^a + \Delta_q^b - N_f)(u_n)\}$ is bounded in $W_0^{1,p}(a,\Omega)^*$ because the nonlinear operators $\Delta_p^a, \Delta_q^b, N_f : W_0^{1,p}(a,\Omega) \to W_0^{1,p}(a,\Omega)^*$ are bounded. Due to the reflexivity of the space $W_0^{1,p}(\Omega)^*$, we can pass to a relabeled subsequence such that for a $\zeta \in W_0^{1,p}(\Omega)^*$ it holds that

$$(-\Delta_p^a + \Delta_q^b - N_f)(u_n) \rightharpoonup \zeta \text{ in } W_0^{1,p}(\Omega)^*. \tag{27}$$

Let $v \in X_m$ for some m. Assertion (ii) in the definition of Galerkin basis renders $v \in X_n$ for every $n \geq m$. Then, (25) and (27) imply

$$\langle \zeta, v \rangle_{W_0^{1,p}(a,\Omega)} = 0.$$

By (iii) in the definition of Galerkin basis $\{X_n\}$, the set $\bigcup_n X_n$ is dense in $W_0^{1,p}(a,\Omega)$. Therefore, $\zeta = 0$, so that (27) becomes

$$(-\Delta_p^a + \Delta_q^b - N_f)(u_n) \rightharpoonup 0 \text{ in } W_0^{1,p}(\Omega)^*,$$

which establishes property (jj) in Definition 1.

Setting $v = u$ in (jj) provides

$$\lim_{n\to\infty} \langle -\Delta_p^a(u_n) + \Delta_q^b(u_n) - N_f(u_n), u \rangle_{W_0^{1,p}(a,\Omega)} = 0,$$

which, with (24), produces

$$\lim_{n\to\infty} \langle -\Delta_p^a(u_n) + \Delta_q^b(u_n) - N_f(u_n), u_n - u \rangle_{W_0^{1,p}(a,\Omega)} = 0. \tag{28}$$

Proposition 4 and (28) ensure that

$$\lim_{n\to\infty} \langle -\Delta_p^a(u_n) + \Delta_q^b(u_n), u_n - u \rangle_{W_0^{1,p}(a,\Omega)} = 0$$

which shows the validity of part (jjj) in Definition 1. Summarizing, $u \in W_0^{1,p}(a,\Omega)$ is a generalized solution to problem (2) in the sense of Definition 1. □

Remark 1. *The notion of a generalized solution can be introduced for problem* (2)*, too. Precisely,* $u \in W_0^{1,p}(a,\Omega)$ *is called a generalized solution to problem* (1) *if there exists a sequence* $\{u_n\} \subset W_0^{1,p}(a,\Omega)$ *such that (j) in Definition 1 holds with*

(jj)′ for every $v \in W_0^{1,p}(a,\Omega)$ *one has*

$$\lim_{n\to\infty} \int_\Omega ((a(x)|\nabla u_n|^{p-2}\nabla u_n + b(x)|\nabla u_n|^{q-2}\nabla u_n)\nabla v - f(x,u_n,\nabla u_n)v)dx = 0;$$

(jjj)″with $u \in W_0^{1,p}(a,\Omega)$ *in (j),*

$$\lim_{n\to\infty} \int_\Omega ((a(x)|\nabla u_n|^{p-2}\nabla u_n + b(x)|\nabla u_n|^{q-2}\nabla u_n)\nabla(u_n - u)dx = 0.$$

In the case of problem (1)*,* $u \in W_0^{1,p}(a,\Omega)$ *is a generalized solution if and only if it is a weak solution in the sense of* (19)*. Indeed, if* $u \in W_0^{1,p}(a,\Omega)$ *is a weak solution to problem* (1)*, then the constant sequence* $\{u_n = u\} \subset W_0^{1,p}(a,\Omega)$ *verifies (j), (jj)′, (jjj)″; thus, u is a generalized solution. Conversely, let* $u \in W_0^{1,p}(a,\Omega)$ *be a generalized solution for* (1) *with the sequence* $\{u_n\} \subset W_0^{1,p}(a,\Omega)$ *satisfying (j), (jj)′, (jjj)″. Condition (jjj)″ reads as*

$$\lim_{n\to\infty} \langle -(\Delta_p^a + \Delta_q^b)(u_n), u_n - u \rangle_{W_0^{1,p}(a,\Omega)} = 0.$$

By (j) and Proposition 3 we deduce that $u_n \to u$ in $W_0^{1,p}(\Omega)$. Then from (jj)′ we get (19), *where u is a weak solution of problem* (1).

6. An Application

The goal of this section is to illustrate the effective applicability of our results. For the sake of simplicity, we focus on problems of types (1) and (2) on the unit open ball $B = \{x \in \mathbb{R}^3 : |x| < 1\}$ in $\mathbb{R}^3$ and for degenerated and competing $(3,2)$-Laplacians with weights.

Consider the Dirichlet problems

$$\begin{cases} -\mathrm{div}(|x|^r|\nabla u|\nabla u + (1-|x|^2)^h\nabla u) = g(x,u) + k_0\frac{|x|^r u}{1+u^2}|\nabla u|^\mu - k_1 u|\nabla u|^\nu & \text{in } B \\ u = 0 & \text{on } \partial B \end{cases} \tag{29}$$

and

$$\begin{cases} -\mathrm{div}(|x|^r|\nabla u|\nabla u - (1-|x|^2)^h\nabla u) = g(x,u) + k_0\frac{|x|^r u}{1+u^2}|\nabla u|^\mu - k_1 u|\nabla u|^\nu & \text{in } B \\ u = 0 & \text{on } \partial B \end{cases} \tag{30}$$

on B, with constants $r \in (0, \frac{3}{2})$, $h \geq 0$, $k_0 \in [0,1)$, $k_1 \geq 0$, $\mu \in [0, \frac{5}{3})$, $\nu \in [0, \frac{5}{6})$, and a Carathéodory function $g : \Omega \times \mathbb{R} \to \mathbb{R}$ satisfying

$$|g(x,t)| \leq a_0 t^2 + b_0 \text{ for a.e } x \in \Omega, \quad \forall t \in \mathbb{R},$$

with constants $a_0 \geq 0$ and $b_0 \geq 0$ provided $(a_0 + b_0)\lambda_1^{-1} + k_0 < 1$, where λ_1 represents the first eigenvalue of $-\Delta_3^a$ on $W_0^{1,3}(a,B)$ with $a(x) = |x|^r$. Notice that (29) and (30) are particular cases of problems (1) and (2), respectively, with $N = 3$, $p = 3$, $q = 2$, $\Omega = B$, $a(x) = |x|^r$, $b(x) = (1-|x|^2)^h$ and

$$f(x,t,\xi) = g(x,t) + k_0\frac{|x|^r t}{1+t^2}|\xi|^\mu - k_1 t|\xi|^\nu.$$

Let us check the conditions (H1)–(H4). Condition (H1) requires having $a^{-s} = |x|^{-rs} \in L^1(B)$ for some $s \in \left(\max\left\{\frac{N}{p}, \frac{1}{p-1}\right\}, +\infty\right) = (1, +\infty)$, which amounts to choosing $1 < s < \frac{3}{r}$. Taking into account that $r \in (0, \frac{3}{2})$, condition (H1) is fulfilled for instance with $s = 2$, a choice that we keep in the sequel.

Since $2r < 3$, we have

$$a^{-\frac{q}{p-q}} b^{\frac{p}{p-q}} = |x|^{-2r}(1-|x|^2)^{3h} \in L^1(B),$$

therefore, assumption (H2) is verified. For $s = 2$, it holds $p_s = ps/(s+1) = 2$, so we are in the situation of $N = 3 > p_s = 2$, where $p_s^* = \frac{Np_s}{N-p_s} = 6$, so $(p_s^*)' = \frac{6}{5}$ and $\frac{p_s}{(p_s^*)'} = \frac{5}{3}$.

We note that

$$\begin{aligned} |f(x,t,\xi)| &\leq a_0 t^2 + b_0 + k_0|x|^r|\xi|^\mu + k_1|t||\xi|^\nu \\ &\leq a_0 t^2 + b_0 + k_0|\xi|^\mu + \frac{k_1}{2}(t^2 + |\xi|^{2\nu}) \\ &\leq b_0 + k_0 + \frac{k_1}{2} + (a_0 + \frac{k_1}{2})t^2 + (k_0 + \frac{k_1}{2})|\xi|^\gamma \end{aligned}$$

for a.e $x \in B$ and all $(t,\xi) \in \mathbb{R} \times \mathbb{R}^3$, where

$$\gamma := \max\{\mu, 2\nu\} < \frac{5}{3} = \frac{p_s}{(p_s^*)'}.$$

Therefore assumption (H3) is satisfied with $\sigma(x) = b_0 + k_0 + \frac{k_1}{2}$, $c_1 = a_0 + \frac{k_1}{2}$, $c_2 = k_0 + \frac{k_1}{2}$, $\alpha = 2$ and $\beta = \gamma$. We also derive

$$\begin{aligned} f(x,t,\xi)t &= g(x,t)t + k_0 \frac{|x|^r t^2}{1+t^2}||^{\mu} - k_1 t^2 |\xi|^{\nu} \\ &\le a_0|t|^3 + b_0|t| + k_0|x|^r|\xi|^{\mu} \\ &\le b_0 + k_0 + (a_0 + b_0)|t|^3 + k_0|x|^r|\xi|^3 \end{aligned}$$

for a.e $x \in B$ and all $(t, \xi) \in \mathbb{R} \times \mathbb{R}^3$. Assumption (H4) is verified with $\rho(x) = b_0 + k_0$, $d_1 = a_0 + b_0$ and $d_2 = k_0$ having been supposed that $\lambda_1^{-1}(a_0 + b_0) + k_0 < 1$.

Since the assumptions (H1)-(H4) are satisfied, Theorems 1 and 2 can be applied to ensure the existence of a weak solution to problem (29) and of a generalized solution to problem (30). The weak solution to problem (29) can be approximated as described in Theorem 1.

Funding: This research received no external funding.

Conflicts of Interest: The author declares that he has no conflict of interest.

References

1. Motreanu, D.; Nashed, M.Z. Degenerated (p,q)-Laplacian with weights and related equations with convection. *Numer. Funct. Anal. Optim.* **2021**, in press.
2. Motreanu, D. *Nonlinear Differential Problems with Smooth and Nonsmooth Constraints*; Elsevier/Academic Press: Amsterdam, The Netherlands, 2018.
3. Drabek, P.; Kufner, A.; Nicolosi, F. *Quasilinear Eliptic Equations with Degenerations and Singularities*; De Gruyter Series in Nonlinear Analysis and Applications, 5; Walter de Gruyter & Co.: Berlin, Germany, 1997.
4. Motreanu, D.; Tornatore, E. Quasilinear Dirichlet problems with degenerated p-Laplacian and convection term. *Mathematics* **2021**, *9*, 139. [CrossRef]
5. Liu, Z.; Livrea, R.; Motreanu, D.; Zeng, S. Variational differential inclusions without ellipticity condition. *Electron. J. Qual. Theory Differ. Equ.* **2020**, *43*, 1–17.
6. Motreanu, D. Quasilinear Dirichlet problems with competing operators and convection. *Open Math.* **2020**, *18*, 1510–1517. [CrossRef]
7. Motreanu, D.; Motreanu, V.V. Nonstandard Dirichlet problems with competing (p,q)-Laplacian, convection, and convolution. *Stud. Univ. Babes-Bolyai Math.* **2021**, *66*, 95–103. [CrossRef]
8. Kufner, A. *Weighted Sobolev Spaces*; John Wiley & Sons, Inc.: New York, NY, USA, 1985.
9. Kufner, A.; Opic, B. How to define reasonably weighted Sobolev spaces. *Comment. Math. Univ. Carol.* **1984**, *25*, 537–554 .
10. Showalter, R.E. *Monotone Operators in Banach Space and Nonlinear Partial Differential Equations*; Mathematical Surveys and Monographs; American Mathematical Society: Providence, RI, USA, 1997; Volume 49.

axioms

MDPI

Article

Global Directed Dynamic Behaviors of a Lotka-Volterra Competition-Diffusion-Advection System

Lili Chen , **Shilei Lin and Yanfeng Zhao** *

College of Mathematics and Systems Science, Shandong University of Science and Technology, Qingdao 266590, China; chenlili0819@foxmail.com (L.C.); linshilei2021@126.com (S.L.)
* Correspondence: zhaoyanfeng1101@126.com

Abstract: This paper investigates the problem of the global directed dynamic behaviors of a Lotka-Volterra competition-diffusion-advection system between two organisms in heterogeneous environments. The two organisms not only compete for different basic resources, but also the advection and diffusion strategies follow the dispersal towards a positive distribution. By virtue of the principal eigenvalue theory, the linear stability of the co-existing steady state is established. Furthermore, the classification of dynamical behaviors is shown by utilizing the monotone dynamical system theory. This work can be seen as a further development of a competition-diffusion system.

Keywords: competition-diffusion-advection; principal eigenvalue; dynamic behaviors; global asymptotic stability

MSC: 35B40; 35K57; 37C65; 92D25

Citation: Chen, L.; Lin, S.; Zhao, Y. Global Directed Dynamic Behaviors of a Lotka-Volterra Competition-Diffusion-Advection System. *Axioms* **2021**, *10*, 195. https://doi.org/10.3390/axioms10030195

Academic Editors: Shengda Zeng, Stanisław Migórski and Yongjian Liu

Received: 7 July 2021
Accepted: 18 August 2021
Published: 20 August 2021

1. Introduction

In the past few decades, the dynamic behaviors of competition-diffusion systems (see [1]) in homogeneous or heterogeneous environments have been extensively studied. Until 2017, He and Ni [2,3] studied the dynamics of two organisms by changing their random diffusion coefficients, resource carrying capacity and competitiveness, and they also described the global dynamics of two organisms. Their research has made outstanding contributions to the competition-diffusion systems. For the competition model of two organisms, either both organisms survive or win with the extinction of the other organisms (see [4–6]). In 2019, Du et al. [7,8] studied a Lotka-Volterra competition system with periodic habitat advection. From a biological point of view, this pulsating travel front provided a way for two competing species to interact in heterogeneous habitats. Based on the assumption that the resource function in spatial variables is decreasing, Lou et al. [9] described the competition between two aquatic organisms with different diffusion strategies for the same resource in the Lotka-Volterra reaction-diffusion-advection system in 2019. Md. Kamrujjaman [10] studied the impact of diffusion strategies on the outcome of competition between two populations while the species are distributed according to their respective carrying capacities in competition-diffusion systems. However, in the competition-diffusion-advection systems, the study of different species with different distribution functions will be more complex. Tang and Chen [11] and Xu et al. [12] studied the population dynamics of competition between two organisms from the perspective of river ecology in 2020. One interesting feature of their system was that the boundary conditions at the upstream end and downstream end can represent the net loss of individuals. In some cases, both organisms leave the site of competition, neither coexisting nor becoming extinct. Such an environment is important enough to demonstrate how organisms change their density and survival time in competition (see [13]). In 2021, Ma and Guo [14] described the feature of the coincidence of bifurcating coexistence steady-state solution branches and the effect of advection on the stability of the bifurcating solution. However, it is worthwhile to point out that all the aforementioned works focus on the global dynamic behaviors of competition-diffusion systems (see [10,15,16]) or advection systems (see [17,18]), in which the diffusion rates and spatial carrying capacity are changed, or the periodic habitat of advection systems is studied, or the upstream and downstream boundary conditions are changed.

Motivated by the effort of the aforementioned studies, we investigate the problem of the global directed dynamic behaviors of a Lotka-Volterra advection system between two organisms in heterogeneous environments, where two organisms are competing for different fundamental resources, their advection and diffusion strategies follow the dispersal towards a positive distribution, and the functions of inter-specific competition ability are variable.

Hence, we discuss the following global dynamics of the advection system:

$$\begin{cases} U_t = \nabla \cdot [\kappa_1(x)\nabla(\frac{U}{Q(x)}) - \mu_1(x)\frac{U}{Q(x)}\nabla\omega_1(x)] + U[r_1(x) - U - \rho_2(x)V], & \\ & in\ \Omega \times \mathbb{R}^+, \\ V_t = \nabla \cdot [\kappa_2(x)\nabla(\frac{V}{Q(x)}) - \mu_2(x)\frac{V}{Q(x)}\nabla\omega_2(x)] + V[r_2(x) - \rho_1(x)U - V], & \\ & in\ \Omega \times \mathbb{R}^+, \\ \kappa_1(x)\frac{\partial}{\partial n}(\frac{U}{Q}) - \mu_1(x)\frac{U}{Q}\frac{\partial\omega_1(x)}{\partial n} = 0, & on\ \partial\Omega \times \mathbb{R}^+, \\ \kappa_2(x)\frac{\partial}{\partial n}(\frac{V}{Q}) - \mu_2(x)\frac{V}{Q}\frac{\partial\omega_2(x)}{\partial n} = 0, & on\ \partial\Omega \times \mathbb{R}^+, \\ U(x,0) = U_0(x) \geq, \not\equiv 0, & in\ \Omega, \\ V(x,0) = V_0(x) \geq, \not\equiv 0, & in\ \Omega, \end{cases} \tag{1}$$

where $U(x,t)$ and $V(x,t)$ are the population densities of biological organisms, location x *in* Ω and time $t > 0$, which are supposed to be nonnegative; $\kappa_1(x), \kappa_2(x) > 0$ correspond to the dispersal rates of two competing organisms U and V, respectively. ∇ is the gradient operator. $\mu_1(x), \mu_2(x) > 0$ correspond to the advection rates of two competing organisms U and V, and $\omega_1(x), \omega_2(x) \in C^2(\overline{\Omega})$ are the nonconstant functions and represent the advective direction. The intrinsic growth rates of the two competing organisms are bounded functions $r_1(x)$ and $r_2(x)$, respectively, two positive distributions are $Q(x)$. $\rho_1(x), \rho_2(x) > 0$ show the inter-specific competition ability. The habitat Ω is a bounded smooth domain in $\mathbb{R}^N$, $1 \leq N \in \mathbb{Z}$; n denotes the outward unit normal vector on the boundary $\partial\Omega$. For the sake of simplicity, we can suppose the initial data U_0 and V_0 not identically zero. The system (1) satisfies no-flux boundary conditions.

When $\kappa_1(x) = \kappa_1, \kappa_2(x) = \kappa_2, \mu_1(x) = \mu_1, \mu_2(x) = \mu_2, Q(x) \equiv 1, \rho_1(x) = \rho_1, \rho_2(x) = \rho_2, \omega_1(x) = \omega_2(x)$, the system (1) becomes the advection system studied by Zhou and Xiao [19]:

$$\begin{cases} U_t = \kappa_1\Delta U - \mu_1\nabla \cdot [U\nabla\omega(x)] + U[r_1(x) - U - \rho_2 V], & in\ \Omega \times \mathbb{R}^+, \\ V_t = \kappa_2\Delta V - \mu_2\nabla \cdot [V\nabla\omega(x)] + V[r_2(x) - \rho_1 U - V], & in\ \Omega \times \mathbb{R}^+, \\ \kappa_1\frac{\partial U}{\partial n} - \mu_1 U\frac{\partial\omega(x)}{\partial n} = 0, & on\ \partial\Omega \times \mathbb{R}^+, \\ \kappa_2\frac{\partial V}{\partial n} - \mu_2 V\frac{\partial\omega(x)}{\partial n} = 0, & on\ \partial\Omega \times \mathbb{R}^+, \\ U(x,0) = U_0(x) \geq, \not\equiv 0, & in\ \Omega, \\ V(x,0) = V_0(x) \geq, \not\equiv 0, & in\ \Omega, \end{cases} \tag{2}$$

where $\kappa_1, \kappa_2, \mu_1, \mu_2, \rho_1$ and ρ_2 are positive constants. $\Delta = \sum_{i=1}^{N}\frac{\partial^2}{\partial x_i^2}$ is the usual Laplace operator. If $\mu_1, \mu_2 > 0$, readers can take a look at the relevant literature [20] and for the case $\mu_1 > 0 = \mu_2$, please see the references [21–25].

If $\mu_1 = \mu_2 = 0$, the system (2) becomes a diffusion model (see [2,3,5,26]):

$$\begin{cases} U_t = \kappa_1 \Delta U + U[r_1(x) - U - V], & in\ \Omega \times \mathbb{R}^+, \\ V_t = \kappa_2 \Delta V + V[r_2(x) - U - V], & in\ \Omega \times \mathbb{R}^+, \\ \frac{\partial U}{\partial n} = \frac{\partial V}{\partial n} = 0, & on\ \partial\Omega \times \mathbb{R}^+, \\ U(x,0) = U_0(x) \geq, \not\equiv 0, V(x,0) = V_0(x) \geq, \not\equiv 0, & in\ \Omega. \end{cases} \tag{3}$$

According to the research of the above models, the purpose of our paper is to deal with a more broader model (1) in a high spatial dimensions. In this system, we consider that the diffusion and advection strategies follow the dispersal towards a positive distribution, growth rates and competitiveness of the two organisms are different. Thus, we have the following basic assumptions in this paper.

(A_1) $\quad \frac{\mu_1(x)}{\kappa_1(x)}\omega_1(x) - \frac{\mu_2(x)}{\kappa_2(x)}\omega_2(x) := \zeta_1\omega_1(x) - \zeta_2\omega_2(x) \geq 0, \Lambda := \min_{x\in\overline{\Omega}} e^{\zeta_2\omega_2(x)-\zeta_1\omega_1(x)}, \zeta_1$ and ζ_2 are positive constants;

(A_2) $\quad (\rho_1(x), \rho_2(x)) \in \Pi_\Lambda := \{(\rho_1(x), \rho_2(x)) : \rho_1(x), \rho_2(x) > 0, \rho_1(x)\rho_2(x) \leq \Lambda\}$;

(A_3) $\quad r_1(x) > 0, r_2(x) > 0$ in $L^\infty(\Omega)$;

(A_4) $\quad Q(x) > 0$ is nonconstant, and $\frac{Q(x)}{r_1(x)}, \frac{Q(x)}{r_2(x)}$ are also nonconstant.

Conditions $(A_3) - (A_4)$ ensure that the distribution of resources is heterogeneous for two species and the positivity is imposed here to guarantee the existence of two semi-trivial steady states for later discussion convenience. Under the conditions of $(A_1) - (A_4)$, we show a complete classification of the global dynamics of the system (1). The rest of this paper is arranged as follows. In Section 2, we mainly do some preparatory work. Some related properties of the system (1) are deduced from the properties of a single organisms model (4). Besides, some lemmas are proved. In Section 3, we investigate our main results. By using principal eigenvalue theory, we obtain the linear stability of coexisting steady states (see Theorem 2). Then, the most important thing is that in virtue of the monotone dynamical system theory (see [4]), we show the classification of global dynamic behaviors (see Theorem 3). A discussion on the main results and problems that deserve future investigation is presented in Section 4.

2. Preliminaries

In order to describe our main results, we show a competition-diffusion-advection system for a single organisms as follows:

$$\begin{cases} U_t = \nabla \cdot [\kappa(x)\nabla(\frac{U}{Q(x)}) - \mu(x)\frac{U}{Q(x)}\nabla\omega(x)] + U[r(x) - U], & in\ \Omega \times \mathbb{R}^+, \\ \kappa(x)\frac{\partial}{\partial n}(\frac{U}{Q}) - \mu(x)\frac{U}{Q}\frac{\partial\omega(x)}{\partial n} = 0, & on\ \partial\Omega \times \mathbb{R}^+, \\ U(x,0) = U_0(x) \geq, \not\equiv 0, & in\ \Omega, \end{cases} \tag{4}$$

where $\kappa(x) > 0, \mu(x) > 0, Q(x) > 0$ and $r(x) > 0$, $r(x)$ is bounded. According to the relevant description in [27] and the case that $r(x) > 0$, there is a unique positive steady state $\theta_{d,Q,\mu,r}$ in the system (4). If we apply this result to the system (1) and the conditions $(A_3) - (A_4)$, there are two semi-trivial steady states $(\theta_{\kappa_1,Q,\mu_1,r_1}, 0)$ and $(0, \theta_{\kappa_2,Q,\mu_2,r_2})$, respectively.

Lemma 1. *Assume that $\kappa(x) > 0, \mu(x) > 0, Q(x) > 0$ and $r(x) > 0$, $r(x)$ is bounded. The elliptic boundary value Problem:*

$$\begin{cases} \nabla \cdot [\kappa(x)\nabla(\frac{\theta}{Q(x)}) - \mu(x)\frac{\theta}{Q(x)}\nabla\omega(x)] + \theta[r(x) - \theta] = 0, & in\ \Omega, \\ \kappa(x)\frac{\partial}{\partial n}(\frac{\theta}{Q}) - \mu(x)\frac{\theta}{Q}\frac{\partial\omega(x)}{\partial n} = 0, & on\ \partial\Omega, \end{cases} \tag{5}$$

has a unique positive solution denoted by θ.

Proof. It is known in [27] that the problem (5) admits a solution and the solution is positive, denoted by θ, owning to the positivity of $\kappa(x), \mu(x), Q(x), r(x)$. Next, assume that θ_1, θ_2 are any two positive solutions of (5) and $0 < \theta_1 \le \theta_2$. It is not difficult to see that

$$\kappa\nabla(\frac{\theta}{Q}) - \mu\frac{\theta}{Q}\nabla\omega = \kappa e^{\frac{\mu}{\kappa}\omega}[\nabla(e^{-\frac{\mu}{\kappa}\omega}\frac{\theta}{Q})].$$

Then

$$\begin{aligned}
&\int \nabla \cdot \{\kappa e^{\frac{\mu}{\kappa}\omega}[\nabla(e^{-\frac{\mu}{\kappa}\omega}\frac{\theta_1}{Q})]\}(e^{-\frac{\mu}{\kappa}\omega}\frac{\theta_2}{Q})\,\mathrm{d}x \\
=& -\int \kappa e^{\frac{\mu}{\kappa}\omega}[\nabla(e^{-\frac{\mu}{\kappa}\omega}\frac{\theta_1}{Q})]\,[\nabla(e^{-\frac{\mu}{\kappa}\omega}\frac{\theta_2}{Q})]\,\mathrm{d}x \\
=& -\int [r-\theta_1]e^{-\frac{\mu}{\kappa}\omega}\frac{\theta_1\theta_2}{Q}\,\mathrm{d}x \\
=& -\int [r-\theta_2]e^{-\frac{\mu}{\kappa}\omega}\frac{\theta_1\theta_2}{Q}\,\mathrm{d}x. \qquad (6)
\end{aligned}$$

We deduce

$$\int [\theta_1-\theta_2]e^{-\frac{\mu}{\kappa}\omega}\frac{\theta_1\theta_2}{Q}\,\mathrm{d}x = 0.$$

Therefore, $\theta_1 = \theta_2$. □

To give a complete classification of the global dynamic system (1), we define

$$(\kappa_1, \kappa_2, \mu_1, \mu_2) \in \Gamma := \mathbb{R}^+ \times \mathbb{R}^+ \times \mathbb{R}^+ \times \mathbb{R}^+.$$

Based on the approach in [2], we define

$$\begin{aligned}
\Sigma_U &:= \{(\kappa_1, \kappa_2, \mu_1, \mu_2) \in \Gamma : (\theta_{\kappa_1,Q,\mu_1,r_1}, 0) \ \textit{is linearly stable}\}; \\
\Sigma_V &:= \{(\kappa_1, \kappa_2, \mu_1, \mu_2) \in \Gamma : (0, \theta_{\kappa_2,Q,\mu_2,r_2}) \ \textit{is linearly stable}\}; \\
\Sigma_- &:= \{(\kappa_1, \kappa_2, \mu_1, \mu_2) \in \Gamma : (\theta_{\kappa_1,Q,\mu_1,r_1}, 0) \ \textit{and} (0, \theta_{\kappa_2,Q,\mu_2,r_2}) \ \textit{are linearly unstable}\}. \qquad (7)
\end{aligned}$$

We first recall the well-known Krein-Rutman Theorem:

Theorem 1 (Krein-Rutman Theorem [28])**.** *Let X be a Banach space, $K \subset X$ a total cone and $T : X \to X$ a compact linear operator that is positive (i.e., $T(K) \subset K$) with positive spectral radius $r(T)$. Then $r(T)$ is an eigenvalue with an eigenvector $u \in K \setminus 0 : Tu = r(T)u$. Moreover, $r(T^*) = r(T)$ is an eigenvalue of T^* with an eigenvector $u^* \in K^*$.*

In order to better describe the linear stability of semi-trivial steady states, we give the definition of elliptic eigenvalue problem:

$$\begin{cases} \nabla \cdot [\kappa(x)\nabla(\frac{\phi}{Q}) - \mu(x)\frac{\phi}{Q}\nabla\omega(x)] + h(x)\phi + \sigma\phi = 0, & in\ \Omega, \\ \kappa(x)\frac{\partial}{\partial n}(\frac{\phi}{Q}) - \mu(x)\frac{\phi}{Q}\frac{\partial\omega(x)}{\partial n} = 0, & on\ \partial\Omega, \end{cases} \qquad (8)$$

where $\kappa(x) > 0, \mu(x) > 0, Q(x) > 0$ and $h(x) \in L^\infty(\Omega)$. Let

$$A\phi = \nabla \cdot [\kappa(x)\nabla(\frac{\phi}{Q}) - \mu(x)\frac{\phi}{Q}\nabla\omega(x)] + h(x)\phi.$$

Since A is uniformly strongly elliptic operator, we declare that the operator A satisfies the conditions in Theorem 1. An eigenvalue σ_1 of the problem (8) is called a principal eigenvalue if $\sigma_1 \in \mathbb{R}$ and for any eigenvalue σ with $\sigma \ne \sigma_1$, we have $Re\ \sigma > \sigma_1$. Hence, the problem (8) has a principal eigenvalue, denoted by $\sigma_1(\kappa, Q, \mu, h)$, and its corresponding eigenfuntion $\phi(\kappa, Q, \mu, h) > 0$ in Ω. The principal eigenvalue is expressed as

$$\sigma_1(\kappa, Q, \mu, h) = \inf_{0 \neq \phi \in H^1(\Omega)} \frac{\int \kappa e^{\frac{\mu}{\kappa}\omega}[\nabla(e^{-\frac{\mu}{\kappa}\omega}\frac{\phi}{Q})]^2\,\mathrm{d}x - \int h \cdot e^{-\frac{\mu}{\kappa}\omega}\frac{\phi^2}{Q}\,\mathrm{d}x}{\int e^{-\frac{\mu}{d}\omega}\frac{\phi^2}{Q}\,\mathrm{d}x}. \tag{9}$$

Next, we give a useful lemma related to eigenvalue comparison results, which is used for Lemma 3 and Theorem 3.

Lemma 2 ([5]). *If $h_1(x) \leq h_2(x)$ within Ω, then $\sigma_1(\kappa, Q, \mu, h_1) \geq \sigma_1(\kappa, Q, \mu, h_2)$ and the equality holds if and only if $h_1(x) \equiv h_2(x)$ in Ω.*

According to the description of theory of monotone semi-flow in the literature [6], let X denote the standard Banach space consisting of all continuous functions from $\overline{\Omega}$ to $\mathbb{R}$, i.e., $X := C(\overline{\Omega})$, and X^+ be the set of all non-negative continuous functions from $\overline{\Omega}$ to $\mathbb{R}^+ \cup 0$. Define $K := X^+ \times (-X^+)$ as the usual cone for the study of competitive systems with nonempty interior. Then we define the notion of linear stability of a given steady state (U, V). Linearizing the steady state problem of (1) at (U, V), we obtain

$$\begin{cases} \nabla \cdot [\kappa_1(x)\nabla(\frac{\varphi}{Q(x)}) - \mu_1(x)\frac{\varphi}{Q(x)}\nabla\omega_1(x)] + [r_1(x) - U - \rho_2(x)V]\varphi & \\ -U[\varphi + \rho_2(x)\psi] + \lambda\varphi = 0, & in\ \Omega, \\ \nabla \cdot [\kappa_2(x)\nabla(\frac{\psi}{Q(x)}) - \mu_2(x)\frac{\psi}{Q(x)}\nabla\omega_2(x)] + [r_2(x) - \rho_1(x)U - V]\psi & \\ -V[\rho_1(x)\varphi + \psi] + \lambda\psi = 0, & in\ \Omega, \\ \kappa_1(x)\frac{\partial}{\partial n}(\frac{\varphi}{Q}) - \mu_1(x)\frac{\varphi}{Q}\frac{\partial\omega_1(x)}{\partial n} = 0, & on\ \partial\Omega, \\ \kappa_2(x)\frac{\partial}{\partial n}(\frac{\psi}{Q}) - \mu_2(x)\frac{\psi}{Q}\frac{\partial\omega_2(x)}{\partial n} = 0, & on\ \partial\Omega. \end{cases} \tag{10}$$

Similar to the scalar problem (8), we can define the principal eigenvalue for the system (10), that is, an eigenvalue λ_1 of the problem (10) is called a principal eigenvalue if $\lambda_1 \in \mathbb{R}$ and for any eigenvalue λ with $\lambda \neq \lambda_1$, we have $Re\,\lambda > \lambda_1$. Based on the approach in [6], by using Theorem 1, the problem (10) has a principal eigenvalue $\lambda_1 \in \mathbb{R}$. In fact, we can select the corresponding eigenfunction (φ_1, ψ_1), which satisfies $\varphi_1 > 0 > \psi_1$ in $\overline{\Omega}$. Here, for the convenience of readers to better understand the problem (10), we provide a simple illustration. Let us do this simple transformation

$$\Phi = e^{-\frac{\mu_1}{\kappa_1}\omega_1}\varphi \ and\ \Psi = -e^{-\frac{\mu_2}{\kappa_2}\omega_2}\psi,$$

then the problem (10) can be changed to

$$\begin{cases} \nabla[\kappa_1(x)\nabla(\frac{\Phi}{Q(x)})] + \mu_1(x)\nabla\omega_1(x) \cdot \nabla[\frac{\Phi}{Q(x)}] + [r_1(x) - 2U - \rho_2(x)V]\Phi & \\ +\rho_2(x)Ue^{(\zeta_2\omega_2(x) - \zeta_1\omega_1(x))}\Psi + \lambda\Phi = 0, & in\ \Omega, \\ \nabla[\kappa_2(x)\nabla(\frac{\Psi}{Q(x)})] + \mu_2(x)\nabla\omega_2(x) \cdot \nabla[\frac{\Psi}{Q(x)}] + \rho_1(x)Ve^{(\zeta_1\omega_1(x) - \zeta_2\omega_2(x))}\Phi & \\ +[r_2(x) - \rho_1(x)U - 2V]\Psi + \lambda\Psi = 0, & in\ \Omega, \\ \frac{\partial}{\partial n}(\frac{\Phi}{Q}) = \frac{\partial}{\partial n}(\frac{\Psi}{Q}) = 0, & on\ \partial\Omega, \end{cases} \tag{11}$$

which is a linear cooperative elliptic system. Suppose now L is the elliptic operator, let

$$\begin{aligned} L\Phi &= \nabla[\kappa_1(x)\nabla(\frac{\Phi}{Q(x)})] + \mu_1(x)\nabla\omega_1(x) \cdot \nabla[\frac{\Phi}{Q(x)}] + [r_1(x) - 2U - \rho_2(x)V]\Phi, \\ L\Psi &= \nabla[\kappa_2(x)\nabla(\frac{\Psi}{Q(x)})] + \mu_2(x)\nabla\omega_2(x) \cdot \nabla[\frac{\Psi}{Q(x)}] + [r_2(x) - \rho_1(x)U - 2V]\Psi. \end{aligned}$$

According to [28,29], the problem (11) has $C^{\alpha}(\overline{\Omega})$ coefficients and is strictly uniformly elliptic in the bounded domain Ω which has $C^{2,\alpha}$ boundary. Let K be the positive cone in $X := C_0^{1,\alpha}(\overline{\Omega})$ consisting of nonnegative functions. For any $\Phi_1, \Psi_1 \in X$, then we can deduce that $T : X \to X$ defined by $T(\Phi_1, \Psi_1) = (\Phi, \Psi)$ is a positive compact linear operator. By applying Theorem 1 for positive compact linear operators and the Neumann type boundary condition, the problem (11) admits a principal eigenvalue $\lambda_1 \in \mathbb{R}$, and the corresponding eigenfunction (Φ, Ψ) can be chosen to satisfy $\Phi \geq 0$ and $\Psi \geq 0$ in $\overline{\Omega}$. Notice that (Φ, Ψ) is the solution of the problem (11). Moreover, since the off-diagonal elements $\rho_2(x)Ue^{(\zeta_2\omega_2(x)-\zeta_1\omega_1(x))}$ and $\rho_1(x)Ve^{(\zeta_1\omega_1(x)-\zeta_2\omega_2(x))}$ are strictly positive in Ω, it can be further concluded that λ_1 is simple and it is the unique eigenvalue corresponding to a pair of strictly positive eigenfunctions, i.e., $\Phi > 0$ and $\Psi > 0$ in Ω. In fact, we have $\Phi > 0$ and $\Psi > 0$ in $\overline{\Omega}$ due to Hopf boundary lemma, which in turn allows us to choose $\varphi > 0 > \psi$ in $\overline{\Omega}$. See [30] using semi-group theory and [31] using maximum principle, [1,6] for detailed explanation. For the principal eigenvalue theory of general linear cooperative elliptic systems, we refer the interested readers to [29]. If $\lambda \neq \lambda_1$ is an eigenvalue of (10) and the boundary condition is Neumann type, then $Re\,\lambda > \lambda_1$ in the coexistence case.

Based on [26], (Corollary 2.10), the following lemma is about the linear stability of $(\theta_{\kappa_1,Q,\mu_1,r_1}, 0)$ and $(0, \theta_{\kappa_2,Q,\mu_2,r_2})$.

Lemma 3. *The linear stability of $(\theta_{\kappa_1,Q,\mu_1,r_1}, 0)$, $(0, \theta_{\kappa_2,Q,\mu_2,r_2})$ and $(0,0)$ in the system (1) are determined by the sign of $min\{\sigma_1(\kappa_1, Q, \mu_1, r_1), \sigma_1(\kappa_2, Q, \mu_2, r_2)\}$, $\sigma_1(\kappa_2, Q, \mu_2, r_2 - \rho_1\theta_{\kappa_1,Q,\mu_1,r_1})$ and $\sigma_1(\kappa_1, Q, \mu_1, r_1 - \rho_2\theta_{\kappa_2,Q,\mu_2,r_2})$.*

Proof. For the linear stability of $(\theta_{\kappa_1,Q,\mu_1,r_1}, 0)$, when $(U, V) = (\theta_{\kappa_1,Q,\mu_1,r_1}, 0)$ in (10), we have

$$\begin{cases} \nabla \cdot [\kappa_1(x)\nabla(\frac{\varphi}{Q(x)}) - \mu_1(x)\frac{\varphi}{Q(x)}\nabla\omega_1(x)] + [r_1(x) - 2\theta_{\kappa_1,Q,\mu_1,r_1}]\varphi & \\ +\lambda\varphi = \theta_{\kappa_1,Q,\mu_1,r_1}\rho_2(x)\psi, & in\ \Omega, \\ \nabla \cdot [\kappa_2(x)\nabla(\frac{\psi}{Q(x)}) - \mu_2(x)\frac{\psi}{Q(x)}\nabla\omega_2(x)] + [r_2(x) - \rho_1(x)\theta_{\kappa_1,Q,\mu_1,r_1}]\psi & \\ +\lambda\psi = 0, & in\ \Omega, \\ \kappa_1(x)\frac{\partial}{\partial n}(\frac{\varphi}{Q}) - \mu_1(x)\frac{\varphi}{Q}\frac{\partial\omega_1(x)}{\partial n} = 0, & on\ \partial\Omega, \\ \kappa_2(x)\frac{\partial}{\partial n}(\frac{\psi}{Q}) - \mu_2(x)\frac{\psi}{Q}\frac{\partial\omega_2(x)}{\partial n} = 0, & on\ \partial\Omega. \end{cases} \tag{12}$$

Let λ be an principal eigenvalue of (12) with the eigenfunction (φ, ψ). We get

$$\lambda = min\{\sigma_1(\kappa_1, Q, \mu_1, r_1 - 2\theta_{\kappa_1,Q,\mu_1,r_1}), \sigma_1(\kappa_2, Q, \mu_2, r_2 - \rho_1\theta_{\kappa_1,Q,\mu_1,r_1})\}. \tag{13}$$

If $\psi \neq 0$, then λ belonging to an eigenvalue of the second equation in (12), is real and the inequality $\lambda \geq \sigma_1(\kappa_2, Q, \mu_2, r_2 - \rho_1\theta_{\kappa_1,Q,\mu_1,r_1})$ holds. Perhaps, if $\psi = 0$, then $\varphi \neq 0$ and λ is an eigenvalue of the first equation, we get

$$\begin{cases} \nabla \cdot [\kappa_1(x)\nabla(\frac{\varphi}{Q(x)}) - \mu_1(x)\frac{\varphi}{Q(x)}\nabla\omega_1(x)] + [r_1(x) - 2\theta_{\kappa_1,Q,\mu_1,r_1}]\varphi + \lambda\varphi = 0, & in\ \Omega, \\ \kappa_1(x)\frac{\partial}{\partial n}(\frac{\varphi}{Q}) - \mu_1(x)\frac{\varphi}{Q}\frac{\partial\omega_1(x)}{\partial n} = 0, & on\ \partial\Omega. \end{cases} \tag{14}$$

Due to the fact that λ is real and satisfies $\lambda \geq \sigma_1(\kappa_1, Q, \mu_1, r_1 - 2\theta_{\kappa_1,Q,\mu_1,r_1})$. It follows

$$\lambda \geq min\{\sigma_1(\kappa_1, Q, \mu_1, r_1 - 2\theta_{\kappa_1,Q,\mu_1,r_1}), \sigma_1(\kappa_2, Q, \mu_2, r_2 - \rho_1\theta_{\kappa_1,Q,\mu_1,r_1})\}.$$

If now $\sigma_1(\kappa_1, Q, \mu_1, r_1 - 2\theta_{\kappa_1,Q,\mu_1,r_1}) \leq \sigma_1(\kappa_2, Q, \mu_2, r_2 - \rho_1\theta_{\kappa_1,Q,\mu_1,r_1})$, letting φ be the first eigenfunction corresponding to $\sigma_1(\kappa_1, Q, \mu_1, r_1 - 2\theta_{\kappa_1,Q,\mu_1,r_1})$, then $\sigma_1(\kappa_1, Q, \mu_1, r_1 - 2\theta_{\kappa_1,Q,\mu_1,r_1})$ is an eigenvalue of (12) with the eigenfunction $(\varphi_1, 0)$, which deduces $\lambda = \sigma_1(\kappa_1, Q, \mu_1, r_1 - 2\theta_{\kappa_1,Q,\mu_1,r_1})$.

Suppose that $\sigma_1(\kappa_1, Q, \mu_1, r_1 - 2\theta_{\kappa_1,Q,\mu_1,r_1}) > \sigma_1(\kappa_2, Q, \mu_2, r_2 - \rho_1\theta_{\kappa_1,Q,\mu_1,r_1})$. Let ψ be the first eigenfunction corresponding to $\sigma_1(\kappa_2, Q, \mu_2, r_2 - \rho_1\theta_{\kappa_1,Q,\mu_1,r_1})$, then $\sigma_1(\kappa_2, Q, \mu_2, r_2 - \rho_1\theta_{\kappa_1,Q,\mu_1,r_1})$ is an eigenvalue of (12) with the eigenfunction $(\varphi, \psi) = (\varphi^*, \psi)$, that means $\lambda = \sigma_1(\kappa_2, Q, \mu_2, r_2 - \rho_1\theta_{\kappa_1,Q,\mu_1,r_1})$. Here φ^* satisfies

$$\begin{cases} \nabla \cdot [\kappa_1(x)\nabla(\frac{\varphi^*}{Q(x)})-\mu_1(x)\frac{\varphi^*}{Q(x)}\nabla\omega_1(x)] + [r_1(x) - 2\theta_{\kappa_1,Q,\mu_1,r_1}]\varphi^* \\ +\sigma_1(\kappa_2, Q, \mu_2, r_2 - \rho_1\theta_{\kappa_1,Q,\mu_1,r_1})\varphi^* = \theta_{\kappa_1,Q,\mu_1,r_1}\rho_2(x)\psi, & in\ \Omega, \\ \kappa_1(x)\frac{\partial}{\partial n}(\frac{\varphi^*}{Q}) - \mu_1(x)\frac{\varphi^*}{Q}\frac{\partial\omega_1(x)}{\partial n} = 0, & on\ \partial\Omega. \end{cases} \tag{15}$$

The existence of φ^* is inferred from

$$\begin{aligned} &\sigma_1(\kappa_1, Q, \mu_1, r_1 - 2\theta_{\kappa_1,Q,\mu_1,r_1} + \sigma_1(\kappa_2, Q, \mu_2, r_2 - \rho_1\theta_{\kappa_1,Q,\mu_1,r_1})) \\ =&\sigma_1(\kappa_1, Q, \mu_1, r_1 - 2\theta_{\kappa_1,Q,\mu_1,r_1}) - \sigma_1(\kappa_2, Q, \mu_2, r_2 - \rho_1\theta_{\kappa_1,Q,\mu_1,r_1}) > 0. \end{aligned}$$

So our claim is right. Owing to (6) and (9), it is inferred that $\sigma_1(\kappa_1, Q, \mu_1, r_1 - \theta_{\kappa_1,Q,\mu_1,r_1}) = 0$. Hence, according to Lemma 2, we gain

$$\sigma_1(\kappa_1, Q, \mu_1, r_1 - 2\theta_{\kappa_1,Q,\mu_1,r_1}) > \sigma_1(\kappa_1, Q, \mu_1, r_1 - \theta_{\kappa_1,Q,\mu_1,r_1}) = 0,$$

then λ has the same sign as the first eigenvalue $\sigma_1(\kappa_2, Q, \mu_2, r_2 - \rho_1\theta_{\kappa_1,Q,\mu_1,r_1})$. Applying the definition of λ and linear stability, we deduce that the linear stability of $(\theta_{\kappa_1,Q,\mu_1,r_1}, 0)$ is determined by the sign of $\sigma_1(\kappa_2, Q, \mu_2, r_2 - \rho_1\theta_{\kappa_1,Q,\mu_1,r_1})$.

Through completely similar arguments, we demonstrate that the stability of $(0,0)$ and $(0, \theta_{\kappa_2,Q,\mu_2,r_2})$, is determined by $min\{\sigma_1(\kappa_1, Q, \mu_1, r_1), \sigma_1(\kappa_2, Q, \mu_2, r_2)\}, \sigma_1(\kappa_1, Q, \mu_1, r_1 - \rho_2\theta_{\kappa_2,Q,\mu_2,r_2})$ respectively. □

Remark 1. *From the variational characteristics of the first eigenvalue, we can see that* $(0,0)$ *is linearly unstable for any* $\kappa_1(x), \kappa_2(x), \mu_1(x), \mu_2(x), \rho_2(x), \rho_1(x) > 0$.

Therefore, we give equivalent descriptions of (7) below:

$$\begin{aligned} \Sigma_U :=&\{(\kappa_1, \kappa_2, \mu_1, \mu_2) \in \Gamma : \sigma_1(\kappa_2, Q, \mu_2, r_2 - \rho_1\theta_{\kappa_1,Q,\mu_1,r_1}) > 0\}; \\ \Sigma_V :=&\{(\kappa_1, \kappa_2, \mu_1, \mu_2) \in \Gamma : \sigma_1(\kappa_1, Q, \mu_1, r_1 - \rho_2\theta_{\kappa_2,Q,\mu_2,r_2}) > 0\}; \\ \Sigma_- :=&\{(\kappa_1, \kappa_2, \mu_1, \mu_2) \in \Gamma : \sigma_1(\kappa_2, Q, \mu_2, r_2 - \rho_1\theta_{\kappa_1,Q,\mu_1,r_1}) < 0\ and \\ &\sigma_1(\kappa_1, Q, \mu_1, r_1 - \rho_2\theta_{\kappa_2,Q,\mu_2,r_2}) < 0\}. \end{aligned}$$

The neutrally stable case is defined as follows

$$\begin{aligned} \Sigma_{U,0} :=&\{(\kappa_1, \kappa_2, \mu_1, \mu_2) \in \Gamma : \sigma_1(\kappa_2, Q, \mu_2, r_2 - \rho_1\theta_{\kappa_1,Q,\mu_1,r_1}) = 0\}; \\ \Sigma_{V,0} :=&\{(\kappa_1, \kappa_2, \mu_1, \mu_2) \in \Gamma : \sigma_1(\kappa_1, Q, \mu_1, r_1 - \rho_2\theta_{\kappa_2,Q,\mu_2,r_2}) = 0\}; \\ \Sigma_{0,0} :=&\{(\kappa_1, \kappa_2, \mu_1, \mu_2) \in \Gamma : \sigma_1(\kappa_2, Q, \mu_2, r_2 - \rho_1\theta_{\kappa_1,Q,\mu_1,r_1}) \\ &= \sigma_1(\kappa_1, Q, \mu_1, r_1 - \rho_2\theta_{\kappa_2,Q,\mu_2,r_2}) = 0\}. \end{aligned}$$

By the definition, it is easy to see $\Sigma_{0,0} = \Sigma_{U,0} \cap \Sigma_{V,0}$.

In the following, "*g.a.s*" is used to mean that the steady state is globally asymptotically stable among all non-negative and not identically zero initial conditions.

Lemma 4 ([5]). *For any* $\kappa_1, \kappa_2, \mu_1, \mu_2 > 0$, *assume that* $(A_1) - (A_4)$ *hold and every coexistence steady state of the system (1), if it exists, is asymptotically stable. Then one of the following alternatives holds:*

(i) There exists a unique coexistence steady state of (1) that is g.a.s.
(ii) The system (1) has no coexistence steady state and either one of $(\theta_{\kappa_1,Q,\mu_1,r_1}, 0)$ *or* $(0, \theta_{\kappa_2,Q,\mu_2,r_2})$ *is g.a.s, while the other is unstable.*

3. Main Results

In this section, we present the results which are related to the co-existence steady state and the classification of global dynamic behaviors of the system (1).

Theorem 2. *Suppose that* $(A_1)-(A_4)$ *hold. For any* $(\kappa_1, \kappa_2, \mu_1, \mu_2) \in \Gamma \setminus \Sigma_{0,0}$, *then every co-existence steady state of the system* (1), *if exists, is linearly stable, i.e.,* $\lambda_1 > 0$.

Theorem 3. *Suppose that* $(A_1)-(A_4)$ *hold. Then we have the mutually disjoint decomposition of* Γ:

$$\Gamma = (\Sigma_U \cup \Sigma_{U,0} \setminus \Sigma_{0,0}) \cup (\Sigma_V \cup \Sigma_{V,0} \setminus \Sigma_{0,0}) \cup \Sigma_- \cup \Sigma_{0,0}. \tag{16}$$

Moreover, the following statements hold for the system (1):

(i) *For all* $(\kappa_1, \kappa_2, \mu_1, \mu_2) \in (\Sigma_U \cup \Sigma_{U,0} \setminus \Sigma_{0,0})$, $(\theta_{\kappa_1,Q,\mu_1,r_1}, 0)$ *is g.a.s;*
(ii) *For all* $(\kappa_1, \kappa_2, \mu_1, \mu_2) \in (\Sigma_V \cup \Sigma_{V,0} \setminus \Sigma_{0,0})$, $(0, \theta_{\kappa_2,Q,\mu_2,r_2})$ *is g.a.s;*
(iii) *For all* $(\kappa_1, \kappa_2, \mu_1, \mu_2) \in \Sigma_-$, *the system* (1) *has a unique coexistence steady state that is g.a.s;*
(iv) *For all* $(\kappa_1, \kappa_2, \mu_1, \mu_2) \in \Sigma_{0,0}$, $\theta_{\kappa_1,Q,\mu_1,r_1} \equiv \rho_2(x)\theta_{\kappa_2,Q,\mu_2,r_2}$ *in* $\overline{\Omega}$ *and the system* (1) *has a compact global attractor consisting of a continuum of steady states*

$$\{(\eta(x)\theta_{\kappa_1,Q,\mu_1,r_1}, (1-\eta(x))\frac{\theta_{\kappa_1,Q,\mu_1,r_1}}{\rho_2(x)}) : \eta(x) \in [0,1]\}$$

connecting with two semi-trivial steady states.

3.1. Co-Existence Steady State

In order to prove Theorem 2, we assume that (U, V) is the co-existence steady state of the following system (1):

$$\begin{cases} \nabla \cdot [\kappa_1(x)\nabla(\frac{U}{Q(x)}) - \mu_1(x)\frac{U}{Q(x)}\nabla\omega_1(x)] + U[r_1(x) - U - \rho_2(x)V] = 0, & in\ \Omega, \\ \nabla \cdot [\kappa_2(x)\nabla(\frac{V}{Q(x)}) - \mu_2(x)\frac{V}{Q(x)}\nabla\omega_2(x)] + V[r_2(x) - \rho_1(x)U - V] = 0, & in\ \Omega, \\ \kappa_1(x)\frac{\partial}{\partial n}(\frac{U}{Q}) - \mu_1(x)\frac{U}{Q}\frac{\partial\omega_1(x)}{\partial n} = 0, & on\ \partial\Omega, \\ \kappa_2(x)\frac{\partial}{\partial n}(\frac{V}{Q}) - \mu_2(x)\frac{V}{Q}\frac{\partial\omega_2(x)}{\partial n} = 0, & on\ \partial\Omega. \end{cases} \tag{17}$$

Similar to the problem (10), then we get the linear eigenvalue model by linearize system (1) at (U, V),

$$\begin{cases} \nabla \cdot [\kappa_1(x)\nabla(\frac{\varphi}{Q(x)}) - \mu_1(x)\frac{\varphi}{Q(x)}\nabla\omega_1(x)] + [r_1(x) - U - \rho_2(x)V]\varphi & \\ -U[\varphi + \rho_2(x)\psi] + \lambda\varphi = 0, & in\ \Omega, \\ \nabla \cdot [\kappa_2(x)\nabla(\frac{\psi}{Q(x)}) - \mu_2(x)\frac{\psi}{Q(x)}\nabla\omega_2(x)] + [r_2(x) - \rho_1(x)U - V]\psi & \\ -V[\rho_1(x)\varphi + \psi] + \lambda\psi = 0, & in\ \Omega, \\ \kappa_1(x)\frac{\partial}{\partial n}(\frac{\varphi}{Q}) - \mu_1(x)\frac{\varphi}{Q}\frac{\partial\omega_1(x)}{\partial n} = 0, & on\ \partial\Omega, \\ \kappa_2(x)\frac{\partial}{\partial n}(\frac{\psi}{Q}) - \mu_2(x)\frac{\psi}{Q}\frac{\partial\omega_2(x)}{\partial n} = 0, & on\ \partial\Omega. \end{cases} \tag{18}$$

According to the problem (8) and using Theorem 1, we can deduce that the problem (18) has a principal eigenvalue λ_1. Moreover, we can choose the corresponding eigenfunction (φ, ψ), it satisfies $\varphi > 0 > \psi$ in $\overline{\Omega}$.

Now, we are ready to discuss Theorem 2.

Proof of Theorem 2. Obviously, as long as we can obtain $\lambda_1 > 0$ when $(\kappa_1, \kappa_2, \mu_1, \mu_2) \in \Gamma \setminus \Sigma_{0,0}$. Multiplying the first equation in (18) and (17) by $\frac{U}{Q(x)}$ and $\frac{\varphi}{Q(x)}$, respectively, and subtracting the obtained equations, we obtain

$$\begin{aligned}&[\nabla(\kappa_1\nabla(\frac{\varphi}{Q}) - \mu_1\tfrac{\varphi}{Q}\nabla\omega_1)]\tfrac{U}{Q} - [\nabla(\kappa_1\nabla(\frac{U}{Q}) - \mu_1\tfrac{U}{Q}\nabla\omega_1)]\tfrac{\varphi}{Q}\\ &\quad -\tfrac{U^2}{Q}[\varphi + \rho_2(x)\psi] = -\tfrac{\lambda_1 U\varphi}{Q}.\end{aligned} \tag{19}$$

In the similar way, it can be derived from the second equation in (17) and (18) that

$$\begin{aligned}&[\nabla(\kappa_2\nabla(\frac{\psi}{Q}) - \mu_2\tfrac{\psi}{Q}\nabla\omega_2)]\tfrac{V}{Q} - [\nabla(\kappa_2\nabla(\frac{V}{Q}) - \mu_2\tfrac{V}{Q}\nabla\omega_2)]\tfrac{\psi}{Q}\\ &\quad -\tfrac{V^2}{Q}[\rho_1(x)\varphi + \psi] = -\tfrac{\lambda_1 V\psi}{Q}.\end{aligned} \tag{20}$$

Furthermore, multiplying (19) by $e^{-\frac{\mu_1}{\kappa_1}\omega_1} \cdot \frac{\varphi^2}{U^2}$, then we integrate over Ω and deduce (for simplicity, we replace $\int_\Omega$ with $\int$)

$$\begin{aligned}&\lambda_1 \int e^{-\frac{\mu_1}{\kappa_1}\omega_1}\frac{\varphi^3}{UQ}\,\mathrm{d}x\\
=&-\int [\nabla(\kappa_1\nabla(\frac{\varphi}{Q}) - \mu_1\frac{\varphi}{Q}\nabla\omega_1)]e^{-\frac{\mu_1}{\kappa_1}\omega_1}\frac{\varphi^2}{UQ}\,\mathrm{d}x\\
&+\int [\nabla(\kappa_1\nabla(\frac{U}{Q}) - \mu_1\frac{U}{Q}\nabla\omega_1)]e^{-\frac{\mu_1}{\kappa_1}\omega_1}\frac{\varphi^3}{U^2Q}\,\mathrm{d}x\\
&+\int e^{-\frac{\mu_1}{\kappa_1}\omega_1}\frac{\varphi^2}{Q}[\varphi + \rho_2(x)\psi]\,\mathrm{d}x\\
=&\int [\kappa_1\nabla(\frac{\varphi}{Q}) - \mu_1\frac{\varphi}{Q}\nabla\omega_1][\nabla\cdot(e^{-\frac{\mu_1}{\kappa_1}\omega_1}\frac{\varphi^2}{UQ})]\,\mathrm{d}x\\
&-\int [\kappa_1\nabla(\frac{U}{Q}) - \mu_1\frac{U}{Q}\nabla\omega_1][\nabla\cdot(e^{-\frac{\mu_1}{\kappa_1}\omega_1}\frac{\varphi^3}{U^2Q})]\,\mathrm{d}x\\
&+\int e^{-\frac{\mu_1}{\kappa_1}\omega_1}\frac{\varphi^2}{Q}[\varphi + \rho_2(x)\psi]\,\mathrm{d}x\\
:=&I_1 - I_2 + I_3.\end{aligned} \tag{21}$$

By using the similarly method for the Equation (20), we get

$$\begin{aligned}&\lambda_1 \int e^{-\frac{\mu_2}{\kappa_2}\omega_2}\frac{\psi^3}{VQ}\,\mathrm{d}x\\
=&-\int [\nabla(\kappa_2\nabla(\frac{\psi}{Q}) - \mu_2\frac{\psi}{Q}\nabla\omega_2)]e^{-\frac{\mu_2}{\kappa_2}\omega_2}\frac{\psi^2}{VQ}\,\mathrm{d}x\\
&+\int [\nabla(\kappa_2\nabla(\frac{V}{Q}) - \mu_2\frac{V}{Q}\nabla\omega_2)]e^{-\frac{\mu_2}{\kappa_2}\omega_2}\frac{\psi^3}{V^2Q}\,\mathrm{d}x\\
&+\int e^{-\frac{\mu_2}{\kappa_2}\omega_2}\frac{\psi^2}{Q}[\rho_1(x)\varphi + \psi]\,\mathrm{d}x\\
=&\int [\kappa_2\nabla(\frac{\psi}{Q}) - \mu_2\frac{\psi}{Q}\nabla\omega_2][\nabla\cdot(e^{-\frac{\mu_2}{\kappa_2}\omega_2}\frac{\psi^2}{VQ})]\,\mathrm{d}x\\
&-\int [\kappa_2\nabla(\frac{V}{Q}) - \mu_2\frac{V}{Q}\nabla\omega_2][\nabla\cdot(e^{-\frac{\mu_2}{\kappa_2}\omega_2}\frac{\psi^3}{V^2Q})]\,\mathrm{d}x\\
&+\int e^{-\frac{\mu_2}{\kappa_2}\omega_2}\frac{\psi^2}{Q}[\rho_1(x)\varphi + \psi]\,\mathrm{d}x\\
:=&J_1 - J_2 + J_3.\end{aligned} \tag{22}$$

We now simplify the formulas I_1, I_2, J_1 and J_2. Then we find

$$\begin{aligned}
I_1 :=& \int [\kappa_1 \nabla(\frac{\varphi}{Q}) - \mu_1 \frac{\varphi}{Q} \nabla\omega_1] [\nabla \cdot (e^{-\frac{\mu_1}{\kappa_1}\omega_1} \frac{\varphi^2}{UQ})] \, dx \\
=& \int e^{-\frac{\mu_1}{\kappa_1}\omega_1} [\kappa_1 \nabla(\frac{\varphi}{Q}) - \mu_1 \frac{\varphi}{Q} \nabla\omega_1][\frac{2\varphi U \nabla\varphi - \varphi^2 \nabla U}{U^2 Q}] \, dx \\
&- \int \frac{\mu_1}{\kappa_1} \frac{\varphi^2}{UQ} e^{-\frac{\mu_1}{\kappa_1}\omega_1} [\kappa_1 \nabla(\frac{\varphi}{Q}) - \mu_1 \frac{\varphi}{Q} \nabla\omega_1] \cdot [\nabla\omega_1] \, dx \\
&- \int \frac{\varphi^2}{UQ^2} e^{-\frac{\mu_1}{\kappa_1}\omega_1} [\kappa_1 \nabla(\frac{\varphi}{Q}) - \mu_1 \frac{\varphi}{Q} \nabla\omega_1][\nabla Q] \, dx \\
=& \int e^{-\frac{\mu_1}{\kappa_1}\omega_1} \frac{\varphi^3}{UQ^2} [\kappa_1 \nabla(\frac{\varphi}{Q}) \frac{Q}{\varphi} - \mu_1 \nabla\omega_1][2\frac{\nabla\varphi}{\varphi} - \frac{\nabla U}{U}] \, dx \\
&- \int \frac{\mu_1}{\kappa_1} \frac{\varphi^3}{UQ^2} e^{-\frac{\mu_1}{\kappa_1}\omega_1} [\kappa_1 \nabla(\frac{\varphi}{Q}) \frac{Q}{\varphi} - \mu_1 \nabla\omega_1] \cdot [\nabla\omega_1] \, dx \\
&- \int \frac{\varphi^3}{UQ^3} e^{-\frac{\mu_1}{\kappa_1}\omega_1} [\kappa_1 \nabla(\frac{\varphi}{Q}) \frac{Q}{\varphi} - \mu_1 \nabla\omega_1][\nabla Q] \, dx \\
:=& \Delta_1 - \Delta_2 - \Delta_3,
\end{aligned}$$

and

$$\begin{aligned}
I_2 :=& \int [\kappa_1 \nabla(\frac{U}{Q}) - \mu_1 \frac{U}{Q} \nabla\omega_1] [\nabla \cdot (e^{-\frac{\mu_1}{\kappa_1}\omega_1} \frac{\varphi^3}{U^2 Q})] \, dx \\
=& \int e^{-\frac{\mu_1}{\kappa_1}\omega_1} [\kappa_1 \nabla(\frac{U}{Q}) - \mu_1 \frac{U}{Q} \nabla\omega_1][\frac{3\varphi^2 U^2 \nabla\varphi - \varphi^3 2U \nabla U}{U^4 Q}] \, dx \\
&- \int \frac{\mu_1}{\kappa_1} \frac{\varphi^3}{U^2 Q} e^{-\frac{\mu_1}{\kappa_1}\omega_1} [\kappa_1 \nabla(\frac{U}{Q}) - \mu_1 \frac{U}{Q} \nabla\omega_1] \cdot [\nabla\omega_1] \, dx \\
&- \int \frac{\varphi^3}{U^2 Q^2} e^{-\frac{\mu_1}{\kappa_1}\omega_1} [\kappa_1 \nabla(\frac{U}{Q}) - \mu_1 \frac{U}{Q} \nabla\omega_1][\nabla Q] \, dx
\end{aligned}$$

$$\begin{aligned}
=& \int e^{-\frac{\mu_1}{\kappa_1}\omega_1} \frac{\varphi^3}{UQ^2} [\kappa_1 \nabla(\frac{U}{Q}) \frac{Q}{U} - \mu_1 \nabla\omega_1][3\frac{\nabla\varphi}{\varphi} - 2\frac{\nabla U}{U}] \, dx \\
&- \int \frac{\mu_1}{\kappa_1} \frac{\varphi^3}{UQ^2} e^{-\frac{\mu_1}{\kappa_1}\omega_1} [\kappa_1 \nabla(\frac{U}{Q}) \frac{Q}{U} - \mu_1 \nabla\omega_1] \cdot [\nabla\omega_1] \, dx \\
&- \int \frac{\varphi^3}{UQ^3} e^{-\frac{\mu_1}{\kappa_1}\omega_1} [\kappa_1 \nabla(\frac{U}{Q}) \frac{Q}{U} - \mu_1 \nabla\omega_1][\nabla Q] \, dx \\
:=& \Delta_4 - \Delta_5 - \Delta_6.
\end{aligned}$$

Next, we have

$$
\begin{aligned}
&\Delta_1 - \Delta_4 \\
=&\int e^{-\frac{\mu_1}{\kappa_1}\omega_1}\frac{\varphi^3}{UQ^2}[\kappa_1\nabla(\frac{\varphi}{Q})\frac{Q}{\varphi} - \mu_1\nabla\omega_1][2\frac{\nabla\varphi}{\varphi} - \frac{\nabla U}{U}]\,\mathrm{d}x \\
&-\int e^{-\frac{\mu_1}{\kappa_1}\omega_1}\frac{\varphi^3}{UQ^2}[\kappa_1\nabla(\frac{U}{Q})\frac{Q}{U} - \mu_1\nabla\omega_1][3\frac{\nabla\varphi}{\varphi} - 2\frac{\nabla U}{U}]\,\mathrm{d}x \\
=&\int \kappa_1 e^{-\frac{\mu_1}{\kappa_1}\omega_1}\frac{\varphi^3}{UQ^2}\{[\nabla(\frac{\varphi}{Q})\frac{Q}{\varphi}][2\frac{\nabla\varphi}{\varphi} - \frac{\nabla U}{U}] - [\nabla(\frac{U}{Q})\frac{Q}{U}][3\frac{\nabla\varphi}{\varphi} - 2\frac{\nabla U}{U}]\}\,\mathrm{d}x \\
&+\int e^{-\frac{\mu_1}{\kappa_1}\omega_1}\frac{\varphi^3}{UQ^2}[\mu_1\nabla\omega_1][\frac{\nabla\varphi}{\varphi} - \frac{\nabla U}{U}]\,\mathrm{d}x \\
=&\int \kappa_1 e^{-\frac{\mu_1}{\kappa_1}\omega_1}\frac{\varphi^3}{UQ^2}\{[\frac{\nabla\varphi}{Q} - \frac{\varphi\nabla\varphi}{Q^2}]\frac{Q}{\varphi}[2\frac{\nabla\varphi}{\varphi} - \frac{\nabla U}{U}] - [\frac{\nabla U}{Q} - \frac{U\nabla Q}{Q^2}]\frac{Q}{U}[3\frac{\nabla\varphi}{\varphi} \\
&- 2\frac{\nabla U}{U}]\}\,\mathrm{d}x + \int e^{-\frac{\mu_1}{\kappa_1}\omega_1}\frac{\varphi^3}{UQ^2}[\mu_1\nabla\omega_1][\frac{\nabla\varphi}{\varphi} - \frac{\nabla U}{U}]\,\mathrm{d}x \\
=&\int 2\kappa_1 e^{-\frac{\mu_1}{\kappa_1}\omega_1}\frac{\varphi^3}{UQ^2}(\frac{\nabla\varphi}{\varphi} - \frac{\nabla U}{U})^2\,\mathrm{d}x \\
&+\int \kappa_1 e^{-\frac{\mu_1}{\kappa_1}\omega_1}\frac{\varphi^3}{UQ^3}[\frac{\nabla\varphi}{\varphi} - \frac{\nabla U}{U}][\nabla Q]\,\mathrm{d}x \\
&+\int e^{-\frac{\mu_1}{\kappa_1}\omega_1}\frac{\varphi^3}{UQ^2}[\mu_1\nabla\omega_1][\frac{\nabla\varphi}{\varphi} - \frac{\nabla U}{U}]\,\mathrm{d}x.
\end{aligned}
\tag{23}
$$

By the similar method, we deduce that

$$
\Delta_2 - \Delta_5 = \int e^{-\frac{\mu_1}{\kappa_1}\omega_1}\frac{\varphi^3}{UQ^2}[\mu_1\nabla\omega_1][\frac{\nabla\varphi}{\varphi} - \frac{\nabla U}{U}]\,\mathrm{d}x, \tag{24}
$$

and

$$
\Delta_3 - \Delta_6 = \int \kappa_1 e^{-\frac{\mu_1}{\kappa_1}\omega_1}\frac{\varphi^3}{UQ^3}[\frac{\nabla\varphi}{\varphi} - \frac{\nabla U}{U}][\nabla Q]\,\mathrm{d}x. \tag{25}
$$

Thus

$$
\begin{aligned}
I_1 - I_2 =&[\Delta_1 - \Delta_4] - [\Delta_2 - \Delta_5] - [\Delta_3 - \Delta_6] \\
=&\int 2\kappa_1 e^{-\frac{\mu_1}{\kappa_1}\omega_1}\frac{\varphi^3}{UQ^2}(\frac{\nabla\varphi}{\varphi} - \frac{\nabla U}{U})^2\,\mathrm{d}x.
\end{aligned}
\tag{26}
$$

By a similar method, one obtains

$$
J_1 - J_2 = \int 2\kappa_2 e^{-\frac{\mu_2}{\kappa_2}\omega_2}\frac{\psi^3}{VQ^2}(\frac{\nabla\psi}{\psi} - \frac{\nabla V}{V})^2\,\mathrm{d}x. \tag{27}
$$

Replace (21) and (22) with (26) and (27), respectively. Multiplying (22) by $\rho_2(x)^3$ and subtracting it from (21), we can obtain

$$
\begin{aligned}
&\lambda_1 \int [e^{-\frac{\mu_1}{\kappa_1}\omega_1} \frac{\varphi^3}{UQ} - e^{-\frac{\mu_2}{\kappa_2}\omega_2} \frac{\rho_2(x)^3\psi^3}{VQ}] \,\mathrm{d}x \\
&= \int 2\kappa_1 e^{-\frac{\mu_1}{\kappa_1}\omega_1} \frac{\varphi^3}{UQ^2} (\frac{\nabla\varphi}{\varphi} - \frac{\nabla U}{U})^2 \,\mathrm{d}x + \int e^{-\frac{\mu_1}{\kappa_1}\omega_1} \frac{\varphi^2}{Q} [\varphi + \rho_2(x)\psi] \,\mathrm{d}x \\
&\quad - \int 2\kappa_2 e^{-\frac{\mu_2}{\kappa_2}\omega_2} \frac{\rho_2(x)^3\psi^3}{VQ^2} (\frac{\nabla\psi}{\psi} - \frac{\nabla V}{V})^2 \mathrm{d}x \\
&\quad - \int e^{-\frac{\mu_2}{\kappa_2}\omega_2} \frac{\rho_2(x)^2\psi^2}{Q} [\rho_1(x)\rho_2(x)\varphi + \rho_2(x)\psi] \,\mathrm{d}x \\
&\geq \int e^{-\frac{\mu_1}{\kappa_1}\omega_1} \frac{\varphi^2}{Q} [\varphi + \rho_2(x)\psi] \,\mathrm{d}x - \int e^{-\frac{\mu_2}{\kappa_2}\omega_2} \frac{\rho_2(x)^3\psi^3}{Q} \,\mathrm{d}x \\
&\quad - \int e^{-\frac{\mu_1}{\kappa_1}\omega_1} \frac{\rho_2(x)^2\psi^2\varphi}{Q} [\rho_1(x)\rho_2(x) e^{(\frac{\mu_1}{\kappa_1}\omega_1 - \frac{\mu_2}{\kappa_2}\omega_2)}] \,\mathrm{d}x \\
&\geq \int e^{-\frac{\mu_1}{\kappa_1}\omega_1} \frac{\varphi^2}{Q} [\varphi + \rho_2(x)\psi] \,\mathrm{d}x - \int e^{-\frac{\mu_1}{\kappa_1}\omega_1} \frac{\rho_2(x)^3\psi^3}{Q} \,\mathrm{d}x \\
&\quad - \int e^{-\frac{\mu_1}{\kappa_1}\omega_1} \frac{\rho_2(x)^2\psi^2\varphi}{Q} \,\mathrm{d}x \\
&= \int e^{-\frac{\mu_1}{\kappa_1}\omega_1} \frac{1}{Q} [\varphi + \rho_2(x)\psi]^2 [\varphi - \rho_2(x)\psi] \,\mathrm{d}x \geq 0,
\end{aligned}
\tag{28}
$$

where we use the facts $(A_1), (A_2)$ and $\varphi > 0 > \psi$ in $\overline{\Omega}$. So, $\lambda_1 \geqslant 0$.

Next, we will prove that $\lambda_1 = 0$ can not happen. According to (28), we infer that $\lambda_1 = 0$ if and only if

$$
\rho_1(x)\rho_2(x) = 1, \ \frac{\mu_1}{\kappa_1}\omega_1 = \frac{\mu_2}{\kappa_2}\omega_2, \ \frac{\nabla\varphi}{\varphi} = \frac{\nabla U}{U}, \ \frac{\nabla\psi}{\psi} = \frac{\nabla V}{V}, \ \varphi = -\rho_2(x)\psi, \tag{29}
$$

which means that

$$
\frac{\nabla U}{U} = \frac{\nabla V}{V},
$$

i.e.,

$$
\nabla[lnU] = \nabla[lnV].
$$

Then, one obtains

$$
U = dV \quad \text{for some constant} \quad d > 0. \tag{30}
$$

In addition, by applying (30) to (17), and the uniqueness of the positive steady state of the system (4), it can be concluded that

$$
(1 + \frac{\rho_2(x)}{d})U = \theta_{\kappa_1,Q,\mu_1,r_1} \quad \text{and} \quad (\rho_1(x)d + 1)V = \theta_{\kappa_2,Q,\mu_2,r_2}.
$$

Noting that $\rho_1(x)\rho_2(x) = 1$, we deduce

$$
\frac{\theta_{\kappa_1,Q,\mu_1,r_1}}{\theta_{\kappa_2,Q,\mu_2,r_2}} = \frac{(1 + \frac{\rho_2(x)}{d})U}{(\rho_1(x)d + 1)V} = \frac{U + \rho_2(x)V}{\rho_1(x)U + V} = \rho_2(x) = \frac{1}{\rho_1(x)}. \tag{31}
$$

Based on (31), one can easily check

$$
\sigma_1(\kappa_2, Q, \mu_2, r_2 - \rho_1\theta_{\kappa_1,Q,\mu_1,r_1}) = \sigma_1(\kappa_2, Q, \mu_2, r_2 - \theta_{\kappa_2,Q,\mu_2,r_2}) = 0,
$$

and

$$\sigma_1(\kappa_1, Q, \mu_1, r_1 - \theta_{\kappa_1,Q,\mu_1,r_1}) = \sigma_1(\kappa_1, Q, \mu_1, r_1 - \rho_2\theta_{\kappa_2,Q,\mu_2,r_2}) = 0.$$

According to the assumption $(\kappa_1, \kappa_2, \mu_1, \mu_2) \notin \Sigma_{0,0}$, we get $\lambda_1 \neq 0$. Therefore, $\lambda_1 > 0$. $\square$

3.2. Classification of the Global Dynamics

In this subsection, we are ready to discuss the complete global dynamic behaviors of the system (1).

Proof of Theorem 3. According to the proof procedure (see [2,5]), this proof can be divided into two steps.

Step 1. On the proof of the disjoint decomposition in (16).

Obviously, we can get the decomposition in (16). According to the relevant conclusion and definitions, we only need to prove

$$(\Sigma_U \cup \Sigma_{U,0} \setminus \Sigma_{0,0}) \cap (\Sigma_V \cup \Sigma_{V,0} \setminus \Sigma_{0,0}) = \emptyset. \tag{32}$$

By Lemma 3, the linear stability of $(\theta_{\kappa_1,Q,\mu_1,r_1}, 0)$, $(0, \theta_{\kappa_2,Q,\mu_2,r_2})$ can be determined by the sign of $\sigma_1(\kappa_2, Q, \mu_2, r_2 - \rho_1\theta_{\kappa_1,Q,\mu_1,r_1})$, $\sigma_1(\kappa_1, Q, \mu_1, r_1 - \rho_2\theta_{\kappa_2,Q,\mu_2,r_2})$ respectively. For the sake of convenience of in writing, let

$$\theta_{\kappa_1,Q,\mu_1,r_1} := \theta_1,\ \sigma_1(\kappa_2, Q, \mu_2, r_2 - \rho_1\theta_{\kappa_1,Q,\mu_1,r_1}) := \sigma_1(\theta_1^*),$$
$$\theta_{\kappa_2,Q,\mu_2,r_2} := \theta_2,\ \sigma_1(\kappa_1, Q, \mu_1, r_1 - \rho_2\theta_{\kappa_2,Q,\mu_2,r_2}) := \sigma_1(\theta_2^*).$$

According to the properties of the variational characterization and (6), we obtain

$$\begin{aligned}
\sigma_1(\theta_2^*) &= \inf_{0\neq\phi\in H^1(\Omega)} \frac{\int \kappa_1 e^{\frac{\mu_1}{\kappa_1}\omega_1}[\nabla(e^{-\frac{\mu_1}{\kappa_1}\omega_1}\frac{\phi}{Q})]^2\,\mathrm{d}x - \int [r_1 - \rho_2(x)\theta_2]e^{-\frac{\mu_1}{\kappa_1}\omega_1}\frac{\phi^2}{Q}\,\mathrm{d}x}{\int e^{-\frac{\mu_1}{\kappa_1}\omega_1}\frac{\phi^2}{Q}\,\mathrm{d}x} \\
&\leq \frac{\int \kappa_1 e^{\frac{\mu_1}{\kappa_1}\omega_1}[\nabla(e^{-\frac{\mu_1}{\kappa_1}\omega_1}\frac{\theta_1}{Q})]^2\,\mathrm{d}x - \int [r_1 - \rho_2(x)\theta_2]e^{-\frac{\mu_1}{\kappa_1}\omega_1}\frac{\theta_1^2}{Q}\,\mathrm{d}x}{\int e^{-\frac{\mu_1}{\kappa_1}\omega_1}\frac{\theta_1{}^2}{Q}\,\mathrm{d}x} \\
&= \frac{\int e^{-\frac{\mu_1}{\kappa_1}\omega_1}\frac{\theta_1^2}{Q}[\rho_2(x)\theta_2 - \theta_1]\,\mathrm{d}x}{\int e^{-\frac{\mu_1}{\kappa_1}\omega_1}\frac{\theta_1^2}{Q}\,\mathrm{d}x},
\end{aligned} \tag{33}$$

and

$$\begin{aligned}
\sigma_1(\theta_1^*) &= \inf_{0\neq\phi\in H^1(\Omega)} \frac{\int \kappa_2 e^{\frac{\mu_2}{\kappa_2}\omega_2}[\nabla(e^{-\frac{\mu_2}{\kappa_2}\omega_2}\frac{\phi}{Q})]^2\,\mathrm{d}x - \int [r_2 - \rho_1(x)\theta_1]e^{-\frac{\mu_2}{\kappa_2}\omega_2}\frac{\phi^2}{Q}\,\mathrm{d}x}{\int e^{-\frac{\mu_2}{\kappa_2}\omega_2}\frac{\phi^2}{Q}\,\mathrm{d}x} \\
&\leq \frac{\int \kappa_2 e^{\frac{\mu_2}{\kappa_2}\omega_2}[\nabla(e^{-\frac{\mu_2}{\kappa_2}\omega_2}\frac{\theta_2}{Q})]^2\,\mathrm{d}x - \int [r_2 - \rho_1(x)\theta_1]e^{-\frac{\mu_2}{\kappa_2}\omega_2}\frac{\theta_2^2}{Q}\mathrm{d}x}{\int e^{-\frac{\mu_2}{\kappa_2}\omega_2}\frac{\theta_2{}^2}{Q}\,\mathrm{d}x} \\
&= \frac{\int e^{-\frac{\mu_2}{\kappa_2}\omega_2}\frac{\theta_2^2}{Q}[\rho_1(x)\theta_1 - \theta_2]\,\mathrm{d}x}{\int e^{-\frac{\mu_2}{\kappa_2}\omega_2}\frac{\theta_2^2}{Q}\,\mathrm{d}x}.
\end{aligned} \tag{34}$$

Since $0 < \rho_1(x)\rho_2(x) \leq 1$, combining with (33) and (34) together, we have

$$
\begin{aligned}
&\sigma_1(\theta_2^*) \cdot \int e^{-\frac{\mu_1}{\kappa_1}\omega_1} \frac{\theta_1^2}{Q} \, dx + \sigma_1(\theta_1^*) \cdot \int e^{-\frac{\mu_2}{\kappa_2}\omega_2} \frac{\rho_2(x)^3\theta_2^2}{Q} \, dx \\
\leq &\int e^{-\frac{\mu_1}{\kappa_1}\omega_1} \frac{\theta_1^2}{Q} [\rho_2(x)\theta_2 - \theta_1] \, dx - \int e^{-\frac{\mu_2}{\kappa_2}\omega_2} \frac{\rho_2(x)^3\theta_2^3}{Q} \, dx \\
&+ \int e^{-\frac{\mu_1}{\kappa_1}\omega_1} \frac{\rho_2(x)^2\theta_2^2\theta_1}{Q} [\rho_1(x)\rho_2(x) e^{(\frac{\mu_1}{\kappa_1}\omega_1 - \frac{\mu_2}{\kappa_2}\omega_2)}] \, dx \\
\leq &\int e^{-\frac{\mu_1}{\kappa_1}\omega_1} \frac{\theta_1^2}{Q} [\rho_2(x)\theta_2 - \theta_1] \, dx - \int e^{-\frac{\mu_1}{\kappa_1}\omega_1} \frac{\rho_2(x)^3\theta_2^3}{Q} \, dx \\
&+ \int e^{-\frac{\mu_1}{\kappa_1}\omega_1} \frac{\rho_2(x)^2\theta_2^2\theta_1}{Q} \, dx \\
= &- \int e^{-\frac{\mu_1}{\kappa_1}\omega_1} \frac{1}{Q} [\rho_2(x)\theta_2 - \theta_1]^2 [\theta_1 + \rho_2(x)\theta_2] \, dx \\
\leq &0,
\end{aligned}
\tag{35}
$$

where all the inequalities become equalities if and only if

$$
\rho_1(x)\rho_2(x) = 1, \; \frac{\mu_1}{\kappa_1}\omega_1 = \frac{\mu_2}{\kappa_2}\omega_2 \; and \; \theta_{\kappa_1,Q,\mu_1,r_1} \equiv \rho_2(x)\theta_{\kappa_2,Q,\mu_2,r_2} \; in \; \overline{\Omega}.
$$

It follows from (35) that the conclusion (32) holds.

Step 2. On the proof of the statements $(i) - (iv)$.

Firstly, we will prove the statements $(i) - (iii)$ hold. In consideration of (16) in Theorem 3 and (35) in step 1, we see that for any $(\kappa_1, \kappa_2, \mu_1, \mu_2) \in (\Gamma \setminus \Sigma_{0,0})$, there are five possibilities as follows:

(b_1) $(\kappa_1, \kappa_2, \mu_1, \mu_2) \in \Sigma_U$, i.e., $(\theta_{\kappa_1,Q,\mu_1,r_1}, 0)$ is linearly stable, $(0, \theta_{\kappa_2,Q,\mu_2,r_2})$ is linearly unstable;

(b_2) $(\kappa_1, \kappa_2, \mu_1, \mu_2) \in \Sigma_V$, i.e., $(\theta_{\kappa_1,Q,\mu_1,r_1}, 0)$ is linearly unstable, $(0, \theta_{\kappa_2,Q,\mu_2,r_2})$ is linearly stable;

(b_3) $(\kappa_1, \kappa_2, \mu_1, \mu_2) \in \Sigma_-$, i.e., both $(\theta_{\kappa_1,Q,\mu_1,r_1}, 0)$ and $(0, \theta_{\kappa_2,Q,\mu_2,r_2})$ are linearly unstable;

(b_4) $(\kappa_1, \kappa_2, \mu_1, \mu_2) \in \Sigma_{U,0} \setminus \Sigma_{0,0}$, i.e., $(\theta_{\kappa_1,Q,\mu_1,r_1}, 0)$ is neutrally stable, $(0, \theta_{\kappa_2,Q,\mu_2,r_2})$ is linearly unstable;

(b_5) $(\kappa_1, \kappa_2, \mu_1, \mu_2) \in \Sigma_{V,0} \setminus \Sigma_{0,0}$, i.e., $(0, \theta_{\kappa_2,Q,\mu_2,r_2})$ is neutrally stable, $(\theta_{\kappa_1,Q,\mu_1,r_1}, 0)$ is linearly unstable.

By Lemma 4, we immediately deduce the following conclusion:

$(\theta_{\kappa_1,Q,\mu_1,r_1}, 0)$ and $(0, \theta_{\kappa_2,Q,\mu_2,r_2})$ are $g.a.s$ based on the assumptions (b_1) and (b_2), respectively, and there is a unique co-existence steady state under the condition (b_3).

We now claim that there is no coexistence steady state under the condition (b_4) or the condition (b_5). Then we can infer that $(\theta_{\kappa_1,Q,\mu_1,r_1}, 0)$ and $(0, \theta_{\kappa_2,Q,\mu_2,r_2})$ are also $g.a.s$ based on the assumptions (b_4) and (b_5), respectively, from Lemma 4.

We only need to verify the above statement for the case (b_4). Indeed, if the system (1) has a co-existence steady state $(\widetilde{U}, \widetilde{V})$ for some $(\kappa_1, \kappa_2, \mu_1, \mu_2) = (\widetilde{\kappa_1}, \widetilde{\kappa_2}, \widetilde{\mu_1}, \widetilde{\mu_2}) \in \Sigma_{U,0} \setminus \Sigma_{0,0}$ and $(\widetilde{U}, \widetilde{V})$ satisfies

$$
\begin{cases}
\nabla \cdot [\widetilde{\kappa_1}(x)\nabla(\frac{\widetilde{U}}{\widetilde{Q}(x)}) - \widetilde{\mu_1}(x)\frac{\widetilde{U}}{\widetilde{Q}(x)}\nabla\omega_1(x)] + \widetilde{U}[r_1(x) - \widetilde{U} - \rho_2(x)\widetilde{V}] = 0, & in \; \Omega, \\
\nabla \cdot [\widetilde{\kappa_2}(x)\nabla(\frac{\widetilde{V}}{\widetilde{Q}(x)}) - \widetilde{\mu_2}(x)\frac{\widetilde{V}}{\widetilde{Q}(x)}\nabla\omega_2(x)] + \widetilde{V}[r_2(x) - \rho_1(x)\widetilde{U} - \widetilde{V}] = 0, & in \; \Omega, \\
[\widetilde{\kappa_1}(x)\frac{\partial}{\partial n}(\frac{\widetilde{U}}{\widetilde{Q}}) - \widetilde{\mu_1}(x)\frac{\widetilde{U}}{\widetilde{Q}}\frac{\partial\omega_1(x)}{\partial n}] \mid_{\partial\Omega} = [\widetilde{\kappa_2}(x)\frac{\partial}{\partial n}(\frac{\widetilde{V}}{\widetilde{Q}}) - \widetilde{\mu_2}(x)\frac{\widetilde{V}}{\widetilde{Q}}\frac{\partial\omega_2(x)}{\partial n}] \mid_{\partial\Omega} = 0.
\end{cases}
\tag{36}
$$

We have

$$
\sigma_1(\widetilde{\kappa_2}, \widetilde{Q}, \widetilde{\mu_2}, r_2 - \rho_1\theta_{\widetilde{\kappa_1},\widetilde{Q},\widetilde{\mu_1},r_1}) = 0 \; and \; \sigma_1(\widetilde{\kappa_1}, \widetilde{Q}, \widetilde{\mu_1}, r_1 - \rho_2\theta_{\widetilde{\kappa_2},\widetilde{Q},\widetilde{\mu_2},r_2}) < 0. \tag{37}
$$

Define the operator $G : \mathbb{R}^+ \times \mathbb{R}^+ \times \mathbb{M}_1 \times \mathbb{M}_1 \to \mathbb{M}_2 \times \mathbb{M}_2$

$$G : (\varrho_1, \varrho_2, w_1, w_2) \longmapsto \begin{pmatrix} \widetilde{\kappa_1}\Delta(\frac{w_1}{Q}) - \widetilde{\mu_1}\nabla \cdot [\frac{w_1}{Q}\nabla\omega_1] + w_1[r_1 - w_1 - \varrho_2 w_2] \\ \widetilde{\kappa_2}\Delta(\frac{w_2}{Q}) - \widetilde{\mu_2}\nabla \cdot [\frac{w_2}{Q}\nabla\omega_2] + w_2[r_2 - \varrho_1 w_1 - w_2] \end{pmatrix},$$

with

$$\mathbb{M}_1 := \{\varphi \in W^{2,p}(\Omega) : [\widetilde{\kappa_1}\frac{\partial}{\partial n}(\frac{\varphi}{Q}) - \widetilde{\mu_1}(\frac{\varphi}{Q})\frac{\partial\omega_1}{Q}] \mid_{\partial\Omega} = 0\},\ \mathbb{M}_2 := L^p(\Omega), p > N.$$

From (36), $G(\rho_1(x), \rho_2(x), \widetilde{U}, \widetilde{V}) = 0$ and Theorem 2, it yields that

$$\frac{\partial G(\varrho_1, \varrho_2, w_1, w_2)}{\partial(w_1, w_2)} \mid_{(\varrho_1, \varrho_2, w_1, w_2) = (\rho_1(x), \rho_2(x), \widetilde{U}, \widetilde{V})} \ \textit{is invertible.}$$

Applying implicit function theorem, one gets (ϱ_1, ϱ_2) is closed to $(\rho_1(x), \rho_2(x))$. We have a positive solution $(\widetilde{U}, \widetilde{V})$ to the equation $G(\varrho_1, \varrho_2, w_1, w_2) = 0$. Let us choose $(\overline{\varrho_1}, \overline{\varrho_2})$, which implies (the solution corresponding to $(\overline{\varrho_1}, \overline{\varrho_2})$ is denoted by $(\overline{U}, \overline{V})$)

$$\overline{\varrho_1} > \rho_1(x),\ 0 < \overline{\varrho_2} < \rho_2(x) \quad \textit{and} \quad \overline{\varrho_1} \cdot \overline{\varrho_2} \le \Lambda. \tag{38}$$

Let us see the following auxiliary problem

$$\begin{cases} U_t = \nabla \cdot [\widetilde{\kappa_1}(x)\nabla(\frac{U}{Q}) - \widetilde{\mu_1}(x)\frac{U}{Q}\nabla\omega_1(x)] + U[r_1(x) - U - \overline{\varrho_2}V] = 0, & in\ \Omega \times \mathbb{R}^+, \\ V_t = \nabla \cdot [\widetilde{\kappa_2}(x)\nabla(\frac{V}{Q}) - \widetilde{\mu_2}(x)\frac{V}{Q}\nabla\omega_2(x)] + V[r_2(x) - \overline{\varrho_1}U - V] = 0, & in\ \Omega \times \mathbb{R}^+, \\ [\widetilde{\kappa_1}(x)\frac{\partial}{\partial n}(\frac{U}{Q}) - \widetilde{\mu_1}(x)\frac{U}{Q}\frac{\partial\omega_1(x)}{\partial n}] \mid_{\partial\Omega} = 0, \\ [\widetilde{\kappa_2}(x)\frac{\partial}{\partial n}(\frac{V}{Q}) - \widetilde{\mu_2}(x)\frac{V}{Q}\frac{\partial\omega_2(x)}{\partial n}] \mid_{\partial\Omega} = 0, \end{cases} \tag{39}$$

which has the same semi-trivial steady states $(\theta_{\widetilde{\kappa_1}, \widetilde{Q}, \widetilde{\mu_1}, r_1}, 0)$ and $(0, \theta_{\widetilde{\kappa_2}, \widetilde{Q}, \widetilde{\mu_2}, r_2})$. From (37), (38) and Lemma 2, it then follows that

$$\sigma_1(\widetilde{\kappa_2}, \widetilde{Q}, \widetilde{\mu_2}, r_2 - \overline{\varrho_1}\theta_{\widetilde{\kappa_1}, \widetilde{Q}, \widetilde{\mu_1}, r_1}) > 0 \ \textit{and}\ \sigma_1(\widetilde{\kappa_1}, \widetilde{Q}, \widetilde{\mu_1}, r_1 - \overline{\varrho_2}\theta_{\widetilde{\kappa_2}, \widetilde{Q}, \widetilde{\mu_2}, r_2}) < 0. \tag{40}$$

According to the case (b_1), $(\theta_{\kappa_1, Q, \mu_1, r_1}, 0)$ is also *g.a.s* in the system (39) which contradicts with the existence of $(\overline{U}, \overline{V})$. Therefore, there is no coexistence steady state under the condition (b_4). Similarly, we can get the conclusion that there is also no coexistence steady state under the condition (b_5). The above descriptions of the cases $(b_1) - (b_5)$ represent the expected results described in the statements $(i) - (iii)$.

Secondly, we prove the statement (iv). We will show

$$\Sigma_{0,0} = \Sigma^{\sim} := \{(\kappa_1, \kappa_2, \mu_1, \mu_2) \in \Gamma : \rho_1(x)\rho_2(x) = 1, \theta_{\kappa_1, Q, \mu_1, r_1} \equiv \rho_2(x)\theta_{\kappa_2, Q, \mu_2, r_2}\ in\ \overline{\Omega}\}. \tag{41}$$

It makes the same description of $\Sigma_{0,0}$, which means the expected result in the statement (iv).

Let $(\kappa_1, \kappa_2, \mu_1, \mu_2) \in \Sigma^{\sim}$, then

$$\rho_1(x)\rho_2(x) = 1 \ \textit{and}\ \theta_{\kappa_1, Q, \mu_1, r_1} \equiv \rho_2(x)\theta_{\kappa_2, Q, \mu_2, r_2}\ in\ \overline{\Omega}.$$

Based on the proof of Theorem 2, we get

$$\sigma_1(\kappa_2, Q, \mu_2, r_2 - \rho_1\theta_{\kappa_1, Q, \mu_1, r_1}) = \sigma_1(\kappa_1, Q, \mu_1, r_1 - \rho_2\theta_{\kappa_2, Q, \mu_2, r_2}) = 0, \tag{42}$$

which implies $\Sigma^{\sim} \subset \Sigma_{0,0}$. When (42) holds, the last three inequalities in (35) become equalities, we have

$$\rho_1(x)\rho_2(x) = 1, \ \ \theta_{\kappa_1,Q,\mu_1,r_1} \equiv \rho_2(x)\theta_{\kappa_2,Q,\mu_2,r_2} \ in \ \overline{\Omega},$$

which shows $\Sigma_{0,0} \subset \Sigma^{\sim}$. Hence, the equality (41) is confirmed.

Let $(\kappa_1, \kappa_2, \mu_1, \mu_2) \in \Sigma_{0,0}$ and (U, V) be the corresponding coexistence steady state of (1). We claim that $\frac{U}{V} \equiv$ constant. Let λ_1 be a principal eigenvalue for (U, V). Moreover, we choose the corresponding eigenfunction (φ, ψ), which satisfies $\varphi > 0 > \psi$ in $\overline{\Omega}$ and $\|\varphi\|_2^2 + \|\psi\|_2^2 = 1$. In order to prove it, it is enough to show that (29) holds. Suppose that (29) is not true. Then (28) means $\lambda_1 > 0$. Similar to the proof of the case (b_4), we get (29) holds, i.e., $\frac{U}{V} \equiv$ constant. This yields that

$$(U, V) = \big(\eta(x)\theta_{\kappa_1,Q,\mu_1,r_1}, (1 - \eta(x))\frac{\theta_{\kappa_1,Q,\mu_1,r_1}}{\rho_2(x)}\big) : \eta(x) \in [0, 1].$$

Therefore, we conclude that for any $(\kappa_1, \kappa_2, \mu_1, \mu_2) \in \Sigma_{0,0}$, the set of equilibria of (1) is

$$\{(0, 0)\} \cup \{\big(\eta(x)\theta_{\kappa_1,Q,\mu_1,r_1}, (1 - \eta(x))\frac{\theta_{\kappa_1,Q,\mu_1,r_1}}{\rho_2(x)}\big) : \eta(x) \in [0, 1]\},$$

where $(0, 0)$ is a repeller by Remark 1. Then each solution of (1) converges to a single equilibrium $\{\big(\eta(x)\theta_{\kappa_1,Q,\mu_1,r_1}, (1 - \eta(x))\frac{\theta_{\kappa_1,Q,\mu_1,r_1}}{\rho_2(x)}\big) : \eta(x) \in [0, 1]\}$. □

4. Discussion

In this paper, by using principal eigenvalue theory and monotone dynamical system theory, we mainly analyzed the global directed dynamic behaviors of a Lotka-Volterra competition-diffusion-advection system between two organisms in heterogeneous environments. The two organisms compete for different fundamental resources, their advection and diffusion strategies follow a positive diffusion distribution, the functions of inter-specific competition ability are variable. Our work can be seen as a further development of Wang [5] for the competition-diffusion system, where we bring new ingredients in the arguments to overcome the difficulty caused by the involvement of advection.

In the future, exploring the global directed dynamic behaviors under the condition of cross-diffusion may be an interesting research point. We leave this challenge to future investigations.

Author Contributions: All authors contributed equally and significantly in writing this article. Conceptualization, L.C.; Formal analysis, Y.Z.; Funding acquisition, L.C.; Writing—original draft, S.L. All authors have read and agreed to the published version of the manuscript.

Funding: This research was funded by Shandong Provincial Natural Science Foundation under grant ZR2020MA006 and the Introduction and Cultivation Project of Young and Innovative Talents in Universities of Shandong Province.

Institutional Review Board Statement: Not applicable.

Informed Consent Statement: Not applicable.

Data Availability Statement: Not applicable.

Acknowledgments: We would like to express our thanks to the anonymous referees and the editor for their constructive comments and suggestions, which greatly improved this article.

Conflicts of Interest: The authors declare no conflict of interest.

References

1. Smith, H. *Monotone Dynamical System. An Introduction to the Theory of Competitive and Cooperative Systems*; American Mathematical Society: Providence, RI, USA, 1995; Volume 41.
2. He, X.; Ni, W. Global dynamics of the Lotka-Volterra competition-diffusion system: Diffusion and spatial heterogeneity I. *Commun. Pure Appl. Math.* **2016**, *69*, 981–1014. [CrossRef]
3. He, X.; Ni, W. Global dynamics of the Lotka-Volterra competition-diffusion system with equal amount of total resources, II. *Calc. Var. Partial Differ Equ.* **2016**, *55*, 25. [CrossRef]

4. Hess, P. *Periodic-Parabolic Boundary Value Problems and Positivity*; Wiley: New York, NY, USA, 1991.
5. Wang, Q. Global directed dynamics of a Lotka-Volterra competition-diffusion system. *Nonlinear Anal. Real World Appl.* **2020**, *55*, 103144. [CrossRef]
6. Zhou, P.; Tang, D.; Xiao, D. On Lotka-Volterra competitive parabolic systems: Exclusion, coexistence and bistability. *J. Differ. Equ.* **2021**, *282*, 596–625. [CrossRef]
7. Du, L.; Li, W.; Wu, S. Propagation phenomena for a bistable Lotka-Volterra competition system with advection in a periodic habitat. *Z. Angew. Math. Phys.* **2019**, *71* , 2402–2435. [CrossRef]
8. Du, L.; Li, W.; Wu, S. Pulsating fronts and front-like entire solutions for a reaction-advection-diffusion competition model in a periodic habitat. *J. Differ. Equ.* **2019**, *266*, 8419–8458. [CrossRef]
9. Lou, Y.; Zhao, X.; Zhou, P. Global dynamics of a Lotka-Volterra competition-diffusion-advection system in heterogeneous environments. *J. Math. Pures Appl.* **2019**, *121*, 47–82. [CrossRef]
10. Kamrujjaman, M. Interplay of resource distributions and diffusion strategies for spatially heterogeneous populations. *J. Math. Model.* **2019**, *7*, 175–198.
11. Tang, D.; Chen, Y. Global dynamics of a Lotka-Volterra competition-diffusion system in advective homogeneous environments. *J. Differ. Equ.* **2020**, *269*,1465–1483. [CrossRef]
12. Xu, F.; Gan, W.; Tang, D. Global dynamics of a Lotka-Volterra competitive system from river ecology: General boundary conditions. *Nonlinearity* **2020**, *33*, 1528–1541. [CrossRef]
13. Tang, D.; Zhou, P. On a Lotka-Volterra competition-diffusion-advection system: Homogeneity vs heterogeneity. *J. Differ. Equ.* **2020**, *268*, 1570–1599. [CrossRef]
14. Ma, L.; Guo, S. Bifurcation and stability of a two-species reaction–diffusion–advection competition model. *Nonlinear Anal. Real World Appl.* **2021**, *59*, 103241. [CrossRef]
15. Guo, Q.; He, X.; Ni, W. Global dynamics of a general Lotka-Volterra competition-diffusion system in heterogeneous environments. *Discret. Contin. Dyn. Syst.* **2020**, *40*, 6547–6573. [CrossRef]
16. Korobenko, L.; Braverman, E. On evolutionary stability of carrying capacity driven dispersal in competition with regularly diffusing populations. *J. Math. Biol.* **2014**, *69*, 1181–1206. [CrossRef]
17. Lou, Y.; Zhou, P. Evolution of dispersal in advective homogeneous environment: The effect of boundary conditions. *J. Differ. Equ.* **2015**, *259*, 141–171. [CrossRef]
18. Ma, L.; Tang, D. Existence and Stability of Stationary States of a Reaction-Diffusion-Advection Model for Two Competing Species. *Int. J. Bifurc. Chaos* **2020**, *5*, 2050065. [CrossRef]
19. Zhou, P.; Xiao, D. Global dynamics of a classical Lotka-Volterra competition-diffusion-advection system. *J. Funct. Anal.* **2018**, *275*, 356–380. [CrossRef]
20. Averill, I.; Lam, K.; Lou, Y. *The Role of Advection in a Two-Species Competition Model: A Bifurcation Approach*; American Mathematical Society: Providence, RI, USA, 2017; Volume 245.
21. Cantrell, R.; Cosner, C.; Lou, Y. Movement toward better environments and the evolution of rapid diffusion. *Math. Biosci.* **2006**, *204*, 199–214. [CrossRef]
22. Cantrell, R.; Cosner, C.; Lou, Y. Advection-mediated coexistence of competing species. *Proc. Roy. Soc. Edinb. Sect. A* **2007**, *137*, 497–518. [CrossRef]
23. Chen, X.; Lou, Y. Effects of diffusion and advection on the smallest eigenvalue of an elliptic operator and their applications. *Indiana Univ. Math. J.* **2012**, *61*, 45–80. [CrossRef]
24. Lam, K. Concentration phenomena of a semilinear elliptic equation with large advection in an ecological model. *J. Differ. Equ.* **2011**, *250*, 161–181. [CrossRef]
25. Lam, K. Limiting profiles of semilinear elliptic equations with large advection in population dynamics II. *SIAM J. Math. Anal.* **2012**, *44*, 1808–1830. [CrossRef]
26. Lam, K.; Ni, W. Uniqueness and complete dynamics in heterogeneous competition-diffusion systems. *SIAM J. Appl. Math.* **2012**, *72*, 1695–1712. [CrossRef]
27. Cantrell, R.; Cosner, C. *Spatial Ecology via Reaction-Diffusion Equations*; Wiley: New York, NY, USA, 2003.
28. Krein, M.; Rutman, M. Linear operators leaving invariant a cone in a Banach space. *Uspekhi Mat. Nauk.* **1948**, *3*, 3–95.
29. Sweers, G. Strong positivity in $C(\overline{\Omega})$ for elliptic systems. *Math. Z.* **1992**, *209*, 251–271. [CrossRef]
30. Nagel, R. Operator matrices and reaction-diffusion system. *Rend. Semin. Mat. Fis. Milano* **1989**, *59*, 185–196. [CrossRef]
31. De Figueiredo, D.; Mitidieri, E. Maximum principles for linear elliptic systems. *Rend. Istit. Mat. Univ. Trieste* **1990**, *22*, 36–66.

MDPI
St. Alban-Anlage 66
4052 Basel
Switzerland
Tel. +41 61 683 77 34
Fax +41 61 302 89 18
www.mdpi.com

Axioms Editorial Office
E-mail: axioms@mdpi.com
www.mdpi.com/journal/axioms

www.ingramcontent.com/pod-product-compliance
Lightning Source LLC
Chambersburg PA
CBHW061613210926
51850CB00009B/2307
* 9 7 8 3 0 3 6 5 7 9 9 7 9 *